THE LAST BASEBALL TOWN

*How Campbell, California achieved the unprecedented,
and still unduplicated, in American youth baseball*

By Chuck Hildebrand

ISBN: I-4392-3444-2
ISBN-13: 9781439234440

Visit www.booksurge.com to order additional copies.

DEDICATION

This book is dedicated to Kevin Allison, Jeff Baxter, Todd Boyd, Jon Middlekauff, Jeff Mitchell, Todd Phillips and other absent friends from so long ago – and to Jimmy Shockley, whom I wish I'd known.

TABLE OF CONTENTS

Introduction: Why Campbell was The Last Baseball Town   i

PART I: THE PLACE AND THE PINNACLES

1909–1953: Beginnings   I

1954–1958: Organization   II

1959–1962: Transition   29

1962 Moreland Little League: 'Big Ben and a flock of pocket watches'   43

1964 Campbell Moreland Pony League: The best Campbell team ever?   59

1963–1969: Emergence   67

1970 Campbell Little League: The Cardiac Kids   83

1970–1975: Close, but ...   107

1976 Campbell Little League: Daydream believers   123

1978 Campbell Moreland Pony League: Unfinished business   145

1979 Campbell Little League: The Campbell Clones   165

1979 Campbell Moreland Pony League: The Truman Show   181

PART II: THE PEOPLE

John Oldham: He came first   223

Duane Kubo: The enabler   229

The defining managers: Gordon Huntze, Jack Zogg, Bud Stallings   235

Jim Saeger: A top hat and a half-century of tales   253

Jimmy Shockley: Death on a diamond   261

Kent Ohmann: The grownup amongst us   267

Mark Paquin: Enduring   275

Paul Sargis: Two generations   279

Steve Clinton: Quality of life   285

Dominic Costantino: The heart and soul   293

Bobby Straight: The teeth   301

Matt Christian: Persistence   305

Dave Roberson: On again   317

PART III: REQUIEM FOR A DYNASTY

The Long Goodbye: The start of Campbell's decline   323

Now: Campbell baseball today, and those who carry on   343

Epilogue: Final thoughts   359

INTRODUCTION

The final tears, the unfamiliar uniforms, the immensity and the tension of a world championship game had been happily shed, and the 14 players on the Campbell Little League All-Star team finally had their childhoods back. They were swimming with their new friends from other teams and other nationalities, playing ping-pong or billiards or crisscrossing the pool deck. They were reacquainting themselves with families from which they'd been virtually sequestered for the previous two weeks, and they were free of a baseball cocoon for the first time in nearly two months.

They were back to being 12-year-old kids. We'd been on a six-week, 15-victory whitewater ride with them, a ride that was at once an odyssey and an ordeal and had brought us to the last destination possible for them to attain, or for any of us to have imagined – Williamsport, Pennsylvania, for the 1976 Little League World Series. An hour or so before, in the championship game before a crowd of 40,000, a guest list that included Joe DiMaggio and Ernie Banks, and an international television audience, we'd done all of the things we'd forced the 15 teams we'd vanquished to do. We undermined ourselves with five errors and six passed balls, stranded more people than the *Andrea Doria*, and lost 10-3 to Chofu, Japan.

Even as poorly as we played, it wasn't a total mismatch; we were within 5-3 before we kicked over the final traces. The Japanese team, in the Far East Regional, had beaten the representative from Taiwan, then and for many years thereafter the dominant force in international Little League baseball, and the Japanese manager was quoted as saying after the game against us that if Taiwan had reached the World Series instead of his team, Campbell likely would have won. Even so, our kids initially were inconsolable as we greeted them immediately after the game, but they were as resilient emotionally as they had been on the field during the winning streak. They were ready to move on.

As we looked, wordlessly, at each other while we were standing around that swimming pool, and reflected on what they the team and we as a community had achieved during this most improbable and unexpected of journeys, I think most of us knew that we had a bond that would endure beyond whatever triumphs and tribulations our lives would subsequently include. In their way, the kids were celebrating not only their imminent return to normalcy, but also what had happened over the past six weeks, and what possibilities lay ahead for each of them, within and beyond baseball.

So were we, in our way. We still do.

There was one player for whom the immediate disappointment seemed to linger – Brian Hughes, our utility infielder, who'd made only a couple of cameo appearances in the World Series. Brian was normally a fountain of ebullience, and then and later, he always seemed to have a knack for saying the right thing to the right person at the right time. But while we were standing on that pool deck, and his teammates were cavorting, Brian was off by himself, staring off without seeing anything, looking as if the entire burden of playing for a world championship had fallen squarely on him.

Brian and I already were good friends, and remained so long after this day, but as I went over to talk to him, I wasn't sure I would have the right words. He looked up at me, his blue eyes clouded over. "We let Campbell down," he said. "We lost. We let Campbell down. We were on national TV. Everybody saw it. We embarrassed Campbell."

"Brian," I said, "how much money do you have on you?"

"A couple of bucks, I guess," he said. "Why?"

"Because I want to bet you that couple of bucks. I'm betting you that when you guys get home, there will be a thousand people waiting for you at the airport. You haven't let anybody down."

"No way. You're on," he said, finally grinning a little.

A few days later, after Little League Baseball had taken all the World Series teams to Baltimore to see an Orioles game, and then to Washington, D.C., to tour the Capitol and the other historic sites and meet their Congressional representatives, our team flew home. (There were probably 100 or so of us supporters in Williamsport, and we had the largest following of all the participants even though we were the most distant of the four U.S. participants. The rest of us had driven or flown home right after the championship game.)

We were there at the San Jose airport when they arrived, of course, and it wasn't long before it was apparent that my thousand-people estimate had been wildly inaccurate. I never heard or saw a crowd count at the airport, and since the team's plane arrived at 6 p.m., a time when the terminal normally would be busy, it's hard to say exactly how many Campbell celebrants were there. But there's no question that I won the bet with Brian (who still hasn't paid up), because one could hardly move outside the team's arrival gate, and the tarmac – this was long before security checkpoints in airport terminals – was jammed. I later heard that some flights were delayed because of the mass of humanity that descended on the airport that day. The kids were whisked away to a waiting motorcade, led by Campbell police chief Don Burr and anchored by a Rolls-Royce that carried manager Jack Zogg and coach Bob Holman, that would take them the eight miles to a reception at the Campbell High football stadium, which had a seating capacity of perhaps 2,500 and was visibly overflowing when we arrived. People were waving, and signs were billowing from every overpass. Three thousand miles away in Williamsport, the kids had no way of knowing it because they'd gone directly to the World Series after winning the Western Regional tournament in San Bernardino, Calif., but it was pretty obvious that our young daydream believers had imparted their sense of imminent and eminent destiny on many thousands of other people, most of whom they didn't even know.

I was 19 years old at the time, seven years older than the kids – an age difference that didn't matter much back then and doesn't matter at all now that we've all attained middle age. I went on to a career in sports journalism, during which I covered World Series, Super Bowls and NCAA basketball tournaments. There were four seminal events in Bay Area sports during the 1980s – the Dallas Cowboys-San Francisco 49ers NFC championship game and the Stanford-Cal five-lateral football game in 1982, Kirk Gibson's one-legged pinch-hit home run in the 1988 World Series, and the earthquake that halted the 1989 World Series – and I may be the only sportswriter who covered all four. I interviewed and wrote about the famous and occasionally the infamous throughout the sports world. I've written two books (this will be the third) and was a contributor to two others.

All of that, for me, was sequel. The main text of my life in sports will always be the years I spent, the level of excellence I saw, and most of all, the friends I made in the Campbell baseball community during the 10 years I was part of it. And no season or event or team I've seen or covered since could ever equal the impact of that summer of 1976, which started with thousands of teams playing for a world championship and ended with only two teams left – one of which was us, just as it had been in 1970, just as it would be again in 1979, and just as it would be in Pony League for a lot of these same kids in 1978 (and again in 1979, with a different group).

Yet during the 33 years that have passed since that summer, I've often thought of two other games our 1976 Campbell team played. They were in our very first tournament, for the championship of District 44, and all four of the games we played in that tournament were against opponents within a 15-mile radius of our home field. It was an established fact in the 1970s that the team that emerged from the District 44 tournament had a real chance of making a national splash. Moreland, Campbell's sister league, had won the event in 1962, becoming the first and still the only Northern California team to do so. Campbell itself had reached the World Series title game in 1970, losing 2-0 to Wayne, N.J. In 1969, a Santa Clara Briarwood team led by eventual major league All-Star Carney Lansford had also advanced to the world title game before losing 2-0 to Taiwan, and in 1971 Cupertino American got to the Western Regional final before losing a one-run decision to Hawaii. Nobody we played in District 44 was intimidated by us, because many of the other leagues had talent comparable to our own. Two, maybe even three of our four District 44 opponents in 1976 could have barricaded our road to Williamsport not far from our own garage, since postseason play in Little League was single-elimination in those days.

After winning our first game 7-0, we won the second 1-0 in seven innings — a game I didn't see because I had announcing duties at the Campbell ballpark, where another District 44 game was taking place at the same time we played. I was at the next game, in which we were trailing Sunnyvale Southern 1-0 in the sixth and final regulation inning and had our most aggressive baserunner and best overall player, Bobby Straight, on third base with two outs when a wild pitch got past the Sunnyvale Southern catcher. He retrieved it and threw to the pitcher covering the plate. The pitcher and Bobby arrived simultaneously. Bobby slid as the pitcher applied a tag. I was in the announcer's booth, maybe 20 feet away and 10 feet above ground level, and I had as good a view of the play as anyone in the ballpark, including the home-plate umpire.

It was an excruciatingly close play. I thought Bobby was out. I waited for the umpire to thumb Bobby out and us out of the postseason. He never did. He called Bobby safe.

The batter walked on the pitch on which Bobby scored, went to second on another wild pitch and scored on a walk-off single. We won, 2-1 ... and we weren't seriously challenged again, outscoring our next 11 opponents 94-20, until the U.S. championship game, in which we beat Richmond, Virginia 3-0 to earn a shot at the Japanese team in the world title game.

So, I had occasion to ask myself, what if we'd lost either of those district games? What if we'd never had the Williamsport experience? What if the Campbell program hadn't been able to use that run as a springboard to three more national championships in the next three years while producing at least two dozen college players, including two — Greg Gohr and George Tsamis — who reached the major leagues?

I've thought about whether I would still feel the same about Campbell — the place that in baseball terms was more of an attitude than it was a locale — if we'd lost either of those games and never won any national titles. And the answer always is an unequivocal yes. I had made all of those friends long before the start of the 1976 postseason. Many of the people to whom I was closest never played on a national championship team or had a son do so.

And it wasn't as if we were treading where no Campbell team had ever trod before. During the 28 seasons from 1960 through 1987, Campbell-area teams played in 14 World Series of legitimate international scope (four in Little League, four in Pony League, five in Colt League, and one in American Legion), winning six and finishing second in five. That's a remarkable total under any circumstances for a city Campbell's size, and even more remarkable when one considers that the rosters weren't bulging with future major league stars. During the first 100 years of Campbell's youth baseball existence, only five players who played in Campbell long enough to be considered true products of the area youth baseball system – John Oldham, Don Hahn, Steve Davis, George Tsamis and Greg Gohr – reached the major leagues. (Four others – Rich Troedson, Joe Ferguson, Dan Gladden and Doug Capilla – spent significant time in the Campbell system, although they are more readily identified with other areas and systems.) And none of those five "true Campbell" players were high-impact performers in the majors. They played a combined total of 14 big league seasons, seven by Hahn. Tsamis, Davis and Oldham played only one season each; Davis appeared in three major league games, Oldham one.

It was a system that was greater than the sum of its parts, by any yardstick. But Campbell wasn't a great baseball system because it challenged for national and worldwide supremacy so often. It challenged for national and worldwide supremacy so often because it was a great baseball system.

As you might imagine, I have many incandescent memories of our championship teams, the long trips to regional and national tournaments, and the kids who played on those teams – great kids who became even better adults and parents and workers and citizens. I'll write about some of those moments, and the players will reminisce about them from the vantage point of middle age, in this book. But I remember other Campbell people and events just as vividly. I remember sharing childhoods and adolescences, and later young adulthoods and weddings and kids of kids, and having my life immeasurably enriched because those young men and their families were in it.

None of the 14 kids on the '76 Williamsport team played in the game that I think defined Campbell baseball more than any other single contest, and one I remember with as much fondness as any of the others. That game was five years later, in 1981, when our Colt League All-Star team was down 9-2 with two outs and one runner on base in the seventh and final inning against Matt McCormick, a pitcher who went on to excel at Santa Clara University. We got nine straight runners on base and scored seven runs to win 10-9. (The game was in Santa Cruz, and a couple of the kids rode back to Campbell with me. One of them, Cameron Comick, had this glazed-over look in his eyes for a full hour after that game. Finally, he looked across the car seat at me and said, disbelief still tinging his voice, "Man, I got to do me some *thinkin'*.")

I remember when I was buying my first new car and had probably a dozen families offer, without being asked, to co-sign the loan for me. I remember the impromptu parties we had, the pizza nights, the hayrides, the Fourth of July celebrations, the San Jose Bees and San Jose Earthquakes games, the trips to the beach. I remember parents coming to their kid's game at 10 a.m. and then hanging out for the rest of the day, watching other kids because of the friendships between families. "You know, I never even *liked* baseball," Marisa Costantino, whose older brother Dominic was on both the 1976 Little League national championship and 1978 Pony League World Series title squads, told me in 2008. "I just never got into the sport. But I hardly ever missed a game. My mom had friends like Betty Freear and Arlene Catalana (whose sons Scott and Mike played in both leagues, Scott as an All-Star) and I was friends with their daughters. I played soccer, and

I'd be running around those baseball parks in my soccer uniform all day. I have so many great memories of Campbell, and I hardly ever even watched a whole game."

Subby Agliolo, who managed the 1979 Campbell Little League All-Stars to the most improbable of all our national championships, remembers the Campbell environment the same way.

"The World Series (appearances in the 1970s) really had nothing to do with it," Subby said. "I was there eight years, and the thing was, we were family. We had dinner dances, pancake breakfasts, trips to the (San Jose) Bees games. That's what I tell people when I watch my grandson play ... it was a family. My kids tell me it's not the same (in the leagues in which Subby's grandchildren play) ... even if our kids weren't playing, we'd be there all day and root for other parents' kids because we were friends with them. We all cheered for each other.

"We lived in San Jose then, but Campbell was my home. I guess it's like that angel on all of our shoulders. We (the 1979 players and coaches) got a blue pin (for winning the national championship) and I want to be buried with that pin."

I remember people like the Kephart family.

Tony Kephart probably should have made that 1976 All-Star team, but didn't, for reasons I still don't understand. In most leagues, then and especially now, the family would have distanced itself from everything connected with the league, except to bitch about the "politics" of the All-Star selection process and badmouth the kids who made the team while Tony was left off. In this case, Tony's father P.H., a plumber, and his wife Bev and Tony's sister Sandi immediately made plans to follow the team everywhere it went, and they even threw a couple of barbecues at their home for the team. The Kepharts were with us in San Bernardino and they were with us in Williamsport, driving their motor home cross-country to reach the World Series, and Tony was as involved in the games as a fan and friend as anybody in the Campbell camp. What we did was as much the Kepharts' triumph as it was anyone else's.

We had a unique group of parents, managers, coaches and other supporters, literally from 8 to 80, throughout our town during the 10 years (1974-83) I was involved with youth baseball in Campbell. A lot of the managers and coaches, and most of the people who were responsible for steering the league, didn't even have kids in the league at the time; they were volunteering their time and expertise simply because they wanted to be positive forces in young lives and because they loved baseball enough to want to convey that love to the kids. Campbell, as a baseball town, was unique because these people weren't individual strands. Together, they created a tapestry that was the fabric of our community. All the kids were *their* kids. And I think that, more than any other factor, was the reason we won as much as we did for as long as we did — because very little that was done was done selfishly.

You don't see that sentiment, or that belief and commitment to shared goals, on the baseball diamond much anymore. In fact, you hardly ever see it at all, in sports or in any other aspect of life.

I coached at a lot of levels, from high school to anthill baseball, and in a lot of places after I left Campbell, and my first priority always remained the same: I didn't want to be anybody's last coach because that kid had a bad experience with me. That's what I had been taught in Campbell, and I've never heard that phrase repeated anywhere else. The postseason, I was constantly reminded during my time in Campbell, would take care of itself. It was a separate, and until it began, secondary entity. That changed after 1979, after we won the Pony League World Series and reached the Little League World Series title game (losing 2-1 to Taiwan in eight innings) within a five-day span — something that had never been done in the same year, and hasn't been done since.

Right after that, parents from outside Campbell started moving within our boundaries and even faking addresses to get their kids into the Campbell system, and the 12 World Series participants that had come out of Campbell from 1960-79 came to represent a mandate rather than a affirmation of a system run the right way. Almost all of the people who made Campbell baseball what it had been left the system over the next few years, many doing so in protest, and my last involvement was in 1982 and 1983, when I revived and ran the Campbell American Legion program.

Before the 1980s were long underway, Campbell had became just another youth baseball system and just another town — especially after Campbell High, the geographical, social and historical epicenter of the city, closed in 1980. The mosaic we once had became a pile of shards. No Campbell-area team has been to a World Series since 1987, and more important, kids don't clamor to play baseball in Campbell anymore. There were 32 teams and over 500 players in Campbell Little League when I was there, including eight on each of four levels. In 2009, there were 22 teams with fewer than 300 players, even though Campbell's population has increased from about 30,000 in 1979 to about 40,000 three decades later.

Of course, other places — the Tampa, Houston and Atlanta areas, Long Beach and other communities in Southern California — have supplanted Campbell as citadels of youth baseball, at least if the criteria are championships won and professional and college players produced. But everything in youth baseball has changed since the period during which Campbell dominated. That's why I call Campbell, and this book, The Last Baseball Town.

In the late 1970s, the first primitive video games were starting to show up in arcades, but our kids still belonged to the pinball generation, and they also represented the last generation of kids whose preferred location in their houses was the door leading outside. You used computers to send men to the moon or steer airplanes, not as home entertainment or as a forum for opinions of little interest and even less value. There was no hip-hop culture to glamorize gangs and crime and drugs and rebellion, and you didn't worry about your kids riding their bikes from one end of town to the other, even at night. You could still be a kid in Campbell in the late 1970s without feeling that you had to do all your growing up in one sitting. Most of the negative influences that beckon to kids today didn't exist then and there, and while a few of our kids got sidetracked from time to time, most of them were able to find their way, often with the help of baseball.

Just as there is far more to detour kids away from baseball now than there was then, the baseball protocol itself has changed radically, and that change also began right after our program reached its apex in 1979 with the simultaneous appearances in the Little League and Pony League World Series.

Our players didn't have personal instructors or instructional DVDs or backyard batting cages or pitching machines, and "travel teams," where the emphasis is on individual showcasing and advancement, did not exist. Our facilities were (and still are) good, but Campbell has never had a lighted baseball field — in fact, the only regulation-sized diamond that ever existed within the city limits, on the former Campbell High campus, has been converted into a soccer pitch — and the ballparks we used were nothing like the industrial mall-like complexes you see today. It can be said that Campbell was the last American city to become a youth baseball leviathan without ever really intending to do so. It was a confluence of positive tributaries, many of which will be outlined in this book, rather than the culmination of any master plan. The only overriding objective was, as former Campbell Little League president John Hanrahan once put it to me, "dedication to the best of everything."

Campbell, just to the west of San Jose, in the 1970s was like a lot of the other suburban cities in the Santa Clara Valley before the phrase "Silicon Valley" came into vogue. It was a blue-collar bedroom community built on land that once had made the valley one of the most productive agricultural regions in the world. (Campbell still officially refers to itself as the Orchard City, yet the last orchards in town were gone for good by the time I left in 1983.) Most of the fathers of the kids in our system were plumbers or electricians or pipefitters or car assemblers or bartenders or small businessmen, and a lot of moms worked as well. The parents were more concerned with their children going to college and leading quality lives and being quality citizens and learning the value of hard work than they were about cashing in on them through baseball. Baseball was something to be played and enjoyed. One should try to excel at it, the parents thought, and my previous disclaimers notwithstanding, don't think for one minute that winning wasn't profoundly important in Campbell. It was. We expected to win every time we took the field in postseason play. But baseball remained something that our kids *did*. It never was *who they were*, even after we won all the national championships and even after some of them went on to star in high school and beyond, and it was never perceived as a career path.

That began to change right after our halcyon years, and today, many kids who are skilled in base-ball are perceived, even by their parents, as commodities whose "careers" start in Little League or on travel teams, and whose every move must be orchestrated so that they stay on track to make their careers in baseball or at least earn a scholarship to play in college. I think Campbell was the very last place within the continental U.S. where a youth baseball program won multiple world and national championships with kids who learned how to play by *playing*, and who took up and excelled in baseball not because they were pressured to do so, but because they *wanted* to do so, collectively and individually.

My early involvement with Campbell baseball was as Campbell Little League's $40-a-week announcer/groundskeeper/scorekeeper/statistician, and as such, I had to get there a couple of hours before that day's first game to groom and chalk the field. Early on, I'd sometimes do it after the previous day's last game, but I soon gave that up because when I'd get there the next day, I'd see that the field had been in continuous use since early morning, and looked as if the Chisholm Trail had been redirected through it. I'd chase them off, eventually – "C'mon Chuck, just *one more inning!*" – and only then could I start preparing the diamond for the upcoming game. In Campbell, kids played baseball – at the league- and city-maintained diamonds, on every playground and park in town, and on the residential streets, some of which sometimes seemed like siege zones because of wayward balls from impromptu games. Neighbors rarely parked their cars on the street because they knew doing so would put their cars squarely in the middle of a game of 500 or Three Flies Up or Over the Line. Even at night, it wasn't uncommon to drive down a residential street and see kids playing under streetlights.

Baseball was the peer pressure in Campbell then. You didn't plan to play baseball. You just did. Between those countless pickup games, and the 28-game schedule that was played every year at every level in the Campbell system, just about every baseball-oriented kid in Campbell had a fairly complete portfolio of baseball instincts by the time he had reached high school. And Campbell High had one of the best programs in Northern California, one that could serve as a pathway to college baseball and beyond for the kids who were talented and serious enough to contemplate that course.

I lived and worked in a lot of communities since I left Campbell, and I've never seen anything resembling that mentality, even in cities that poured far more material resources into their youth baseball programs than Campbell did.

Campbell baseball kids of my era often played other sports, and for some of them, baseball became a gateway to excellence in their subsequent athletic endeavors. John Aimonetti, who played on the 1976 Campbell All-Star team, completed only two more years of baseball before switching to football and authoring a career that took him to San Jose State – where one of his teammates was John Murphy, another '76 All-Star – and then to the Kansas City Chiefs. In 1981, Bellarmine Prep and Saratoga High met in the Central Coast Section football championship game, and each team had a 1976 Campbell Little League All-Star – Dominic Costantino with Bellarmine, which won the game, and John Lawson with Saratoga. Alan Spehar played baseball in Campbell Little League, but he was far more proficient in aquatic sports, and turned his attention to pool pursuits in earnest after his Little League days. By 1981, his junior season at Westmont High, he was a high school All-America, and in 1984, he came close to making the 1984 U.S. Olympic team. (A resident of Carmel in 2008, he was still a national-caliber age-group swimmer at age 44.) Andy Buchanan, a 1977 Campbell Little League All-Star, continued playing baseball through age 18 and participated in the Palomino World Series in 1983. But both his parents were Canadian, and his main priority, even as a Little Leaguer, was ice hockey. He played in the Youth Hockey Junior "A" national championships, and in 2008, he was coaching in the San Jose Sharks' youth hockey program.

Such athletic multi-tasking, however, became less common in the 1980s and 1990s, and now, even very young kids are told that if they want to achieve anything beyond the norm in any sport, they must focus exclusively on that sport. That postulate, patently false though it is, is impressed upon kids even more forcefully once they arrive in high school. Future wealth and fame never even entered into the kids-sports equation in the 1960s and 1970s. Now, too often they control the equation.

The end of the Campbell baseball era coincided with the advent of free agency and ballooning salaries in major league baseball, and it was at about that point that the carnivores among the parents began to descend on the local diamonds. They wanted the big money and the 48-point headlines for their kids and themselves, and the team and the joy stopped mattering. The kids became manufactured products. The game became scripted and regimented, and kids played in pain and wrecked their pitching arms because the adults were more interested in exploiting them than they were in protecting them. Fun and friendship and shared sacrifice and accomplishment didn't matter anymore. I saw the start of that phenomenon in the Bay Area early in the 1980s, ironically as one of the unintended results of our success, and today it has largely shrouded and deadened the sport, from tee ball to the major leagues and in just about every community where baseball is considered important.

In a lot of ways, the Campbell of our era was like today's Latin America or Caribbean, where there are few organized leagues to temper the sheer passion and joy of baseball played spontaneously — and not coincidentally, more proficiently — than it is in this country. Today, if you fly into just about any American city, almost every baseball diamond you see from the air is empty. Kids are told when, where and how they will play. The spontaneity and the joy are gone.

No place in America since the 1970s has done what Campbell has done in baseball the way Campbell did it. That's why Campbell was The Last Baseball Town. The story of Campbell baseball will never be written again, anywhere, and that's one of the main reasons I'm writing it now.

This book consists partly of a chronological history of Campbell youth baseball, going all the way back to 1909 when Campbell's first true youth baseball team won a championship in its first season of play. I will document the evolution of the formal Campbell youth baseball system, which dates to 1954 when Campbell Little League and the first version of what is now Campbell Pony League were formed. It was in 1954 that future NFL quarterback Craig Morton played alongside Robert Straight, father of the aforementioned Bobby who led us to two national championships. In the second part of the book, I will let some of the people who made our success possible tell the human side of the story.

The story of Campbell youth baseball in many ways parallels the story of Campbell itself, and while boys played baseball and grew up to be fine men in Campbell, Campbell itself grew up to be a fine community while they were here. That process will be intertwined with the baseball narrative in this book. I also intend for this book to be a cautionary story – a description of why the winning stopped and never resumed – and the epilogue will include my thoughts on whether there can ever be a Last Baseball Town II.

These are people and times that have great meaning to me, and I hope I can do them justice here. I also hope some of you feel some pangs of emotion after you read this book, even if you've never heard of Campbell or don't know about, or remember, what once happened here.

Chuck Hildebrand
Campbell, California
February 23, 2009

PART I:
THE PLACE AND THE PINNACLES

1909–1953: Beginnings

Campbell Avenue, Campbell's primary east-west artery, neither begins nor ends in Campbell. It begins in a high-end Sputnik-era neighborhood in west San Jose and ends about eight miles west on the northeastern edge of Saratoga, one of the most affluent communities in the western United States with a median home value of $1,660,000 in 2007. On a map, and economically, Campbell is in-between. The city's median home value in 2007 was $707,500, making it middle-class by Silicon Valley standards, and throughout the town's recent history, one could drive the length of Campbell Avenue and change municipalities at least a half-dozen times without any knowledge of having done so.

Campbell became an entertainment and commercial entity in the 1990s and 2000s, with a re-furbished downtown and dozens of high-end restaurants, nightclubs, specialty shops and condo-miniums. In the 1960s and 1970s, though, it was a middle-class bedroom community with few landmarks. Then as now, it afforded its residents a high quality of life, but most of its commercial establishments existed to serve Campbell residents and not to attract outsiders. Before the 1960s, when youth baseball excellence and Campbell first became synonymous, the community was an agricultural enclave with a high level of contentment, but little to call attention to itself from the historical or cultural perspectives.

Its founder and first resident was a farmer-surveyor named Benjamin Campbell, who in 1851 bought a 160-acre tract that once had been part of a Spanish land grant, and established a wheat farm near what is now Campbell's main intersection, at what is now Winchester Boulevard and Campbell Avenue. After returning to his native Missouri to marry, Campbell and his wife led a wagon train consisting of 43 settlers back to his tract, and they became the township of Campbell's first residents. A few other farmers and orchardists bought plots of land near Campbell's, and a modest settlement began to emerge in the 1870s and 1880s between Winchester and the Southern Pacific railroad tracks about a mile to the east.

The commercial district, bisected by Campbell Avenue — a dirt road until it was graveled in 1912 and paved shortly thereafter — consisted of a few shops, churches, mercantile stores and liveries. Benjamin Campbell, who until the 1880s owned about two-thirds of the land currently within the Campbell city limits, was an austere, church-going teetotaler, and whenever he sold commercial lots, he included a clause in the contract stipulating that liquor could not be sold there. Not long after the township was founded, a man opened a saloon in a shack next to the Campbell Avenue Bridge on the banks of Los Gatos Creek. Benjamin Campbell and other citizens formed a vigilante committee and attempted to pull down the structure with a team of horses. The effort failed, but the building slid into Los Gatos Creek shortly thereafter during one of Campbell's frequent floods, and no attempt was made to rebuild it. In fact, Campbell never was home to a permanent saloon until after the repeal of nationwide Prohibition in 1933, and it was a distinction in which the citizenry took pride. Even for many years after 1933, relatively few establishments that served or sold liquor operated in Campbell.

Another reason Campbell had little liquor-related activity throughout most of its early history was more practical than philosophical: The early inhabitants were so consumed with working their orchards and farmlands that recreational time was at a premium. And because the Santa Clara Valley was then a sparsely populated agricultural area that included only one city (San Jose, which is now the 10th-largest city in the country but didn't exceed the 10,000 population mark until 1905) of significant size, Campbell had few visitors and was largely its own sphere of influence. In fact, only two Campbell news stories prompted much widespread attention outside the Santa Clara Valley before Campbell became an incorporated city in 1952.

The first such story unfolded on May 26, 1896, when a ranch hand named James Dunham murdered his wife and five other members of Campbell's McGlincy family, one of the most prominent in the Santa Clara Valley. The crime, and its lurid details, made national headlines and prompted one of the most extensive manhunts in California's early history. (It failed; Dunham was never apprehended, and the case remains unsolved.) The horror and rage that the McGlincy case prompted is reflected by the tomb at San Jose's Oak Hill cemetery that contains the remains of the victims. It's a horizontal concrete slab, about 400 square feet in size. Inscribed on the tomb, along with the victims' names, dates of birth and death, is a line from Romans 12:19: "Vengeance is Mine, I will Repay Saith the Lord" in enormous black lettering.

Seven years later, on May 11, 1903, President Theodore Roosevelt — who in 2009 was still the only sitting U.S. president to have set foot in Campbell — planted a *Sequoia sempervirens* sapling near the southeast corner of Winchester Road and Campbell Avenue, on the original Campbell High campus. It was cut down in 1964 when the city widened Winchester Road and renamed it Winchester Boulevard, but Campbell Union High School District superintendent Laurence Hill — who also was the first president of Campbell Little League — had carved a burl from the original tree shortly before it was cut down. In 1966, that burl was planted on the "new" Campbell High campus (now the Campbell Community Center), which had been completed in 1938 on the northwest corner of the Campbell-Winchester intersection. In 2009, the tree that emerged from that burl was about 70 feet high.

Campbell High, which had opened in 1900, already had started to field track, tennis and basketball teams when Roosevelt visited in 1903, and TR, who spoke and wrote often of the benefits of sports and in 1906 would prod university presidents into founding what is now the National Collegiate Athletic Association, told the assembled Campbell students and the other assembled townspeople: "I want to see you play hard when you play, and when you work, do not play at all."

Before and after the McGlincy murders and the Roosevelt visit, though, Campbell was little more than a speck on an uncluttered map, and its growth until the late 1940s was steady but slow. The first building that attracted outsiders' attention for its architecture and scope was Campbell Grammar School, which opened in 1922 and cost $155,000 – a sum of no small magnitude at the time – to build. After it was closed as a grammar school in 1964, it served as the new West Valley College's temporary campus from 1964-76, and after a period of abandonment and decay, it was finally demolished in the 1980s and subsequently rebuilt as the Campbell Heritage Village Offices building – the exterior of which looks almost exactly like the school did when it was first constructed.

While Campbell didn't develop a reputation for athletic excellence until much later, sports represented a part of the local culture from the township's earliest days. The first Campbell resident to gain widespread notoriety for his athletic prowess was Cornelius Erwin "Swede" Righter, who was born in 1897 in the family home on 599 El Patio Avenue, a Victorian structure that had just been rebuilt after a fire in 1896, and still stood in 2009. His father, Francis Marion Righter, was one of Campbell's earliest inhabitants, having settled there in 1873. Swede Righter graduated from Campbell High in 1912 at the age of 15, and was an All-Coast football and basketball player at Stanford after serving in the Army during World War I. He was a member of the 1920 U.S. rugby team that won a gold medal at the Olympic Games in Antwerp, Belgium. In 1921, after becoming one of several early Campbell High graduates to earn a degree at Stanford, Righter began a 40-year teaching and coaching career, first at College of the Pacific (located in San Jose before it moved to Stockton in the early 1920s) and then at Burlingame High in San Mateo County. He died in 1985 at age 88.

Righter also played baseball at Campbell High, which fielded its first baseball team in 1909 in the Interurban Athletic Union. The IAU had been founded the previous year around the Interurban Railway, which was the precursor of the light-rail lines that bisect the Santa Clara Valley today. The Interurban connected San Jose, Campbell, Saratoga, Los Gatos and Congress Springs. Eventually, the IAU would evolve into the Peninsula Athletic League, which extended from the southern end of Santa Clara County to the San Francisco city limits. Campbell, Mountain View, Santa Clara, Fremont of Sunnyvale, Los Gatos, and Live Oak of Morgan Hill withdrew from the

PAL in 1930 to form the Santa Clara Valley Athletic League, in which Campbell remained until the West Valley Athletic League was formed in 1961. San Jose and Palo Alto, the two largest high schools in Santa Clara County, remained in the PAL after 1930 along with Sequoia of Redwood City, Burlingame, San Mateo, Jefferson of Daly City, and South San Francisco.

Like virtually every community in America before World War I, when baseball was the only widely-played team sport and was rivaled in popularity only by boxing and horse racing, Campbell had a town team that competed against squads representing nearby communities. The team was called the Athletics – presumably after the Philadelphia Athletics, who won four American League pennants and three World Series from 1910-1914. The Athletics sometimes took the Southern Pacific's "Suntan Special" train into the Santa Cruz Mountains, and played the team from Wright's Station (near present-day Scotts Valley), which served several nearby resorts in the days before the Suntan Special was discontinued in 1940, dooming the resorts and Wright's Station. But Campbell High was too tiny to field a baseball team in its earliest years. Its first graduating class, in 1901, had consisted of one person – Charles Beardsley, who went on to graduate from Stanford and later became a prominent East Bay attorney and president of the American Bar Association. By 1912, its 12th year of existence, Campbell High had graduated a *total* of only 137 students, including 14 that year, so when the school competed in baseball for the first time in 1909, it couldn't do so without almost all of the enrolled boys lending their varying talents.

The catalyst for the establishment of baseball at Campbell High in 1909 was a donation by the Santa Clara Valley outlet of the Spalding Company, the nation's largest sporting-goods dealer at the time. A silver loving cup, to be given annually to the IAU baseball champion, was commissioned and created, and that first Campbell team established a winning precedent. It won the first IAU Cup, going 5-0 against Los Gatos (which had opened the previous fall), Mountain View and Live Oak, and capturing two non-league wins over much-larger Santa Clara High. A rudimentary diamond was built on a lot adjoining the Campbell High campus, and through fund-raising by the players and donations from local businesses, new white-with-green-trim uniforms, described by the *Campbell Interurban Press* as "stunning," were purchased. Maurice Weeks, the team's top pitcher, was doing double duty that spring; he also was the lead pitcher for the town team. The Campbell High batting order, which included no seniors, usually read this way: Harold Lancaster, third base; D. Currier, center field; Claud Vollman, second base; Marshman, left field; Crow, shortstop; Nic Dunphy, right field; Maurice Weeks, pitcher; and Herbert Scholz, first base.

Claud Vollman, a freshman that year, was a senior along with Swede Righter on the 1912 team that claimed the IAU Cup again. That team also included Herman Freyschlag at third base, Frank Harris at second base, Freeman Duncan at first base, Vollman catching, Charles Brandenberg in center field, Arnold in right field, Sibley Dawley pitching, Goodridge at shortstop, and Swede Righter in left field and batting ninth. Although that team won the coveted championship cup, it stumbled against Los Gatos in a 10-2 loss, resulting in an upbraiding from the *Campbell Interurban Press*: "The Campbell team needs a course of rigorous coaching which, with the material at hand, would produce a very fast high school team." The Campbell-Los Gatos rivalry, which would endure until Campbell High closed in 1980, already was intense; instead of referring to the Wildcats by their correct nickname, the *Interurban Press* sneeringly called them the "Meows."

Oliver Righter, Swede's younger brother, played on the 1915 team that won another IAU Cup, with Ed Pierce doing the bulk of the pitching. In 1916, Campbell was in an expanded IAU that also included San Jose, Santa Clara and Palo Alto for baseball, and the team, though considered Campbell's best up to that time, finished third in the stronger league. Campbell lost 19-9 at home to Santa Clara in a game that reportedly attracted 800 spectators. It traveled all the way to Santa Cruz for one game — a trip that would be the equivalent of crossing the Sierra Nevada mountains now — and beat San Jose Normal (the future San Jose State University) 19-3.

Although big games, like the ones against Los Gatos, often attracted large crowds for the time, high school sports were of limited general appeal during this time, because the majority of teenagers of the period entered the work force before graduation. (Ironically, high school athletic programs, especially those in rural areas, were among the few beneficiaries of the Great Depression. Because jobs were scarce in the 1930s, more 17- and 18-year-olds stayed in school until graduation, and townspeople found high school sports to be an inexpensive diversion from the hardships of the day.) Because Campbell High was on a microscopic budget and couldn't travel far for games, its baseball schedule in the early years included some exotic opponents. Besides San Jose Normal, which Campbell played several times in the first decade of its baseball existence, Campbell in 1910 and 1911 played Heald Business College of San Jose. It also had occasional matchups with Montezuma Mountain School, a private boys school that had opened in 1911 on Bear Hill Road in the Santa Cruz Mountains overlooking Los Gatos. Montezuma had sports teams only intermittently before its closure in 1955, but as an academic institution, it was almost a century ahead of its time. *History of the Santa Clara Valley*, written in 1922 by Eugene Sawyer, described Montezuma this way:

"Eleven years ago, Ernest A. Rogers and William J. Meredith, both teachers in the schools of California, became dissatisfied with the restrictions imposed, by the methods of instruction employed in the average school, upon the initiative and opportunity for the expression of personal convictions by teachers. Through years of teaching and studying methods of instruction and the results accomplished they saw a great gap between what the public school is equipped to do and what is demanded of it. They had reached the point where their experience pointed to a better way of doing things intimately related to the very foundation of human education. Since they did not have the opportunity for putting their ideas into practice while teaching in the public schools nor the natural environment conducive to natural education, at their own expense and by making sacrifices, they established the Montezuma Mountain School for boys ... The student body is an actual democratic state in miniature, self-governing through a mayor and board of commissioners, acting under a simple constitution and elected by ballot, holding office subject to recall on petition at the pleasure of the electorate. Legislation and administration are actually subject to review, of course, by the faculty, which functions in this respect as a court of appeals. Constitutional amendment and by-laws are initiated from time to time by the commissioners, or petition, as experience shows the need ... The boys lead an outdoor, pioneer life, in keeping with the principles of the school ... They sleep on the open porches of the school dormitories, where they are constantly under the supervision of directors. The open air gymnasium, the library, the assembly hall, the swimming hole, the pond with its boats and slides, the teeters and the merry-go-round add varied interest to the day's program of events after school hours."

After 1909, Campbell High assembled baseball teams annually until 1918, when the final convulsions of World War I and the worldwide influenza outbreak diverted all attention away from sports. After the U.S. entered the war in April 1917, the Athletics played a benefit game that attracted about 600 people, but the Athletics also were unable to operate in 1918, and they did not reappear after the war, although Campbell had several town teams that operated at various times between the world wars.

Campbell High did not play baseball again until 1921, when its senior class – 29 – was the school's largest up to that time. As one of the smallest schools in the PAL and after 1930 in the Santa Clara Valley Athletic League, its baseball teams often struggled. But a surprising number of Campbell athletes became prominent well beyond the township over the next three decades.

Henry Oliver, who had played for Campbell High and the Athletics before World War I, became the first Campbell resident to play professional baseball, competing for several teams in the lower minors before a short stint with Seattle of the Pacific Coast League in 1923. Tony Sunzeri, Campbell High Class of 1936, became Campbell's second Olympian (after Swede Righter) in 1940. Using a bamboo pole, he cleared 14 feet in the pole vault at the U.S. team trials to win a spot on the American track and field team. However, those 1940 Olympics, which had been scheduled for Tokyo, were cancelled because of the outbreak of World War II in 1939. Sunzeri went on to serve in the Army Air Forces during the war, and was a successful San Jose businessman for many years before his death in 2004 at age 85.

Bert Robinson was a football, baseball and basketball star at Campbell High, from which he graduated in 1939. He went on to excel in football and basketball at San Jose State, and is a member of that school's sports Hall of Fame. Robinson was with the SJS football team in 1941 when it traveled to Hawaii for two season-ending games – against the University of Hawaii on December 13, and against Willamette College of Oregon three days later. Neither game was played, of course, and after the Japanese attacked Pearl Harbor on December 7, Robinson and some of the other players were commandeered to serve as Honolulu policemen until December 19, when they finally were able to obtain ship passage back to the mainland.

Soon after Robinson got back to California, he joined the Army Air Forces, from which today's U.S. Air Force originated. During his three years in the AAF, he flew 51 B-17 missions over Europe, and was discharged from the service as a first lieutenant after earning a number of decorations, including the Distinguished Flying Cross. After his discharge, he spent two seasons as a football and basketball coach at Bakersfield College before being hired as Campbell High's basketball coach in the fall of 1948. Robinson coached the Buccaneers for 20 years and won six league championships before starting the program at Prospect when it opened in 1968, and he remained there for more than a decade before retiring. He died in 2008 at age 86.

Mitch Lobrovich, a 1940 Campbell High graduate, could have become the township's first major league player had his baseball career not been interrupted, first by World War II and later by options outside baseball that he couldn't pass up in good conscience.

Lobrovich, whose father Mitchell was a prominent Santa Clara Valley orchardist, earned a baseball scholarship from Santa Clara University, which at the time was one of the most successful college baseball programs in the country. (It also was a national power in football, winning two Sugar Bowls and finishing 15th or better in the final *Associated Press* rankings five times in seven seasons from 1936-42.) At the time Lobrovich first enrolled there in the fall of 1940, Santa Clara already had sent 22 of its former players to the major leagues, including Marv Owen, who'd been the starting third baseman for the Detroit Tigers when they won the 1935 World Series. One of Lobrovich's Santa Clara teammates, Duane Pillette, also went on to play in the majors.

Lobrovich enlisted in the Army in April 1943, graduated from Officer Candidate School in Fort Sill, Okla., and saw combat as an artillery officer throughout the Pacific theater, including Okinawa. By the time he was discharged from the Army in 1946, he was 24 and torn between his passion for baseball, his sense of responsibility to the family business, and his desire to further his education through the GI Bill. For the next five years, he juggled all three.

In 1947, despite his advanced baseball age, the New York Giants signed Lobrovich and sent him to their Reno affiliate in the Class C Sunset League. He batted .353 that year and .316 in 1948 despite taking more than a month of each season off, with the Giants' approval, to return to Campbell and oversee the harvest at the family's 27 cherry orchards throughout the Santa Clara Valley. By 1949, though, the Giants wanted Lobrovich to commit fulltime to baseball. Rather than do so, he retired, returning to the Santa Clara Valley to complete work on his degree at Santa Clara and then going to Columbia University in New York City to earn a masters degree.

Upon returning from New York, he went back to Reno, took a job as a teacher and coach at Reno High, and played for the Reno Silver Sox in the Class D Far West League in 1950 and 1951. The Far West League folded after the 1951 season, leaving Reno without a professional team, but Lobrovich stayed there for another year, playing semipro ball, before leaving in the fall of 1952 to accept a job as a regional manager for a book publisher in San Jose. Lobrovich later moved to Texas and was successful in various business ventures, including an oxygen-equipment firm in Dallas. In 2009, at age 87, he was living in retirement in Sarasota, Fla.

In 1945, Billy Wilson, a native of Oklahoma who had come to Campbell as a teenager as part of the Dust Bowl migration, graduated from Campbell after a stellar four-year varsity career during which he led Campbell High to a long-awaited athletic breakthrough.

Particularly vexing to Campbell athletes and their supporters in the pre-World War II era was the Buccaneers' paucity of success against archrival Los Gatos High. Los Gatos was much larger than Campbell, which grew steadily after World War I but still had only 85 graduates in its Class of 1935, and their football rivalry didn't begin until 1934, when Campbell fielded a football team for the first time. Campbell went scoreless in the first six matchups against Los Gatos before finally beating the Wildcats 7-0 in 1940. As a senior in 1944, Wilson, a two-way end, made the new T formation incendiary under new coach Walt Hill; in a 40-0 victory over Fremont, Campbell threw 21 passes and completed 11, both unheard-of totals at the time. The Buccaneers were unbeaten, although they tied with Washington of Centerville (now part of the city of Fremont), and won the school's first SCVAL football championship.

Wilson also was one of the SCVAL's best basketball players, and during the 1945 track season, he set a school triple-jump record (40 feet, 8 inches) that stood for almost a decade. He played a year of freshman football at San Jose State before serving an 18-month Navy hitch. After his discharge, he returned to San Jose State and played football and basketball for the Spartans from 1948-50, and in 1951 he joined the San Francisco 49ers, who were beginning their second year in the National Football League. Wilson was a wide receiver for 10 seasons (1951-60) with the 49ers, for whom he caught 407 passes for 5,902 yards. He made the Pro Bowl six times and led the NFL in receptions three times. After the end of his playing career, he remained with the 49ers for many years as an assistant coach and scout before his death in January 2009 at age 81.

Wilson's family was among many to migrate from the Midwest to the Santa Clara Valley in search of agricultural work during the Dust Bowl calamity of the 1930s, and after the U.S. began incremental military mobilization in the late 1930s as the Axis war machine terrorized Europe and Asia, some of the valley's industries entered into military contracts and expanded to fulfill them. As a result, the population in the vast area that Campbell High serviced had begun to swell, making it apparent that a new campus was needed. It was finished in 1938 after two years of construction, and with the completion of the athletic complex – including new football, basketball, track and baseball facilities and six tennis courts – two years later, Campbell had a state-of-the-art sports plant for the first time. Enrollment was up to 712 in 1940, although most of the new arrivals did not live in Campbell township, where the economy remained agriculture-driven and growth stayed modest.

The township wasn't rousted from its bucolic idyll until Pearl Harbor, after which the erstwhile "Valley of Heart's Delight" saw its first full-scale industrial and population boom, with companies such as General Electric, Sylvania, IBM and Hewlett-Packard establishing wartime plants. Even after the war ended in 1945, the growth continued unabated, as the wartime industries converted to a peacetime footing. Many who had come to the area seeking war work stayed with those companies and the dozens of others that followed, and servicemen who had been transported through the valley during the war liked it and decided, with the help of the GI Bill, to plant roots there.

A.P. "Dutch" Hamann became San Jose's city manager in 1950, and made no secret of his intention to transform San Jose into a major West Coast metropolis. With the support of developers, Hamann began a series of land annexations that pushed San Jose's city limits to the borders of adjoining townships, including Campbell, and sometimes beyond.

These encroachments prompted Campbell, where the voters had turned down three previous incorporation measures, to finally take that step by a 686-633 margin in 1952. Self-preservation was one of two major reasons Campbell finally opted for incorporation — flood control, a major problem in Campbell throughout its early history, was the other — but the "annexation wars" between San Jose and Campbell persisted throughout Hamann's tenure, which ended in 1969. By that time, San Jose had completed more than 1,500 annexations under his stewardship. (He died in 1977 in the Tenerife disaster on the Canary Islands, where two Boeing 747s collided on a runway, killing 583 people, the highest single-accident toll in world aviation history.)

Throughout the 1950s and 1960s, Hamann and Campbell leaders played a game of real-estate hopscotch. Every time San Jose annexed an unincorporated parcel, Campbell tried to blunt or encircle that extension by claiming surrounding tracts. The impact of that process is seen now by the jagged edges of both cities' maps, and that indiscriminate sprawl is the reason that somebody traveling along Campbell's transportation arteries will cross into and out of Campbell several times over a stretch of only a few miles. It's also the reason Campbell became decentralized, especially after the opening of regional shopping centers just outside the city limits, particularly Cambrian Plaza in 1953 and the mammoth Valley Fair in 1955.

With its new territorial acquisitions, Campbell, which couldn't match San Jose in terms of what it could offer new or relocated industries, began to emerge as a bedroom community for San Jose. Many returning World War II and Korean War veterans, able through the GI Bill to afford to become first-time home-buyers, settled into the new housing tracts within the city limits. In 1948, the Campbell Union School District opened two new schools, Moorpark and San Tomas, to augment the existing Campbell Grammar School. Campbell High's enrollment topped the 1,000 mark in 1949, prompting the high school district to float a $950,000 bond issue for an expansion that was obsolete before it was completed in 1950. Another bond issue, this one for $2.5 million in 1953, financed the construction of Camden High, which opened in 1955. (By 1968, when Prospect High opened, the district included eight schools. The high school district's enrollment reached a peak of 15,700 in 1972 before it began to decline steadily, forcing the closure of Camden and Campbell in 1980 and Blackford and Branham in 1991. Branham was later reopened.)

With the new families came a widespread interest in providing recreational baseball for their children. Campbell and Moreland grammar schools had organized interscholastic teams sporadically before the war, and for some time thereafter, but the first attempt to institutionalize Campbell youth baseball came in 1947, when a civic-improvement group called the Campbell Coordinating Council teamed with Lloyd Nelson, a local sporting-goods dealer, to form the Junior Hardball League. It was divided into two divisions, one for seventh and eighth graders and one for younger boys, and everybody who lived in the Campbell Union High School District was eligible.

The Junior Hardball League, which wasn't affiliated with any national organization and did not schedule games against outside teams, was immediately popular, with 130 boys competing. Games were played at Campbell High and Campbell Grammar School. For unknown reasons, it wasn't reorganized the following year, but local kids teams were assembled from 1948-52, and played informally among each other and against opponents from Los Gatos, Cupertino and other nearby communities. Other kids signed up for junior softball leagues, which proliferated after a fund-raising drive in 1949 yielded $3,000 to install lights at the Campbell Grammar School softball field. A few of the better high school players honed their skills in the various semipro baseball leagues that operated in the Santa Clara Valley at the time.

By 1953, it was apparent that a more permanent outlet for Campbell's baseball-playing youth was needed, and it was at that point that the nascent Little League program began to intrigue Campbell's baseball-minded citizens.

Begun in Williamsport, Pa., in 1939, Little League didn't make its way into Northern California until 1950, when *San Jose Mercury* sportswriter Wes Mathis (whose son Kevin much later played in Campbell Little League) helped found San Jose American Little League, headquartered at the Santa Clara Valley Youth Village on Newhall Street near the Santa Clara-San Jose border. Several other Santa Clara Valley leagues started soon after, including now-defunct Burbank Little League on San Jose's near west side. Campbell entered two teams in the new Burbank league in 1953, and from that seed, Campbell Little League sprouted in 1954.

1954–58: Organization

In 1953, two Campbell teams – the Campbell Merchants and the Campbell Pirates, sponsored by Western Gravel – had played in the new Burbank Little League. In 1954, interest was such that Campbell Little League split from Burbank and played under its own name for the first time. The league president was Laurence Hill, who also was the superintendent of the Campbell Union High School District, and the vice president was Ken Robinson. The secretary-treasurer was Guy Troedson, a longtime teacher and physical education instructor in the Cambrian School District just outside Campbell. Much later, Troedson's son Rich pitched for the San Diego Padres in 1973-74 after starring at Camden High and Santa Clara University.

Four teams played an 18-game schedule on the Campbell Grammar School softball field during Campbell Little League's inaugural season. Craig Morton, the future University of California and NFL quarterback who today is probably Campbell's best-known former athlete, played for the Campbell Stamps team, as did Robert Straight, whose son Bobby was the centerpiece player on the 1976 national championship team. The Campbell Stamps name, which was to remain a sponsorship fixture in the league throughout its early years, was a product of the Campbell Merchants Association's sale of redeemable stamps – similar to the S&H Green Stamps and Blue Chip Stamps programs that were familiar to shoppers nationwide in the 1950s and 1960s. Throughout the merchants' sponsorship, plural and singular references to the team were used interchangeably, although most team uniforms of the period included the final "S."

Interestingly, neither Morton nor Straight made the first Campbell Little League All-Star team, which played only one game, a 1-0 loss to Spartan Little League of San Jose. Jack Puma, who did make the '54 All-Star team, had the distinction of being the first batter in Campbell Little League history. Representing the Cambrian Plaza team, he faced Western Gravel pitcher Tony DiCenzo, an 11-year-old who also was chosen for that first All-Star team.

The Campbell Pony League also came into existence in 1954, outfitting eight teams, drawn from throughout the western Santa Clara Valley, for its first season, which was conducted at Campbell High. It was one of the first western affiliates of the Pony baseball program – the name is an acronym for Protect Our Nation's Youth – that had started in 1950 in Washington, Pa., as a transition program for boys who wished to continue playing beyond Little League, but weren't ready to begin play on a regulation-sized diamond. (In Pony League, the pitching rubber is 54 feet from home plate, compared to 46 feet in Little League and 60 feet, 6 inches on regulation-sized diamonds.) Max Kinsey, who pitched for the team sponsored by the local Campbell American Legion post, highlighted the season by pitching two no-hitters. George Miskulin was the first president of the league; he was the athletic director at Campbell High at the time, and in 1959, he became Del Mar High's first principal.

The level of youth baseball interest in Campbell at that point was such that the weekly *Campbell Press* – the "Interurban" had long since been removed from the name – routinely printed full box scores for both leagues, and once the 1954 Little League season was underway, so many kids signed up that the league stitched together a six-team farm league in time to play a season that started in July and extended through the third week of August.

Although the city had incorporated only two years before, it already had 7,662 people in 1954, almost twice its population at the start of World War II. The Campbell High district was geographically massive, extending well into south-central San Jose to the east and into Cupertino to the west. It was fed by the Union, Moreland and Cambrian elementary-school districts as well as the local Campbell Union School District, and the high school's enrollment – 1,687 at the beginning of the 1953-54 school year, compared to only 712 in 1940 – had prompted the Campbell Union High School District to float a bond issue to build a second high school, Camden.

The area's economy was still driven primary by agriculture – in 1954, 90 percent of the world's prunes were grown within a 25-mile radius of Campbell – but that was about to change. The California Department of Transportation already had announced plans to build a freeway through town as part of the expansion of Route 5 (now Highway 17) between San Jose and Santa Cruz, and three more Campbell-district elementary schools – Dover, Hamilton and Monroe – were either ready for occupancy or under construction. A three-bedroom home in the Sunnyside Gardens tract, near the intersection of Budd and Kenneth avenues, cost $8,195 – a price that would have been prohibitive before World War II, but had been made feasible for many World War II and Korean War veterans because of the GI Bill, which President Franklin Roosevelt had signed into law in 1944.

Despite the urban sprawl, many still felt (or at least hoped) Campbell would remain a rural outpost. "The horn of plenty is not yet choked with too many subdivisions," intoned a *Campbell Press* editorial in late 1953, "and let's hope that it never will be."

Alas, 1955 was the year that Campbell and the rest of the Santa Clara Valley reached the no-turning-back point in their commitment to an urban future.

That year, rural traditions such as the 63-year-old Old Settlers Day parade were still being celebrated, and the new Cherry Lane School's home-and-school club raised funds by conducting a whist tournament. (Whist, one of the most popular card games of the 18th and 19th centuries, is virtually extinct today.) But urban encroachment and urban ways were taking over. Two new shopping centers were opened in 1955 – the Campbell Shopping Center at Latimer and Winchester, and another on Hacienda Avenue. Cambrian Plaza, at the intersection of Union and Camden avenues just outside the Campbell city limits, in 1953 had become the first full-blown shopping center in the western Santa Clara Valley, and the mammoth and futuristic Valley Fair center, which featured a merry-go-round on its roof, would open in 1955 on Stevens Creek Road in west San Jose only two miles from the San Jose-Campbell border. Valley Fair's main tenants when it opened were department-store chains that had tried in vain to obtain property in downtown San Jose. By 1970, most shoppers had abandoned downtown San Jose in favor of Valley Fair and other shopping centers in the outlying areas, and San Jose's original commercial core virtually ceased to exist.

Campbell also installed its first permanent traffic light in 1955, at the intersection of Campbell and Winchester, and for the first time, Campbell, which hadn't even had direct-dial telephone service until 1942, was assigned telephone numbers that included seven digits. In those days, telephone numbers consisted of two letters (corresponding with the letters on the telephone dial) and five digits. Campbell was assigned FR, or 37, as its prefix. In the post-Franklin Roosevelt years, the FR morphed in casual speech into Franklin, so if someone had, say, the 378-2500 phone number, it was called "Franklin 8-2500." That system stayed in place until the mid-1960s, when the two-letter prefix faded from popular use and seven-digit references became the norm. Campbell and the rest of Santa Clara County were in the 415 area code at the time; the current 408 code area wasn't split off until 1959.

The Ford auto-assembly plant in Milpitas, which was to employ many Campbell youth baseball parents over the years before it was closed in 1983 and later converted into a shopping mall, also opened in 1955. At least a half-dozen more schools were under construction in the Campbell-Cambrian Park area. Jonas Salk's polio vaccine was widely distributed for the first time that spring, and Campbell school children were among the 16,000 Santa Clara County youngsters who were given the new vaccine for the first time in April as part of the nationwide "Polio Pioneer" program.

It's difficult for people in the 21st century to comprehend the terror that polio once spawned, especially among parents. Even after polio patient Franklin Roosevelt's Presidency, relatively little was known about the disease, although nobody had to be told about its capacity for crippling and killing. In 1954, more than 50,000 infantile paralysis cases were reported nationwide, and the random nature of the disease left even the youngest and strongest at risk. In nearby Los Gatos, Don Panighetti had become one of the best athletes in Los Gatos High history – and as such, a prime tormenter of rival Campbell – by the time he graduated in 1947. After being recruited by Notre Dame and many other major-college football powers, Panighetti chose St. Mary's College in Moraga. In November 1948, just after his second football season with the Gaels, he was stricken by polio during a visit home. In less than a month, he was dead at age 19.

Almost as soon as Salk's vaccine became available, the scope of its potential was immediately apparent. (By 1963, the national total of reported cases was down to 400.) In Campbell, it was proposed during the summer of 1955 that one of the new elementary schools be named after Salk. Instead, the new campus, at the intersection of San Tomas Aquino and Bucknall roads, became Bucknall School.

Another construction project took place early that year on the western edge of the grounds of Rosemary School, which had opened in 1953 at the intersection of Hamilton Avenue and Millich Drive, about three miles northwest of downtown Campbell. This was a modest under-taking compared to some of the other building projects in town at the time, but it was one of the few facilities built in the city at that time that still was used for its original purpose more than 50 years later.

"Little League Stadium" was primarily the result of the foresight and labor of the Campbell Rotary Club, which had proposed a Little League-specific ballpark not long after Campbell Little League had made its debut the year before. The Rotarians and not the Little League itself were primarily responsible for its construction, although many of the people involved belonged to both organizations. The Campbell Union School District leased the plot to the Little League, under a permanent $1-per-year arrangement, and the ballpark was built by volunteers on week-ends over a six-month period. The Rotarians spearheaded the project as part of the national organization's 50-year anniversary. Merv Willoughby, the Campbell Stamps manager, supervised the project, Hal Beatty of Western Gravel donated all of the necessary concrete and the labor required to pour it, and the wood was donated by Campbell Lumber's Doc Arends, the local Rotary chapter's president.

The first games at the new ballpark were played on June 4, 1955, and several hundred people turned out, including players, coaches and parents from the 10 teams – four major, six farm – that comprised the league as it began its second season. The first batter in the ballpark's history was Western Gravel leadoff man Frankie Testa, whose sister Darlene's two sons, Paul and Jim Balbas, both played in the league during the 1970s. (Paul's son Ian played there too, finishing up in 2008.) Mayor Richard Morton, no relation to Craig, threw out the first ball, and the Rosemary School band, directed by Ed Tonini, played. Tonini remained at Rosemary as music director until his death of a heart attack at age 55 in 1977, two years before his grandson Steve was on the 1979 Campbell Little League national championship team.

When it first opened, the facility had only one diamond, and home plate was beyond the present-day left-field corner. Any balls that went over the left-field fence wound up on Hamilton Avenue, which then was a two-lane road that had no businesses adjoining it and dead-ended a couple of blocks west of the park. "There was nothing around it except orchards," Jack Zogg, who came to Campbell Little League as a minor-division coach in 1958, remembered. "You'd park on Hamilton, behind the fence. The first year I managed in the majors there (1959), Ranny Baldinger hit a home run over the fence and broke my windshield."

The main building that is the hub of the Campbell Little League complex today was not part of the original construction – it was built in 1963 when the complex was completely overhauled – and the fences and the original dugouts were made of wood. Little visible landscaping was done, although some of the trees that much later were to give the park a bucolic quality had been planted. Cherry and apricot orchards bracketed the ballpark, and San Tomas Creek, which was rerouted when San Tomas Expressway was built in the mid-1960s, adjoined the property. Photographs taken on the ballpark's opening day show almost nothing in the background except sky, the Santa Cruz Mountains to the south, and orchards.

The project might be considered austere by 21st-century standards, and because of its wood-based construction, the park looks ramshackle in the photographs that were taken during its first day of service. But it was hailed at the time as state-of-the-art and visionary. One reason was that it was one of the first attempts to centralize a multi-tiered youth baseball organization in one permanent hub. In 1955 and for many years afterward, most youth baseball organizations didn't have formal homes any larger than the inside of a post-office box. They played at multiple sites that usually were hastily-converted playgrounds used for other sports and activities when baseball wasn't played there. Almost all of the early Little League facilities had skinned all-dirt infields that originally had been designed for softball, and some didn't even grass in the outfield. If a Little League park of the 1950s had outfield fences at all, they were temporary barriers that were dismantled when the baseball season ended. But Little League Stadium's main diamond had permanent wooden fences and bleachers, and its most conspicuous feature was a carefully manicured grass infield that onlookers said gave it the appearance of a miniature major league park. It was a statement on the part of everyone involved in its planning and construction that this park was permanent, and would be used for Little League baseball and nothing else. Although the original wooden fences and stands have long since given way to chain-link barriers and metal bleachers, what's now Bob Holman Field remains a sanctuary where only baseball is played.

The Opening Day games of 1955 were preceded by a league fund-raising breakfast, during which 900 meals were served. It was the beginning of a Campbell Little League tradition that still was observed more than a half-century later. On the first day of play at Little League Stadium, Jay's Sheet Metal edged Campbell Stamps 7-6 on a two-run single by David Hill (Laurence's son) and John Ezzie pitched the first of several no-hitters he was to craft that season as Mac's Market beat Western Gravel 2-1.

Although Craig Morton is the best known of the early Campbell Little League alumni, Ezzie can be described as the league's first dominant player. "He wasn't a real big guy," recalled John Oldham, who later coached against Ezzie when Oldham was at Campbell High and Ezzie was pitching for Camden, "but he had a whole lot of breaking pitches, and in those days, if you could master more than one breaking pitch, you were darn near impossible to hit."

Later that summer of 1955, in the first All-Star game ever played at Little League Stadium, Ezzie pitched a two-hitter and struck out 15 of a possible 18 as Campbell defeated Santa Clara 13-3. Catcher Tony DiCenzo, a returning All-Star, went 4 for 5 and drove in four runs and Raleigh Hill had three RBI as a crowd estimated at 700 watched.

Campbell then beat Lincoln Glen and Willow Glen before losing 1-0 to Burbank even though Ezzie pitched another no-hitter and struck out 17; he lost the game on a two-base infield error, a wild pitch and a passed ball. David Hill then pitched yet another no-hitter as Campbell beat Los Altos 10-3 to finish third behind Burbank and Palo Alto in the first Santa Clara Valley-wide All-Star tournament, featuring teams from Palo Alto to Gilroy.

Reports of Ezzie's prowess at the time indicated that he might have a limitless future in baseball, and he went on to play at Camden High, graduating in 1960 after earning all-league designation as a senior. But so far as is known, he never played after that. He died on August 13, 1989, from liver and colon cancer.

Meanwhile, at Campbell High, the Pony League completed its second season under the direction of Wade Wilson, who also was an assistant football and baseball coach at the high school. The league included six teams, two fewer than the year before, playing a double round-robin schedule. The league's pre-eminent player was Campbell Lumber's Benny Lujan, who had six pitching wins during the regular season. Lujan, despite being small even by the standards of the day, went on to become a three-sport standout at Campbell High, and was elected student body president his senior year, 1958-59.

Already, the question of whether Little League did the children it purportedly served more harm than good was becoming a nationally debated issue. *Sport* magazine in 1955 asked Bob Feller and Tommy Henrich to write pro-and-con essays regarding Little League. Feller, nearing the end of his Hall of Fame career with the Cleveland Indians, lauded Little League as a vehicle by which baseball could withstand the encroachment of other sports and remain the National Pastime, while Henrich, a five-time All-Star who had retired in 1950, condemned Little League as an attempt by overzealous parents to impose lock-step regimentation on a sport that he felt children should play informally and strictly for fun. (Of course, the same debate has been part of the national sports dialogue ever since.)

In an editorial in 1955, the *Campbell Press* noted the opposition that already was mounting nationally to Little League, describing the disbanding of one league in Los Angeles because the local PTA contended that it had become "too emotionally disturbing to the boys, and too much pressure has been put on them as the result of the commercial aspects of team sponsorship." The *Press* editorial expressed relief that the new Campbell Little League had not strayed from its mission of providing wholesome recreation for the city's youth, and said sportsmanship had prevailed during the league's first two seasons. "We have no fear that Little League baseball has become a menace to society," the writer of the piece opined dryly.

While organized youth baseball in Campbell was seen from the beginning as a possible municipal athletic incubator as well as a healthy outlet for the town's youth, it wasn't because of formal youth baseball's advent that Campbell became a baseball-minded community. As detailed earlier, its baseball tradition had begun not long after the turn of the 20th century, and the progress of local players like John Oldham was closely monitored in the city. Oldham, who had graduated from Campbell High in 1950, in 1955 was pitching for the Seattle Rainiers in the open-classification Pacific Coast League. PCL teams usually owned their players' contracts and didn't have Player Development Contracts with major league clubs – hence the "open-classification" designation – but Oldham was the property of the Cincinnati Redlegs, who had signed him in 1954 out of San Jose State, and he was sent to Seattle with the understanding that he would be on the Redlegs' major league roster in 1956. Campbell had other baseball dignitaries within the city limits at the same time. Duane Pillette, a Santa Clara University graduate who pitched for four major league teams from 1949-56, lived in town, and so did Sal Taormina, who was playing for the PCL's San Francisco Seals and worked as a milkman in Campbell during his offseasons. Taormina later became the baseball coach at Santa Clara, winning a school-record 511 games from 1965 until his death in 1979.

Still, Campbell's most visible claim to athletic fame in the mid-1950s was in the person of a football player – Billy Wilson, Campbell High Class of 1945. In 1954, Wilson, in his fourth season with the NFL's San Francisco 49ers, had ascended to the top of his profession with a 60-catch season that had landed him in the Pro Bowl for the first time. Beyond the fact he had grown up in Campbell and still lived there (and continued to do so after his retirement from the 49ers), the citizenry also admired him because he had turned down a lucrative offer, probably involving more money than he was making with the 49ers, to stay with them.

The Canadian Football League wasn't officially formed until 1967, previously operating as separate western and eastern leagues whose teams met only in the national championship game, the Grey Cup. During the 1950s, several Canadian franchise owners, operating independently of each other, tried to raid NFL teams in the hope of attaining competitive parity and, perhaps, eventually having their teams considered for membership in the NFL (which had taken three teams, including the 49ers, from the defunct All-America Football Conference in 1950). Wilson, who also owned Billy Wilson's Bottle Shop at the intersection of San Jose-Los Gatos Road and Hamilton Avenue, said at the time that one of his reasons for turning down the Canadian offer was because he considered Campbell the best city anywhere to live, and in February 1955 Campbell thanked him with a Billy Wilson Day. Frankie Albert, the 49ers' quarterback during their formative years and later their coach, delivered a speech. During a talk Wilson gave at a father-son banquet at Rosemary School that day, he posed with sixth-grader Craig Morton, whose father Ken had organized the event, for a *Campbell Press* photograph. It was the first time Morton had his picture in the paper, but hardly the last.

By the mid-1950s, Campbell High was a championship contender in almost every sport, and was known for having athletes who also were serious students. Tony Schraub, a three-sport All-Santa Clara Valley Athletic League selection during the 1954-55 school year, was also a straight-A student who earned an engineering scholarship from Stanford. His younger brother Jack later would become Craig Morton's favorite football receiver at both Campbell and Cal.

The basketball program may have been Campbell's strongest, winning SCVAL titles in 1953 and 1954 and losing to Santa Clara in the game that decided the 1955 championship.

Coach Bert Robinson had played basketball for San Jose State coach Walt McPherson, one of the most respected tacticians and basketball teachers of his era, and like McPherson, Robinson was a mild-mannered man who maintained classroom decorum and structure during practices and games. He was remembered, beyond his success in the won-lost column, for treating his players with deference and respect instead of resorting to intimidation, as many coaches did in an era during which their authority was almost never challenged. Many of his former players went on to become coaches themselves, and Robinson's coaching career continued into the 1980s, at Campbell and then at Prospect High after it opened in 1968. In 1978, 25 years after his first title at Campbell and 30 years after he began his coaching career there, Robinson's Prospect team won the West Valley Athletic League championship and took eventual Central Coast Section champion Silver Creek to the brink before losing 59-56 in the first round of the CCS playoffs.

Campbell's baseball reputation was enhanced during the summer of 1956 when Bob Sutton, the star pitcher of coach Mel Stein's 1956 Campbell High title team, signed a contract with the New York Yankees shortly after graduation. Sutton had gone 11-0 during his final two high school seasons, striking out 59 in 40 innings during league play as a senior and earning the SCVAL's MVP award.

Sutton was signed for $4,000 — the maximum allowed at the time under Major League Baseball's bonus role, which stipulated that any player signing for more than that had to be frozen on the team's major league roster for two years. Eleven of the 16 major league teams in existence at the time had sought Sutton, according to a story in the *Modesto Bee* that announced his assignment to the Modesto Reds of the Class C California League.

"He's the top prospect in California," Yankees scout Tony Robello told the *Bee*.

However, Sutton's professional career was short-lived. In his first game, on July 19, he came on in relief against Stockton in the eighth inning of a game the Reds led 15-7. Sutton faced seven batters and didn't retire any of them, giving up four hits, three walks and three runs before being lifted. He fared only slightly better in his first start, on August 1 at Salinas, giving up 10 hits and seven runs in five innings and taking the loss. The Yankees were willing to be patient with him, to a point, and Sutton was reassigned to Modesto at the start of the 1957 season. But he showed no progress. The Yankees soon released him, and by 1958 he was pitching for the independent Tucson Cowboys of the Class C Arizona-Mexico League, finishing his final pro season 9-10.

Sutton's efforts as a senior at Campbell, though, had helped make the 1955-56 school year one of Campbell High's best, especially during the spring when the Buccaneers won league titles in baseball, track, swimming and tennis. The school's athletic reputation was such that it was attracting coaches with qualifications that would have been considered excellent even in much larger urban areas. First-year track coach Bill Priddy, for example, had just graduated from San Jose State, where he earned a share of the national pole-vault title at the 1952 NCAA finals. He moved over to Del Mar when that school opened in 1959, and still was on the Del Mar faculty in the mid-1970s.

The city and the surrounding area continued to grow beyond even the loftiest projections; the Campbell Union School District enrolled 5,300 students in the fall of 1955 and would exceed 6,000 by the spring of 1957. (The CUSD's total enrollment for the 2008-09 school year was not much higher, at 7,300, even though Campbell by that time had almost 40,000 residents.) Three more elementary schools opened in the fall of 1956, and the elementary and high school districts hired 91 new teachers to accommodate the latest influx of pupils. The Campbell Union High School District had opened its second high school, Camden, in the fall of 1955, and by 1956 had already purchased the sites on which its next two schools, Del Mar and Blackford, would be built. The growth within the Campbell city limits had proceeded without any attempt to create a citywide addressing system, and by 1956 tracking down certain addresses, especially on the rural fringes of Campbell, was like trying to translate the Rosetta Stone. Consequently, in early 1956 the City Council approved a uniform system with Campbell Avenue and Winchester Road as the east-west and north-south baselines, forcing almost every business and residence in town to change its address or face a fine of up to $500.

The City Council did its deliberating in a brand-new City Hall, built on Central Avenue where the Campbell Congregational Church previously had stood. Almost 3,000 people attended the opening of the new Campbell Drugs and Pharmacy in the Campbell Shopping Center on the corner of Winchester and Latimer, and 17,000 from all over the county lined Campbell Avenue for the 64th annual Old Settlers Day parade. Campbell no longer was a quiet rural settlement, and with the population increase came hikes in the cost of living. A GE washing machine sold for $189 and a refrigerator went for $339 at Accardi's Appliances on East Campbell Avenue. A 1956 Chrysler Windsor, with push-button transmission and power steering (both innovations at the time), could be purchased for $3,417 — a year's salary for a typical blue-collar worker at the time — at Fox Motors in Los Gatos. Another outgrowth of the burgeoning population numbers was an increase in crime. The Campbell Police Department processed 854 crime reports in 1956, up from 399 only one year before, although most of those complaints involved traffic citations.

The *Campbell Press* also grew its staff, adding sports columnist Marvin Moore — a hiring that wouldn't have elicited much attention had it not been for the fact Marvin was only 9 years old. The *Press* proclaimed him to be the youngest sportswriter in the country, and he was so acknowledged in wire-service stories.

Marvin, whose father Jim had a TV sales-and-repair store in town, "was uncanny in his ability to rattle off averages of current and former major league players," the *Press* reported, although he acknowledged his fan loyalty was to the PCL's San Francisco Seals. Marvin continued to write his column, consisting of snippets about major league baseball and other non-Campbell sports, until his retirement in 1960 at the ripe old age of 13.

He was the first of several Campbell residents to attract national attention for precocity. In 1972, 18-year-old Rusty Hammer was elected to the Campbell City Council, making him the youngest elected public official in U.S. history at the time, and three years later, at age 21, he became the youngest elected mayor ever in California. (Hammer, a Del Mar graduate who later became the CEO of the Los Angeles and Sacramento chambers of commerce, died in January 2008 at age 54 after a five-year battle with leukemia.) In 1976, after playing for the Campbell Little League All-Star team that won the national championship, John Lawson was appointed to the Santa Clara County Youth Commission by county supervisor Rod Diridon, who had watched him deftly handle master-of-ceremonies duties at a banquet that followed the team's return from Williamsport. John, who had just turned 13 at the time he accepted the appointment, was the youngest public official in the state and one of the youngest in the country during his three-year term.

Like Campbell itself, Campbell Little League also grew dramatically in 1956. Or rather, it morphed.

The major division expanded from four teams the previous season to eight in 1956, and was divided into four-team Campbell and Cambrian divisions. Cambrian Park Little League actually was chartered for the 1956 season, but its new ballpark at Steindorf School on Leigh Avenue in west San Jose was not finished in time for the start of the season, so the four Cambrian teams played under Campbell Little League auspices at Rosemary School and Campbell Grammar School until the Steindorf facility was ready at the end of July. One of the new Cambrian teams was sponsored by the Ainsley Packing Company, a first-year participant that in 1957 switched its sponsorship to Campbell. The Robins team it sponsored has been in the major division ever since.

Another Cambrian team, the Methodist Men, was managed by John Morgan, then a sergeant in the Campbell Police Department. Morgan, who had joined the department in 1955, became chief of police in 1960 and was revered for his work in modernizing the Campbell PD and weaving it closely into the fabric of the community. He was incapacitated by a stroke in 1971, but amazingly, he was able to write two books and dozens of essays and columns before his death in 1980. He used a system in which he blinked his eyes to indicate letters as family members recited the alphabet. John D. Morgan Park, which has housed Campbell Pony League's home diamond since 1969, is named after him.

Campbell Lumber, Campbell Stamps and Western Gravel returned as Campbell sponsors for the 1956 season. No sponsor for the fourth team could be found by Opening Day, so the team's manager, Herb Raymond, paid the sponsorship fee himself and the team was known as the Herb Raymonds. The Campbell and Cambrian divisions played two nine-game halves, with each team facing the others six times. There was no regular-season interleague play.

Opening Day for Campbell Little League's second season at Rosemary School was on June 2, and Dave Buck of Campbell Stamps pitched a no-hitter with 12 strikeouts, although he also issued eight walks as his team beat Campbell Lumber 3-0. Buck was the league's best pitcher that year as well as one of its most prolific hitters; he finished the first half with a .524 average, 10 RBI and a 3-1 pitching record with 47 strikeouts (and 38 walks) in 29 innings.

Campbell Lumber went through the entire first half and the first seven games of the second without winning a game, but it concluded its season admirably by beating both Campbell Stamps and Western Gravel in the final week. Western Gravel, the second-half champion, beat first-half titlist Campbell Stamps 4-1 in the championship game. Campbell and Cambrian then played an eight-team postseason tournament, which the Herb Raymonds won by beating Mac's Market 12-0 in the championship game in early August.

The late starting and finishing dates of the early Campbell years represented a desire by the league's founders to emphasize the regular season, provide recreation for the players throughout the summer, and attach only secondary importance to the Little League national All-Star tournament, which began in 1947. In 1954 and 1955 Campbell had participated in the All-Star playoffs while its regular season was still underway, but in 1956 the decision was made to limit Campbell's All-Star involvement so that it didn't interfere at all with the regular season. As a result, Campbell's All-Star season consisted of a best-of-three series between the Campbell and Cambrian divisions. Campbell won 8-3 and 13-4.

"The Campbell All-Stars planned to enter (an) independent Little League tournament in Santa Monica, but cancelled its entry this week," the *Campbell Press* reported on August 10.

After two years of operation, the Campbell Pony League did not organize for the 1956 season. The void temporarily was filled by the Campbell Union High School District's recreation department, which also was responsible for the day-to-day operation of Campbell Little League. Guy Troedson, the baseball director for the rec department, organized an ad hoc league for players ages 13-15. More than 100 players signed up, underscoring the need for post-Little League baseball in Campbell, and in 1957 two competing leagues for players in that age group surfaced – a revived Campbell Pony League, and a new Babe Ruth League that covered Los Gatos and Campbell. Both leagues played most of their games at Campbell High; Craig Morton chose the Babe Ruth League and starred for its Avila's team, and John Ezzie played for the Cambrian Park squad.

This was one of the few seasons during which two age-group programs competed against each other for Campbell players. The Babe Ruth league lasted only two years, and the Pony League's subsequent monopoly on 13- and 14-year-old players was key to Campbell's ascent to regional and national baseball prominence in the 1960s and 1970s. While Moreland and Quito Little Leagues fielded teams in Senior League, the Little League-affiliated program for players ages 13-15, from time to time, it was generally understood that those programs were supplementary and were intended for players not yet ready for Pony League. Campbell Little League, unlike most organizations under the Little League umbrella, has never underwritten programs for children older than 12 (or softball programs for girls) and has maintained a close relationship with the Pony League throughout both organizations' histories.

On June 2, 1957, Campbell Little League began its fourth season with the same four-team, 18-game schedule it had utilized the year before, although it no longer had to share its facilities with Cambrian because that league had moved fulltime into its new complex. Campbell signups were up dramatically, with 275 boys taking part in tryouts early in May. Campbell's farm system only included four teams that year, so it's to be presumed that the rest of the candidates simply didn't play that summer – a situation league officials knew they would have to address in 1958.

"We only had the one field," said Jack Zogg, who joined the league as a minor division manager in 1958. "We had only eight teams, four major and four minors. We had 17 kids on each team. We (the minor league teams, which played at Campbell Grammar School during the week) would play the first game on Saturday, usually at 8 or 8:30 in the morning. We always had this big debate about cutting kids – now, you'd call them 'reassignments' – and finally we just decided, no more cuts, we'll just keep everyone. That was when we started adding teams."

Campbell Stamps, Campbell Lumber and Western Gravel returned as major division sponsors for the 1957 season. The fourth team, which had been called the Herb Raymonds the year before after its manager stepped in to sponsor the team out of his own pocket, assumed what was to become the league's most recognizable team brand – Robins, which remained a major division participant more than 50 years later. The Ainsley Packing Company, one of Campbell's early mercantile powers, originally sponsored the team, and even after the company halted its fruit-production operations as the last of Campbell's orchards gave way to commercial and residential development, the Ainsley family stipulated that the sponsorship continue in perpetuity.

According to Jack Zogg, who managed the Robins team from 1959 to 1980, the company's president, William Lloyd, had a grandson named Robin Hicks, who grew up in Pasadena and was 10 in 1957 when the name first was used. Lloyd thought using Robin's name would reflect the fact that the family and company were making an investment in the future of Campbell's children. "I'd always bring over the team picture, and (Lloyd) would always say, 'I'll make sure Robin gets this.'" Jack said. "But I think he only came to one Opening Day. I always talked to (Lloyd) a little ... very nice man."

The Robins name, Jack said, didn't become universally used in common conversation right away, but when Jack became the Robins manager in 1959, he had a personal reason for wanting it to become permanent – the fact he could use the name to tease his players.

"I'd always been a Dodgers fan," Jack said, "and just about all of the boys on the team naturally were Giants fans. One day, I was talking to them, and I said, 'All you guys are Robins, right? Well, this will break your hearts, but did you know that the Dodgers were called the Robins at one time?'"

(The Brooklyn Dodgers were known as the Robins from 1914-31, in honor of their manager, Wilbert "Uncle Robbie" Robinson.)

"The kids would always say, 'Mr. Zogg, you're not telling us the truth,'" Jack said, laughing. "But one of the dads researched it and found out it was true."

As it turned out, though, the team formerly known as the Herb Raymonds could have been called the Lonny Raymonds in 1957. Robins won the championship, its first of many, and Raymond finished with a statistical manifesto. In 18 games, he batted .529 with 11 home runs and 31 runs scored. He twice hit two home runs in one game, and he had seven RBI in a 14-9 victory over Campbell Lumber. On the mound, he was 8-0 with 99 strikeouts in 40□ innings. (In one of the few games all season in which Raymond was usurped, 10-year-old Joe Anderson of Campbell Stamps pitched the season's first complete-game shutout.)

As in previous years, the 1957 All-Star season was bracketed by the start and finish of the regular season, which extended into late August. In 1956, the league had limited its All-Star participation to the one series against Cambrian, but in 1957 the All-Star team was sent into the district tournament with the understanding that it would continue to play as long as it kept winning. And with Raymond as impactful as he had been during the regular season, Campbell won two postseason tournaments and advanced beyond Santa Clara County for the first time.

The first tournament involved Campbell, Cambrian, Cupertino and Burbank, and Raymond flung a two-hitter and struck out 14 as Campbell beat Cambrian 13-1 in the championship game. Then, in the sectional championship game in Santa Clara, Raymond hit a game-deciding two-run homer and earned the pitching victory in relief as Campbell beat Menlo-Atherton 4-2. That sent Campbell to the divisional tournament in Hayward, where the host team took advantage of four Campbell errors to score eight third-inning runs and prevail 9-6. Raymond hit yet another home run, his fourth in five tournament games, in the defeat. On August 3, he capped his season by striking out the first 17 batters he faced in a 4-0 win in a regular-season finale against Campbell Lumber. A walk to the 18th hitter cost Raymond a perfect game, but the runner was thrown out trying to steal, completing the no-hitter.

Raymond maintained his excellence throughout his Campbell amateur career. By the time he completed his freshman year at Campbell High in 1959, he'd already made honorable mention All-West Santa Clara Valley Athletic League in both basketball (in which he led the Buccaneers in scoring) and baseball. After graduating from Campbell in 1962, he went on to play one baseball season (1964) at Stanford University. One of his '64 Stanford teammates was Pete Middlekauff, a slugging first baseman who later played in the Minnesota Twins organization. Middlekauff's two sons, Jon and Craig, played in the Campbell youth baseball system in the late 1970s and early 1980s, and Craig subsequently played for Santa Clara University.

The Campbell area's growth continued unabated in 1957; it was reported in May that the Campbell telephone exchange, which covered much of the western Santa Clara Valley, had just activated its 11,000th receiver. (When direct-dial telephone service was first introduced in Campbell in 1942, it had only 1,000 phones.) The loss of one of the town's last links to its distant past was reported in the *Press* in January, when Lucia Whitney died at home at age 92. Whitney, who lived alone at 175 E. Campbell Ave., had come to Campbell as a teenaged bride in 1884 and had helped organize the first Old Settlers Day celebration in 1892. She was the widow of George Whitney, an architect who designed many of Campbell's early buildings. Mrs. Whitney's father, Horace Foote, was a prominent San Jose attorney who had purchased much of the land surrounding downtown Campbell after it was put up for sale by the Benjamin Campbell estate. Foote, who has a Campbell street named after him, donated several of those parcels to the town of Campbell, including the strips of land on which Campbell Avenue — known as "Campbell's Lane" into the 20th century because it had been Benjamin Campbell's private access road — was extended west from downtown.

The Campbell youth baseball front was relatively quiet in 1958, although the same couldn't be said for the political arena. Two issues, both of them directly related to the Santa Clara Valley's urban sprawl, brought Campbell's leaders and their constituents to a level of anger rarely seen when Campbell was a sleepy orchard town.

While Campbell's growth continued – a $1.32 million bond issue for fire stations, road improvements and storm drains passed in November 1957 – San Jose, with which Campbell and other Santa Clara Valley communities had been feuding over land since Dutch Hamann took over as San Jose city manager in 1950, in 1958 took its most brazen annexation step yet.

Despite protests from Campbell leaders, San Jose began annexation of the Cherry Lane area, surrounding what's now John D. Morgan Park. The area, which was unincorporated but was surrounded by Campbell and was only about a mile from downtown, was clearly in Campbell's legally-defined sphere of influence – or so Campbell officials thought. (The Campbell Union School District in 1953 had opened Cherry Lane School, which now is Campbell Middle School, adjoining the future John D. Morgan Park.) *Campbell Press* headlines and stories screamed as loudly as did Campbell's city officials, but San Jose officials ignored them. So in early 1959, Campbell filed a lawsuit against San Jose, claiming San Jose violated a non-annexation "gentlemen's agreement" by going after the parcel, and had broken a state law by failing to call an election of the affected residents. The lawsuit dragged through the state Attorney General's office and then through the courts for more than a year before Campbell's final appeal was rejected in early 1960, officially deeding the tract to San Jose. In 1961 and 1962, Campbell went back to court to try to wrest the area away from San Jose, and was rebuffed twice more. Consequently, the 253-acre annexation – derogatorily called "The Fist" by Campbell planners because of its shape and the manner in which San Jose seized it – remains a San Jose isthmus, surrounded by Campbell. A final secessionist effort, in 1983, by the residents was voted down by the San Jose City Council, and by the turn of the 21st century, most residents accepted their status as San Jose citizens, even if they still identified with Campbell.

The highlight of the 1957-58 Campbell High sports year was provided by Campbell High senior Steve Skold, who set a national high school 100-freestyle record during the SCVAL swim finals. Skold the following year became one of the first Campbell athletes to travel far outside California to compete on the college level, accepting a scholarship to the University of Oklahoma, where he set two national records as a freshman. The AAU-sponsored Campbell Swim Club, to which Skold belonged, had an extensive program, and one of its enrollees in 1958 was 9-year-old Mitch Ivey, who later moved to the famous Santa Clara Swim Club and won two Olympic medals – a silver in 1968 and a bronze in 1972. Claudia Clevenger, who graduated from Blackford High in 1973, was another world-class swimmer from the Campbell area during that period. She was the national AAU 200-meter breaststroke champion in 1970 and 1971, and in 1972 finished fourth in the Munich Olympics in the same event.

Campbell Little League, meanwhile, planned on only modest growth in 1958 as it prepared for its May 31 season opener. Even though the Campbell area was growing faster than ever before, the league – which continued under the direction of the high school district's recreation department – functioned with the same four-team, 18-game alignment of previous years. Another new league, Los Gatos, siphoned off players from Campbell's western and southern fringes, while

Cambrian, in its second full season at its home complex, expanded from four to six major teams. One of those teams was sponsored by Western Gravel, which switched its affiliation to Cambrian after sponsoring one of Campbell's teams in Burbank Little League in 1953 and then becoming one of the original Campbell Little League major division sponsors the following year.

Western Gravel, founded in 1940, employed more people than any other non-agricultural Campbell industry in the 1940s and 1950s, but it would cease to exist in 1960 after its gravel pits were depleted by the construction of Route 5 (now Highway 17), which opened between San Jose and Santa Cruz in 1959. During the early 1960s, it sold some of its land to a developer that built the Winchester Drive-In theater.

The city in 1958 signed a deal with Cascade Research Co., which manufactured components for aircraft and missiles, to build the first electronics plant in the city. (IBM built a plant that manufactured computer cards in 1960, on East Hacienda.) At the same time, it was revealed that the 1958 apricot harvest had yielded less than half the quantity of fruit that had been picked the previous year.

Campbell Lumber, another original Campbell Little League major division sponsor, also bolted for Cambrian in 1958, although it would return the following year and remain as a sponsor until 1975. The 1958 sponsor lineup consisted of Robins, Campbell Stamps, Walgrove Manor and Big Boy Market, and six teams comprised the minor league. The Campbell-Los Gatos Babe Ruth league returned for another season, which turned out to be its last, with 13-year-old Lonny Raymond starring for Avila's. The Pony program, which then included a "Grad League" in which Craig Morton participated, also was active.

As in previous years, the Little League All-Star postseason was conducted within the regular season, which again extended into August — for the last time, as it turned out. Ronnie Taniguchi, who led Big Boy Market to the regular-season championship, was selected to pitch Campbell's All-Star opener July 17 against Burbank. Campbell lost 4-1, and the Pony League All-Star team also had a one-and-done postseason, losing to Mountain View 12-10. However, after Big Boy Market won the Campbell title, it went on to win a Santa Clara County-wide tournament of champions, beating Odd Fellows of Sunnyvale Little League 4-3 in the final.

In many ways, 1958 marked the end of the country-to-city transitional period for Campbell baseball and for Campbell itself. By the end of 1959, both had largely become what they would remain for the next quarter-century, at least structurally.

The Cherry Lane dispute with San Jose had established, even to the least pragmatic Campbell residents, that if Campbell wanted to maintain its autonomy, establish a regional identity and solidify its economy, it would have to be as aggressive as its larger neighbor in terms of land acquisition. This made it clear that the end of the Orchard City's agricultural existence was imminent, although the last of the orchards within the city limits weren't leveled until the 1980s.

During 1959, Campbell either annexed or absorbed into its sphere of influence subdivisions in the Budd Avenue, South Winchester and McGlincy Lane neighborhoods, pushing its population to 11,944 in 1960. The city's largest shopping center to date, Hamilton Plaza at the intersection of Hamilton and San Jose-Los Gatos Road, opened in 1959, and so did Saratoga Lanes, near the intersection of Saratoga Avenue and Campbell Avenue just west of the Campbell city limits. The 32-lane facility, which featured Brunswick's then-novel automatic pinsetters and underground ball-return system, was a recreational and social center for Campbell residents of all ages before its closure in 2004. It also was the site of the Professional Bowlers Association's annual San Jose Open, starting in 1961 and continuing into the 1970s. During the 1969 San Jose Open, Johnny Guenther became only the second bowler to throw a perfect 300 game in a televised PBA tournament.

The Route 5 freeway, which extended from San Jose to Santa Cruz and bisected Campbell just east of downtown, was formally dedicated on May 1. The Los Gatos-to-Santa Cruz segment of what is now Highway 17 had been opened in 1940, but before 1959, southbound motorists had to take Winchester Road or San Jose-Los Gatos Road to reach Los Gatos. Responding to complaints about the unkempt appearance of Los Gatos Creek, which paralleled the new freeway, Campbell and Santa Clara County officials created a beautification district that eventually converted the acreage into the scenic and recreational greenbelt that still exists today.

Enrollment in the Campbell Union School District reached 7,800 students – an increase of 2,500 in less than four years – occupying 14 campuses (compared to 12 in 2009) with more on the way. The Campbell Union High School District was up to 4,500 students, and Del Mar High, adjoining San Jose-Los Gatos Road (now Bascom Avenue) in west San Jose just north of the Campbell border, conducted its first classes on September 24. Three weeks later, California Gov. Pat Brown was among the dignitaries at the formal dedication. On the east edge of the $3 million campus, a bowl that had been excavated by the adjoining San Jose Brick & Tile Company as part of the construction project was donated to the district and transformed into a football stadium that was designed to eventually seat 12,000, although it was never expanded beyond its original capacity of 4,000. During the early 1960s, San Jose City College reached an agreement with Del Mar officials that called for the college to install lights in the stadium – free of charge to the high school – in exchange for its use for SJCC games. But the Campbell Union High School District inexplicably vetoed the idea, and it wasn't until 2007 that lights finally were installed in the bowl. The '59 Dons lost their first game in the new stadium 33-6 to Fremont and went on to a 1-8 season that portended decades of football misery there, but one of the Del Mar assistant coaches was to move on to much bigger and better things. Dick Vermeil stayed at Del Mar only one school year before taking the head coaching job at Hillsdale High in San Mateo.

Much later, he coached UCLA to a Rose Bowl win and the Philadelphia Eagles to a Super Bowl, and in 1999 he steered the St. Louis Rams to victory in Super Bowl XXXIV.

Camden, which in 1958 had graduated its first senior class, had become an instant athletic behemoth, and its basketball team went undefeated in 1958-59, winning the Peninsula Basketball Tournament (the precursor of the Central Coast Section playoffs) at Stanford and extending its two-season winning streak to 42 games. The Cougars' star player was Mel Profit, the MVP of the PBT. Many thought Camden was on the way to establishing a basketball juggernaut, but amazingly, the Cougars never won another postseason basketball game before the school was closed in 1980. Camden slipped to 3-7 in league play in 1959-60 and never participated in another PBT. Its only CCS playoff appearances, which lasted just one game each, came in 1974 (when it had future UCLA and NBA star Raymond Townsend) and 1975. Camden's original coach, Chuck Crampton, resigned after the 1958-59 season to start the program at Foothill College in Los Altos Hills, and the Cougars' second-best player, junior Rich Gugat, transferred to Del Mar when it opened and led the Dons to a share of the West Santa Clara Valley Athletic League title in their first season, 1959-60.

(The old SCVAL split into East and West divisions in 1958. In 1961 the WSCVAL was itself divided, with the Campbell Union High School District and Los Gatos Joint Union High School District forming a six-team West Valley Athletic League. The WVAL's membership peaked at 10 schools from 1968-76. In 1991, the WVAL was left with just four schools after Los Gatos left and Blackford and Branham closed. It disbanded after the 1992-93 school year, and Leigh, Prospect, Westmont and Del Mar were absorbed into the new Blossom Valley Athletic League.)

A few years before 1959, of course, all of the athletes who brought Camden and Del Mar immediate prominence would have matriculated at Campbell High. The Bucs struggled with their depleted talent pool, losing 10 straight games at one point during the 1958-59 basketball season and going 5-7 during the 1959 WSCVAL baseball season. But they won five of their last seven basketball games, and freshman Lonny Raymond and sophomores Craig Morton and Jack Schraub, all three-sport performers, provided Campbell supporters with hope that the school could return to athletic excellence even though a fourth district high school (Blackford) was under construction and two more campuses (Leigh and Westmont) were in the planning stages.

John Oldham, who was to bring Campbell's baseball team three league championships and two runner-up finishes in his five years as the head coach, joined the faculty in the fall of 1959 after ending his professional baseball career that spring. He was one of the prime movers as baseball started to become the Campbell area's *nom de plume*.

1959–1962: Transition

The Campbell youth baseball system, like the community it served, continued to undergo whole-sale changes in 1959. Some of those changes reflected Campbell's growth; others resulted from the new corporate structure and postseason emphasis of the national Little League Baseball hierarchy.

In their earliest years, Campbell and other area Little Leagues had tailored their schedules to co-incide with schools' summer vacations, beginning play during the first week of June, continuing it into August and shoehorning the All-Star tournaments between the two halves of the season. That ended in 1959, when Little League Baseball Inc., mandated that the regular season end before the postseason started. Consequently, Campbell Little League's 1959 opening day was May 18, two weeks earlier than in previous years, and the regular season ended on July 18. In 1960, Opening Day was advanced again, to April 30. In the 1970s, the season typically started in the first or second week of April, and by the end of the first decade of the 21st century, league seasons were getting underway in mid-March.

Before 1959, the league had been overseen by Guy Troedson of the Campbell Union High School District's recreation department. It had a sitting board of directors, but that board tended primarily to procedural functions while the school district determined broader policy. In 1959, though, the league was reorganized in accordance with new guidelines set forth by the national governing body. Campbell Little League was incor-porated for the first time as an independent volunteer recreational body, with a board of directors that was responsible for the entire operation. "Guy was a little angry with us for breaking away," Jack Zogg said. "He'd worked very hard at that job; there was a lot of responsibility. "

In reality, though, Campbell Little League might have not had any choice but to sever its ties with the high school district. The recreation program headed by Troedson had just been absorbed by the City of San Jose, which had no interest in operating a Little League outside its city limits. The City of Campbell might have assumed responsibility for the league had the only other alternative been to fold it, but that became a moot issue after the league's officers decided to go independent.

In response to another national Little League edict, decreeing that each Little League should have firm boundaries and serve a population of no more than 15,000, Campbell Little League's territorial limits were redrawn so that the league would include players from five public elementary schools — Campbell, San Tomas, Hamilton, Cherry Lane and Rosemary. The Moreland area, which had been the westernmost Campbell Little League territory, was given to the new Moreland Little League, which commenced play in the spring of 1959. Despite the advent of Moreland, Campbell expanded its major division for the first time, with Campbell Lumber returning as a sponsor after a one-year hiatus and Thomas Shell underwriting a fifth major division team.

Les Baldinger, who also managed Big Boy Market in the major division, was elected as the first president of the restructured league. Two of the men who arguably did the most to shape the league over its first three decades assumed leadership positions for the first time. Jack Zogg began a two-decade tenure as the manager of Robins in addition to his duties as league treasurer. "We had $135 in the bank when I started," Jack remembered, five decades later.

Bob Holman, after whom the Rosemary School complex is now named, became the manager of Campbell Stamps in 1959 after having entered the league as a coach the year before. Holman's managerial career began with one of the most bizarre games in Campbell annals. Big Boy Market led Holman's Campbell Stamps team 3-0 entering the bottom of the sixth and final regulation inning, whereupon Allan Jackson of Campbell Stamps hit a three-run homer to send the game into extra innings. In the top of the seventh, Big Boy Market scored 19 runs on only six hits, one of which was a grand slam by Les Baldinger's son Ranny, and won 22-3.

Zogg, meanwhile, managed the 1959 season's best player, Joe Anderson, who had first made his mark by pitching a complete-game shutout as a 10-year-old two years before. Anderson batted a league-best .520 for the season, and as a pitcher, became the league's equivalent of the Cincinnati Reds' Johnny Vander Meer, who in 1938 had become the first and only major leaguer to fashion back-to-back no-hitters. In the first of his two no-nos, Anderson walked a batter in the first inning and struck out each of the other 18 in a 5-0 win over Campbell Lumber. He wound up with eight pitching wins for the season, including four shutouts.

"Big Joe Anderson ... he was the fastest pitcher I ever had," Zogg said in 2009. "We did not have a catcher who could catch him, which was a shame ... later on we became better at coaching each of the positions. We had one kid, Jimmy Bernal, who came up to me and said, 'Mr. Zogg, I'll catch Joe Anderson.' He really wanted to make the All-Star team and he figured that might be a way he could do it. I'm not saying he was the greatest at it, but he did a hell of a job. Joe was not only extremely fast, he was accurate, and I used to tell (Bernal), 'Just stick the glove up there, and he'll hit it.' And he did. He didn't play again in Campbell, though ... I believe he moved after that season."

Thomas Shell and Robins won the first- and second-half titles respectively, but no playoff was held because of the new Little League rule requiring the regular season to conclude before All-Star play started. That postseason was Campbell's most successful yet, as the team, managed by Les Baldinger, won the District 12 title (District 44, in which Campbell still plays, was not created until the following year) and advanced to the sectional playoffs in Watsonville, where it defeated Madera but lost to Tulare. In the district tournament, Anderson hit a three-run homer to give Campbell an 8-6 semifinal win over Willow Glen. He then pitched eight innings in the title game against San Jose American, giving up only three hits and two runs, and singled off the first-base bag in the 10th to give Campbell a 3-2 win with relief pitcher Jim McMonagle registering the victory and Duane Peterson scoring the winning run.

Meanwhile, the Babe Ruth organization disappeared from the Campbell area for good, and Campbell Pony League assumed its permanent status as the area's primary program for post-Little League players. The league, which fielded eight teams in 1959, continued to play at Campbell High, but was formulating plans for its own Pony League-sized diamond on the grounds of the new Castro Middle School, which had opened in 1957 near the intersection of Campbell and Hamilton avenues. As in 1958, the Pony program also operated a "Grad League" for 15- and 16-year-olds. This eventually became the current Colt League.

Lonny Raymond led Ryan's Sport Shop to a 13-1 record and the Pony League championship; afterward, the league's All-Star team won two tournaments to earn a trip to Redding for the state finals, where it lost to Carmichael and Redding after beating Ukiah.

In 1960 and early 1961, Campbell High's athletic program achieved the loftiest heights of the school's 80-year history.

During the spring of 1960, new baseball coach John Oldham led his team to the WSCVAL title, and junior Craig Morton was named the league and Central Coast region player of the year — honors that would have gone to Walt Christiana had he not ran afoul of Oldham's rules with two games left in the season.

Christiana, a 6-foot-3, 195-pound left-hander, had major league scouts drooling during the 1960 WSCVAL season, during which he struck out 19 in an 8-1 victory over Buchser — breaking the league record of 18 that Oldham himself had set as a Campbell senior in 1950 — and fashioning a 7-0 pitching record while batting .545. But with two games left in the season and Campbell closing in on an unbeaten season, Christiana violated a team rule and Oldham kicked him off the squad. Campbell lost its last game, to Santa Clara, but still took the WSCVAL title with a 9-1 mark.

It was well known that Christiana was in a position to cash in on the fact that the Major League Baseball bonus rule, which required teams to keep all players who had signed for $4,000 or more on the major league roster for two years, had been repealed. Some felt his disciplinary issues might spook the scouts who were eying him so eagerly, but after playing a month or so of semi-pro ball in the San Jose area, he signed with the Boston Red Sox for a financial package worth $50,000, according to a report in *The Sporting News*.

On July 28, Christiana reported to the Waterloo Hawks in the Class D Midwest League, and made his pro debut in the second game of a doubleheader at Dubuque two nights later. Like fellow Campbell High graduate Bob Sutton in his first minor league game four years earlier, he impressed few, giving up three earned runs and walking six in his three innings of work. He began the 1961 season with Waterloo, but soon was assigned to Alpine, Texas in the Sophomore League, another Class D circuit. He finished the season with Alpine, accidentally shot himself during the off-season, and did not pitch professionally again. He was one of many young, untested players on whom major league teams lavished outrageous bonuses in the early 1960s, and that trend was one of the reasons the major league draft, which limited amateurs' bargaining power and protected organizations from their own financial recklessness, was implemented in 1965.

In the fall of 1960, while Christiana was contemplating his future in baseball, Morton, Jack Schraub and some of Christiana's other former baseball teammates were helping Campbell High achieve the first perfect football season in school history. The Buccaneers, who went 9-0 overall and 8-0 in the WSCVAL, had only one close call, a 14-12 win over Los Altos that was decided by Raleigh Johnson's two extra-point kicks. They concluded the season with a 46-26 victory over rival Los Gatos before a home crowd estimated at 10,000 – undoubtedly the largest crowd ever at Campbell High's stadium, which seated no more than 2,500 comfortably. Morton was held to just 62 passing yards – 48 on a touchdown pass to Schraub, his preferred receiver all season – in that game, but he returned two interceptions for touchdowns and fullback Ron Oburn scored four touchdowns, all in the second half.

No playoff system existed at the time, and many newspaper reporters conjectured at the time about a "dream" matchup between Campbell and Sequoia of Redwood City, which went unbeaten in 1960 while starting a 33-game winning streak. It would have been a showdown of teams on opposite ends of the football spectrum; Sequoia ran a power-oriented single-wing offense and almost never passed, while Campbell coach Jim Muir, whose 37-player team included only three players who weighed more than 200 pounds, used a pro-style, pass-based offense built around Morton and Schraub, both of whom subsequently earned scholarships from a Cal program that had reached the Rose Bowl in 1959. Morton in 1960 set several SCVAL passing records that stood until Peterson's Ben Bennett, who later starred at Duke, surpassed them in 1978 and 1979.

On the local baseball front, Campbell Little League expanded from five to six major league teams for the 1960 season. Moreland Little League, in only its second season, already was attracting numbers that marked the league as a postseason force of the future. Six major division squads, up from four in 1959, and eight minor division teams began the season May 1. The league, which was based at Strawberry Park School (on Blackford Avenue west of Saratoga Avenue) but also used several other west San Jose diamonds, unveiled a "C" division that allowed younger players to be switched from the minor league to the C league or vice versa as their abilities and progress dictated. Bob Miailovich, who would claim a permanent place in local baseball lore two years later, was the manager of the Giants in the major division. Other managers in the league's top tier were Dell Park (Dodgers), Nick Margherita (Pirates), Cal Adams (Braves), Dick Hannah (Bears) and Morris Focht (Cubs).

For the first time, the Campbell Pony organization used the age and name designations – Pony League for 13- and 14-year-olds and Colt League for 15- and 16-year-olds – that were to become permanent. The national Pony Baseball organization had created the Colt League in 1953, originally calling it the Grad League.

The 1960 youth baseball season was marred on June 29 when John Ezzie, manager of the Campbell Merchants entry in the Pony League, collapsed and died during a game at Campbell High. Ezzie was only 49, but as it turned out, he outlived his son of the same name, an all-league choice as a senior at Camden High that spring, by two years.

Jack Zogg's Robins team won the Campbell Little League championship, beating the Italian-American Club 12-11 in the deciding game of a best-of-three playoff. Zogg was the All-Star coach under Les Baldinger, who managed the team for the second straight year and was still the league president. Campbell lost 7-0 to Sunnyvale National in its first game, and the Pony League All-Star team lost its first two games in the sectional tournament after winning the area round. The Colt team, which was known as West Valley and was considered a San Jose entry because it drew players from throughout the western Santa Clara Valley, reached and won the 1960 Colt League World Series in Ontario, Calif. It was the first time a team with Campbell components had reached a youth baseball World Series, but the tournament and the fact West Valley won it elicited little attention, even in Campbell, because the scope of Colt League baseball was so limited at the time, and because the majority of the West Valley players did not reside in Campbell.

One of the Pony All-Stars that year already was far more renowned for his mastery of another sport. Playing for a Campbell Grammar School basketball team that went 15-1 in 1960 and won the Santa Clara County championship, Bob Burton was so diminutive that he was in the front row of the team picture. But in a 51-12 victory over Castro, Burton scored 41 points – breaking the county record of 34 that had belonged to Rich Gugat, who was on his way to WSCVAL Player of the Year honors as he led Del Mar to a league championship in its first season of existence. Burton, who also set a county junior-high season scoring record in 1960, was still making basketball news almost a half-century after that achievement. After graduating from Campbell High in 1964, playing for two years at West Valley College and getting his degree from Fresno State in 1968, he began a basketball coaching career that included a 21-season stint at West Valley, where he went 488-158, reached the state community college title game three times, and sent more than 80 of his players on to Division I programs. In 2003, Burton landed his first D-I head coaching job, at Cal State Fullerton, and in 2008 he directed the Titans to a Big West Conference title and their first NCAA tournament appearance since 1979.

Joe Grewohl of Auto Mechanics won the 1960 Pony League batting title with a .500 average, and made the All-Star team. Surprisingly absent from that group was the league's third-leading hitter, who was omitted despite a .450 average, but it was probably the last honor-team slight that Joe Ferguson would have to endure as an amateur. After starring at Camden and at University of the Pacific, Ferguson was drafted by the Los Angeles Dodgers in 1968, reached the majors in 1970 and went on to a 14-season major league career during which he caught for the Dodgers in two World Series. He has the distinction of being the first player from the Campbell Pony League to play in the major leagues.

Most Campbell sports discussion through 1961 continued to center around the cadre of Campbell High athletes that was erasing all doubt that it was the best in the school's history – a distinction it still held when the school was closed in 1980.

After Campbell ran the 1960 football table, coach Bert Robinson's Campbell basketball team similarly rampaged through the final WSCVAL season in 1960-61, going unbeaten in league and taking a 21-1 record into the Peninsula Basketball Tournament at Stanford. The Buccaneers blew out defending champion Del Mar 57-35 in midseason and were ranked sixth in Northern California at the time; their only league challenge came from Camden, which Campbell defeated 37-34 in the final game of the regular season. In the PBT, the Bucs were toppled 55-48 by Bishop O'Dowd of Oakland in the opening round. But Campbell regrouped to beat Carmel and Menlo-Atherton to earn the consolation championship and finish 23-2, the best record in school history.

Each of Campbell's five starters led the team in scoring at least once during the league season; it was rare when any player scored as many as 20 points, and equally rare when at least three of them didn't end up in double figures. With 6-foot-5 Jack Schraub at center and 6-3 Craig Morton and 6-4 junior Lonny Raymond, Campbell had imposing size for the period, and 6-foot Mike Smith and 6-2 Randy Hain comprised the backcourt. All five were named to the all-league team at the end of the season, with Morton making first team. Hain and Smith were chosen to the second team and Raymond and Schraub were honorable-mention selections.

The only downside to Campbell's basketball *tour de force* was that it meant Morton, Raymond, Smith and Raleigh Johnson all were missing from the baseball team when it opened defense of its WSCVAL title. The Bucs lost three early games, including a league contest against Los Gatos, before the basketball players were baseball-ready, and that cost them a chance to repeat. Morton also was hip-deep in the recruiting process, with several major league baseball teams joining dozens of college football programs in pursuit of his future services. Morton, who also was Campbell High's student body president and carried a B average despite his tri-sport athletic commitments, was a true student-athlete and thus was a rarity in an era when most major-college football programs knew little and cared less about their players' academic credentials or anything else that they did away from the field.

Marv Levy, who many years later was to coach the Buffalo Bills to four straight Super Bowls, was the Cal coach at the time Morton was recruited. In his book, *Marv Levy: Where Else Would You Rather Be?*, he described the process by which Morton became a Golden Bear.

"Prior to the beginning of my second year at Cal, I paid a visit to the admissions office," Levy wrote. "There was a quarterback at Campbell High School, 50 miles from campus, who was the nation's most coveted college football prospect. He was a good student, but by a very narrow margin, he was going to fall shy of qualifying for admission to Cal. My plea to the director of admissions was a model of abject self-degradation, but I finally managed to gain mercy – and a concession – from that admissions officer. He agreed that he would accept the lad's application. That was the easy part. Now we had to go recruit him. How we managed to get that done is material for a book in itself, but we succeeded."

Morton didn't announce his commitment to Cal until April 26, and in the meantime continued with his Campbell High baseball season. In a WSCVAL game at Buchser, he hit a three-run homer that cleared five rows of trees in an orchard beyond the left-field fence, but he didn't re-peat as MVP of the league, and a 5-1 loss to Los Altos in the final game of the season relegated Campbell to second place in the final standings. Morton did join Raymond and outfielder Bob Lewis on the all-league first team.

Morton completed his high school career during the summer, when he threw an 88-yard touch-down pass for the North's only score in a 7-2 victory over the South in the North-South Shrine high school All-Star game before 43,902 at the Los Angeles Coliseum. At Cal, he became an All-America quarterback as a senior, ahead of Alabama's Joe Namath and Navy's Roger Staubach, even though he never played on a winning team during his three varsity seasons in Berkeley. (Freshmen were not eligible for varsity competition then.) Despite injury problems, Morton passed for 4,501 yards and 36 touchdowns, both school records at the time.

Campbell teammate Jack Schraub, who had signed with Cal during the summer of 1961 to complete a comparatively low-profile recruiting process, was Morton's favorite target at Cal — just as he had been when the two first started flinging footballs to each other on Campbell playgrounds at age 10. In 1963, Schraub caught two touchdown passes from Morton to help Cal tie three-time Atlantic Coast Conference champion Duke 22-22. In 1964, he had an 11-catch, 133-yard performance against Illinois. At the end of the 1964 season, Schraub joined Morton on the Pacific-8 all-conference team, and the two collaborated on a 6-yard scoring play with 1:04 remaining to give the West an 11-7 win over the East in the East-West Shrine Game at Kezar Stadium in San Francisco.

In 1965, Morton was taken by the Dallas Cowboys with the fifth pick of the NFL draft, and after understudying Don Meredith for four years, he became the starter in 1969 and in 1970 took the Cowboys to Super Bowl V, which they lost to the Baltimore Colts. He was supplanted by Staubach midway through the 1971 season, which ended with the Cowboys winning Super Bowl VI, and although he regained the starting job briefly the following season, in 1974 he was traded to the New York Giants, and then was sent along to Denver in 1977. There, he was named NFL Comeback Player of the Year after he shepherded the modestly-talented Broncos to Super Bowl XII, which they lost to Staubach and the Cowboys. Until Kurt Warner took the Arizona Cardinals to the Super Bowl in 2009, nine years after doing the same for the St. Louis Rams, Morton was the only quarterback to start for two different teams in Super Bowl play.

During his 18-year NFL career, Morton passed for 29,708 yards and 183 touchdowns. He was elected to the Broncos' Ring of Honor in 1998 and to the San Jose Sports Hall of Fame in 2002. In 2008, he was working in Cal's Athletic Development Department as a gifts officer, and was a partner in a San Francisco restaurant run by Mel Hollen, his Cal roommate. He remains part of a three-way dead heat with Billy Wilson and Swede Righter for the distinction as the best all-around athlete ever to emerge from the Orchard City.

Schraub also was drafted by the Cowboys in '65, in the 13th round, but was cut before the start of the preseason. The San Francisco 49ers signed him to their taxi (reserve) squad in November, and invited him to training camp in July of 1966, but he was released before participating in a game. In September, he played briefly with the Edmonton Eskimos of the Western Interprovincial Football Union (which in 1967 became the Western Division of the Canadian Football League), and in 1967 he landed with the San Jose Apaches of the Continental Football League — a team that was noteworthy only because it was coached by Bill Walsh, who was between pro-assistant jobs. Walsh, of course, later coached the San Francisco 49ers to three Super Bowl titles, but after he gained fame, he never allowed his Apaches sojourn to be mentioned in any biography distributed by the 49ers. To the end of his life in 2007, he flatly refused to talk about that "missing season" in interviews. He wouldn't even say why he wouldn't talk about it.

Schraub spent the entire 1967 season with the Apaches, but his major contribution to the team was as a punter – he finished third in the league in average yards per kick – and that season marked the end of his football career. While he was never able to establish himself in the pros, he's almost certainly the only man who never played in the NFL himself, yet worked under two head coaches (Walsh and Levy) who piloted seven Super Bowl teams between them.

While Schraub, Morton and their 1960-61 Campbell teammates presided over the Santa Clara Valley prep scene, their home city's residents and officials were beginning to ask themselves what they wanted Campbell to be when it grew up.

Campbell still was small enough that neighbors interconnected freely with each other, and the city tried to maintain a personal touch in its dealings with the public. In early 1961, a frantic telephone call was received at police headquarters, and chief John D. Morgan personally responded and rescued two boys who had pried loose a manhole cover, crawled inside and become lodged in a sewer pipe. But by 1961, Campbell had all the commercial trappings of a metropolitan area. In addition to the banks and grocery stores that had been in place for several years, Campbell had attracted national fast-food retailers such as the Henry's 15-cent-burger joint across from Campbell High and the Me-n-Eds pizza parlor on Casey Road. Such establishments provided visual proof that Campbell's exponential growth would continue indefinitely; the statistical indications were even more indisputable.

The San Francisco Bay Area Council in 1960 had undertaken a study to try to determine what the region's population numbers might be in the immediate and distant future. Its projections for Campbell were remarkably prescient: 20,090 by 1970, 26,400 by 1980, 34,600 by 1990, 37,400 by 2000 and 45,000 by 2010. Partly because of those findings, Campbell hired its first city manager, Milton Hetzel, in August 1960, and he immediately set about compartmentalizing city services and bringing a businesslike approach to what had been a largely informal municipal operation. In 1961 he consolidated Campbell's developmental functions into an Urban Planning Department, which was charged with creating short- and long-term mechanisms by which Campbell would manage its future growth. His tenure in Campbell, though, would be short. City Council members, thinking Hetzel was usurping their authority, clashed with him almost continuously, and he was forced to resign in April 1962.

It was apparent to city officials by 1961 that the "original" Campbell, along with the city's easternmost and southernmost districts, had largely been built out. Everybody knew that the next major growth area would be in and around the southwestern part of the city, near the site where Westmont High would be built, and that downtown was petering out because of the decentralization of the previous decade and the advent of the regional shopping mall. In 1961, a proposal that a decade and a half later would come to fruition first made the news. It called for two one-way traffic loops to be built parallel to East Campbell Avenue, with the idea that the city's oldest thoroughfare would become a downtown pedestrian mall, alleviating the downtown area's acute parking problem. (A *Campbell Press* headline in early 1962 shrieked: "Parking Must Be Solved Or Campbell Will Die.") The loops were built in the mid-1970s, but the plan to close Campbell Avenue itself to traffic was never carried out, mainly because of the protests of downtown merchants whose interests the bypasses were designed to serve in the first place. Those business owners wound up with the worst of both worlds: They lost the existing through traffic, and they never got the projected pedestrian patronage. Before long, most of them shuttered their businesses. No new establishments took their places, and by 1980 downtown Campbell was so desolate that nobody would have been surprised to see sagebrush skittering along Campbell Avenue.

Meanwhile, the Moreland School District, which included some Campbell pockets but mostly served west San Jose, could not build schools fast enough to accommodate the increasing population. The San Tomas neighborhood was growing fastest of all, and in fact had considered incorporation before being voluntarily annexed by Campbell in 1961. Blackford, the Campbell high school district's fourth campus, was intended as a Moreland-specific school. It opened in the fall of 1961 at the intersection of Blackford Avenue and Boynton Avenue, just west of the current San Tomas Expressway in west San Jose. Moreland Little League continued to grow as well; it was up to eight major and eight minor division teams and a C league on May 6 when it opened its third season.

The expanded major division played a 21-game schedule in 1961. The Giants, again managed by Bob Miailovich, won the championship, but the league's most productive player that year was 12-year-old Don Hahn of the Pirates. Mike Ucci, a 10-year-old, hit five home runs in the first two weeks of the season, and Moreland opened the district All-Star tournament auspiciously, beating Sunnyvale National 9-0 with Gary Parkes pitching a one-hitter and Hahn doing the catching. Moreland won only one more postseason game before being eliminated, but with Ucci and many other promising players returning, league parents and supporters had lofty hopes for 1962 and beyond.

Campbell Little League conducted its seventh season at Rosemary School, which the league had been ready to abandon as its operational base during the offseason. Upon the completion of Route 5, the city of Campbell had acquired from the state a parcel of land adjoining the new freeway at its intersection with Hamilton Avenue, and tentative plans to build a park there were announced. The Rosemary complex, which still had most of its original wood fencing and seating, was in need of repairs and upgrades, and the league wanted to build a new facility within the proposed park. That plan was thwarted early in 1961 when the land was sold for $135,000 to the Brueners furniture store chain, which built a huge showroom on the site. That location now is occupied by a Kohl's department store and a Bedroom Bath and Beyond retail outlet.

Resigned to the fact it would remain at Rosemary permanently, the league began the 1961 season with the same configuration – six major teams, six minor teams – it had used in 1960, although a Pee Wee league, similar to Moreland's C circuit, was added. Towne Pride Market replaced Big

Boy Market as a major-league sponsor. Over at Campbell High, the Campbell Pony League dropped its Cambrian arm and operated with four Campbell-based teams, and the league's two Colt League teams combined with their four Santa Clara counterparts to form a league. This was advantageous to Campbell because many of the Colt League games were scheduled at Santa Clara's Washington Park, one of only a half-dozen or so lighted baseball-specific diamonds in the Santa Clara Valley at the time.

Campbell Stamps manager Bob Holman won his first Campbell Little League championship, beating Jack Zogg and Robins in a playoff for the second-half title and then defeating first-half champion Italian-American Club for the overall crown. Play during the season was unremarkable, and the All-Star team lost its only game, 9-1 to Santa Clara Briarwood. The Pony and Colt All-Star teams also made quick postseason exits.

Overall, 1961 was a quiet year in the Campbell area, save for the explosion that leveled the Sherman Oaks Bowl, on San Jose-Los Gatos Road a few blocks from Del Mar High, on the night of February 22. *Campbell Press* editor and publisher George Vierhus, whose weekly column almost always included a lengthy diatribe against anything and everything San Jose, mentioned the explosion – which was heard all over the valley – only in passing in his next column, even though it happened less than a mile outside of Campbell and was considered the valley's most spectacular human-error disaster in decades, perhaps ever. Instead, Vierhus manufactured a parallel non-story, complaining that San Jose police did not publicly express gratitude for the help they received from their Campbell counterparts that night. When a reader complained about Vierhus and his San Jose bashing, he made a thin promise – one he didn't keep – to "endeavor in the future to be more charitable in our outbursts (toward all things and people San Jose). We hope our halo stays on straight."

Vierhus was a Madera native and Fresno State graduate who had run unsuccessfully for a state Assembly seat in 1938, and had served in the Army during World War II before turning to journalism and serving as editor of several small Southern California papers in the 1940s and early 1950s. He purchased the *Press* in 1956. Like many small-town editors of that era, Vierhus took himself and his self-assigned role as the voice and conscience of Campbell ultra-seriously, even though he had never set foot in the city before purchasing the *Press*. When he wasn't lambasting San Jose, he was shrill in his municipal boosterism, especially when it came to growing Campbell and establishing it as a destination community. But by 1961 most of his readers had tuned him out and, in defiance of his urgings, began voting down bond issues and other tax-raising propositions. In early 1962, Vierhus left Campbell to take over as the managing editor of a newspaper in Temple City, in southern California. He retained ownership of the paper, leasing it to advertising director Joseph Anello, who became publisher.

For the first time since Campbell's growth spree had begun a decade earlier, voters in 1961 decisively defeated property-tax increases for both the elementary and high school districts, along with a bond issue to fund municipal improvements. Campbell had never been an activist town in the past, but its ennui was even more pronounced than usual in 1961. Voter turnout was low, often below 30 percent, and Campbell citizens seemed indifferent even on issues (like the Cherry Lane annexation battle) that had bestirred them only a few years earlier. Even the Old Settlers Day parade, which attracted crowds estimated at 20,000 or larger throughout the late 1950s and early 1960s, was affected. "Community participation in Old Settlers Day is at a low ebb," a *Press* editorial read. "More and more, it seems to be dependent on outside marching units and bands." (The Old Settlers Day parade diminished in scope after 1961, and was discontinued in 1966.)

It was as if Campbell-area residents were waiting for something monumental, something that would give residents a more proprietary interest in their area. In 1962, that something came from the youth baseball community.

As 1962 began, Campbell High celebrated a repeat basketball championship — Bert Robinson's fifth title as head coach — as the Buccaneers defeated Del Mar 65-39 in the final regular-season game to finish 9-1 in the new West Valley Athletic League. Mike Smith and Lonny Raymond, the two returning starters from 1960-61, were all-league selections, and 6-foot-6 senior Jeff Goodere provided Campbell with a third go-to scorer. Campbell then finished fourth in the PBT, beating San Mateo 70-57 before losing to Ravenswood of East Palo Alto 57-46 and Sunnyvale 51-47. The Bucs finished the year 20-4, and in the spring, with many of the same athletes, John Oldham's baseball team won its second league title in three years, beating Blackford 5-3 in its last game to finish 13-2. Mike Smith hit a two-run homer in the clinching game, and Lonny Raymond capped his high school athletic career, one of the most successful in Campbell's history, by pitching six innings of one-hit ball. He had not started the game, but relieved in the first inning after Blackford had scored all three of its runs.

The 10-year-old city's maturity continued. Real estate now was both plentiful and affordable, even for the time; a four-bedroom house in the Linda Park development cost $15,995, with only $195 required as a down payment. Ground was broken on the city's first hospital, Campbell Community Hospital on North Winchester Road, and funding was being finalized for Good Samaritan Hospital, a $6.4 million regional project in nearby Los Gatos. A new post office opened at 90 E. Latimer Ave. Campbell police chief John D. Morgan now headed a department that included 14 uniformed officers and two dispatchers. Among the schools scheduled to open in the fall of 1963 was Rolling Hills Junior High; its construction enabled the Campbell Union School District, in June 1962, to announce plans to shut down aging Campbell Grammar School, which had been a K-8 school, after the 1963-64 school year. (It was subsequently leased to the new West Valley College, which used it until moving into its permanent Saratoga campus in 1976.) The Campbell district's need for new teachers remained pressing, but with an attractive pay scale for the period — averaging $6,105 — it had little trouble finding and keeping qualified applicants.

Leigh High, the fifth Campbell Union High School District campus and the first that didn't serve any part of Campbell itself, opened in the fall of 1962. Leigh immediately joined the West Valley Athletic League, giving it seven members for the 1962-63 school year. Camden in 1961-62 had won the Bill Perry Award, given to the school that amassed the best overall athletic record among the 26 public high schools in the Santa Clara Valley, but Leigh would absorb the eastern, more affluent areas of Camden's attendance area while leaving it with the austere GI Bill neighborhoods that had fueled Camden's early growth but already were deteriorating by the early 1960s. The school never resurfaced again as an athletic power, and declined further after Branham opened in 1967 and siphoned off more enrollment and athletes. Leigh, meanwhile, quickly emerged as a contender in almost every sport.

At Campbell Little League, an expansion of the plant was on the drawing board now that the Highway 17 site was off the table, and expenses were such that the league needed more money than it could generate through business sponsorships and fundraisers such as its annual pancake breakfast.

Eventually, the pancake breakfast, which usually was held on Mothers Day, outgrew the Rosemary School cafeteria and in later years was held at Campbell High. "When it first started, I'd always be selling candy bars or pancake-breakfast tickets, and the guys at work would always run from me (to avoid his sales pitch)," Jack Zogg said. "But later they'd always be saying, 'When are you going to have tickets for that breakfast for sale again?' It was really a good breakfast."

Even so, the breakfast alone couldn't cover all the league's expenses, so it began to produce and sell a season program for which it solicited advertising, bringing in more revenue. It also began to charge players' parents for the first time, although the fee in 1962 was only $1 and was to cover insurance costs.

Bob Holman's Campbell Stamps team won its second straight league title, defeating Big Boy Market (which had returned as a sponsor after a one-year absence) two games to one in a best-of-three playoff series. The league again fielded six major teams and six minor teams. Since Campbell had begun play in 1954, Cambrian, Moreland, Los Gatos and Quito had been formed, and had all carved pieces from Campbell's district upon their formation. But by 1962, the boundaries that were to stay in effect for the next 30 years were in place. As a result, Campbell Little League's signup numbers began to increase faster than ever before, and that factor would begin to manifest itself on the field later in the decade.

The 1962 season marked the first time the Campbell Moreland Pony League played under that title, adding the Moreland designation. The league also expanded from four teams to six and moved into its first Pony League-specific home, at Castro Middle School, where it would play until 1971. Although the Castro move was considered temporary, it enabled the area's 13- and 14-year-olds to play, for the first time, on a field that was permanently laid out according to

Pony League specifications – larger than Little League but smaller than a regulation major league diamond. Les Baldinger, who had been Campbell Little League's president the previous three seasons, moved over to the Pony League and assumed the presidency there. He also managed a team, as he had done in Little League. The '62 Campbell Moreland Pony League All-Star team included Don Hahn, who just seven years later become the league's second graduate (after Joe Ferguson) to make the major leagues. On the Colt League level, Campbell Moreland (or West Valley, as the Colt division still was called) terminated its one-year partnership with Santa Clara, and reorganized the 15-16 age-group teams to parallel the WVAL. It operated with six teams, each representing a WVAL school, that year; there was no Del Mar team, but Leigh, which hadn't yet opened, was represented.

While most of the changes in Campbell-area youth baseball in 1962 were incremental, the season ended with a sea change, one that was to impact every Campbell-area team and player to come along after it.

1962 MORELAND LITTLE LEAGUE: 'Big Ben and a flock of pocket watches'

As Moreland Little League's 13-win rampage to Northern California's first – and as of 2009, still only – Little League World Series championship unfolded, even some San Joseans scratched their heads and had to consult their maps when they saw the Moreland team associated with their city.

In point of fact, there was and is no Moreland, at least as a distinct community with a social or economic hub. Most municipalities, including Campbell, built schools to accommodate their communities. Moreland, on the other hand, originally built its community to accommodate a school.

The Moreland School District, formed in 1851, claims the distinction of being the first rural school district in California, which had attained statehood only one year before. (The San Francisco and San Juan Capistrano districts also were created in 1851.) Students were initially taught in a private home by the district's first teacher, Charles La Follette. In 1852, Zecheriah Moreland sold his home, at what is now the intersection of Saratoga and Payne avenues, to be used as a schoolhouse. Moreland sold his home for $350, donating $50 from the sale to the school district. The district was formally recognized by Santa Clara County in 1853, and officially took the Moreland name in 1862. In 1894, a new Moreland School was constructed on the same site as the original. It was the district's only school until the early 1950s, and it served the children of a loose collection of orchardists and farmers who lived far apart and were primarily focused on raising their crops and educating their offspring. Most people in the Moreland area had little interest in creating a collective civic entity, so no effort to incorporate the region was ever made.

The Moreland area was identified on maps as Strawberry Park because several strawberry farms existed there, most notably Harold and Louise Easterbrook's spread on Doyle Road. Louise Easterbrook was a longtime Moreland School District trustee, and after she and her husband retired and sold their land to developers, the school that was built adjacent to their acreage was named Easterbrook School. Many of the orchard owners and workers were of Japanese ancestry, and after World War II, the Easterbrook family played a major role in helping them regain their land and other possessions after they were forcibly removed to inland concentration camps in 1942 by President Franklin Roosevelt's infamous Executive Order No. 9066.

After the war, the Strawberry Park area was one of the first Santa Clara Valley agricultural zones targeted by developers, who began to build homes there even before Dutch Hamann became San Jose City manager in 1950 and began all-out annexation. By 1962, most of the former farms and orchards had been given over to housing, but at the time of the one event that made many outsiders want to know where and what Moreland was, it had only its schools, the businesses that lined the four thoroughfares that roughly defined its boundaries – Hamilton Avenue, Saratoga Avenue, San Tomas Aquino Road and Stevens Creek Road – and block upon block of residential tracts. Some of those new units, especially on the western side of the school district, were upscale; more were built along the same lines as the postwar housing in Cambrian Park. They were modest units designed to sell quickly to GI Bill recipients and to alleviate a national housing shortage in the years immediately following World War II.

As late as 1949, Moreland School had fewer than 100 students, and only 14 eighth-graders were graduated that year. But the population mushroomed in the 1950s, and by 1962 the Moreland School District was almost as big as the Campbell Union School District, with 6,790 students attending nine schools. Area high school students attended Blackford, which had opened the previous year in the midst of Strawberry Park.

Moreland Little League, headquartered at Strawberry Park School, began operating in 1959. With all the newcomers came an immediate confluence of baseball capabilities. Don Hahn, the future major leaguer who was a Moreland All-Star as a 12-year-old in 1961, had been born in San Francisco, and so had Bob Miailovich, a construction superintendent who had moved to the Moreland area in 1958 at the age of 46 and had immediately immersed himself in the new Little League program.

Miailovich had been a lifelong resident of San Francisco, which during his youth and young adulthood was one of the most fertile baseball areas in the country. Unlike residents of the Eastern Seaboard and Midwest cities that constituted the major leagues before the New York Giants and Brooklyn Dodgers arrived in California in 1958, San Franciscans could play baseball virtually year-round because of the superior weather, and the sport flourished there, even though the city was so densely populated that field space was scarce. The list of pre-eminent names that emerged from San Francisco during the first 50 years of the 20th century is almost endless. Joe DiMaggio, Joe Cronin, Harry Heilmann, Tony Lazzeri, Lefty Gomez and George "Highpockets" Kelly are in the Hall of Fame; Dolph Camilli, Dominic DiMaggio, Lefty O'Doul, and Duffy Lewis were among the best players of their generations; and other top-tier players – Gil McDougald, Frank

Crosetti, Mark Koenig, Jim Gentile, Eddie Joost and Willie Kamm, among many others – dotted the rosters of major league teams over the years.

Miailovich – the name usually was misspelled "Mialovich" in contemporary accounts – was two years older than Joe DiMaggio, and often played against DiMaggio and his brothers Vince and Dominic on San Francisco's sandlots and streets. In 1932 he received a tryout with the Pacific Coast League's San Francisco Seals, with whom "Joltin' Joe" began his professional career that same year. Miailovich didn't make the Seals, and never played professionally, but he competed in the area's formidable semipro leagues well into his 30s, and managed many teams in those leagues as well. His background and his knowledge made him an ideal choice to orchestrate the development of the new Moreland Little League, and his team, the Giants, dominated the league in Moreland's early years. He has been variously described as aloof yet hands-on, calm yet demanding, and quiet yet intense, and his style and demeanor dovetailed with the talent on hand in 1962 as the Moreland All-Star team prepared for the District 44 tournament.

"Miailovich was kind of an old-school kind of guy," Duane Kubo, a starter on the 1962 Moreland All-Star team, remembered in 2009. "He didn't really talk a lot, didn't give a lot of motivational speeches. He was pretty straight-forward. His son Ray really was part of a management of the team. Ray was a few years (actually only two years) older than us, and he was sort of the surrogate for Bob. He'd work out with us, and he kept all the data ... we had great baseball statistics available to us, for that time. Between the two, we got a good combination – old school, and maybe a guy who would offer a little different interpretation.

"Bob's wife Mary was a big fan. She organized the parents and she was one of our chief cheerleaders. She had the loudest voice; you could hear her very clearly on the field. That was a big part of it, a big presence."

Ray Miailovich indeed had a knack for numbers, and his work as scorekeeper with the Moreland team in 1962 would serve as prelude to his life's work. In 1971, he joined the faculty at Piedmont Hills High in east San Jose as a math teacher and basketball coach, and stayed there 34 years before accepting a position as events coordinator for the California Interscholastic Federation's Central Coast Section, the governing body for high school sports between King City and San Francisco. In 2009, he resided in Campbell, and proudly shows the museum-quality scrapbook he compiled during that summer of 1962.

Ray was playing in Campbell Moreland Pony League at the time Moreland began its World Series odyssey, and he actually missed a couple of the early games because his Pony League team was playing at the same time. He was surprised and flattered by Duane Kubo's characterization of him as virtually an assistant coach without portfolio, but he says he shared the same sense of wonderment as the players – and his father – as Moreland's win total mounted.

"The team and I kind of reflected my dad, and he was surprised at every step," Ray recalled. "When we flew up to Vancouver for the Western Regional, it was the first time my dad had ever been in an airplane. I wonder what would have happened if they'd put one of those field microphones on my dad, like they do now. My dad was quiet, and he wasn't an elegant speechmaker. I think the thing he was most worried about was whether he'd be able to get off work if we were to go to Williamsport; he was so dedicated to his work. Fortunately, his boss was a big Little League fan. His son had played for my dad (on his regular-season team)."

"I think the one word that comes to mind about how all of us felt when this was happening was 'wow.'"

In Williamsport during the 1962 Little League World Series, *Associated Press* reporter Jim Becker described the Moreland squad as "a team whose topography resembles Big Ben amid a flock of pocket watches." Big Ben was Ted Campbell, a pitcher-first baseman whose size – 6-foot-1, 210 pounds – astounded those who were seeing him for the first time. He was the largest player ever to appear in the Little League World Series up to that time, and many must have mistaken Campbell for Bob Miailovich or Moreland coach Don Van Shook, because few of his teammates were even half his size. Campbell's regular catcher, Don Silva, weighed 93 pounds. Vaughn Takaha, the team's No. 2 pitcher and one of its most dangerous hitters, was one of the larger Moreland players at 115 pounds, and despite his pitching and batting prowess, he was less than intimidating at first sight, perhaps because of the glasses he wore on the field.

"Ted Campbell got beat during league play a couple of times that year," Duane Kubo said, "but if you're seeing him for the first time, like in All-Stars, he was pretty intimidating. He wasn't the most accurate thrower. Certainly during that period he was still trying to gain control and figure out the whole phenomenon of being so huge."

In contemporary accounts, Campbell is described as unfailingly modest and self-effacing, and no doubt those were key components of his makeup. Ray Miailovich describes Campbell as "a big teddy bear kind of a guy, not cocky at all." But he also may have harbored inner insecurities, at least at first, because the 1962 regular season represented his first fulltime commitment to pitching. "He never became a pitcher until this spring," his father Sid said after the World Series. "He tried pitching last season, but was afraid of hitting batters, and as a result his control was poor. He was (primarily) a right fielder as a 10-year-old and a first baseman last year."

Campbell played for Miailovich's Giants for three years, leading them to 17 straight wins to complete the 1962 regular season. Miailovich wisely did not force Campbell to pitch, waiting until the youngster felt he was ready, and the result was that Campbell was able to build on each new success and maintain his quest for improvement even though he overwhelmed most opposing batters, both physically and psychologically.

The Little League postseason format at the time featured four-team, single-elimination tournaments at each level prior to the World Series, instead of the much larger and longer preliminary playoffs that became the norm later. That meant that a team could push deep into the postseason with only two dominant pitchers, which Miailovich knew he had in Campbell and Takaha. In fact, Miailovich never had to make an in-game pitching change at any time during his team's 13-game postseason. Campbell and Takaha pitched six complete games each during the postseason, and only one other Moreland player – Milt Murata, who went the distance in the World Series opener against France – saw the mound at all.

The presence of Campbell and Takaha also meant Miailovich was able to work with a set lineup. Silva did almost all of the catching. Murata played exclusively at third (except for the one game he pitched), and Mike Ucci, Tony Riley and Duane Kubo were fixtures in left field, center field and shortstop respectively . When Campbell pitched, David Schneider went to first base, Takaha was at second base, and Mike Ganson was in right field. With Takaha on the mound, Campbell moved to first, Ganson went from right field to second base, and Schneider moved from first base to right field. Most of Moreland's position players were smallish, but almost all of them were well above average in terms of speed, hands, and throwing accuracy, three assets that Miailovich valued above power. The reserves, who played sparingly, were Randy Dickson, Phillip Kagel, Craig Ratkovich, Steve Smith and John Whitton.

"Vaughn Takaha was pound for pound one of the best players I've ever seen," Kubo said. "He was about average size for a Japanese-American, but pretty small (by Caucasian standards). Mike Ucci was one of the most talented guys I ever played with. He and I were both 11. He was just a great natural athlete, and we grew up together and I knew him quite well. There were a lot of similarities between my family and his; his dad was a (first generation) Italian-American who just loved the game. One time (in a regular-season game) Mike hit a ball that must have been 150 feet behind the home run line, but it curved around the foul pole. It was inside the foul pole but it landed in foul territory and the umpire called it foul. Of course, that was the wrong interpretation, but it wound up costing us that game.

"Ganson was really versatile. He probably could have been the frontline catcher. In that final (World Series) game when Don Silva got hit in the eye, Mike went in to catch, and with Ganson back there, there probably were fewer pitches dropped. He was a little outspoken and had things to say; I think that came from his father. I heard he gave Miailovich a black eye once in a dispute over how much time Mike was getting. He was a little bit of a hothead, and Mike probably got that from him. Silva was a friend of mine; he was the frontline catcher because he was Ted Campbell's personal catcher. We had that, and it was kind of unique." (It was another 30-plus years before Atlanta Braves manager Bobby Cox came up with the idea of regularly assigning pitcher Greg Maddux a "personal catcher.")

Although Moreland broke a tournament single-game scoring record and pounded out 19 hits in a 22-2 rout of Poitiers Post, France — a team made up of American dependents living on the U.S. military base there — on Wednesday, August 22 in its first World Series game, Miailovich's team won most of its games primarily with pitching and defense, and it rarely bludgeoned its foes, hitting only four home runs in its first eight games and 11 in all 13 games. The team batting average, .260, was pedestrian, and David Schneider (.394) and Campbell (.322) were the only regulars who batted above .300.

As was later the case with all three of Campbell Little League's World Series entrants during the 1970s, Moreland surmounted its most serious pre-Series obstacles before leaving the Santa Clara Valley.

In its area tournament, Moreland struggled before eliminating Cupertino National 3-2, then defeated Sunnyvale American 10-5 to advance to the District 44 tournament. Its first opponent was Campbell, the league from which Moreland had been split only three years before. Most of the players and parents knew each other, and to this day, long-time Campbell supporters frown when they remember this game.

"We knew in our heart and soul we had beaten them," said John Emery, a Campbell major-division manager in 1962, who later coached with Jack Zogg on the Robins team and for most of the 1976 postseason that ended with Campbell losing in the Little League World Series final.

The game was tied 2-2 going to the bottom of the sixth and final regulation inning when Campbell's Chucky Hawthorne reached third base and tried to score on an infield grounder. He and the throw arrived at the plate simultaneously.

"Chucky Hawthorne slid into home plate with (what would have been) the winning run," Emery said. "He slid under the catcher. The tag was high, but the umpire called him out."

Ted Campbell kept Campbell scoreless through the next three innings. In the top of the ninth, Moreland scored two runs and held on to win 4-2.

"The other thing I remember about that game was Mike Ucci hitting a home run over the left-field wall, across Hamilton Avenue to where the post office is now," Emery said. "He was a *hitter*. They had an outstanding team, especially their infield defense. But I still wonder how our team might have done if we'd gotten past them that day."

Moreland then won the District 44 title by edging Santa Clara Eastside 3-1, and moved on to the Section 3 tournament in Santa Cruz, where it defeated Mid-County from the Capitola-Soquel area 4-2 and San Jose American 6-0. The next stop was the divisional tournament at Sunnyvale's Washington Park, where Moreland beat West Sacramento 7-0 and Clovis 4-2. Then, it was on to Vancouver, British Columbia, Canada for the Western Regional tournament. In Vancouver, where Moreland became the only Campbell-area team ever to play outside the U.S., Miailovich's team earned its Williamsport trip by beating Rolling Hills, the Southern California representative, 3-2 and Kailua, Hawaii, 3-1.

Against Rolling Hills, Campbell completed a three-hitter, striking out 10 and walking three, but Moreland had to come from behind twice. Ucci drove in a run with a single in the third to tie the game at 1-1, and he put Moreland ahead for good with a sacrifice fly in the fifth. Against Hawaii, Takaha pitched a one-hitter – the only hit was a home run in the fourth – and Campbell and Silva hit solo homers. That game was postponed a day by rain, and the field was made playable only after Vancouver officials poured gasoline on the mound and the dirt portion of the infield and ignited it.

Because of the rainout, Moreland was the last of the eight teams to arrive in Williamsport for the 16th annual World Series, and aside from the gawking to which Campbell was subjected because of his size, relatively little attention was paid to the Californians. The main curiosity for the assembled reporters and fans was the team from Kunitachi, Japan – the first Far East squad ever to play in the World Series, which until then had been limited to teams from the Western Hemisphere. Some perceived the presence of the Japanese at such a quintessentially American event as a harbinger of future world unity after the horrors of World War II only a generation before. The *Williamsport Sun-Gazette* noted bemusedly that the Japanese players had brought their own kimonos and instant-noodle snacks, were fed rice with every meal in the players' communal mess hall, and seemed more regimented than the other teams. Although the language barrier was obvious, the *Sun-Gazette* reported that the Japanese players were popular in the barracks and recreation areas that the eight teams shared, and were unfailingly polite to their hosts and to the other boys.

The Japanese team also had the smallest player in the tournament, 4-foot-3, 65-pound Jun Sato. A photo was taken of Sato and 6-foot-1, 210-pound Ted Campbell standing alongside each other. Campbell is patting Sato on the head, and he is reaching almost down to waist level to do it.

Ray Miailovich's most enduring memories of Williamsport are of the players' accommodations and their admirers.

"I watch that tournament on TV now, and the first thing I think about is how rustic our barracks were compared to what they have now," Ray said. "The walls were all wood, and there was dirt outside. It was like a big campout for us. And our guys were like mini-major leaguers, with all these little girls asking them for their autographs. I'm 14 years old and I'm watching this and I'm thinking, 'This is just *crazy*.'"

The team's arrival in Williamsport also meant the players would be wearing identical uniforms for the first time. Like many Little Leagues of the period, Moreland did not buy All-Star uniforms, and the players simply wore their regular-season outfits during their first 10 games. Only their caps, with a block M, identified them as Moreland representatives. In Williamsport, though, they were issued uniforms reading "West."

Joining Moreland, Poitiers Post and Kunitachi in the World Series field were Kankakee, Ill.; Pitman, N.J.; Del Rio, Texas; Monterrey, Mexico; and Stoney Creek, Ontario, Canada. Kankakee and Monterrey were mentioned most frequently as favorites, perhaps because both were familiar names in Williamsport. In 1957, Monterrey had become the first foreign team to win the World Series, and had repeated in 1958, the year before Moreland came into existence. Kankakee had lost in the finals to Monterrey in 1958, and had finished third in the 1950 Series. Observers were as impressed with Kankakee's ace pitcher, Danny Brewster, as they were with Ted Campbell. At 5-foot-3, Brewster was dwarfed by Campbell when a *Sun-Gazette* photographer posed the two of them pretending they were arm-wrestling, but the paper reported that Brewster's curveball broke two feet and that he could throw it for strikes consistently.

Some predicted major league futures for Campbell and Brewster, but as it turned out, the only player in that World Series who eventually got to the big leagues was Del Rio's Larvell Blanks, an outfielder for the Atlanta Braves, Cleveland Indians and Texas Rangers from 1972-80.

Knowing that the French team was the weakest in the tournament, and not wanting to pitch Campbell on only one day of rest, Miailovich took a calculated risk and broke from his Campbell-Takaha pitching rotation, going with Murata on the mound in Moreland's Series opener. If the move worked, Miailovich knew, he would have his two top pitchers fully rested for what figured to be far stiffer competition in the semifinals and finals. Murata responded with a six-hit complete game, and Moreland put the game out of reach immediately by hitting three home runs (by Takaha, Murata and Schneider) in the first inning. Moreland led 21-0 after four innings, with Schneider hitting another homer and Ucci driving in five runs, before reserves completed the 22-2 victory.

Kankakee joined Moreland in the semifinals by beating Stoney Creek, the Canadian team, 13-1 as Brewster pitched a no-hitter, while Pitman beat Del Rio 2-1 and Monterrey edged Kunitachi 3-2. On Thursday, August 23, Moreland was matched against Monterrey in one semifinal, while Pitman took on Kankakee in the other.

Moreland's Takaha and Monterrey's Mario Torres befuddled hitters through the first two innings before Moreland broke through in the third with the only run Takaha would need. Silva doubled and Ucci singled him home. In the sixth and final inning, Moreland tacked on an insurance run as Takaha led off with a double and Ucci registered his seventh RBI of the tournament with another single.

Ucci, playing left field as usual, also made the defensive play of the Series in the fourth, with Raul Lozano on first base after parachuting a single into short left field for Monterrey's only hit of the game. "(Ucci) hauled in the ball by stretching his gloved hand skyward," reported the *Sun-Gazette*. "Had he not caught the ball, it more than likely would have cleared the fence and the score would have been tied at 2-2."

It didn't and it wasn't, and Takaha did the rest, walking only one and striking out nine while completing his one-hit, 2-0 victory before 5,500 at Lamade Stadium in only 1 hour, 2 minutes. Just five Monterrey players reached base, and only one – Miguel Blanco, who was marooned after reaching second on a double error by shortstop Kubo – advanced beyond first.

Kankakee, meanwhile, came from behind to defeat Pitman 9-5 and set up the much-anticipated mound showdown between Brewster and Campbell on Saturday, August 25. Jackie Robinson, the first black major league player of the 20th century and six years removed from his retirement from baseball after the 1956 season, was on hand to serve as color commentator for New York television station WPIX, which carried the only live telecast of the game. (The WPIX telecast was shown nationally a week later on a tape-delay basis. ABC's Wide World of Sports began covering the World Series the following year.) No live radio broadcast was available on the West Coast either, although NBC, CBS and Hearst all sent newsreel crews to the game. Also in attendance was Ted Williams, who had retired from baseball two years earlier and was in Williamsport as an invited guest of the tournament organizers. Williams was introduced to many of the players one day before the championship game; when he met Ted Campbell, Williams told him, "I'm glad I don't have to bat against you."

Other guest at the Series included former Postmaster General James Farley, who was on the international Little League Board of Trustees; Walter Kennedy, the mayor of Stamford, Conn., who in 1963 would begin a 12-year tenure as commissioner of the National Basketball Association; and longtime California Congressman Charles Gubser, in whose district Moreland was located. Gubser had said he would treat the Moreland players to lunch in Washington, D.C., after the Series; all eight teams already were scheduled to travel to Washington anyway to attend a game between the Washington Senators and Baltimore Orioles at brand-new D.C. Stadium (now RFK Stadium) on August 27, two days after the conclusion of the LLWS.

At 2 o'clock on the afternoon of August 25, 1962, a Series-record turnout of 20,000 filled the modest stands – at that time, they extended only about 10 rows deep from dugout to dugout – and the grassy hillside that framed Lamade Stadium. They saw Ted Campbell, concluding his first full season as a pitcher, flirt with perfection while lifting a league that had not even existed four years before to the zenith of American youth baseball.

At of this writing, Campbell's no-hitter in Moreland's 3-0 victory that day is one of only five such manifestos consummated in Little League championship-game play. (The most recent, in

1979 by Taiwan's Dai Han-Chou, came against Campbell Little League.) Kankakee hit only one ball out of the infield, and Campbell struck out 11, giving him 63 in 38 postseason innings. After Campbell walked Brewster with two outs in the first, he retired the final 16 batters he faced. His stuff was as uncatchable as it was unhittable; his catcher, Don Silva, had to come out of the game before the start of the second inning after one of Campbell's warmup pitches swerved suddenly and struck Silva on his forehead above his left eye. (He was not severely injured, although he sported a black eye for some time afterward.)

Moreland didn't exactly belabor Brewster, who struck out 10 and surrendered only three hits while doling out just a single walk. But his throwing error in the fourth inning enabled Moreland to score two unearned runs. After David Schneider walked with two outs and moved to second on a passed ball, Milt Murata hit a comebacker. Brewster fielded the ball cleanly, but threw wildly to first. Schneider scored and Murata was safe at first. Tony Riley then singled, sending Murata to third, and he scored when the Kankakee catcher fumbled the relay throw to the plate.

Takaha's home run in the sixth inning concluded the scoring, and shortly thereafter, Moreland reigned supreme among the 5,851 Little Leagues that existed at the time. Counting the 17 straight wins by Miailovich's Giants at the end of the regular season, it was the 30th straight managing victory for Miailovich over a three-month period.

The *Sun-Gazette* reported that Miailovich placidly surveyed the celebration scene, during which Campbell's teammates tried unsuccessfully to tackle their giant pitcher, from the top step of the Moreland dugout. "It's the greatest thrill that could come to a fellow," he was overheard saying. Later, he told the media: "I'm sure glad Takaha hit that home run. I felt real good about it because our first two runs were unearned. With the homer as the extra run, in itself enough to win, nobody can ever say we won on tainted runs."

Afterward, the paper reported, Campbell sought out Brewster and attempted to console him. "I know how you feel," Campbell reportedly said. "I've been a loser myself. But you must forget it. You pitched a great game, and your team played great ball. You must get ready to pitch the next game."

Most of the Moreland players were from working-class families, and few of their parents and supporters had the money or the vacation time to make the trip to Williamsport. About 100 friends and family showed up at the Miailovich house on game day, and they were kept up to date on the game's progress by Ray Miailovich, who called his house every inning to provide play-by-play from the scorebook he was keeping.

After word of Moreland's triumph circulated and more fans and well-wishers showed up, the Miailovich house looked and sounded like Times Square on New Year's Eve.

"It's fantastic," league president Gus Millat said as parents sang a fight song, "Go All The Way To Victory," that some of them had composed as Moreland neared its ultimate destination. "We are so thrilled, so happy that our little kids came through. You see these little kids running through the neighborhood, and here they are, the best team in the world. It's unbelievable.

"That was a terrific team victory," Sid Campbell said, "and Ted outdid himself."

The *Associated Press*, meanwhile, synopsized Moreland's championship thusly in its second-day story:

"Observers in this home of Little League baseball were talking today about (Moreland), winner of the 16th World Series, as possibly the best Little League team ever assembled ... Observers who have seen most or all of the 16 World Series pointed out that (Moreland) produced two of the finest pitchers in the history of the organization in Takaha and Campbell, a slick infield, good catching and a fine outfield, anchored by Mike Ucci in left field ... Hall of Famer Jackie Robinson, who did the television broadcast of the final game, said Takaha was the outstanding player in the tournament."

After the game, the Moreland group had little time either to rest or to celebrate, because they were due to board a bus at 6 o'clock the following morning for their trip to Washington, D.C. Their tour of the capital, on Sunday, August 26, was ill-organized. After their early wakeup call, they spent two hours of idle time at an Army base outside of D.C. after the 300-mile bus ride from Williamsport, and several players expressed disappointment that they weren't able to go to Washington's primary landmarks, such as the Lincoln Memorial, the Washington Monument or the Smithsonian Institution. They did visit the Capitol and the White House, where they were greeted briefly by one of President John Kennedy's staff members, but were otherwise ignored and wound up taking the standard tourist excursion through the presidential residence.

During their lunch with Gubser, the congressman asked how many of them hoped to become major league players. Not surprisingly, all raised their hands. Then, Gubser asked how many of them aspired to serve in Congress. Only Mike Ganson raised his hand. Why? "Because I like to argue," he replied.

At one point during the White House tour, the guide pointed out a sofa that supposedly had been purchased for $30,000. "Wow," David Schneider said. "That's more than a house costs in San Jose." (Actually, it probably was twice as expensive as most of the players' homes.) Ganson, though, was unimpressed. "I'll give them $300 for it," he said.

The players also lamented that they had not yet been able to see the highlights of their game on television. "We had to go to a barbecue (after the game) and watch some guys playing the banjo," Ted Campbell said. "We couldn't even get near a set."

The next night, the players went to the Orioles-Senators game, where the eight teams formed the only recognizable fan bloc at a game attended by only 6,526. Finally, three days after their championship-game victory, the Moreland players boarded a jet for their trip from Washington to San Francisco. Understandably, they vented some of their pent-up enthusiasm and energy on the flight. "They were all up and down the aisles and all over the plane," a stewardess told a *San Jose Mercury* reporter. "Everybody loved them." Said another traveler: "I aged 12 years on that flight. They're a lively bunch of kids."

When they arrived at San Francisco International Airport, they were met by about 400 parents and supporters who had made the 40-mile drive from Santa Clara County. (The team couldn't fly into what was then San Jose Municipal Airport, which in 1962 was too small to accommodate jets and used a converted Quonset hut as a main terminal.) Then, it was off to a reception at Moreland School. The next night, they were guests of the San Jose Bees at a California League game at Municipal Stadium. In early September, they made an appearance at a Giants game at Candlestick Park, and on September 15, they were feted at a banquet at Lou's Village in San Jose.

And that was it.

When Campbell Little League made its three World Series appearances in the 1970s, the players remained celebrities for months and even years afterward because they were seen as representatives of a distinct city. In 1962, the Moreland players faded from public view soon after the welcome-home festivities were concluded, and all that was left for them was to enjoy the afterglow of the season, focus on the new school year, and look forward to returning to baseball the next year.

For Moreland, though, there would never be another next year in terms of reaching the Little League World Series. (In fact, Moreland would win only two more District 44 championships, in 1974 and 1991, during the next 41 seasons, and it didn't survive the next tournament in either of those seasons.) And while the *Mercury* and other large newspapers all over the world carried extensive coverage of Moreland's victory, the approach taken by the closest thing Moreland had to a local paper can be seen in retrospect as a portent of the indifference that was to mark much of Moreland Little League's future existence.

After George Vierhus turned over operation of the *Campbell Press* to Joseph Anello early in 1962, the paper's journalistic quality, rarely above average, deteriorated to the point of incoherence, with far more emphasis placed on advertising volume than on editorial content. Boorish as Vierhus could be when he got on one of his anti-San Jose jags, the *Press* under his stewardship generally was tidy in appearance and was thorough, if not always completely objective, as a source of local goings-on. It also endeavored to cover the neighborhoods surrounding Campbell, including Strawberry Park.

But under Anello, whose journalism background had been in advertising, the paper began to look more like a ransom note, with most of its editorial content devoted to gossip columns and "stories" that were of no apparent interest to anyone except the people directly involved in them. Moreland Little League, which the *Press* had covered consistently under Vierhus' editorship, was completely ignored all season. And when the biggest sports story ever to emanate from the Campbell area up to that time began to unfold, the *Press* made no mention of it at all until after Moreland's win over Kankakee. At that point, a Moreland parent collected individual photos — almost all of them school portraits — and gave them to the *Press*, which dutifully printed them along with a caption that ran alongside a larger photo of a nondescript church event. No other mention of Moreland's triumph appeared in the *Press* during the ensuing weeks.

Campbell, Murata, Takaha, Kubo and Ucci were starters in 1964 when Campbell Moreland won the Pony League World Series. But the majority of the players on that team were not from Moreland, and in 1970, when Campbell Little League made the first of its three trips to Willliamsport during the 1970s, Moreland yielded the Santa Clara Valley youth baseball stage and never regained it.

One reason was that the league was uprooted several times for a number of reasons, including a temporary split that was mandated by national Little League officials after they determined that Moreland's district was too large. After beginning its existence at now-closed Strawberry Park School, the Moreland major division at various times played at Hathaway Park, Rogers Middle School, Easterbrook School and Payne School, while the lower divisions played at various sites, including Moreland School. Moreland came close to folding or being absorbed into adjoining leagues more than once because of financial problems and a lack of players. In 2009, even after an upsurge in signups as it prepared to celebrate its 50th anniversary, it had only five major division teams, and played an interlocking schedule with Campbell and Santa Clara Westside.

In 1978 when Campbell Moreland won the Pony League World Series, only two of the 15 players on the team (Billy Roberts and Brett Blackwell) were from Moreland. Later, Moreland's participation in the Pony-Colt program became so minimal that the Pony League took the Moreland reference out of the name of the league, which in 2009 was simply called by the same name it had used when it was originally formed in 1954: Campbell Pony Baseball.

Blackford High, like Moreland Little League, began promisingly from the athletic standpoint but couldn't extend early success. The Braves' first basketball coach was Carroll Williams, who later was the head coach at Santa Clara University for 23 years, and their build-around player from 1962-66 was 6-foot-9 center Dennis Awtrey, who became an All-America at Santa Clara and played in the NBA from 1970-82. Blackford won WVAL titles during all four of Awtrey's seasons there. But when the Campbell Union High School District closed Blackford High in 1991, its loss was not widely mourned. Blackford had become an underperforming institution with high dropout and juvenile-delinquency rates. Its athletic program had little community support, mainly because it wasn't very good (or maybe it wasn't very good because it had little community support). Blackford won only two Central Coast Section team titles during its 30-year existence – in boys soccer in 1987, and in baseball in 1991 after the decision to close the school that summer already had been made. It made the CCS football playoffs only twice, in 1981 and 1982 when the Braves benefitted from the addition of key Campbell High players after that school's closure, and Blackford reached the CCS basketball playoffs just once, in 1988.

What happened to the players who did what no other Northern California Little League team has ever done, as of 2009? From a baseball standpoint, not as much as one might expect.

Ted Campbell kept growing and dominating, for a while. In 1964, at 6-foot-3, his pitching spurred Campbell Moreland Pony League to a World Series title. But the following year, when it came time for him to begin pitching from the regulation 60-foot, 6-inch distance in high school, he found that power alone was not enough, and it may have been that some of the insecurities that had made him reluctant to pitch before 1962 resurfaced. He was cut from the Blackford frosh-soph team as a freshman, and never played organized baseball again. For years, the rumor in Campbell baseball circles was that Campbell had suffered in his post-baseball life and had committed suicide, but after that rumor found its way into print in the late 1980s, Campbell contacted some of his old Moreland friends to assure them that he was alive and well. He lived in Southern California, and was working construction.

Mike Ucci, probably the best all-around athlete on the team, played through high school at Blackford, but knee problems prevented him from extending his career beyond that. Ironically, Ucci's father refused to give him permission to play football at Blackford because of the possibility of injury, so Ucci played basketball there instead – and injured his knees doing so. Only one of the 1962 Moreland players is known to have played beyond high school: Milt Murata, who played at West Valley College after graduating from Blackford, and concluded his career in 1971 at Cal State Hayward (now Cal State East Bay). In 1982 the team had a 20-year reunion, organized by Ray Miailovich and attended by most of the players, but has not gathered as a group since.

Bob Miailovich continued managing in Moreland Little League until his retirement in 1966. In 1980, he reappeared on the national Little League stage with his grandson, Richard, who played for the Kirkland, Wash., team that won its state tournament to earn a trip to the Western Regional in San Bernardino. Bob Miailovich threw out the ceremonial first pitch at that tournament, and Kirkland went on to win the regional and advance to the Little League World Series, where it finished third. (Richard Miailovich went on to play at Gonzaga, and had a brief professional career.) Bob Miailovich died in 1998.

It can be written, in retrospect, that the four most resounding one-hit wonders of 1962 were "Wild Weekend" by the Rebels, "Al Di La" by Emilio Pericoli, "Telstar" by the Tornadoes, and "World Series championship" by Moreland Little League. Nevertheless, Moreland's all-conquering 1962 season created a set of standards for Campbell-area youth baseball. For the next quarter-century, winning was not a hope but an expectation in the Campbell area when the postseason began. Moreland's success was the catalyst that spurred many teams and individuals, especially in the 1970s when Campbell became as much of an adjective in baseball circles as it was a proper noun.

By the end of the 1960s, Campbell's youth baseball network, along with that of rival Santa Clara, had produced dozens of players who excelled in high school and beyond over the next generation. Don Hahn, the former Moreland player who graduated from Campbell High in 1966 and had been drafted by the San Francisco Giants that June, in 1969 became his high school's second major leaguer (after John Oldham) when he played four games for the Montreal Expos. He wound up playing seven seasons with five teams, batting .236, and is best remembered today as Willie Mays' late-inning defensive replacement when Mays finished his career with the New York Mets in 1972 and 1973.

Campbell High's league, the West Valley Athletic League, dominated the CCS in the 1970s and into the 1980s. Camden graduates Joe Ferguson and Rich Troedson, both residents of nearby Cambrian Park and former Campbell Moreland Pony-Colt League participants, had reached the majors, as did Branham's Roger Samuels, Westmont's Dan Gladden and Doug Capilla, and Leigh's Ken Caminiti and Rick Foley. Capilla, who returned to Campbell after his retirement and coached in Campbell Moreland Pony League for a time, had played in Quito's Senior Big League program, and Gladden had played in Quito as well as in the Cupertino system. Caminiti, the 1996 National League MVP, honed his skills in Union Little League, which had split off from Cambrian in the early 1960s. Steve Davis, formerly of Campbell Little League, went on to star at Campbell High and Stanford University, and in 1979 became the third player from Campbell High to reach the major leagues, playing three games for the Chicago Cubs.

At a time when Santa Clara County was approaching its athletic zenith, especially in baseball, Campbell won CCS titles in 1972 and 1973 under Gordon Huntze, who had replaced John Oldham when the latter left for Westmont after the 1964 season. During the 20 seasons from 1972 through 1991, WVAL schools won nine section titles – Campbell in 1972 and 1973, Leigh in 1974 and 1976, Branham in 1971, 1979 and 1989, Prospect in 1982 (by beating Westmont in a final that was more like a Campbell-system intrasquad game) and Blackford in 1991 in its last baseball season before its closure. All the championships except Blackford's came when the CCS playoffs consisted of a single division in which all schools competed, regardless of size or location.

All of that began with Moreland Little League in 1962.

"It's kind of standard to watch it on TV now," Ray Miailovich says, "and every time I do, the same thing goes through my mind: 'Wait a minute. We were there. Wow. We were *there*.'"

"We had one thing in common, and that was baseball," Ted Campbell said a few years later. "Then and forever."

1964 CAMPBELL MORELAND: The best Campbell team ever?

For profit, Joe Gagliardi was a partner in his family's successful insurance business, San Jose-based Gagliardi Brothers. For profit and fun, Gagliardi was professional baseball's youngest club owner, one of the Bay Area's most successful boxing promoters, and the president of minor league baseball's California League for almost three decades.

In 1964, purely for fun, he managed the Campbell Moreland Pony League All-Star team to a World Series championship. And while he had six players who had been on Moreland Little League's title team two years before, Gagliardi's squad transcended even its Little League counter-part, and arguably all of the other 12 Campbell-system teams that reached youth baseball World Series from 1960-87.

In 1962, Moreland manager Bob Miailovich essentially needed only two pitchers to navigate its championship journey, and while Moreland had Ted Campbell as a fright factor on the mound, the team didn't often scare opposing pitchers. In its final nine games, Moreland scored more than seven runs only once (in its 22-2 rout of a bad French team in the first round of the World Series), and it recorded 32 runs in the other eight games — a sufficient and respectable total, to be sure, but hardly monumental.

The 1964 Pony League team, by comparison, was a fright factory. It scored *at least* 11 runs in eight games (including several that were shortened by the Pony League's mercy rule) spanning three of the tournaments leading up to the Pony League World Series in San Diego. Only three teams seriously challenged them during their 18-0 stampede. One of those teams used a future major league pitcher against Campbell Moreland. One of the others had no less than three players who reached the major leagues. (Moreland, by comparison, never played against a major leaguer-to-be during its Little League championship run.) Campbell Moreland's other difficult game, against Gadsden, Ala., lasted 16 innings, a still-standing Pony League World

Series record – but when the teams met again in the Series final, Moreland wasted little time eliminating any doubt about its superiority.

In 1962, Miailovich never had to make a single in-game pitching change during any of his team's 13 wins. The '64 Pony League team had its pitching depth tested to a much greater degree because of the double-elimination Pony League format. At 6-foot-3, Ted Campbell was almost as overpowering as he had been in Little League, and Vaughn Takaha was still more than capable. But he became the team's No. 4 pitching option because Campbell Moreland also had Tom Stanford and Mark Taku, both of whom came from Campbell Little League (and went on to play for Campbell High). Because of Stanford and Taku, Gagliardi was able to play Takaha at shortstop and Duane Kubo at second base throughout every game – a move that helped cement Campbell Moreland's infield defense.

In all, six holdovers from the '62 title team – Campbell, Takaha, Milt Murata, Duane Kubo, Phillip Kagel and Mike Ucci – were on the '64 Pony League team, but most of the others were from Campbell Little League. In addition to Stanford and Taku, a key addition from Campbell was catcher Kent McLain, who had made second-team All-WVAL on the frosh-soph level as a freshman at Campbell High that spring. McLain, who later played at UC Santa Barbara, represented a considerable upgrade over his 1962 Moreland Little League counterparts. He commanded the pitching staff, added power at the plate, and helped shut down opponents' running games – a quality that isn't obligatory in station-to-station Little League baseball but is essential in "real" baseball such as Pony League.

Gagliardi was an atypical youth baseball manager in that he didn't have any kids in the league at the time. He was working at his family's insurance agency and dabbling part-time in publicity with the Cal League's San Jose Bees before the 1964 season, when he found out from a friend who was associated with Campbell Moreland that the league was casting about for managers and coaches, as it often was obliged to do during its formative years. Even though he was only 25, he was given a regular-season team and then the league All-Star team, and his team's championship apparently was a springboard to his subsequent successes. In late 1965, at the age of 26, he became professional baseball's youngest owner when he purchased the Cal League's inactive Modesto Reds franchise. He obtained a one-year Player Development Contract with the Kansas City Athletics, who sent Reggie Jackson, Rollie Fingers, Joe Rudi, Dave Duncan and Skip Lockwood to a Modesto team that won the 1966 Cal League title and still is considered one of the best in the league's history.

Gagliardi sold the Reds in 1968 and moved on to other ventures, most notably fight promotion; he managed the closed-circuit television showings of several heavyweight title bouts in the late 1960s and early 1970s in addition to promoting many fights in the San Jose area. Although he managed in Campbell Moreland Pony League only one more season after 1964, he stayed closely connected with the Pony League regional and national organizations for decades, advocating its two-year increments and mid-sized diamonds as the best vehicles by which boys could develop their skills and confidence as they grew. It was largely because of Gagliardi that the Pony system was able to force competing organizations like Senior League, Babe Ruth and even American Legion out of most parts of Santa Clara County.

In 1977, Gagliardi bought a controlling interest in the San Jose Missions, who were about to enter the Class AAA Pacific Coast League. After an unsuccessful two-year stint in the PCL, the franchise was moved to Ogden, Utah in 1979 and Gagliardi bought the San Jose franchise that replaced it in the Cal League. Gagliardi retained the Missions nickname until he sold the franchise in 1982 to assume the presidency of the Cal League – a position he still held as of this writing.

"Joe made sure we had all the ingredients for success – coaches, equipment – and again (as in 1962) we had a pretty sophisticated system and a lot of discipline toward baseball," Duane Kubo remembered. "Joe had a lot of contacts all over the valley, and Pony was different (than Little League) – a lot was organized for us and he was the person mostly responsible for that. All we had to do was play the game, and with the talent we had, we were pretty confident.

"The '64 team had better pitching, better hitting, and the same defense as the '62 team. One thing I remember was that I played both Pony League and on the junior high team at Castro that year. At Castro we played on 90-foot bases, and then we'd come down to 75 for Pony. Just because of that, I thought we might dominate.

"Tom Stanford was as big as Ted (Campbell) was, two years later, and he was a much better pitcher, with control and something other than a fastball. He had an understanding of how to pitch, and he was very effective. Mark Taku had the best left-handed pickoff move I've ever seen. His father was a scout for the Pittsburgh Pirates, and let me tell you, when he started pitching in Pony League, he just *stopped* us, especially guys like me who were good at stealing. Even at 14, he had four pitches and good stuff. The kid who went to CCS with Santa Cruz (in 2008), Alex Taku, got a scholarship from Sac State. He's also a very tall lefthander and looks just like Mark ... he's the son of Dennis, Mark's older brother, and when I saw him pitch, I almost thought I was watching Mark."

In 1964, as Campbell Moreland manager, Gagliardi's Plan A lineup consisted of Takaha leading off and playing shortstop, Kubo at second base, Tom McLachlan (who'd been a Campbell Little League All-Star in 1963) at first base when Campbell was pitching, Ucci in center field, McLain catching, Taku in left, Ed Creech in right, Campbell pitching and batting eighth, and Murata at third base. Bobby Rodriguez, Craig Tritt, Kirk Mackley and Andy Vasquez rounded out the roster.

After cruising through the area tournament without much difficulty, Campbell Moreland began the district tournament in Felton with a 14-0 win over Salsipuedes of Watsonville. At that point,

Campbell Moreland collided with Cambrian Park and Rich Troedson, who two years later would help the Campbell system complete its 1962-64-66 championship trifecta with a Colt League World Series title. In 1973, he reached the major leagues, with the San Diego Padres.

"I played against Rich throughout our careers," Duane Kubo said. "I remember how active his father was in baseball, and (Rich) was far ahead in terms of knowing about baseball. He was also a lefthander, and we hadn't seen many like him before."

Troedson pitched against Campbell Moreland twice in three days. In the first meeting, Campbell Moreland prevailed 4-2, and in the district tournament final, it needed eight innings to pull out a 4-3 triumph. Cambrian Park, trailing 3-0 going to the bottom of the seventh and final regulation inning, scored twice and had the tying run on third and the winning run on first with nobody out when Campbell entered the game in relief of Tom Stanford. Campbell gave up a game-tying hit to the first batter he faced, but he retired the next three Cambrian players to send the game into extra innings. Kubo then won the game with an RBI single in the eighth.

Campbell Moreland wasn't tested in its next two tournaments, winning its six games by a combined margin of 78-13. Gagliardi's team beat Southeastern Sacramento 14-1 to win the divisional tournament in Santa Cruz, and crushed Central Marin 15-2 to claim the sectional title in Springville, Utah. But in the West Regional in San Pedro, Campbell Moreland ran into trouble in the form of Canoga Park, from Southern California.

That team included Rick Dempsey, a catcher who was the fourth-youngest player in the major leagues when he came up to the Minnesota Twins at age 19 in 1969. He stayed in the majors for 24 seasons, and was the fourth-*oldest* player in the bigs at age 42 when he caught his final eight games, in 1992 for the Baltimore Orioles. In-between, he was the MVP of the 1983 World Series for the champion Orioles, and played in 1,765 games, including one in 1971 in which he pitched two innings for the Milwaukee Brewers.

Canoga Park's center fielder was Rick Auerbach, who was a utility infielder for four MLB teams from 1971-81. One of Canoga Park's pitchers was Larry Yount, older brother of Hall of Famer Robin Yount. Larry Yount was signed by the Houston Astros out of high school, and on September 15, 1971, he was called on to make his major league debut in the top of the ninth inning of a game against the Atlanta Braves. He had already been entered into the official box score when he hurt his arm warming up and had to be taken out of the game. He never appeared in another major league game, and he never actually threw a major league pitch, but MLB records list him as having participated in that 1971 contest.

At that time, though, Yount wasn't even Canoga Park's best pitcher.

"The pitcher that faced us (Terry Hankins) was the fastest I've ever seen in youth baseball," Kubo said. "I struck out three times against him, and I think that was the only time in my whole career I ever struck out three times in a game. In one game, we won with a bunt, a stolen base, another bunt and then a suicide squeeze. We could play baseball either way. We had guys like Ucci who could hit the ball out of the park, but we could play small ball if we had to."

The first game against Canoga Park went eight innings, with Campbell Moreland prevailing 2-1 despite a Pony League-record 21 strikeouts by Hankins. Campbell countered with a three-hitter of his own, and Campbell Moreland won the game in the eighth when Ucci beat out a bunt, stole second, advanced to third on a sacrifice and scored on Taku's two-strike suicide squeeze bunt.

The next night, Stanford narrowly missed a perfect game; Riverside's only runner in an 11-0 loss was a hit batsman in the fourth inning, and he was immediately wiped out by a double play. Canoga Park then beat Riverside in an elimination game to get another shot at Campbell Moreland, but Campbell flung a five-hitter and Campbell Moreland won 4-1. Trailing 1-0 after two innings, Campbell Moreland took the lead in the third on Taku's two-run single and iced the game in the fourth on a two-run single by Ucci.

That sent Campbell Moreland to the Pony League World Series at San Diego's Westgate Field, home of the Pacific Coast League's San Diego Padres. The other three participants were Greensboro, N.C., Paducah, Ky., and Gadsden, Ala. Campbell Moreland was matched against Gadsden during the first night — and during the first hour of the following morning as well.

The game began at 8:30 p.m. and trudged along in almost complete silence for 4½ hours before Vaughn Takaha ended it at 1 a.m. with a thunderclap — a three-run homer in the bottom of the 16th inning to give Campbell Moreland a 4-1 victory. It was a game that represents a virtual subsection in the Pony League World Series record book, establishing the following team marks, all of which still stand:

- Longest game, 16 innings.

- Lengthiest game, 4½ hours

- Most strikeouts by one team's pitchers: 25 by Gadsden, including 15 by starter Eddie Lumpkin and 10 by reliever Bill Brooks.

- Most strikeouts, two teams: 43.

- Most runners left on base by one team: Gadsden, 16

- Most runners left on base by both teams: 29

Campbell had given up a run in the third, and that Gadsden lead had held up until the seventh when Campbell Moreland scored to force extra innings. Campbell and Lumpkin soldiered on until the end of the ninth, when both pitchers were lifted per the Pony League rule prohibiting pitchers from working more than nine innings in a single game. Stanford and Brooks kept putting up zeroes until the 16th, when Campbell and Taku reached base ahead of Takaha's walk-off homer. McLean caught the full 16 innings.

"I remember how that game dragged on," Kubo said, "but the thing that comes to mind first was that probably half the Gadsden players were chewing tobacco. They were big ol' Southern boys, and they seemed a lot older than us. Same with Paducah. All three of the (other) teams were Southern teams; I don't know why that was, but I know Pony League wasn't as national as it became later on."

With Stanford unavailable because of his unexpected role against Gadsden, Gagliardi sent Taku to the mound the following night – or, for the players, the *same* night – against Paducah, and he responded with a one-hit, 12-strikeout performance. Bobby Rodriguez drove in three runs as Campbell Moreland advanced to the tournament finals with a 5-0 win. Gadsden stayed alive by beating Paducah in an elimination game, but on August 29, 1964, Stanford pitched $4\frac{2}{3}$ innings of scoreless relief after replacing Campbell and hit a three-run homer to give Campbell Moreland an 8-2 win and complete the team's 18-0 pathway to perfection. Ucci hit a two-run homer and McLean had two singles and a double in the final game.

The team returned home the following day and was greeted by a motorcade that wound its way to Campbell Park for a reception attended by Campbell mayor Peter Lico. The local Jaycees threw them a party that night, and a banquet was held at Villa Felice in Los Gatos a couple of weeks later.

"I think (the title) impacted the 14-year-olds more than Mike (Ucci) and I (the two 13-year-olds on the team)," Duane Kubo said. "I say that because at 14 you're entering high school and you're being talked to by a lot of the high school coaches. I remember that the other guys were talked to a lot more than I was."

As had been the case with the Moreland Little League champions two years before, the players didn't have long to revel in their accomplishments before school started and they resumed their real-world routines. And the real world was infiltrating. As 13- and 14-year-olds, and as baseball players in quest of a world championship, they had been somewhat insulated during their two-month championship quest, but the newspaper headlines they probably never saw at the time reflected events that would affect all of their lives profoundly when they became 18-year-olds eligible for the military draft.

As the summer progressed, the national and international news became increasingly ominous. On August 5, President Lyndon Johnson responded to allegations of an attack by North Vietnamese forces against American ships in Saigon by ordering fighter jets to attack North Vietnamese positions and asking the United Nations to mobilize for an American-led incursion to help the South Vietnamese government withstand its Communist attackers. The Gulf of Tonkin resolution followed, and with it came the start of America's longest war, which was to claim more than 58,000 American lives during the next decade, including 13 residents of Campbell and 142 of San Jose.

About that same time, the bodies of three white civil rights leaders who were in Mississippi to help black citizens exercise their right to vote were found in a ditch outside Philadelphia, Miss. The racial unrest that shook the nation in the mid-1960s also began in earnest while Campbell Moreland was in pursuit of its world championship. Although some think of the Watts riots in Los Angeles in 1965 as the trigger event for that litany of violence, festering anger and distrust escalated into bloodletting in several U.S. cities in the late summer of 1964, including Chicago, Philadelphia, Pa., and Jersey City, N.J. When the Campbell Moreland team returned home from San Diego, the *Mercury* ran a half-page photo layout showing the players posing with their parents and coaches. The bottom half of the page, separated from the Campbell Moreland layout by the fold of the newspaper, was given over to gory photos from a riot in North Philadelphia that lasted three days and resulted in more than 200 injuries.

(One of the headlines on the front page of the August 30 front page of the *Mercury* referred to the rioting in Philadelphia, and another topped the story of Campbell Moreland's victory. A third, though, might have attracted the attention of the boys even before they read the account of their own game. It called readers' attention to a story about a research project by a Texas doctor, and it read: "Flat Chested Gals 'More Intelligent.'")

Major league baseball was not immune from the racial tension. In early August, San Francisco Giants manager Alvin Dark was quoted — inaccurately, he claimed — that black and Latin ballplayers did not respond as well to pennant-race pressure as did their white counterparts. Dark's remarks infuriated players on a team that probably had more black and Latin players than any other major league club at the time. Owner Horace Stoneham did not comment publicly on the matter other than to say Dark remained his manager, and Willie Mays tried to defend Dark, saying the quotes had been taken out of context. But as it turned out, Stoneham already had decided to fire Dark at the end of the season, and after the Giants finished fourth in a five-team National League race won by the St. Louis Cardinals on the final day, Stoneham did just that, even though Dark had taken the Giants to the World Series only two years before.

The 1964 Campbell Moreland All-Star players' lives, and those of young people their age throughout the nation, would never be the same after that tumultuous, euphoric summer. The team's achievements have largely been forgotten by those not directly involved with them, and the players have not stayed in constant touch.

"Vaughn (Takaha) and I were good friends," Duane Kubo said, "but I haven't seen him in many years. I still see Milt (Murata) occasionally. I saw Tony Riley (from the 1962 team) at our (40-year Blackford) high school reunion (in 2008). I correspond with Mike Ganson; he had talked about writing something about those two years. I don't see any of the others on a regular basis, and four or five I've lost track of completely."

But the 1964 Pony League All-Star team's impact on Campbell baseball remains as indelible as those of the Campbell area's other championship-level teams of the 1960s and 1970s ... and none of those teams can front their highlight film with an 18-0 marquee.

"They were saying at the time that this was the best Pony League team ever," Kubo said, "and I don't know if we still are, but I do know we were awfully good – for any time."

1963–69: Emergence

While Moreland needed only four seasons to pole-vault the youth baseball heights, Campbell Little League was ascending slowly, but steadily. It was in 1963 that the league began to take on the look that was to characterize it during the 1970s and beyond. The new look started with the league's Rosemary School complex, which was almost completely overhauled during the offseason.

When the facility was built by the Campbell Rotary Club in 1955, it consisted of one diamond, the infield of which was laid out in the middle of what is now the farm-division field, at the eastern edge of the school playground. While the playing surface itself was perhaps the best in the Santa Clara Valley, the structures surrounding it were made of wood, and more fields were needed to accommodate the league's growth. Before the 1963 season, the league, now knowing that it would be at Rosemary permanently because of the sale of the Route 5 property it had been eying, built the current main diamond on the western end of the property, and added fields for the minor and farm divisions, which previously had played most of their games at Campbell Grammar School. Chain-link fencing and new bleachers were installed with the fields.

Most significant, the league constructed its first true administrative and operations center. It housed (and still houses) the league's first permanent kitchen, snack bar, storage facilities, meeting rooms and restrooms. A scorers booth with a manual scoreboard on its side (an electronic scoreboard was installed in the outfield a few years later) was built on the roof overlooking the major-division field. The park had some quirks; the scorers booth, for example, could only be accessed by climbing over a bathroom urinal on a ladder that dangled precariously from the ceiling. Because residential structures were being built around the facility, parking was beginning to become an issue, and the right-field wall on the new major field was closer to Hamilton Avenue than the old left-field wall had been, creating a potential traffic hazard whenever a home run was hit to right. But for the first time, Campbell Little League was almost entirely self-contained, and

1963 photos of the complex are the first in which the place is instantly recognizable to anyone familiar with the complex as it existed in 2009.

Another soon-to-be-familiar aspect of the 1963 season was Jack Zogg managing the league's All-Star team. Zogg and Bob Holman had become major division managers during the same year, 1959, and their Robins and Campbell Stamps team had quickly emerged as the teams to beat almost every year. In 1963, they teamed for the postseason, with Zogg managing and Holman coaching. It was the same tandem that was to direct the 1976 All-Star team in the Little League World Series, although the 1976 pairing came out of necessity after John Emery, Zogg's original coach, was prevented by a family crisis from accompanying the team to the World Series. In 1963, Emery also was managing in the major division, guiding the Paul's Texaco team, and his team won the championship that year. That would also be the last year that Campbell would operate with six major league teams; in 1964, two more teams were added to the league's top tier, and Campbell would retain that eight-team major-division alignment for almost two decades.

(Emery continued to coach in Campbell Little League until 1990, and even after that, he never lost his passion for working with children. In 2009, John still lived in Campbell, where he had been a masonry contractor, and was coaching his 13-year-old *great-granddaughter* in age-group softball.)

Campbell's 1963 postseason lasted only three games; the team beat Saratoga and San Jose Northern before losing 8-7 to Santa Clara Briarwood. But in a pattern that was to become standard, Campbell stayed alive longer than did Moreland, the defending World Series champion. Even though Moreland had Mike Ucci and Duane Kubo back from its 1962 team, it was beaten 1-0 by Santa Clara Eastside in its first District 44 game.

The Campbell Moreland Pony League All-Star team also made an early tournament exit despite the presence of Don Hahn, who dominated the regular season after being named the WVAL frosh-soph MVP as a freshman that spring. The Colt League remained configured along high school lines; after its postseason, several of its players finished the summer on an ad hoc team organized by Campbell High coach John Oldham.

In the spring of 1964, Oldham's last Campbell High team went 12-0 in the WVAL to earn its third league title in his five years there, with second-place finishes in the other two seasons. Junior Pat Hartigan had seven pitching victories in league play, and concluded the season with 114 strikeouts. Murray Hall won the team's other five league games, and Ranny Baldinger, Randy Knight, Junior Rodriguez and Gary Papa all joined Hartigan and Hall on the all-league team. The team was so good that it never needed to bring Hahn up from the frosh-soph. Vaughn Takaha and Kent McLain, both of whom were on the World Series championship Pony League team that summer, were frosh-soph all-league selections as freshmen.

Even though the extent of Campbell High's talent pool, and the quality of its feeder system, seemed to bode well for Oldham's program in the immediate future, he saw the district's changing demographics. Westmont in the fall of 1964 was to become the Campbell Union High School District's sixth school and the WVAL's eighth, and Oldham knew that most of the younger families that were migrating to the Campbell area were buying houses in the neighborhoods surrounding the Westmont site. Barely two years after its opening, Westmont's enrollment was 2,000, well above its design capacity, and the campus was so cramped that only seniors received lockers of their own.

Asked in a newspaper interview in March 1964 what might happen to Campbell High after the opening of Westmont, Oldham bluntly replied, "Campbell will no longer be a power for a few years." So it wasn't surprising that he took over the new baseball program at Westmont when the school opened, but his replacement, Gordon Huntze, in 1965 led Campbell to its fourth league title in six seasons with Hartigan going 6-1 on the mound and junior Don Hahn 5-1. Oldham's first Westmont team, meanwhile, went 6-8 in the WVAL – a good showing for a first-year program in a league that had become one of the area's strongest.

The Pony League, meanwhile, began 1964 with the first of what became a protracted series of clashes with the city of Campbell over the use of Rincon Park, which the city had decided to build after abandoning its original idea of erecting a storage and operations center on the property. Pony League officials immediately eyed the 7½-acre site as an ideal location for a permanent diamond, and city leaders did not object in principle to that concept. But the Pony League wanted exclusive use of the ballpark and the complex surrounding it, because it planned to build a Pony League-sized field that would not be convertible to any other baseball use, or for softball. Some City Council and city staff members objected strenuously to such a narrow use plan.

Campbell Moreland had already built a rudimentary diamond on the Rincon Park site in 1963. In January 1964, it requested a city-funded expansion of the field's grass area, a permanent water line, and $1,500 for a permanent backstop. Mayor Peter Lico balked, saying he didn't want the city to pay for a "Cadillac park" that benefitted only the Pony League, to which league president Les Baldinger replied testily: "You'll never get a Cadillac in Campbell." Eventually, the parties compromised, with the city providing some of the requested improvements and giving the league exclusivity on a year-by-year basis. In 1965, and in subsequent years, a virtually identical dispute ensued, with the city finally agreeing to move a snack bar onto the property and to keep the grounds, which did not yet have a grass infield, weeded and level. Even the fact Campbell Moreland had won the Pony League World Series the previous August didn't give the league much immediate leverage in its effort to plant roots and build a ballpark tailored to its unique needs.

The site remained largely undeveloped, with few baseball accouterments aside from the diamond itself. It wasn't until 1969 that Campbell Moreland was able to move its entire operation to the Rincon Park site and begin work on a permanent complex that it had to fund itself. The 2,800-square-foot headquarters that became its permanent home wasn't completely done until 1972, and the league continued to ward off complaints from some citizens and city leaders who thought the facility ought to be available to other groups. Softball interests were usually the most vociferous complainers, and in the late 1970s, the city and the Campbell Union School District placated the softball crowd by building separate softball fields on the grass area separating John D. Morgan Park from adjacent Campbell Junior High.

Names, both within and beyond the baseball realm, that remained familiar many years later first surfaced in 1964. Bob Stephens was hired that year as Campbell city manager, a post he was to retain for 17 years, far longer than anyone else, before or since. Charlie Rose, who had been a City Councilman from 1956 to 1960 and had done much to support the local youth baseball leagues in their nascent years, was elected mayor. He is best remembered today for the baseball-equipment store he operated on North Central Avenue, where his specialty was restringing and reconditioning baseball gloves, which were brought to him from all over the Bay Area. George Vierhus also returned as *Campbell Press* on-site publisher after his two-year sojourn in Southern California.

At the same time, irreplaceable people were lost in 1964. Charles Beardsley, who in 1901 had been the only member of Campbell High's first graduating class, died at age 82. And the entire community was stunned on June 13, six days before Campbell High's graduation ceremony, when football and baseball all-leaguer Randy Knight lost his life at age 18.

On that night, a Friday, Knight had attended a yearbook dance at the school, and according to reports, he talked glowingly about his years in Campbell and the fact he had been offered at least two college football scholarships. Afterward, according to the *Los Gatos Times-Observer*, he and two of his classmates headed south on Winchester Road toward Los Gatos, and were seen at a pizza parlor there. Just before midnight, their car, driven by one of Knight's classmates, went out of control on Santa Cruz Avenue and crashed into the side of a house. Both of Knight's companions survived. Knight did not, and his death cast a pall over the community that lasted well beyond graduation ceremonies the following week.

As chronicled previously in this book, Campbell Moreland Pony League's All-Stars brought the summer to a close on a decidedly happier note. Campbell Little League, again managed by Jack Zogg, reached the District 44 semifinals before losing 3-0 to Santa Clara Westside.

While 1964 had been one of Campbell's most tumultuous baseball years — and would represent prelude to an equally eventful 1966 — 1965 was an interregnum. Joe Gagliardi again managed the Pony League All-Star team, and with Mike Ucci, Duane Kubo and Andy Vasquez back from the 1964 title team, hopes were high for a repeat. Campbell Moreland hosted and won its first tournament, with Kubo and Joe Lobrovich both pitching shutouts, but its season ended at the next tournament, in Martinez, where it lost 8-3 to Sacramento and 7-4 to Richmond-San Pablo.

In two different respects and on two different levels of baseball, Campbell bordered on greatness in 1966. That summer, Campbell Little League came closer than it had ever come to duplicating what rival Moreland had achieved four years earlier. Meanwhile, Milt Murata and Vaughn Takaha earned the rare distinction of playing for a third straight World Series championship team, even though that squad and that title belonged more properly to the communities bordering Campbell than to Campbell itself.

Although a wealth of baseball talent flourished in and around Campbell in 1966, the area's basketball teams and players were usurping the headlines. The western Santa Clara Valley, in fact, was in the midst of what remains its most successful basketball era ever.

In March, Blackford and 6-foot-9 center Dennis Awtrey earned the last of their four straight WVAL championships, and ended the 1965-66 regular season on a two-year, 44-game winning streak. With no sectional playoffs at the time, Blackford went to a postseason tournament in Sacramento and ran its streak to 45 before losing in the semifinals. Lincoln, which served San Jose's near west side, had Bud and Ralph Ogden, both of whom later teamed with Awtrey on a Santa Clara frontline that propelled the Broncos to the No. 2 spot in the national rankings behind only Lew Alcindor and UCLA in 1969. Lincoln, like Blackford, went unbeaten (29-0) in 1965-66, but the two teams never met, even though Blackford and Lincoln were only about five miles apart.

That 1966 championship was the last boys basketball crown Blackford would ever win, and it would be immediately supplanted as the WVAL's dominant program by Del Mar, which won WVAL titles in 1967, '68 and '69 behind center Bruce Posey and guard Bill Drozdiak. Both went on to play at the University of Oregon, and Drozdiak attained much wider recognition as a longtime international business reporter for the *Washington Post*. Another Del Mar basketball standout at the time was Gary Radunich, who transferred to Branham when it opened in 1967 and played his senior season there. Radunich later played at Brigham Young and UNLV, but is far better known today as Gary Radnich, the longtime sports commentator on San Francisco television station KRON. (He dropped the "u" from his last name shortly after beginning his TV career.)

Campbell's population reached 21,211 in 1966, and the baseball leagues that served it continued to grow. Moreland Little League added the area's first tee-ball program, and moved into a new complex at Payne School on Phoenix Avenue. Its best-known graduate, Don Hahn, was drafted and signed by the San Francisco Giants in June. He had batted .553 as a senior at Campbell High, which finished second in the WVAL that year. The Campbell Moreland Pony League was operating with eight teams, and had added a four-team minor division. One of its managers was

Bob Devor, who had started with the league in 1960 and was still there in 1978 and 1979 when Campbell Moreland won back-to-back World Series. Bob, though gruff and sometimes impatient with his players, was knowledgeable and knew how to win, and he could be as kind-hearted on the inside as he was abrasive on the outside. Jason Miller, whose older brother played for Bob, tells of the time that Bob, upon hearing that Jason's parents had bought property on the San Joaquin Delta, gave them an aluminum boat that the Miller kids could use when they were there.

Campbell Little League was up to 24 teams (eight majors, eight minors, eight Pee Wee); one of the new major-division sponsors was Campbell Plaza, which in 2009 was still underwriting a team. Jack Zogg and John Emery again combined to direct the Campbell All-Star team, which many compared favorably to the 1962 Moreland Little League championship squad. One reason was that it had Steve Davis, who dominated games almost to the degree that Ted Campbell had done four years earlier, although unlike Campbell, Davis was a shortstop and rarely pitched.

"John (Emery) had Steve in majors," Jack Zogg said. "He and Mitch Vierra (who in 2009 was managing in Campbell Pony League) were the last two 9-year-olds that were allowed into the majors. We played against John that year; we both had good teams, and in one game, Steve Davis was playing shortstop and he made 11 consecutive outs against us. Now, being the strong fundamental coach that I was, I told my team, 'Why don't we try hitting the ball to somebody else?'"

Much was expected of Davis throughout his amateur career, and he seldom disappointed. In 1972, as a senior at Campbell High, he helped the Buccaneers earn the first of their two straight Central Coast Section titles, and accepted a baseball scholarship from Stanford University. With the Cardinal, he set a Pacific-8 Conference record with 237 career hits. He was drafted by the Chicago Cubs after the 1976 season, and played in three games for them in 1979 to become the first Campbell Little League graduate to appear in a major league game, and the third and last Campbell High graduate (after John Oldham and Don Hahn) to do so.

"Sure, I remember Steve well," longtime Stanford coach Mark Marquess, who was an assistant coach for five years before taking over the Cardinal program in 1977, said in 2009. "People didn't think he could be a good defensive shortstop because he was so big and powerful ... he didn't fit the stereotype. But he was a great player for us. He didn't strike out much and he could hit for both power and average.

"When he was playing, that was the era when SC (Southern Cal) gave unlimited scholarships and would recruit guys just to keep them away from other schools like us. But we had good teams when Steve was here, and he was one of the guys who set the stage for what we were able to do later."

Entering the 2009 season, Marquess' Stanford teams had appeared in 13 College World Series and five CWS championship games, winning in 1987 and 1988, and had reached the NCAA tournament 23 times starting in 1981.

Gordon Huntze, Davis' coach at Campbell High, remembers his toughness afield and his gift for getting his point across.

"Steve ... boy, that was a guy that was *tough*," Gordon said. "I remember a few times where he'd get spiked and there'd be blood all over the place and he'd say, 'No, no, don't take me out of the game. Just put some gauze or something on it.' Afterward he'd have to get the thing stitched up, but no way he would come out of a game.

"Later (after the end of his playing career) I had him come talk to our guys about hitting. The kids are sitting there wide-eyed, and he's talking about how you have to use your off hand to pull the bat through the strike zone. Well, the way he explained it was, 'Just go up there and pretend you're slapping a midget in the mouth.' The kids always picked up on that."

In 1966, Davis helped Campbell Little League win its first District 44 title and make its deepest-ever incursion into the Little League national tournament, winning nine games and advancing to the Northern California divisional. Winning District 44 was a monumental achievement in 1966 because the district included 22 leagues (compared to 14 in 2009), but after opening with wins over Sunnyvale Bayshore and Sunnyvale American, Campbell knocked off Sunnyvale Southern 3-0 as Gary Yamamoto pitched a one-hitter. In the district title game, Mitch Vierra and Bob Johns homered as Campbell beat Santa Clara Eastside 5-3.

Yamamoto, who played second base when he wasn't pitching, was the smallest player on the team, and his mound repertoire bewildered many hitters even though it intimidated almost none of them. (In that respect, he was similar to Mike Alvarez, the No. 2 pitcher on Campbell's 1970 Little League World Series finalists four years later.) In a sectional tournament game against Menlo Park at Campbell, Yamamoto came within a second-inning walk of a perfect game as his team won 4-0. Steve Davis had two hits and scored three runs for Campbell, which went on to beat Watsonville 5-1 and Burlingame 5-1 to advance to the divisional tournament in Novato.

In the first round there, Campbell was matched with Airport Little League of Sacramento, and Davis scored on a wild pitch in the first inning to give his team a 1-0 lead. Bob Johns and Kelly Davis combined to limit Airport to four hits, but one of them was a two-run single in the third by winning pitcher Zach Vanegas, and that was enough to send Campbell to a 2-1 defeat. The team went on to finish third in the tournament, routing Petaluma and Hanford by 11-1 scores in the consolation round. Airport won the divisional and then the Western Regional to advance to the Little League World Series, where it lost to eventual champion Houston 4-0 in the semifinals.

If Campbell had beaten Sacramento, won the Western Regional and advanced to Williamsport, it might well have met up with the same league that Moreland had beaten in the 1962 final. Jaycee Little League of Kankakee, Ill., advanced to the World Series in 1966 for a record fourth time, losing 3-1 in its opener to West New York, N.J., and remains the only American league with more World Series appearances than Campbell's three in 1970, 1976 and 1979. Toms River East of New Jersey, probably the country's best-known Little League as this is written, went to Williamsport three times in a five-year span, winning in 1998, but has not made any other trips to the Series. Northridge, Calif., is the only other West Region city to be represented in three World Series, and those three teams were from two separate leagues in Northridge. If Moreland is to be counted as a Campbell league, the city is alone with Kankakee as a claimant to four World Series representatives.

Meanwhile, the West Valley Colt League team remained alive in its quest to add a third World Series title to the championships won by Moreland Little League in 1962 and Campbell Moreland Pony League in 1964.

As had been the case for several years, the Colt League was organized along the lines of the high schools its players attended, with most of the West Valley Athletic League programs maintaining their own distinct teams. That's the reason the Colt League referred to itself, and is referenced in record books, as the West Valley Colt League of San Jose and not as Campbell Moreland, even though it was operated under the auspices of Campbell Moreland Boys Baseball.

In 1966, a number of prominent 15- and 16-year-old players who had come up in the Campbell youth baseball system committed elsewhere for the summer, and Mike Ucci, one of the stars of the '62 and '64 title climbs, did not play on the All-Star team after competing for the Blackford Colt team during the regular season. As a result, the Colt League's All-Star team had only two players – Vaughn Takaha and Milt Murata – who had played on both the 1962 Moreland Little League and 1964 Campbell Moreland Pony League championship teams. (Tom McLachlan had played on the '64 Pony team, and Don Silva had been in the '62 Moreland group.) The '66 Colt All-Star team included players from six different schools. Three of its mainstays were from Los Gatos High, including outfielder Roy Meisner, who was drafted by the St. Louis Cardinals in 1970 out of West Valley College, but instead accepted a baseball scholarship from Cal. The 1966 Colt League team's No. 1 pitcher, Rich Troedson, had been a second-team All-WVAL varsity selection as a freshman at Camden that spring, and while playing in the Cambrian Park Pony League, had twice come close to interrupting Campbell Moreland's run to the 1964 World Series championship.

Perhaps because the players came from youth and high school programs that had long been rivals, the West Valley team didn't coalesce immediately. In the opening tournament, Santa Clara came through the losers bracket and beat West Valley 8-2 to force a deciding game that West Valley won 8-5. The sectional tournament in Santa Cruz began with a defeat that forced West Valley to win five straight elimination games to advance. The next step was the divisional tournament in Ukiah, where West Valley struggled to beat Provo, Utah 5-4 in its second game before defeating Provo again 7-2 in the finals as Troedson crafted a two-hitter.

At the regional tournament in Riverside, the host team handed West Valley its third postseason loss, 6-0, but Campbell again rebounded in the winner-take-all final, beating Riverside 1-0 as Troedson pitched his second shutout of the tournament. Ron Curnutt, like Troedson a Camden student, hit a home run in the seventh inning to break a scoreless tie and send West Valley to the 1966 Colt League World Series in Shawnee, Okla. It was West Valley's third appearance in the Colt League World Series; it had won in 1960, and had returned in 1963.

In Oklahoma, West Valley was matched against the same Paducah, Ky., program that had been in the Pony League World Series with Campbell Moreland in 1964. West Valley was held scoreless through all seven regulation innings, but pitcher Pete Shank, another Los Gatos player, came through with a succession of zeroes of his own. In the top of the eighth, West Valley's Henry Honda walked, Murata was safe on an error, and Meisner walked to load the bases with no outs. Lou Gasper, another Camden player, doubled home two runs, Curnutt singled home another, and the fourth and final run of West Valley's 4-0 win came home on an infield out.

West Valley then beat Hagerstown, Md., 5-4, to clinch a berth in the finals, as Troedson completed a six-hitter and struck out 11. Two days later, West Valley beat El Paso, Texas, 4-1 to win the championship and finish 18-3 in the postseason. Bill Butler, a Del Mar sophomore, came on to pitch in the first inning when starter Ed Creech was injured, and went the rest of the way. West Valley scored four unearned runs in the second inning, during which Takaha and Gasper delivered key hits.

Partly because its ties to the Campbell youth baseball system were loose, the 1966 Colt League championship is considered a part of the Campbell legacy only because of the fact it enabled Vaughn Takaha and Milt Murata to complete their unique Little League-Pony League-Colt League trifecta. Unlike its 1962 and 1964 counterparts, the team's return home virtually was unnoticed, aside from a banquet that previously had been scheduled to honor the regular-season champions and individual standouts.

Even so, that 1966 championship completed a remarkable five-season litany of success for the Campbell youth baseball system, and particularly for the Moreland area. In one respect, that litany came to an end in Oklahoma when Takaha and Murata played their final Colt League games, but in another way, it was only the beginning.

By 1967, Campbell had abandoned all pretenses of rural-urban coexistence. The so-called Orchard City had only two large agricultural parcels within the city limits — the 34-acre Brynteson spread at the intersection of Bascom and Campbell avenues, and the 26-acre Gomes ranch near the center of town — and both would be purchased and leveled by developers within two years. For the first time in memory, Campbell's headlong growth was slowing. Building permits issued in 1965 were for properties valued at a total of $4,677,945; in 1966, the collective valuation of the city's building projects was $3,885,807 — a reflection of the fact that Campbell was approaching its saturation point. In 1967, a citizens advisory committee recommended that the city slash more than $1 million from its projected $4.11 million annual budget before taking its almost-annual bond issue before the electorate. Urban ills were creeping into Campbell as well. The Campbell Police Department reported 344 juvenile arrests – almost one a day – in 1966, and in 1967 a number of large-scale drug busts, most involving upper-middle-class students from local high schools, prompted the Campbell Union High School District to appoint Haskell Bowen, a Westmont teacher and coach, as what would now be known as a drug czar. His job was to do whatever was necessary to determine the extent of the problem and formulate solutions.

Campbell Little League opened its 1967 season on April 29 with 430 players manning 24 teams. The league continued to field eight major division teams, but one of its original 1954 sponsors, Campbell Stamps, was gone because the merchants who had financed the promotional stamp program had abandoned it. Bill McLean, whose son Kent had once played in Campbell Little League and had quarterbacked Campbell High's football team to a 5-2 league record the previous fall, was managing in the league and was shown in a *Campbell Press* photo instructing 9-year-old minor leaguer Ron Colburn. That Colburn surname would become part of league and Campbell baseball lore three years later. Another photo, taken later in the season, featured the Willow Glen Optimist team that won the minor division. The team included three 9-year-olds who, like Ron Colburn, were to play for Campbell in the Little League World Series in 1970 – Kent Ohmann, Lank Rowland and Steve Esau.

As had become the custom on Opening Day at Rosemary School, Mayor Charlie Rose threw out the first ball and other city dignitaries participated in the ceremonies. Former San Francisco Giant Hobie Landrith, who played for seven teams during a 14-year major league career that had ended in 1963, was among Moreland's Opening Day guests; so were San Jose Bees general manager Larry Glissman, former San Jose State pitching star and longtime minor leaguer Pete Mesa, and Bob Fatjo, whose 509 victories as baseball coach at Bellarmine Prep from 1943-68 was a Northern California high school record at the time of his retirement. Gordon Hahn, younger brother of Don, hit a home run on Moreland's Opening Day; he and his twin brother George would become standouts at Campbell High and at Santa Clara University.

Campbell's All-Star team, again managed by Jack Zogg, was knocked out in the semifinals of the District 44 tournament. San Jose West Valley, a new league that bordered Moreland on the north, beat Santa Clara Westside, which had eliminated Campbell, for the title.

In the Pony League, the 1967 season marked the All-Star managing debut of Chuck Calhoun, whose mastery of the nuances of "small ball" was to make him the league's most successful and influential manager over the next decade. With Steve Davis as a 13-year-old starter, Campbell Moreland easily won its first three tournaments and went 9-0 to advance to the regional in San Bernardino. There, Campbell Moreland, hampered by the loss of top pitcher Bob Nickeson to an arm injury, lost 11-2 to Hawaii in the winners-bracket final, and after navigating the losers bracket to get a rematch in the finals, trailed Hawaii 9-0 going to the bottom of the seventh inning.

In the 1970s, one of Calhoun's most salient qualities was his ability to fully milk his team's 21-out quota, and it was in that seventh inning that his reputation first flowered. Campbell Moreland came agonizingly close to pulling off a comeback for the eons, sending 13 men to the plate. Eight of them scored, and two others were on base when Hawaii finally recorded the third out to escape with a 9-8 victory.

Just as Campbell baseball was overshadowed in the early and mid-1960s by the area high schools' emergence as basketball powers, football was the talk of Campbell in 1967 and 1968. During those two seasons, the Buccaneers matched the accomplishments of the Craig Morton/Jack Schraub squads and brought the school what turned out to be its final two WVAL football championships. The program had struggled after Morton and Schraub graduated in 1961, partly because of the advent of new district high schools and partly because of the retirement of veteran coach Jim Muir after the perfect '60 season. But in 1967 the school hired Mike Jones, who promptly directed his first team to a 9-0 season and followed with a 9-0-1 showing in '68, marred only by a non-league tie with Lincoln. Chuck Hawthorne, a former Campbell Little League player who rushed for a WVAL-record 1,263 yards in 1967, was the league MVP for the second straight season. He would go on to play at Washington State, as did Dennis Mitchell, a Campbell teammate. The Buccaneers concluded the '68 season with a 53-14 Thanksgiving Day victory over rival Los Gatos in which quarterback Gary Tomasso completed 11 of 12 passes – five for touchdowns.

Campbell never again came close to matching its football accomplishments of 1967 and 1968; Leigh, Saratoga and Branham took over as the WVAL's dominant programs for the rest of Campbell High's existence, and Campbell's only appearance in the CCS playoffs, which began in 1972, also represented the last football game the school ever played. The Buccaneers entered the 1979 CCS playoffs with a 7-1-2 record, including a win over Los Gatos that sent Campbell to the postseason, but an Oak Grove team quarterbacked by Marty Mornhinweg built a 40-0 halftime lead and coasted to a 48-12 victory. Mornhinweg went on to play at the University of Montana, was the Detroit Lions' head coach in 2001 and 2002, and in 2008 was in his sixth season as an assistant coach (and his fourth as offensive coordinator) with the Philadelphia Eagles.

(The last touchdown in Campbell High history was scored on a kickoff return by Wade Allison, who'd been a Campbell Little League All-Star in 1975. His younger brother Matt was the starting catcher on Campbell's 1979 Little League national championship team. One of Wade Allison's '75 All-Star teammates, Mark Paquin, made the last out of Campbell's baseball history, in a 2-0 loss to Yerba Buena in the first round of the 1980 CCS playoffs.)

By the mid-1970s, Mike Jones had stepped down as varsity coach and was directing the frosh-soph football and baseball teams, and several of the most luminous Campbell youth baseball names of the period played both sports for him. Many remembered Mike's son roaming the football sidelines and sitting in the baseball dugout with his father during those years. As it turned out, Brent Jones went farther in football than any player who ever set foot on Campbell High's football field, even Craig Morton or Billy Wilson. After starring at Leland High and Santa Clara University, Jones was a four-time Pro Bowl selection and won three Super Bowl rings during his 11-season career with the San Francisco 49ers.

Another theme – beyond the ongoing national crises of Vietnam, race relations and drugs – that rendered baseball a secondary topic of discussion in Campbell in 1968 was a controversy involving the disposition of the former Brynteson orchards at the intersection of Bascom and Campbell avenues. The property had been sold to a commercial developer, Fred Sahadi, who proposed a joint venture with the city of Campbell that would result in the construction of a 17-story building that would house all of the city's offices and operations.

Everybody knew that this project would be Campbell's most impactful and ambitious ever, and would transform the city in ways few at the time felt free to predict. Consequently, objections to the original plan were loud and widespread, and in October 1968 the plan was amended to make the development a regional shopping center, without the municipal facilities that had been envisioned. In late 1969, the first phase of the Pruneyard shopping center was opened, and the entire facility was functioning by the end of 1971. Two high-rise office buildings, one encompassing 17 stories and the other 10, opened in 1970 on the adjoining lot between the main shopping center and the Highway 17 freeway. At the time it was completed, the 17-story tower was the tallest building between San Francisco and Los Angeles.

The Pruneyard's growth was episodic at times over the years; both the shopping center and the towers were minimally occupied for many years, but by 2009 the Pruneyard had become a regional shopping, cultural and culinary destination. A hotel was added on the north end of the center, and the larger tower's tenants in 2008 included Rep. Michael Honda (D-Calif.), who maintained his offices there, and the FBI, which had an operational center. Along with East Campbell Avenue, which is promoted as "Historic Downtown Campbell" but in reality is neither historic in the architectural sense nor a true downtown in the commercial-hub sense, the Pruneyard is the face of a rebuilt, redefined, trendy, upscale Campbell that is the antithesis of the slow-paced middle-class bedroom community in which its longtime residents had grown up. The one common denominator between Campbell past and Campbell present is that its municipal services still earn high marks from residents. In November 2008, at the height of the worst American economic downturn since the Great Depression, the city was still operating with almost no reductions in services, and the electorate overwhelmingly approved a local sales tax increase to pay for the continuation and extension of those services. Campbell has not always been a well-planned community, but with very few exceptions, it has been efficiently and honestly run throughout its history.

Meanwhile, the only other large agricultural parcel left in town in 1968, the 26-acre Gomes ranch at the intersection of Hamilton and Latimer, also was leveled to make way for new construction. Joseph Gomes, the patriarch of the family, had died in 1964; a Stanford law-school graduate as well as one of the valley's leading orchardists, he had been on Campbell's first City Council after the city incorporated in 1952 and was heavily involved in municipal affairs throughout his lifetime. Gomes Park, at the intersection of Winchester Boulevard and Alice Avenue, is named for him.

Amidst everything else happening in Campbell, the 1968 baseball season was relatively pedestrian. Campbell was eliminated in the District 44 tournament, which was won by a Santa Clara Westside team that advanced to the regional final before losing 4-3 in seven innings to Bolsa of Garden Grove. It was the deepest postseason streak by a Santa Clara Valley team since Moreland's 1962 championship, and it was the first of four straight seasons in which a District 44 team would reach the Western Regional title game. Camden, which had won the WVAL championship and then finished second in the first CCS playoffs in 1967, repeated as league titlist in 1968 and went to the CCS semifinals before losing 3-2 to Soquel. The Cougars' Rich Troedson, the 1968 league MVP, was a sixth-round pick by the Houston Astros in the 1968 amateur draft, but turned down the Astros' offer to accept a scholarship from Santa Clara University. After he pitched for the Broncos for three seasons, setting school records for career victories and strikeouts, the San Diego Padres made him the sixth selection in the January 1972 supplementary draft. He signed, spent the 1972 season in the minor leagues, and made the Padres' Opening Day roster in 1973. He pitched in 50 games and went 7-9 with a 4.25 earned run average for San Diego that year, but was demoted to Class AAA Hawaii after 15 appearances in 1974. By the end of that season Troedson was playing for Class AA Alexandria, and by 1977 he was out of baseball, having never resurfaced in the major leagues.

The deepest postseason advance among the Campbell teams in 1968 was made by the Campbell Moreland Pony League squad, which again was managed by Chuck Calhoun. Playing at Castro Junior High, Campbell Moreland went undefeated through its first tournament, but was knocked out at the sectional level. After the season, the league, having received long-awaited permission from the city of Campbell to proceed with the preliminary construction stages of its long-awaited complex at the future Rincon Park, finally broke ground. In the meantime, Campbell Moreland played most of its games at Castro while continuing to conduct some games and practices on the primitive Rincon Park diamond.

By April 1969, the ballpark skeleton was complete, with a grass infield, a new concession stand and improved fencing. It had no permanent stands or other amenities, but for the first time, Pony League officials scheduled the Opening Day ceremonies there instead of at Castro. Les Baldinger, whose involvement in Campbell youth baseball dated to the 1950s, was one of the prime movers in the construction project, as was Chuck Cannady, described as the park's "ramrodder" in a *Press* story. However, the question of whether Campbell Moreland would be able to make Rincon

Park its permanent home remained unanswered on Opening Day, because the development of Rincon Park itself depended on a $625,000 bond issue to be placed before the voters on June 10. A similar proposal, in October 1967, had fallen just short of the two-thirds majority needed for passage, and if this bond issue met a similar fate, the city was ready to sell the parcel to a developer that planned to build a 288-apartment complex on it — forcing the Pony League back to a Castro facility that it had always considered temporary.

On June 10, Campbell voters approved the measure, with 74 percent voting yes. At last, Campbell Moreland Pony League could begin working in earnest on what was now certain to be its permanent home.

Elsewhere in town, construction on the Pruneyard towers began, and in January it was confirmed that two theaters would be built within the confines of the main shopping center. The Gaslighter Theatre, in the building that until 1966 had housed the old Campbell Theatre, opened downtown as a venue for melodramatic plays. Laurence Hill, who had been superintendent of the Campbell Union High School District for 22 years (and Campbell Little League's first president), retired in June. The CSUHD had one school, Campbell High, and about 800 students when Hill had assumed command of the district in 1946. At the time of his retirement, enrollment was 14,000 and still rising, and Prospect High, which had opened in the fall of 1968, gave the district eight campuses.

The seemingly unending horror and waste of the Vietnam War continued to gnaw at every American city, including Campbell. As a senior during the 1967-68 school year, Matthew Edward Smith had been the captain of Westmont's football team and one of the key players on the Warriors' baseball squad. By the fall of 1968, he was a private in the Marine Corps. By March 1969, he had been deployed to Vietnam. Six weeks later, on April 11, he was killed in action at age 18. Almost four decades later, he was remembered this way by Carol West Corless, also a member of the Westmont Class of 1968: "Matt was sensitive and wrote poetry. Only a few special people were blessed to share his beautiful words and thoughts. Matt had so much to live for — a wonderful future. He was taken from us much too soon. Matt designated a portion of his will to the Westmont High School library. I have felt Matt's spirit and presence many times over the years and it has helped me through the tough times. We have honored Matt for 35 years and respect his service to our great country every day. He is a true hero and a great American. We will never forget (him)."

Perhaps some parents at the Campbell-area Little Leagues' 1969 opening ceremonies in the days after Smith's death knew him or of him, and offered a silent prayer that the conflagration in Southeast Asia would be doused before the children parading before them would reach draft age. (Happily, none of those kids ever were conscripted for service in Vietnam; the draft was ended in 1973 and the last U.S. combat troops were removed from Southeast Asia two years after that.)

In 1969, Campbell Little League went to greater lengths than usual to make Opening Day an event. Craig Morton was one of the honored guests; so was Don Larsen, who in 1956, pitching for the New York Yankees, had completed the only perfect game in World Series history. The eight major division teams were Campbell Moose Lodge, Fontanetti's, Campbell Plaza, Asquith, Campbell Lumber, Bruener's, Buchholtz, and Robins. Campbell Moose Lodge, managed by Bob Pettit, pulled off a rare double by winning both halves and taking the championship without a playoff. The Moose team included several players who soon would become familiar names in the Campbell baseball community and beyond: Cliff Judd, Mike Alvarez, Kevin Mathis (son of Wes Mathis, the longtime *San Jose Mercury* sportswriter who had helped bring Little League baseball to the Santa Clara Valley two decades before) and Gary Lujan. Willow Glen Optimist, which won the minor division, was managed by John Hanrahan, who in 1971 became league president and remained in that post until 1977, when he went back to managing.

John, who worked for Lockheed, first became involved with the league in 1964, when one of his neighbor's sons began playing, and he began managing the following year. John, whose wife operated the snack bar through much of their time in Campbell, never had a son in the league, and projected a sense of quiet fairness that everyone respected. "I enjoy baseball," he once said, "and I like to see something done for the kids."

When it came time to select the league's 1969 All-Star team, the managers took the unusual step of choosing three 11-year-olds – Ron Colburn, Kent Ohmann and Rickey Roth. That might have been seen at the time as an investment in 1970, but most thought the 1969 team's chances of winning District 44 were promising, especially with Steve McGrody on the mound. In Campbell's first game, McGrody pitched a no-hitter in a 12-0 win over Sunnyvale Pioneer, sending Campbell into a second-round matchup with Santa Clara Briarwood.

If the Briarwood-Campbell matchup had occurred in a game in which McGrody had been eligible to pitch, it's possible that 1969 and not 1970 would be remembered today as the year that Campbell Little League established itself internationally. District 44 was so strong that any team emerging from it had a good chance to make a deep penetration into the postseason, as Santa Clara Westside had demonstrated the previous year by making it to the regional championship game.

As it happened, though, Campbell's '69 team never got past its second game, losing 3-0 to a Briarwood team led by Carney Lansford, who would become a 15-year major league veteran and 1981 American League batting champion. Briarwood went on to win the district title, blew through the next four tournaments to earn the West berth in the Little League World Series, and advanced to the finals in Williamsport before losing 2-0 to the first of the Taiwan teams that were to win 17 of the 28 LLWS championships between 1969 and 1996.

"I thought our All-Star team when I was 11 was, per player, was a better team than we had in '70," Kent Ohmann recalled in 2009. "But it didn't jell; it didn't work."

Even so, all of the components for all-encompassing youth baseball success — both as a recreational medium and as a postseason entrant — were in place at Rosemary School by the end of 1969. But Campbell had won only one District 44 title, in 1966, and three times (1962, 1966 and 1969) the team that had eliminated Campbell from the postseason had gone on to represent the West in the Little League World Series.

In 1970, denial became denouement.

1970 CAMPBELL LITTLE LEAGUE: The Cardiac Kids

Of the nine baseball teams of Campbell composition that reached World Series title games during the 1960s and 1970s, eight tugged at the public imagination either because of the extent to which they won, or because of the players with whom they won, or a combination thereof.

Only the 1970 Campbell Little League All-Star team became the talk of the youth baseball world, and beyond, because of *how* it won.

"The Cardiac Kids nickname came from Ronald Reagan," Kent Ohmann, a frequent third-base starter on that team, said in 2009. "When we got to Williamsport, we were getting a lot of telegrams from aunts, uncles, friends, people like that. But one of the telegrams came from Ronald Reagan (who was governor of California at the time). He knew that we had won all those one-run games, and he wished good luck to the Cardiac Kids. That was the first time we heard it."

It was a team that spent a month teetering on the precipice against teams it couldn't vanquish on the basis of raw talent alone, even though manager Gene Colburn's team had a surfeit of ability, especially on the mound. Tom Davis, Mike Alvarez and Ron Colburn, who did almost all of the pitching, were nicked for a total of 12 runs, just seven of them earned, in their 13 postseason games, and those totals are even more startling when one considers that they were almost always working without a net. Campbell's highest run total in a game was eight, and it didn't score more than four runs in any of its final eight games, including the 2-0 loss to Wayne, N.J., in the World Series championship game in Williamsport, Pa.

No less than five of those final eight games went eight innings (two more than regulation Little League games), and one of them, the West Regional title game against Hawaii, required two days to complete. Campbell owed its win in that game, and its subsequent trip to Williamsport, largely to a wayward newspaper photographer.

Another game was saved by a throw by a part-time center fielder, who hadn't even been part of the original team, to a backup catcher. At a level where leading off base before a pitch crosses the plate isn't allowed and where the distance from the plate to the backstop often isn't more than a few yards, Campbell won another game because another non-starter scored from first on three straight wild pitches. Because of the no-leadoff rule, the suicide squeeze is virtually non-existent in Little League, and yet Campbell scored a crucial run via that method in the victory that sent the team to Williamsport. In that same game, a Campbell batter twice was asked to bunt in a sac-rifice situation, failed twice, and then came through with a single to prolong the decisive rally.

Given those circumstances, it was little wonder that Reagan wasn't the only one who saw these players as "Cardiac Kids." The nickname quickly was picked up by the Williamsport and Bay Area media at the start of the World Series, and following them as they neared and reached Williamsport certainly wasn't for the faint of heart.

The beginning of Campbell's Williamsport excursion elicited little attention, but by the time the team arrived home after its loss to Wayne, the community had erupted in what a *Campbell Press* editorial described as "spontaneous combustion." George Vierhus, the longtime *Press* editor whose interest in sports was minimal, proclaimed Campbell's accomplishments to be "the big-gest thing that has ever happened to Campbell in the history of this community." (It probably was the biggest thing ever to happen to the *Press'* asset-debit ledger as well, because the paper sold dozens of congratulatory ads in the aftermath of the team's return.) The paper's cover page on September 3, the week after their return, was given completely over to a Campbell Little League photo montage – something the *Press* had never done in its 75-year history, not even at the con-clusion of either World War. The *Press* also printed the home addresses of all the players so that any neighbors so inclined could pay appropriate individual homage.

"I don't think what we had done really sank in until after we got home," Kent Ohmann said. "That was when you could go out onto the tarmac to meet the planes at San Jose airport. As we walked down the airplane stairs, you could see banners and people all over the place. I remember somebody said there had never been a procession down Highway 17 like the one we had. They treated us like royalty. It was like we had won (the World Series)."

The cars in which the boys were passengers were cheered by bystanders during an impromptu parade that snaked all over town before ending at the football field at Campbell High. All three theaters in town shoved the titles of their featured films to the sides of their marquees and posted celebratory and welcome-home messages, and markets, gas stations and other businesses did likewise with their displays. More than 400 people bought tickets to the celebratory banquet at Lou's Village in San Jose. Players appeared as guests at service clubs and store openings for weeks after their return. In 1962 when Moreland Little League won the World Series, the only national politician to personally congratulate the team was Charles Gubser, the area's Congressional rep-resentative, and they were whisked around Washington, getting only a cursory tour of the White

House and missing out on many of the iconic historical sites. In 1970, the Campbell team was met at the White House by California Sen. Alan Cranston, who guided them on a tour of all the Washington sites that the Moreland team had missed eight years before. After their return, the San Francisco Giants had a "Campbell Night" at Candlestick Park on September 8, and the players got a loud ovation when they were introduced to the crowd before the Giants' game against Cincinnati.

All this jubilation over a Little League baseball team, and not even a national or world championship team at that? Part of it may have had to do with the fact that the new, suburban Campbell had found, through youth baseball, the municipal definition it had lacked.

After a quarter-century of unmitigated growth and the anticipation and controversy surrounding it, almost all of the orchards in the Orchard City were gone, replaced by dozens of housing tracts that were virtually indistinguishable from each other. Downtown, for all intents and purposes, was gone too, and while Campbell by 1970 had more than enough shopping centers and grocery stores and schools and housing tracts, it had nothing that qualified as a destination even for local residents. The 17- and 10-story Pruneyard Towers were nearing completion, and Reagan attended the formal dedication on March 13 – that may be why the Cardiac Kids' accomplishments registered with him five months later – but as office buildings, they were only visual novelties that had little real impact on day-to-day life in Campbell. The acreage that soon would become Rincon Park was little more than a barren lot dotted only by Campbell Moreland Pony League's still-rudimentary baseball diamond. A first-time visitor to the Santa Clara Valley would have had no way of distinguishing Campbell from Santa Clara or Sunnyvale or Cupertino or Cambrian Park or Burbank, because nothing about Campbell called attention to its uniqueness.

Campbell had neither extreme poverty nor extreme wealth in 1970. It had evolved into a working-class community where people labored long and hard to meet their mortgages and to try to ensure that their children would have better lives. The controversies of the 1950s and 1960s had determined what kind of community Campbell would ultimately be; by 1970, it had become that community. Most of the disputes that had marked its postwar growth had passed, and its residents were stirred into action beyond their daily routines only by NIMBY (Not In My Back Yard) issues. Tax hikes and bond issues were routinely defeated at the polls, as voters made it abundantly clear that they felt Campbell and its school districts needed no more money to fuel more expansion. The *Press* had so little sweepscope news to report that it focused, with blaring headlines, for months on the question of whether the Winchester Drive-In theater should be allowed to erect a third movie screen. (It eventually was granted permission by the city to do so, despite the adjacent NIMBYs.)

Amid the municipal ennui, manager Gene Colburn and coach Ken Aubineau began piecing together the Campbell Little League All-Star team. After having competed on nearly-even terms with eventual national champion Santa Clara Briarwood in a 3-0 loss during the district tournament the previous year, they knew the 1970 squad – with returnees Ron Colburn, Kent Ohmann and Rickey Roth – would be in good position to challenge for the District 44 championship. Ron Colburn and Tom Davis were power pitchers of the type that was a prerequisite for any team thinking about Williamsport, and because of the presence of Paul Rhoades and Mike Alvarez, Gene Colburn had the additional luxury of using his son as the regular catcher and turning to him as a pitcher only in late-inning crises – of which Campbell wound up having more than anyone could have imagined.

Alvarez – who was not related to Rich Alvarez, the star pitcher on the 1976 Campbell Little League All-Star team – was perhaps the team's most compelling human-interest story. That was partly because he was one of the smallest players on the team at 4-foot-11 and 80 pounds, but mostly because he had been born with a club foot, and only a succession of operations had allowed him to walk normally, let alone play baseball. "I remember during my first year in Campbell, as a 9-year-old, seeing him sitting in his wheelchair," Kent Ohmann recalled. "I'm looking at him, and I'm thinking, 'This kid can't even walk.' He still had the club foot when he was 12, but he could move around OK. He had this big ol' roundhouse curve, and he could actually throw harder than most people thought."

Alvarez overcame his limitations by becoming a mound artisan, developing a repertoire of off-speed stuff that left batters beveling themselves into the ground after overswinging. After he defeated Nicaragua 2-1 to put Campbell into the Little League World Series final, the *Associated Press* game story described him as "the world's youngest junk pitcher." After the game, Alvarez was asked by a reporter about the pitches he'd used. "About one out of six pitches I threw were fastballs," he replied.

Ron Colburn was the team's leader and most physically imposing player, and his father didn't want to remove him from his command center behind the plate except in an emergency. But because he had Rhoades, who was on the All-Star team because of his defense and not because of his bat, Gene Colburn felt confident sending his son to the mound as a relief pitcher and having Rhoades replace him at catcher. Campbell's depth would come into play often during its seemingly endless succession of "cardiac" moments. While the other three Campbell-area teams that reached Williamsport in the 1960s and 1970s rarely deviated from their regular starting lineups, the 1970 Campbell squad made extensive use of its reserves, and all made important contributions along the way.

Steve Esau and Rickey Roth were fixtures at second base and shortstop respectively, and in the first two spots of the batting order. Esau, who later became the only player on the team to advance to four-year-college and professional baseball, was versatile, swift and dependable. He was known for his dispassionate efficiency at routine junctures and for his death-stare countenance during game-changing situations. Roth, on the other hand, had flair afield that he made no effort to conceal. He made easy plays look hard and hard plays look easy, but what mattered was that he made them all. Like Esau, he was a contact hitter who could pressure defenses with his speed and ability to use the entire field.

Twins Kelly and Kevin Linnane were wiry, rangy, and long — both became standout basketball players at Del Mar later — and although Kevin played regularly while Kelly was used on a part-time basis, both were defensive standouts who gave Gene Colburn the flexibility to use players whose strength wasn't defense at the other outfield post. At third base, Kent Ohmann and Lank Rowland alternated, with Ohmann playing when defense was the No. 1 priority and Rowland moving in when the lineup needed additional punch. Rowland also played some outfield, as did Gerry Ford and Matt Cary. Greg Oswald was a valuable utility man and fourth pitcher, and Greg Wood started at first base when Davis pitched.

While players on some of the Campbell system's great teams formed their relationships and closeness long before they became All-Stars, Ohmann said that was somewhat less the case with the Cardiac Kids, many of whom attended different schools and knew their All-Star teammates only through their interaction at the Rosemary School ballpark. Some of them had been friends since their first baseball days, but Ohmann said the group's collective spirit — one that endured throughout their youth baseball careers — was more the result of their 1970 experiences than the cause of them. With the exception of the Linnane twins, who then and later were humorous pro-vocateurs, the players submerged their outward personalities, because the personality that always hovered above the team was that of Gene Colburn.

"Boy, Mr. Colburn, there was the fear of God right there," Kent said. "He was scary. He didn't like me because when I pitched during the regular season, I'd blow bubble-gum bubbles during my windup without realizing it, and he thought I was crazy because of that. Before our first game, he was throwing batting practice to us, and I'd never broken a bat in my life (this was before the advent of metal bats, when teams had a limited supply of wooden bats), but I broke one then, and he was pissed. So he threw harder, and I broke another bat, and he said, 'That's it. Get the hell out of there.' In the first tournament, I hardly played at all.

"If you made an error during infield practice, he'd hit the ball to you harder and harder. He was just that kind of man. He was intense, always intense. Ron (his son) had to be a hard-ass on the field because of his dad. He was mean. You might have made a great play but then forgotten there was a guy on first and he had tagged up or something like that, and he'd ream you. (Aubineau) was a more laid-back, easygoing kind of coach, and he was kind of the buffer. But they really didn't have to do a lot of coaching that year, because all of us were pretty well coached coming up through the system."

But even though Campbell Little League by then was well-known for the quality of its players and teams, it did not have a reservoir of tournament success upon which to draw. Entering the 1970 postseason, Campbell had advanced its All-Star team beyond the district level only twice (in 1959, when it was still in District 12, and in 1966 in District 44) since the format then in place had been adopted. Given the success of Briarwood in 1969 and Santa Clara Westside in 1968, Colburn and his players knew that a long postseason was a distinct possibility if they could get out of District 44. But they made a conscious effort to micromanage every game and let the bigger picture resolve itself.

"As kids back then, all we were concerned with was playing the best baseball we could play," Ohmann said. "If we didn't make errors, kept our gloves down on ground balls, ran everything out, we felt like whatever hits we got would take care of it. There wasn't any rah-rah or anything like that. We were just a bunch of kids who seemed to like each other and had gotten real disciplined coaching."

Probably to everyone's surprise, given the strength of District 44 at the time, Campbell emerged from its first tournament unchallenged and only once scored upon. Tom Davis pitched a two-hitter while striking out 12 and Greg Wood belted a pinch-hit home run as Campbell opened tournament play by blanking Sunnyvale Serra 4-0. Against Sunnyvale Metro, Ron Colburn trumped Davis by pitching a no-hitter in a 4-1 victory. Campbell completed its District 44 *tour de force* with two more complete-game shutouts, with Davis beating Santa Clara Westside 6-0 and Alvarez fashioning a two-hit, 10-strikeout performance in a 5-0 win over Sunnyvale American in the tournament final as Kevin Linnane and Lank Rowland hit homers.

That sent Campbell to the sectional tournament at Oak Grove Little League on San Jose's southeast side, and Campbell had little trouble in its first game, an 8-1 victory over San Jose National. Davis pitched a one-hitter, Steve Esau homered and Campbell broke open a close game with a five-run fifth inning. The sectional championship game matched Campbell against Milpitas, and it was in that game that Campbell's continuum of crises began.

Campbell, the visiting team, was locked in a 2-2 tie in the bottom of the sixth and final regulation inning when Milpitas put runners on first and second with no outs against Alvarez, whose energy tank clearly was empty. Davis, of course, had pitched the previous game, and Little League rules prohibited pitchers from taking the mound in successive games. So Gene Colburn had his son take the mound and inserted Paul Rhoades behind the plate. Ron Colburn escaped the predicament to send the game into extra innings.

Neither team scored in the seventh. In the top of the eighth, Campbell took a 4-2 lead as Davis led off with a double and scored on a single by Lank Rowland. Rowland advanced to second on the throw to the plate and then scored on a single by Gerry Ford, who'd taken over in center field earlier in the game.

"Gerry didn't even make the original All-Star team," Kent Ohmann said. "He was an alternate; John McKay was on the team instead of him. But John's family was going to Lake Tahoe on vacation, and his dad said he couldn't be on the team, so that's how Gerry got on. I wonder how John must have felt, picking up the papers while we were in Williamsport and reading all that Cardiac Kids stuff."

Ford probably was the least-used player on the roster during that postseason, but there might not have been any "Cardiac Kids stuff" had it not been for him. After his single against Milpitas extended Campbell's lead to 4-2, Milpitas loaded the bases with two out in the bottom of the eighth against Colburn, who then gave up a single to center field. The runner on third scored easily, but Ford came up throwing and delivered a one-hop laser to Rhoades, who maintained his concentration and tagged the sliding runner to end the game and give Campbell a 4-3 victory.

The divisional tournament was less stressful. Davis and Alvarez pitched shutouts, with Davis authoring a three-hitter and contributing a two-run single in a 4-0 win over Salinas, and Alvarez completing a one-hitter and striking out 11 as Campbell beat host Concord National 4-0. In the Concord game, Ron Colburn narrowly missed a home run in the first inning when his line drive skipped off the warning track and over the fence for a ground-rule double. In the third and fifth innings, he launched two-run homers that cleared the outfield wall with yards to spare. Rickey Roth was on base on both occasions, and the two two-run homers accounted for all of Campbell's runs.

Campbell's first-ever foray beyond the divisional level notwithstanding, its three tournament championships up to this point were acknowledged only in passing by the Santa Clara Valley youth baseball community.

By 1970, valley teams challenging for national and international honors represented the rule rather than the exception. Besides the Moreland/Campbell Moreland/West Valley trifecta of 1962-64-66, and Santa Clara Briarwood's national Little League championship in 1969, the West Valley Colt League team had won a national championships in 1960. Santa Clara had won the same tournament in 1969 after a runnerup finish the year before. In 1970, as Campbell readied for the Little League Western Regional in El Cajon, no less than five other valley teams were still alive in regional tournaments: Branham Hills in the Senior League, the West Valley Colt team, a District 44 Big League squad, a Connie Mack team from Santa Clara, and the Stevens Creek American Legion squad from the Cupertino-Sunnyvale area. Several soon-to-be prominent names were on those rosters. The District 44 team had Mike Vail, a Mitty High graduate who was an outfielder for seven major league clubs from 1975-84. The Santa Clara Connie Mack team included Steve Bartkowski, the future Cal and NFL quarterback who also was a heavily-pursued baseball prospect, having been drafted out of high school and again when he was a junior at Cal. The Stevens Creek Legion team was led by Doug Clarey, who was taken by the Minnesota Twins in the sixth round of the 1972 major league draft after starring at Homestead High in Cupertino. Clarey's major league career consisted of four at-bats in nine games for the St. Louis Cardinals in 1976; his only major league hit was a pinch-hit, two-run, game-winning homer in the 16th inning of the Cardinals' 4-2 victory over the Giants at Candlestick Park on April 28.

However, none of those other teams were still playing beyond August 21. The only Santa Clara Valley team still standing on that day was Campbell Little League.

The team's trip to El Cajon, near San Diego, for the Western Regional represented the longest trek ever taken by a Campbell Little League team in postseason play up to that point. By 1976, when Campbell played in the Western Regional in San Bernardino, the tournament involved 13 teams from as far away as Alaska and Wyoming, and took a full week to complete. In 1970, Campbell was joined in the regional by only three other teams – Coronado, the Southern California champion; Mesa, Ariz.; and Kaneohe, Hawaii – and the tournament was scheduled over only two days on an unlit diamond. The players and coaches knew they would be facing a difficult tournament, but given the degree to which Campbell's pitching had dictated its games up to this point, it also loomed as a quick tournament.

Or so they thought.

Campbell opened against Coronado, whose pitcher, John McClinon, no-hit Campbell through the six regulation innings and the seventh. Tom Davis nearly matched McClinon, permitting just two hits and no runs and amassing 13 Ks through the top of the eighth, and he was thrown a defensive life preserver in the bottom of the seventh as Greg Oswald, who hadn't entered the game until the sixth inning, draped himself over the center-field fence to haul in a drive that otherwise would have been a game-winning homer for Coronado.

Colburn let Osborn hit for himself to lead off the eighth inning, and he responded with a single – Campbell's only hit of the game against McClinon, whose control suddenly deserted him. He threw three pitches out of the reach of his catcher, and Oswald, one of the fastest players on the team, seized each opportunity and advanced. On the third wild pitch, he came home with the game's only, and concluding, run.

That left Campbell and Hawaii, which had beaten Mesa in the other first-round game, to play for the trip to Williamsport. About 2,000 fans attended, and they were treated to one of the most eventful games imaginable – not to mention one of the longest games, in terms of the time elapsed between the first and last pitches, in Little League playoff history.

Campbell took a 1-0 lead in the third on a single by Roth, a fielders choice, a passed ball and a squeeze bunt by Davis that caught the Hawaii defenders unaware. Hawaii tied the game in the fifth, during which Alvarez, who started, was replaced on the mound by Ron Colburn.

Despite the fact Hawaii, then as now, was a baseball hotbed, no team from the islands had ever reached the Little League World Series up to that point. But the Kaneohe fans must have been planning their itineraries after Russell Kagawa hit a two-run homer off Colburn in the top of the sixth to give Hawaii a 3-1 lead. After the homer, Gene Colburn lifted his son and gave the ball to Greg Oswald, who became the first pitcher other than the "big three" to take the mound for Campbell in the postseason. He retired the side without further damage, but Campbell was three outs away from elimination as it came to bat in the bottom of the sixth.

Kaneohe pitcher Curtis Chun, against whom Campbell had had few answers through the first five innings, began the sixth by apparently retiring Davis on a deep but routine fly to center. But as the Hawaiian outfielder settled under the ball, the first-base umpire raced toward second base, frantically waving his arms. A photographer on the field had strayed from his assigned area and come into the umpire's line of vision just as Chun was delivering the pitch, and even though neither the photographer nor the timeout call had interrupted the pitch or the swing, the first-base umpire insisted that the timeout came before, and thus superseded, the play. The crew chief agreed. The out was taken off the scoreboard, and Davis returned to the plate.

"Tommy Davis was our man-child," Kent Ohmann said. "He always had a bigger bat than any of us, a 34, and it had this red handle on it. The thing looked like a club. The first ball he hit was one of his patented shots, but it was right at the center fielder. After they said it was no pitch, he went back up to the plate and hit one to almost the exact same spot, only over a little."

Davis' drive rolled all the way to the left-center field wall for a triple. Lank Rowland doubled him home, advanced to third on a passed ball and scored the tying run on a sacrifice fly by Kevin Linnane.

In the seventh inning, Chun struck out the side and Oswald held Hawaii scoreless – at which point the umpires were confronted with another difficult decision. Even though the game was on a Saturday and could have been started at mid-day, it was scheduled late in the afternoon. The preceding Coronado-Mesa consolation game had extended longer than expected, pushing the Kaneohe-Campbell starting time further back, to about 6 p.m., and although the contest was not high-scoring, pitchers on both sides had trouble pinpointing the plate, resulting in many walks and long counts as the sun continued its descent.

The ballpark did not have lights, so the umpires suspended the game. Tournament officials scheduled the resumption for the next morning, and the players and coaches on both teams were told to be prepared to head straight for the airport after the game to catch a flight that afternoon to Williamsport, where the Western Regional champion's first game was scheduled for Tuesday, two days later.

Whether the players got much sleep that night is questionable, especially since they were housed separately by families in the El Cajon area instead of billeting in team barracks such as those that would be provided to future Western Regional participants in San Bernardino, where the tournament moved permanently in 1971. In any case, they returned to the park the next morning, and Oswald found himself right back on a tightrope in the top of the eighth after walking the bases loaded with one out.

Kent Ohmann, who hadn't pitched at all in the postseason, was in the bullpen warming up. "I thought I was going to have to go in," he said in 2009. "My dad told me later that his first thought was, 'Oh, my God, Kent's going to have to pitch.' When I was warming up, I was thinking that we'd come this far and if we don't make it (to Williamsport), that's fine."

Oswald steeled himself, went back to the mound and struck out the next two hitters to get his team back to the dugout unscathed. In the bottom of the eighth, the baseball gods again became capricious on Campbell's behalf.

Chun, who now had 10 strikeouts, walked Ron Colburn to lead off the inning, and a passed ball advanced him to second, whereupon Kaneohe decided to walk Davis intentionally. With runners on first and second and nobody out, Lank Rowland was given the bunt sign on the first pitch to him. He missed the bunt. The bunt sign was flashed again, and Rowland again was unable to make fair contact.

With the count at 0-and-2, Gene Colburn took the bunt off and let Rowland swing away. He whacked a sharp single to center field on the next pitch. Ron Colburn, not wanting to take any unnecessary chances with no outs and himself as the winning run, stopped at third — but the throw from the outfield wasn't cut off and went through to the catcher, who mishandled it. Colburn, seeing the ball trickle away from the catcher, scored to give Campbell a 4-3 win and its first-ever Little League World Series berth.

"I remember that game maybe better than any of the others," Ohmann said. "I think Hawaii was the best team we played, even better than any of the teams in the World Series. I remember their players crying more than I remember us celebrating. Almost as soon as the game was over, we were on our way to the airport."

The team got to Williamsport Sunday night, and had less than two days to acclimate itself and get settled into its bunkhouse before it had to take the field on Tuesday afternoon against Nashville, Tenn., in the first round of the World Series. The players, though, actually enjoyed the whirlwind itinerary, and quickly made friends with players from the other teams as they swam, played Ping-Pong and exchanged souvenirs. They also discovered that being on a Little League World Series team had unexpected fringe benefits.

"I think every one of us got his first kiss in Williamsport, Pennsylvania," Kent Ohmann said, smiling, in 2009. "Lank Rowland was a good-looking guy, and he was the ladies man of our team. They had visiting hours in the barracks, and you could either spend that time with your parents or with the girls who came to get your autograph. And since most of our parents weren't there yet ... "

At least to that point, the kids were insulated from what was happening outside their compound. By 1970, the scope – and attendant pressure – of the Little League World Series went far beyond what the Moreland Little League team had experienced eight years before.

In 1962, the national news media covered the Series primarily as a gee-aren't-those-kids-cute novelty and not as a serious sporting event. The main grandstand at Lamade Stadium, which hadn't been built until 1959, was not much larger or more elaborate than some regular-season Little League facilities. The only telecast of the Moreland-Kankakee championship game was on a New York station, WPIX, and the game wasn't carried live nationwide even on radio. The estimated crowd of 20,000 spectators, most of whom were perched on the outfield terraces, was considered extraordinary.

That all changed with the introduction of ABC's Wide World of Sports telecast (at first, on a tape-delay basis) of the title game starting in 1963, and the internationalization of the World Series in particular and Little League in general throughout the 1960s. Far East teams, which began playing in the World Series in 1962, won the championship in 1967, '68 and '69, with Japan prevailing in 1967 and 1968 and Taiwan in '69, and the Oriental teams' presence had added an us-against-them, nationalistic element that hadn't existed in 1962. Even the preliminary games, which in 1962 had been played in relative privacy, were now well attended, and Lamade Stadium had been expanded to include about 10,000 permanent seats in addition to the hillside terraces that pushed the facility's capacity to the 40,000 mark. (Attendance estimates at Williamsport were, and still are, just that because the national organization has never charged admission to World Series games and doesn't attempt to get actual crowd counts.)

Mickey Mantle, who had just retired from the New York Yankees the year before, was on hand throughout the week before participating in the Wide World of Sports telecast, and many of the players got autographs and had pictures taken with him. The game program, which had been only a perfunctory product in 1962, was now professionally done, and if Campbell supporters glanced at it before the team's first game, they must have considered it a positive omen that one of the main stories was on Craig Morton. Morton, then the Dallas Cowboys' starting quarterback, was quoted to the effect that his experience in Campbell Little League had been instrumental in his subsequent athletic successes, and he described his Little League coach, Merv Willoughby, as an ongoing influence. (The content of the program, of course, was planned long before it was known that the Little League in which Morton had played would qualify for Williamsport.)

In later years, the eight-team field would be divided into American and non-American brackets to ensure that a foreign team would play a U.S. team in the championship game, but in 1970 each of the brackets included two American teams and two outside teams. The upper bracket, with Campbell, Nashville, Chinandega of Nicaragua and Chayi of Taiwan, was far more difficult than the lower bracket, which included Wayne, N.J.; Highland, Ind.; Valleyfield of Quebec, Canada; and Weisbaden, West Germany.

As usually was the case with the European entry at Williamsport, the Weisbaden team consisted of the children of American military personnel assigned to a U.S. installation, and those teams usually were non-competitive in the World Series. (Moreland trounced a similar team from France 22-2 in its first-round game in 1962.) In 1970, though, the Weisbaden team played well before losing 2-0 to Highland. In the other first-round games, Wayne shut out Valleyfield 10-0 and Nicaragua surprised Taiwan 3-2. The Taiwanese wouldn't lose in Williamsport again until 1982, when Kirkland, Wash., beat them in the championship game.

Nashville National Optimist Little League was the first team from Tennessee ever to reach the Little League World Series, but the team didn't appear cowed by its unfamiliar surroundings or by the weekday-afternoon crowd of 10,000. Against Tom Davis, who had allowed only two earned runs in 40 innings of work entering the Series, Nashville took a 1-0 lead in the third and held it until the fifth when Campbell tied the game. Davis, who finished with a six-hitter and struck out 15, continued his dual with Nashville's Mark Raulston through the seventh inning, sending Campbell into its third straight eight-inning game and fourth in the postseason.

Davis remained strong in the top of the eighth, retiring Nashville in order. Raulston, who had walked seven batters and hit two others, did not appear to be feeling the effects of his pitch count, but his defense betrayed him in the bottom of the eighth.

Gene Colburn again turned to his bench, sending Matt Cary up as a pinch-hitter to lead off the inning. Cary hit a slow ground ball that Nashville's third baseman cuffed for an error. Greg Wood, who was playing first base because Davis was pitching, sacrificed Cary to second, and Kelly Linnane used his speed to leg out an infield hit, leaving runners at first and third with one out.

Steve Esau popped up for the second out, but Roth, after running the count to 2-and-2, lined a single to short right, easily scoring Cary and winning the game 2-1. In 1970 and for some time thereafter, most managers and the Little League hierarchy discouraged players from being demonstrative on the field, but Cary couldn't resist landing on the plate with a triumphant two-footed stomp as he scored the winning run.

Two days later in the semifinals against Nicaragua, Campbell finally appeared to be on the verge of altering its pattern of scoring dangerously late and just enough. With two outs in the first inning, Colburn and Davis singled. Rowland doubled, scoring Colburn and sending Davis to third, and as in the game against Nashville, a throw from the outfield that should have been cut off was allowed to filter through to the catcher, who misplayed it. Davis scored, giving Campbell a 2-0 lead.

That was all Campbell got, but it was all Alvarez would need, and an hour and a half later, Campbell was in the clubhouse with another 2-1 win – its fourth straight one-run victory and its fifth of the postseason – and a berth in the championship game.

Alvarez' one-fastball-for-every-six pitches protocol was as bewildering to the Nicaraguans as it had been in his previous four postseason victories, and he worked more quickly than before to control the tempo of the game and prevent a recurrence of the fatigue that had prevented him from completing his two previous starts. The only run he allowed, in the third, was unearned, and he was touched for only three hits while walking one and striking out five. It was a victory that was hailed, at the time and for years thereafter, as a retort to those who insisted that Little League baseball was exclusively the province of hulking pitchers and home-run hitters. Relatively few pre-teen baseball players could identify with a Ted Campbell because, in 1962, he looked more like a man than most of their fathers. Mike Alvarez in 1970 looked like what he was, a 12-year-old kid, and yet on this day under a level of stress that would immobilize most adults, his adulthood was expressed through the method with which he out-finessed and outsmarted far bigger and more powerful boys. To this day, many Campbell oldtimers remember Mike Alvarez, more than any other player, as the personification of all that was right about their town and its youth baseball program, because of what he achieved and because of what he had overcome.

His performance's immediate impact was to send Campbell into the World Series final with its staff ace, Tom Davis, against Wayne and Steve O'Neill, who had pitched a no-hitter against Canada in his team's Series opener. "We heard later that there were 40,000 people there," Kent Ohmann said. "It didn't seem that way to us, though. We were used to packed stands by then, and we didn't really think of it as anything but another game. We didn't get caught up in all of that."

The crowd – which included Campbell city councilman Bill Podgorsek, who had flown in for the Series even though he didn't have a kid on the team – and the Campbell-area radio audience that had tuned in to Santa Clara FM station KREP's live broadcast settled in for a low-margin-of-error game that might be decided in favor of the first team to score.

Unfortunately for Campbell, that's what they got, and while Campbell played well, Wayne was slightly more proficient and considerably luckier.

Davis was close to his best, striking out 12 and giving up only five hits and a walk during his five-inning stint. Campbell, meanwhile, had O'Neill scrambling, piling up six hits and two walks while putting at least one runner on base in each of the first five innings. "In the first inning my arm felt stiff, and I couldn't throw hard," he said after the game. "It was our defense that saved me. This was not one of my better games."

But at the end, it was O'Neill who was pummeled on the mound by his jubilant teammates.

The lead of the *San Jose Mercury* game story read: "The fuzzy-cheeked Campbell 'Cardiac Kids' got their first introduction to a 'Shaver' Saturday, and ... they got nicked. Applying the wound was 12-year-old Dave Shaver, who knocked in both runs as Wayne defeated the Campbell kids 2-0."

Davis had not given up a run since the sectional tournament, and he wasn't exactly belabored during the second-inning rally that cost him the game. Ron Webb singled to short center, was bunted to second by Bill Lee and advanced to third as Bob Houghton hoofed out an infield hit. Houghton then stole second without a throw, and Shaver, one of the smallest players on either team, got around on a Davis fastball and lined a ball to center field that scooted by Kevin Linnane to the wall as both runners scored.

Upon their arrival in Williamsport, all the players were offered free rubber baseball cleats as part of a shoe manufacturer's sponsorship of the World Series. The Linnane twins, however, declined the new footwear and played in tennis shoes, as they had done throughout Campbell's All-Star tour. Both had bony feet that made wearing cleats uncomfortable. On Shaver's drive, Kevin Linnane slipped while pursuing the ball, and while it's unlikely that he could have prevented the single and the first run under any circumstances, he might have had a play at the plate on the second runner had he been able to keep his feet.

Wayne, meanwhile, was using its own defense to thwart every Campbell threat. In the top of the second inning, Shaver, Wayne's center fielder, had speared a bases-loaded, two-out line drive by Roth to enable O'Neill to escape with the scoreless tie intact. In the fourth, Campbell advanced runners to second and third with two outs, but Esau's bid for extra bases was thwarted by Wayne right fielder Mike Fantau, who made a diving catch.

Campbell was retired in order only once, in the sixth and final inning as O'Neill's fatigue prompted him to abandon his fastball and turn to his sinker, which had Campbell's final three hitters swinging over the ball as it descended. He finished with five strikeouts, two in the final inning.

"I remember I just wanted to get back to the barracks and jump in the swimming pool so I could cry (without anybody seeing his tears)," Kent Ohmann said.

While the Campbell players and coaching staff were understandably disappointed after their near-miss, their spirits had been restored by the time they boarded a bus for Washington, D.C., the next morning for a two-day tour of the capital city. Back home, their supporters' recuperative powers were just as strong. After all, they knew it had been as much of an experience of a lifetime for them as it had been for their Cardiac Kids.

"We are certain that there was probably no one in this community, whether or not familiar with Little League or with baseball in general, who was not affected in some way either directly or indirectly by the excitement that was generated by having a team from Campbell in the World Series," read a *Press* editorial. "Campbell, California has become nationally known because of its Little League team, and the community has had a built-in promotional project that has given Campbell an exposure that could not be obtained in any other way."

At the team banquet at Lou's Village in San Jose a week after the team's return, the players were given commemorative knife-and-fork sets by their coaches, who jestingly were honoring the fact that the kids had proved on the road that they were of championship caliber as trenchermen as well as baseball players. The kids, in turn, presented their mothers with corsages. Joe Gagliardi, who had been the manager of the Campbell Moreland Pony League World Series championship team of 1964, gave a speech, as did Bob Burton Sr., father of the former Campbell High basketball star, and a career baseball operative who at the time was general manager of the Shreveport, La., franchise in the Class AA Texas League.

Surprisingly, the Cardiac Kids never were able to renew their 1970 sorcery on a significant collective scale, even though most of them stayed together through their 16-year-old Colt League seasons.

Six of them – Kent Ohmann, Matt Cary, Mike Alvarez, Rickey Roth, Steve Esau and Lank Rowland – were on the Campbell Moreland Pony League All-Star team two years later, but that team won only one game in its first tournament before being eliminated. Tom Davis, the pitching yeoman of 1970, never played organized baseball again, even in Pony League. Unlike Moreland's Ted Campbell after 1964, his decision wasn't related to any inability to pitch successfully on a larger diamond; according to some who knew him, he simply had never liked baseball, and considered his Williamsport experience a negative one. Davis subsequently turned his attention to football, basketball and track at Campbell High, and wound up at Brigham Young University on an academic scholarship. "That was really a disappointment," Campbell High coach Gordon Huntze said in 2009 of Davis' abrupt departure from baseball. "I had heard he was going to be coming over to our place (Campbell High), and I was looking forward to him pitching for us."

Nobody on the 1970 All-Star team ever played on a championship squad in Colt League or in high school, and the only team member who played baseball at a four-year college was Steve Esau, who had a good career at San Diego State and in 1980 had a 19-game professional stint, with the independent Redwood Pioneers of the California League. As with the Linnane twins, Esau's best sport probably was basketball. He was a starting guard for the 1975-76 Del Mar team that went 29-3 and finished third in the Northern California tournament, losing to eventual titlist Castlemont of Oakland.

Ron Colburn, whose family moved to Saratoga in the early 1970s, starred at Monta Vista High and then at De Anza College. In 1976, while Campbell Little League was making the second of its three trips to Williamsport in the 1970s, Colburn played on a District 44 team that finished third in the Big League World Series (for players ages 16-18) in Fort Lauderdale, Fla.

Other Cardiac Kids enjoyed athletic success after 1970, but most of them carved out niches in other sports.

The Linnane twins played both basketball and baseball at Del Mar before graduating in 1975, and both later went on to play basketball at West Valley. Gerry Ford also played baseball and basketball at Del Mar, but his work as a football quarterback and student (he had a 4.0 grade-point average) prompted Brown University of the Ivy League to give him a full academic scholarship to play there.

Mike Alvarez was an All-Star on the Pony League level, but his career was cut short by arm trouble after one year of frosh-soph baseball at Campbell High. He turned to tennis at that point, and played three years for Campbell High's varsity. Paul Rhoades played baseball through his freshman year at Campbell High before switching sports and emerging as one of the West Valley Athletic League's top soccer players during his final three years of high school.

Greg Oswald, Lank Rowland and Rickey Roth played four years of baseball at Campbell High, although Oswald was better known as a football player for the Buccaneers. Paul Sargis, one of the key players on the 1976 Campbell Little League team, said he got to know Oswald that summer while Oswald was working a summer job at a rockery near Paul's home. Paul said Oswald went out of his way to encourage the 1976 team as it made its way to Williamsport.

Kent Ohmann played baseball at Del Mar, and for a winter season at San Jose City College before leaving school for a job at Westinghouse, and later a successful career in real estate in rural Santa Clara, Santa Cruz and San Benito counties. Matt Cary played on the frosh-soph team at Campbell for two years, but after that, he gave up sports entirely and immersed himself in surfing and music, reportedly developing into a first-rate guitar player.

"I haven't kept in touch with all of the guys, although we had a reunion about 15 years ago," Ohmann said. "But I think most of them have done pretty well beyond baseball. Steve Esau and I are still best friends, and have been since we were 9."

With the possible exception of Esau, the World Series of 1970 represented the apex of the Cardiac Kids' baseball careers, but that didn't change, then or in retrospect, what they had accomplished.

The national and world news headlines of August 1970 were of race riots in Chicago, the expansion of the Vietnam War into Cambodia, the ongoing struggle for fair wages and working conditions by Cesar Chavez's United Farm Workers, and the struggles of California cities (including San Jose) to cope with smog and pollution levels that had become intolerable. But to many in Campbell, that summer of 1970 was made memorable by something else — the 14 kids who made anything and everything seem possible.

"Not at all," Kent Ohmann said when asked if it seemed as if the Cardiac Kids days were almost four decades distant. He grinned. "Has it really been that long? What great memories I still have."

1970–75: Close, but ...

Although Campbell Little League's journey to the Little League World Series championship game remained the prevailing sports story in Campbell through the end of 1970 and into 1971, other soon-to-be-familiar names were appearing on the horizon.

Campbell Moreland Pony League's All-Star team won only one tournament in the summer of 1970, but Mike Codiroli, a 13-year-old, provided one of the first inklings of his imminent eminence. In Campbell Moreland's 5-3 victory over Santa Clara for the championship of the sectional tournament at Rincon Park, Codiroli pitched a complete-game five-hitter and hit a two-run homer in the sixth inning to break a 3-3 tie. George and Gordon Hahn were other prominent players on that All-Star team, as were Tom Guardino and Wayne Hagin. Hagin went on to play baseball at Blackford and San Diego State, and in 1981 he began a baseball broadcasting career that was to make him the radio voice of both the Oakland Athletics and San Francisco Giants at different junctures. He also was a play-by-play man for the Colorado Rockies and St. Louis Cardinals, and in 2008 was hired as a New York Mets broadcaster by New York radio station WFAN.

In the fall of 1970, Campbell High's football team lost to Los Gatos 27-19 – the Buccaneers' first loss to the rival Wildcats in six years. Joe Alvarez, brother of future Campbell Little League icon Rich Alvarez, was an all-league quarterback that year, and running back Steve Davis was an all-league selection as a junior. Leigh, which had emerged as the WVAL's dominant athletic school, won the WVAL football title that year, and went on to take the first Santa Clara County playoffs – a precursor to the Central Coast Section tournament, which began in 1972.

As 1971 dawned, the impact of Campbell Little League's Williamsport trip was manifesting itself in the form of record signup totals for the upcoming baseball season. Campbell Little League alone enlisted more than 500 players, and expanded to 32 teams. (In 1972, Campbell had an all-time high of 34 teams.) Quito, in the midst of the city of Campbell's last growth area, also had approximately 500 players, and Moreland served about 400 that year. Campbell Moreland Pony League, which had eight teams in 1971, organized its first full-scale fall-league program.

However, baseball anticipation was muted after Campbell's 11-year police chief, John D. Morgan, stunningly was stricken by a cerebral hemorrhage on February 3. Morgan, who was only 40, was hospitalized in critical condition, and it soon became apparent that although he had lost no brain function, he was completely and permanently paralyzed. He could not speak, move, or even breathe on his own for months, and his only means of communication was by flickering his eyelids.

Morgan had joined the Campbell Police Department in 1955, three years after Campbell was incorporated as a city, and it was he more than anybody else before or since who put a human, compassionate face on his agency at a time when police departments were maligned and feared in many other U.S. municipalities. He had managed, coached and umpired in Campbell Little League and Campbell Moreland Pony League, had been involved in many of the fund-raising campaigns that had resulted in improvements to all of the city's youth sports facilities, and had been a consistent and convincing champion of youth sports in Campbell from the time he arrived there. Some sadly noted the irony of the fact the stroke had felled him while he was preparing to go on a road trip with a youth basketball team he was coaching.

The outpouring of concern and emotion was unprecedented in Campbell. A special Mass and prayer at the Knights of Columbus hall a few days after Morgan was stricken was attended by several hundred people, and the Methodist Church organized a community-wide prayer chain. Morgan's insurance did not cover all of his medical costs, and fund-raisers were held throughout the community. By June, $15,500, the equivalent of a year's salary for many Campbell families at the time, had been raised. Don Burr was promoted to acting chief, and was given the permanent job in February 1972 when Morgan officially went into retirement.

Barely one month after Morgan was incapacitated, another tragedy struck Campbell. On March 13, two Hazelwood School students – Randy Owens, 10, and his brother David, 9 – were playing, along with a friend, on a vacant lot with what they thought was a harmless World War II souvenir that had been brought to school by another boy that day. The "souvenir" was a 40mm antiaircraft shell, and as the boys banged it against a rock, it exploded, killing the Owens boys instantly and seriously injuring their friend. The Owens boys' father was a single parent with two other children, and Campbell citizens, well underway with fund-raising to help John Morgan's family, redoubled their efforts to assist the Owenses.

(Campbell was thrust into mourning yet again later that year, on December 27, when Craig Chelonis was killed in an auto wreck. Chelonis, 18, had played in Quito Little League, and had graduated in June from Westmont, where he was the quarterback and captain of the football team and the No. I pitcher on the Warriors' baseball team. He had just completed his freshman football season at West Valley College at the time of his death.)

In early 1971, the beginning of the end for two of Campbell's most important consolidating influences – Campbell High and the *Campbell Press* – could be glimpsed, if only in the distance.

Camden, the Campbell Union High School District's second high school, had been built in 1955 to service the Cambrian Park area, which was the first bedroom community to emerge in the west San Jose area after World War II. Cambrian Park was sometimes described as the Bay Area version of Levittown, a planned community adjoining New York City that in 1947 became the U.S.' first mass-produced suburb, and the archetype for postwar suburbs throughout the country. But by the late 1960s, much of Cambrian Park's GI Bill-motivated housing was beginning to decay, and the area's growth had long since subsided. By the start of the 1971-72 school year, the Cambrian School District's enrollment had dropped an average of 37 percent over each of the previous three years, and the district laid off nine teachers – an unheard-of necessity in Santa Clara County throughout the first three decades following World War II.

It should have been evident to Campbell Union High School District officials by the late 1960s that Cambrian Park's population decline soon would render Camden High expendable and obsolete, and that the district would not need any more new high schools in the foreseeable future, if ever. But apparently it wasn't, and the district proceeded, in 1968, to open Prospect, the CUHSD's eighth school.

From the time it opened, Prospect had a still-intact reputation as the district's best academic school, but with the benefit of hindsight, it is obvious that Prospect never should have been built, and that the decision to do so ultimately led to the demise of Campbell High in 1980. The reasons, besides the fact Cambrian Park's population decline made an eighth high school unnecessary, include:

- The portion of the district Prospect served when it opened was neither high-growth nor central, and thus did not reflect long-term district needs. The district's most pronounced growth in the late 1960s and throughout the 1970s was in the Branham and Leigh attendance areas – which, of course, was why Branham was built in the first place. The district's lack of foresight became glaringly apparent in 1999 when the CUHSD had to reopen Branham, eight years after closing it.

- All of the other district schools – including Campbell High after its 1950 renovation – housed most of their classrooms in open-air wings that required little or no daytime lighting. But because Prospect was built on a smaller parcel, it was laid out as a square with many covered passageways and windowless classrooms that had to be illuminated even during sunny days. That made its day-to-day utility costs far higher than any other school in the district. The additional roofing also required maintenance money and manpower that weren't needed at the other seven campuses.

- The district had acquired the land on which Prospect was built in the early 1960s, and by the time construction began on the campus, it was the most valuable parcel the district owned because it was within the city limits of Saratoga, one of the Bay Area's wealthiest cities. Sale of the land in the late 1960s, when choice acreage was becoming hard to get, would have been a financial windfall for the district, and might have buffered it for years to come, even after the district began to hemorrhage enrollment.

- Prospect was geographically redundant three years before it opened. The adjoining Fremont Union High School District had opened Lynbrook, less than a mile to the northwest of Prospect, in 1965, and if foresight had been shown by either district — and if both districts hadn't been greedy for daily-attendance money from the state — Lynbrook, which opened with only 1,026 students and never exceeded 2,000 in enrollment, could have been built with enough capacity to absorb much of the student population that Prospect eventually served. (In 1980, the same year that Campbell and Camden were closed, the Fremont district's own poor long-range planning forced it to shut down one of its schools, Sunnyvale.)

- The CUHSD could have built Westmont or Branham as a mega-school, as San José's East Side Union High School District did when it built Independence High in 1976. Independence's enrollment capacity was approximately 5,000, twice that of any other school in Santa Clara County, and it included elements, such as a 4,000-seat gym and a performing-arts center, that conventional high schools lacked. Building it allowed the East Side district to avoid having to construct the four new high schools that its planners had projected would be needed during the late 1970s. (In fact, even though the ESUHSD's enrollment continued to increase long after the numbers elsewhere in the Santa Clara Valley had begun to decline, the East Side district didn't have to add another campus until 2002 when it opened Evergreen Valley High.) If the Campbell district had built Westmont or Branham as an Independence-like campus, and not built Prospect, it would have had far more flexibility when enrollment began to decline, and keeping Campbell High open would have been a far more viable option in 1980. Campbell Union High School District enrollment peaked at 15,700 in 1972 (compared to 7,700 in 2009). The district could have operated seven high schools with an average of 2,243 students that year (with the mega-school absorbing most of the overflow) rather than eight schools with an average enrollment of 1,963. Even if those seven campuses were overcrowded over the short term, the crowding would have subsided starting in 1973, when district enrollment began a slide that remained continuous through the next two decades.

By 1980, of course, declining enrollment and the passage of Proposition 13 two years earlier had put CUHSD officials in a box, and they claimed they had no alternative but to close two of their eight high schools. After much acrimonious debate, the board of trustees — which did not include a single Campbell resident — opted to close Camden and Campbell, the two oldest schools, at the end of the 1979-80 school year. That Camden was doomed had been a foregone conclusion for years because of Cambrian Park's population decline, but if Prospect had not been built, it's not likely that the district would have found it necessary to close Campbell High as well. Many felt at the time that the decision to close Campbell was motivated by the fact the land on which it stood was perhaps the most valuable parcel in the city, although selling it for industrial development soon was removed as an option because the city rezoned the property.

The district leased and eventually sold the property to the city, which renovated the buildings and transformed it into today's Campbell Community Center. By 2009, the Campbell Community Center was a showplace that served far more residents than it had when it was a high school, and it was in much better structural condition than it had been in 1980 because of city-financed renovations. But with Campbell High's loss came a parallel loss in Campbell's sense of community, and the loss of that element played a role in the decline of the youth baseball program in the 1980s.

The *Campbell Press*, like Campbell High, was an important element in Campbell's ability to maintain its identity even as San Jose ballooned around it. It had been published continuously since 1895, and even though not everyone approved of its editorial bent under editor George Vierhus, it was a congealing influence in Campbell because it was the city's only real information and opinion clearinghouse. But by 1971, the *Press* had descended into irrelevance. Vierhus, known as a curmudgeon who paid little heed to anyone's counsel except his own, by now was running essentially a one-man editorial operation, and rather than covering the broad community that surrounded him, he covered only the narrow community that included him — local politicians, Chamber of Commerce types, school bureaucrats, and the like. Beyond his bland and minimally-newsy reporting on those groups, and his scattershot columns that seemingly went on forever without arriving anywhere, the *Press* in 1971 consisted almost exclusively on stories and photos for which Vierhus had to pay nothing. Legitimate stories — such as the aftermath of the Owens tragedy, which begged the question of how a live World War II shell got into the hands of third- and fourth-graders in a California suburb — were never addressed.

The paper included only two sports constants, neither of which involved or interested more than a small handful of people in Campbell — West Valley College sports, and the local dart league. Vierhus ran weekly write-ups submitted by high school students and other non-staffers, not because they were newsworthy or well-written, but because they filled space at no cost to him. As a result, Campbell High's athletic teams were almost completely ignored. Even Campbell Little League's achievements in 1970 didn't earn it much coverage in the *Press* in 1971 besides a few Opening Day photos, and team pictures of the division champions at the end of the season. In general, the *Press* in 1971 looked and read like an anachronism, and although it revived for a time in the mid- and late 1970s under new ownership and the direction of new editor Pat Safford, it relapsed again after her departure. Its death in 1986 virtually was unnoticed, and although several metro-chain throwaways have tried at various times to replace the *Press*, Campbell never again has had a viable news medium devoted exclusively to Campbell – a circumstance that has been to the community's detriment.

If Vierhus had been so inclined, there was plenty to report on the sports scene in Campbell in 1971, even though there would be no repeat of Campbell Little League's 1970 manifesto. The 1971 team included two future Campbell High stars – Mark Raust, who later played at Fresno State, and Cliff Judd – and Campbell defeated Santa Clara Briarwood 6-0 in a matchup of the World Series runners-up of the previous two seasons, but then lost to Santa Clara Westside 2-0. Cupertino American, which won District 44 and later the divisional tournament at Campbell Little League, advanced all the way to the Western Region championship game, and was within three outs of District 44's third straight World Series trip before Hawaii rallied for two runs in the bottom of the sixth to win 4-3. It was the fourth straight year that a District 44 team advanced at least to the regional finals.

Campbell's other All-Star teams fared better than their Little League counterpart, especially the West Valley Colt League squad, which included Campbell High students George and Gordon Hahn, and Jeff Mason. The team also featured Branham sophomore Pat Hughes, who played baseball primarily as an adjunct to his No. 1 sport, basketball. Hughes briefly played basketball at San Jose State, but as with Wayne Hagin and Gary Radnich, his playing accomplishments served as prelude to a distinguished broadcasting career. Hughes started as the radio voice of Joe Gagliardi's San Jose Missions from 1978-81, moved on to major-league employment with the Minnesota Twins and Milwaukee Brewers, and in 2009 he began his 14th season as the Chicago Cubs' play-by-play man over radio station WGN, alongside color man Ron Santo.

With Los Gatos' Paul Bauer proving almost unhittable, the West Valley Colt team reached the World Series for the fourth time in 12 seasons by winning its sectional at home, its divisional in National City, and the West Regional in Yakima, Wash. In the World Series in Lafayette, Ind., West Valley set a tournament scoring record while winning its opening game 22-7 over Puerto Rico, and also defeated the host team 6-1 before being eliminated as the result of losses to Joliet, Ill, and Hawaii. The team was managed by Wayne Mitchell, a Monroe Middle School teacher who in 1974 would guide many of the same players to Campbell's first and only appearance in the American Legion World Series.

Campbell Moreland Pony League, which included 13-year-olds Kent Ohmann and Lank Rowland from Campbell Little League's 1970 All-Stars, was eliminated in its second tournament, by host Watsonville, but the talk of that tournament was Mitty High freshman-to-be Mike Codiroli. Codiroli, who later was an All-America outfielder at Stanford and played four seasons (1979-82) in the Seattle Mariners minor league system, pitched 12 innings in the Watsonville tournament, including a seven-inning no-hitter against Santa Clara during which he struck out 16. In a relief appearance later in the tournament, he struck out 13 in five innings without giving up a hit – giving him 12 hitless innings and 29 strikeouts in 12 tournament innings. (Mike's younger brother Chris, who went on to play at San Jose State and pitched in the major leagues from 1982-90, is not known to have played in the Campbell system at any point.)

At Campbell Little League, Kiwanis, the minor-division champion, had three players who would go on to achieve athletic excellence at Campbell High and beyond.

Jeff Melrose, described by Gordon Huntze as perhaps the most conscientious player he ever coached at Campbell High, pitched for the Bucs during their final three baseball seasons and then was an all-conference selection at Santa Clara. He was drafted by the Texas Rangers in 1984, and advanced as high as Class AAA in their organization. In the meantime, he completed work on his engineering degree at Santa Clara, and in 2009 was working for an East Bay engineering firm. Steve Aimonetti, whose younger brother John was a starting outfielder on Campbell Little League's 1976 national-championship team, also was on that Kiwanis team. He played football at Campbell High and then at Stanford, where he later was an assistant coach. David Erkman, still another Kiwanis player, became a Campbell Little League All-Star in 1974, and was one of Campbell High's best all-around athletes in its final years of existence. He subsequently played football at Occidental College in Southern California.

The most important baseball event of 1972 was the Central Coast Section championship breakthrough by Campbell High.

After Gordon Huntze took over the Campbell High program in 1965, he won a league title his first year. His next six teams were of similar strength, but the West Valley Athletic League had become a minefield by the late 1960s, and the Central Coast Section playoffs, which began in 1967, did not include non-champions. Camden, which took the WVAL in 1967 and 1968, got to the CCS finals in '67 and to the semifinals the following year. In 1969, Los Gatos won the league and advanced to the CCS semifinals, and Branham was the WVAL champion in 1970 and 1971. In '71, the Bruins beat Cupertino 2-0 to win the CCS championship in only Branham's fourth varsity season.

In 1972, though, nothing could deter Campbell. The Buccaneers went 26-5, with their last loss coming on April 27, and their last victory was a 2-0 conquest of Gunn in the CCS championship game.

"You know the thing I remember most about that team?" Huntze said in 2009. "Just about everybody on our team could hit. Thurl Noonkester, our No. 9 hitter (and best defensive outfielder), batted better than .300 that year. But what was amazing was the baseball knowledge they had. Very heady guys. They just understood the game. Guys would come back to the dugout (after a defensive inning) and they'd say, 'Coach, we got their signs.' So I said, 'Well, go ahead and use them.' We were able to get some outs on pitchouts that way. And they were *dedicated*. We'd have a pretty good practice, and I'd be walking back to my car and there's Ed Hahn standing out there and there's the twins (his sons George and Gordon) hitting. And they weren't the only ones."

Huntze had no less than five future NCAA Division I players on his 16-man roster in 1972. The top two starting pitchers were Steve Garrido, who finished 9-1 for the season, and fourth-year varsity starter Kelly Davis (9-2). Davis went on to play two seasons at Brigham Young University, and later was a baseball and football coach at Juan Diego High near Salt Lake City. Garrido played two seasons at West Valley and one at Gonzaga. The fact Davis and Garrido were entrenched at the top of the Buccaneer rotation might have discouraged a promising sophomore from trying out. He had just moved to Campbell, and made it clear he was unhappy there, for reasons that apparently had nothing to do with baseball. He told acquaintances that he would be moving to Visalia after the school year ended. He also boasted, to their amusement, that he would pitch in the major leagues someday. In 1978, at age 22, Mike LaCoss made his big league debut with the Cincinnati Reds, starting an MLB career that would span 14 seasons and included a World Series appearance with the San Francisco Giants in 1989.

Shortstop Steve Davis, the second and last major leaguer Gordon coached at Campbell, was on his way to Stanford (and eventually the Chicago Cubs). In 1972, he was the WVAL MVP and probably the best all-around player in the Santa Clara Valley. George and Gordon Hahn, who were juniors, quickly made it apparent that they would become college players, as both later did at Santa Clara.

"George Hahn we brought up as a freshman catcher (in 1970)," Huntze recalled. "He only weighed about 120 pounds then, but boy, he was a tough kid. We're playing at Soquel and they had a wire mesh fence surrounding their field. I'm hitting pregame infield and I pop one up to him ... he goes charging back there and runs right into the thing. Just opened him up. We're telling him, 'George, we're going to have to get you out of here,' but he's insisting, 'No, I'm not leaving.' Another time we're at Camden and he catches a foul ball and dislocates his little finger. It had kind of popped out ... I went over there and tried to pull it out a little bit, and I thought I had the thing back in place. He taped it up and continued to play, but when you shake hands with him now and you look at his finger, maybe I screwed it up more. But those guys wouldn't come out of games ... no way."

The Buccaneers were well settled at every defensive position; their preferred lineup was Gordon Hahn at second base, George Hahn catching, Steve Davis at shortstop, Jeff Mason (who later played at Division II San Francisco State) at first base, Kelly Davis pitching, Garrido in left field, Dave Judd at third base, Joe Ferrari in right field and Noonkester in center. Early in the season, they had impressive non-league wins over Carlmont, Aptos and Bellarmine, all strong programs at the time. They struggled at times during the WVAL season, especially on days when the third spot in the pitching rotation came up, but they locked up the league championship by winning their final six games, and then beat Piedmont Hills 5-0 and San Jose 4-0 in the first two rounds of the CCS playoffs as Garrido and Kelly Davis sculpted back-to-back shutouts.

Against Riordan of San Francisco in the semifinals at San Jose's PAL Stadium, Campbell jumped out to a 4-0 lead in the top of the first as Mason hit a three-run homer. Campbell's usually-reliable defense betrayed Garrido in the bottom of the first, committing two errors as the Crusaders tied the game 4-4. But Riordan, which had two hits in the first inning, didn't get another. Campbell scored a run in the third and Garrido made it stand up for a 5-4 victory that sent Campbell into the CCS finals against Gunn of Palo Alto, which had upset pre-tournament favorite Homestead in the second round and then defeated Pacific Grove in the semifinals.

This time, at San Jose Municipal Stadium, Campbell's defense was flawless and Kelly Davis was nearly perfect. He pitched a one-hitter as Campbell earned its first CCS title with a 2-0 victory that gave the Buccaneers a 10-game winning streak to end the season. In 28 postseason innings, the Davis-Garrido tandem had given up only six hits and the four unearned runs against Riordan.

Campbell got Davis the only run he would need in the third on back-to-back doubles by the Hahn brothers, and in the fourth, Mason singled, went to third on an error and scored on Garrido's sacrifice fly.

From that night until the last game of Campbell High's baseball history, a 2-0 loss to Yerba Buena in the 1980 CCS playoffs, Huntze's program was closely intertwined with the area's developmental system. The Bucs would repeat as CCS champions in 1973 and would be WVAL contenders every year after that. Starting in 1972, even the youngest Little League players in the Campbell area began focusing on the long-term goal of playing baseball for Campbell High. A goal as tangible as that naturally made the best players better, benefitting both Huntze and a Campbell youth baseball system that already had achieved much but was destined to achieve much more.

The summer of 1972 brought Campbell Little League its fourth district championship. Pitchers Cliff Judd and Les Lizer each won twice as Campbell prevailed in its four District 44 games, including a 7-5 victory over Moreland in the championship contest. In a 1-0 first-round win over Santa Clara Eastside, Judd led off the game with a home run and then came within a third-inning hit of pitching a perfect game. Some thought Campbell might give District 44 a representative in the West Region title game for the fifth straight year, but those thoughts dissipated quickly as Campbell had to play the host Pacifica team in the first round of the sectional tournament, and lost 7-5.

Despite the presence of six 14-year-olds who had been on the Campbell team that had reached the World Series final in 1970, the Campbell Moreland Pony League team was a disappointment, losing two of its three games in the area tournament it hosted. The Colt League team, again managed by Wayne Mitchell, had the Hahn twins back from the 1971 team that had advanced to the World Series, and it had added two players who would become teammates at Stanford during the late 1970s – Campbell High's Tom Guardino and Mitty's Mike Codiroli, who had pitched 12 no-hit innings while striking out 29 in the Pony League sectional tournament in Watsonville the year before. But after winning its first tournament, the Colt League team exited quickly in the sectionals.

As the 1973 baseball season approached, nobody, including Gordon Huntze, knew what to expect from Campbell High's defending CCS champions. The Hahn twins were back – George behind the plate, Gordon moving from second base to shortstop – but the only other returning starter was outfielder Joe Ferrari, and the entire pitching staff would have to be retooled. Much would depend on callups from the 1972 JV team, particularly junior pitcher Pete Fair, sophomore pitcher Steve McGrody, junior catcher-first baseman Jim Guardino and junior second baseman John McMonagle. Two 1972 varsity reserves, Felix Mancinez and Jim Oswald, would assume starting duties at third base and right field respectively.

As all-encompassing as the pitching skills of Kelly Davis and Steve Garrido had been in 1972, each of them had suffered losses. Fair was 12-0 in 1973, and McGrody would have been the No. 1 pitcher on most WVAL staffs. George Hahn was the league MVP, and was drafted in the 27th round by the San Francisco Giants after the season, although he turned down the Giants' offer and accepted a scholarship from Santa Clara. The team's batting average was .295, down from .315 the previous year, but Fair, McGrody and the Hahn brothers sustained Campbell through an 18-6 regular season during which the Buccaneers defended their WVAL title, again winning their final six games to finish 14-4, two games ahead of Leigh (12-6). The Buccaneers clinched their fifth title in the WVAL's 12-season existence by scoring five runs in the top of the seventh inning to defeat Branham 6-4 in their next-to-last league game.

In the CCS playoffs, Campbell defeated Pioneer 5-3 and Oak Grove 11-7 to earn a berth in the semifinals against Homestead at San Jose Municipal Stadium.

Homestead was the pre-tournament favorite, largely because of pitcher Sandy Wihtol, who had dominated the Santa Clara Valley Athletic League, and would later pitch three seasons for the Cleveland Indians. The SCVAL included the talent-rich Cupertino, Sunnyvale and Santa Clara areas, and was the only league in the CCS that approximated the WVAL in terms of overall quality. Jim Hemphill, the longtime Homestead coach, had been quoted as saying that Wihtol was the best pitcher with whom he had ever worked, and that resonated with Huntze because he and Hemphill were close friends and he knew Hemphill, like himself, was not given to overstatement. He also knew Wihtol, who challenged hitters rather than trying to finesse them, would be in his element at Muni, where a power pitcher could work up in the strike zone without fear of giving up home runs. The ball usually carried so poorly at Muni that even professional hitters rarely could loft the ball over its distant fences during California League games.

But not even Muni could hold the two blows that sent Campbell on to the CCS finals.

"It was a heckuva pitching duel for a while," Huntze said. "It was 1-1 in the fifth and we've got a guy on and George Hahn comes up and pops one out of Muni. Well, you know it took a pretty good poke to get one out of there, so naturally we're pretty happy. So Jim Guardino comes up right behind him and hits one even farther, just an absolutely mammoth shot. We just went *crazy*. I'll never forget that."

Campbell made four errors in the game, but Fair gave up only one unearned run and completed a five-hitter, and Campbell collected eight hits in $6\frac{1}{3}$ innings against Wihtol on its way to a 6-3 victory. Although Wihtol was to reach the major leagues in 1979, he would have to wait a baseball lifetime after 1973 to finally earn a CCS title, which he finally attained as Los Altos' head coach in 2007.

Campbell's pitching opponent in the championship game would be all too familiar to the Buccaneers – Mitty sophomore Mike Codiroli, who had faced the Campbell players innumerable times in Campbell Moreland Pony League and Colt League play. The Monarchs also had shortstop Ray Townsend, the soon-to-be UCLA and Golden State Warriors basketball star.

Huntze had to decide whether to send senior Joe Casares or sophomore Steve McGrody to the mound against Mitty. He chose the latter, making the CCS title game a pitching matchup of 10th graders, and it turned out to be the correct move. McGrody spaced eight hits over the seven-inning distance, Campbell touched Codiroli for nine hits, and Mitty's defensive largesse enabled Campbell to score six unearned runs in its 7-2 victory.

Trailing 1-0 after two innings, Campbell scored four runs in the third, with Guardino, Jim Oswald and Ted Bertron singling home the first three runs and Codiroli wild-pitching home the fourth. That was all McGrody needed as Campbell ended the season with a 10-game winning streak for the second straight year.

"I really wasn't sure what we had going into that season," Huntze said in 2009. "But as I reflect back on it, that team was about character, fundamental ability, and a little luck."

Campbell was the first team to earn back-to-back CCS titles, and as of 2008 remained one of only two public high schools to achieve that feat. Carmel did it three times while winning seven section championships from 1996-2007, but that was after the CCS subdivided its playoffs into large- and small-school playoff divisions, and all of the Padres' championships were in the smallest-school category.

The Buccaneers' second straight section championship set the tone for the summer-league season, during which Campbell Little League won District 44 for the third time in four years. While Campbell High had beaten a pitcher (Wihtol) who would one day work in the major leagues, the Little League All-Stars had to overcome a pitcher who went on to win 179 major league games compared to Wihtol's one, and logged 2,962 $^{2/3}$ big-league innings compared to Wihtol's 57 $^{2/3}$.

For the first time in many years, Campbell Little League signups were down slightly and the league featured "only" 30 teams, down from 34 the previous year. But some – including Jack Zogg, taking still another turn as the All-Star manager – thought the upper-tier talent was as substantial as it had been in 1970, and in Mike Sullivan, Campbell seemed to have the type of pitcher who could keep the team playing well into August.

When he was on the mound during his years in Campbell, Sullivan competed in several shades of red, with his strawberry-colored hair bulging from his cap and his face turning crimson as his pitches emerged from the tangle of limbs that was his windup. He had a temper to match, once heaving a ball over the right-field wall and onto Hamilton Avenue from the mound in a fit of pique. But his appearance, temper, and occasional difficulty locating the strike zone belied his intelligence and competitive zeal, and the degree to which his teammates respected him. In 1981, after he followed ex-Campbell system paragons Steve Davis, Mike Codiroli and Tom Guardino into Stanford's baseball program, he received the Bruce Cameron Memorial Award, given annually to the Stanford player who best combines baseball proficiency, leadership, and academic performance.

To begin Campbell Little League's 1973 All-Star season, Sullivan came within two outs of a perfect game, striking out 14 of the 19 batters he faced as Campbell routed Sunnyvale National 19-0. The only batter to reach base against Sullivan did so on a one-out walk in the sixth and final inning. Mark Izatt had three hits, and Curt Aure hit a home run.

Aure was also a pitcher of considerable ability, but he was No. 3 in the '73 All-Star team's rotation, and Ray Ybarra, who got the second-game start, responded with a two-hitter as Campbell beat Santa Clara Westside 6-4. Kirk Nolte had three hits for Campbell and Tom Mooney's two-run single in the fifth put Zogg's team ahead 4-3. In the semifinal against Sunnyvale Serra, Sullivan fell behind 3-1 early, but Campbell scored eight runs in the fourth inning and Izatt and Billy Tsamis hit homers in a 16-3 blowout that advanced Campbell into the District 44 finals against Santa Clara Eastside and Mark Langston, a lefthanded pitcher who was ahead of his time in more ways than one.

A generation later, when single-sport specialization became the norm in American youth sports, Langston might have chosen soccer over baseball if he had been confronted with an ultimatum. At Buchser High, he was gifted both as a field player and as a goalkeeper, and even after baseball had made him a millionaire, Langston acknowledged that his decision to play baseball and give up soccer while he was attending San Jose State was dictated exclusively by the fact he could make far more money in baseball than in soccer. (He indulged his soccer passion in a different way, buying part of the Major Indoor Soccer League franchise in nearby Tacoma while he was an All-Star pitcher with the Seattle Mariners.)

His interest in soccer notwithstanding, though, Langston also was ahead of his time as a baseball pitcher. While most young power pitchers of the day exaggerated their leg kicks and their arm extension while trying to generate as much velocity as possible, Langston was economical and smooth in all of his mound mannerisms, and could keep hitters off-balance with breaking pitches if blazing it past them didn't work. He still ranks with Rob Ferguson – a youth-baseball prodigy who had a scholarship offer from Fresno State in hand in 1977 when he blew out his arm as a senior at Buchser, and never pitched competitively again – as the best pitcher ever produced by Santa Clara's baseball system. And in 1973, when Langston took the mound against Campbell in the District 44 final, Campbell soon found itself long in its swings and short of ideas.

In an eight-inning game, Langston struck out 13, and he took a 1-0 lead into the bottom of the sixth and final regulation inning as Santa Clara Eastside had scored in the second against Campbell starter Ray Ybarra. Aure had relieved Ybarra with the bases loaded and no outs, and after one run scored on a bad-hop single, he got out of the inning with no further damage. After that, he had been even better than Langston, winding up with 16 strikeouts over seven innings, but Langston's command was such that it didn't appear as if Aure's work would change the outcome.

In the sixth, Aure led off with a single, and an infield error put runners on first and second. Dan Rosewicz bunted, but Eastside got a forceout at third base and then the second out before Billy Tsamis singled to tie the game. In the eighth, Langston's defense betrayed him again. An error by the shortstop, a passed ball and an infield hit by Bobby Cirivilleri put the winning run on third. Rosewicz struck out, but the third strike evaded the catcher. Under Little League rules, Rosewicz was out, but the runner on third scored on the wild pitch, giving Campbell a 2-1 win and its second straight District 44 title.

"District 44 had a lot of great teams and players in those years," Zogg said in 2009. "We knew our '73 team was a good team, top to bottom, but Santa Clara was always the barometer for us. If you beat Santa Clara, you knew you were a good team. They had some big stars, and sometimes they had guys who would strut a little, but they were good, real good."

Campbell went on to win the sectional tournament, beating Branham Hills 1-0 in 12 innings on a home run by Sullivan, but lost to Orange-Olive 3-2 in the divisional tournament at Santa Clara despite a three-hitter by Aure. "Curt Aure had a great breaking ball in that game, but the umpire wouldn't call a breaking ball to save his soul," John Emery said. "And two of our baserunners had line drives hit them (resulting in outs) ... neither one of them was more than a step off the base, and the line drives were just shots ... they were hit so hard that the runners couldn't move."

The Pony League All-Star team didn't survive its first tournament, and neither did the All-Star team from the Colt League, which that year abandoned the high school-based format it had used for more than a decade, opting for a self-contained schedule.

The other significant Campbell baseball development in 1973 was the first flowering of American Legion baseball in the city.

The national American Legion baseball program is the country's oldest, having crowned its first national champion in 1926, 13 years before the formation of Little League. It serves players through the age of 18, and it plays under major league baseball rules, including nine-inning games and the use of metal cleats. (It used National League rules, which prohibit use of a designated hitter, until the late 1980s.) Next to Little League, it is the closest thing American amateur baseball has to national age-group uniformity, and until the advent of "showcase" events such as the Area Code Games in the 1990s, it was scouted more heavily by college recruiters and professional talent-seekers than any pre-college program, including high school.

In Campbell, several abortive attempts had been made to start a Legion program, and Jack Zogg, the most pre-eminent of the Campbell Little League baseball men, was involved with one such effort in 1968. But Joe Gagliardi, who had managed the 1964 Campbell Moreland Pony League All-Star team to a World Series championship and was the guiding force in Bay Area teen baseball for decades, hated the by-invitation-only Legion program because he considered it elitist. (Gagliardi also disliked Campbell Little League, having once managed there for half a season before quitting, telling other managers he couldn't tolerate the kids.) He used his influence and his control over facilities like San Jose Municipal Stadium and Santa Clara's Washington Park to halt Legion ball's growth while promoting Pony baseball extensions such as Palomino League. Although Legion ball thrived elsewhere in the Bay Area, the only Santa Clara County city in which it had a permanent foothold was Palo Alto, which had never had Pony baseball and thus was out of Gagliardi's range of influence.

Challenging Gagliardi in Campbell required more time, money, energy, and access to top players than most could muster, and Legion rules at the time mandated that the manager of a team be a full-fledged member of the sponsoring post. In 1973, Wayne Mitchell qualified on both counts. As a middle-school teacher in the Campbell Union School District and a longtime manager in the local Pony and Colt League programs, Mitchell had close ties to the best available players, and as a member of Campbell Post 158, he was able to convince his lodge mates to lend financial support to a baseball team. He teamed with Al Casino, a Campbell resident and California Highway Patrol officer who had extensive playing experience, to put together a squad comprised of Campbell, Prospect, Blackford and Mitty players. Legion rules allowed teams to draw from as many as four public high schools as long as they had adjoining attendance areas, and private schools like Mitty could be tapped for talent as well if the players in question lived within the appropriate public-school boundaries.

Mitchell's Legion venture also was timely because it coincided with the most profound change in the history of the *Campbell Press*, which George Vierhus, who had owned the paper since 1956, had sold to Suburban Newspapers, Inc., early in 1973. The *Press* was one of about a dozen suburban San Jose-area weeklies purchased by SNI, which converted all of those papers into tabloids and oversaw their editorial and advertising content. Most of the purchased papers, including Vierhus' *Press*, had been glorified gossip sheets with little significant news content, but under SNI, they were restructured along more purposeful journalistic lines. Vierhus gave up most editorial control, although he continued to write his column until the summer of 1975, and maintained a financial interest in the paper until it went out of business in 1986. He died in 2002 at the age of 90.

The takeover by SNI meant, among other things, that for the first time in many years, the *Press* had a full-fledged sports section produced by a fully paid staff. While many sports stories that appeared in the *Press* after the ownership change were chain-generated and did not involve Campbell, SNI, unlike Vierhus, was willing to spend money on free-lancers to cover local events and leagues. Mitchell was smart enough to make sure that information on his Legion team got into the right hands, and lengthy stories on his team began appearing in the new *Press*, enhancing the Legion team's impact on the Campbell youth baseball community.

In its first season, the team went 16-4 to win its league with a roster comprised primarily of 17-year-olds, and although Campbell was knocked out of the postseason early, Mitchell knew he had a chance to take his team far the following year if he could keep it intact. And for that one year, 1974, Campbell American Legion baseball was the overriding sports story in Campbell.

Campbell High was almost as good in 1974 as it had been while winning the previous two CCS championships, but Leigh, which went on to win the WVAL's fourth successive section title, outdistanced the Bucs in the WVAL race. After the high school season, several of Campbell's top players cast their lot with Mitchell and his American Legion team, including pitcher Pete Fair, catcher Jim Guardino, and position players Tom Guardino, Dave Judd, John McMonagle and Ted Bertron. From the underachieving Blackford program, Mitchell culled shortstop Butch Rowe, third baseman Dan Bongiovanni, outfielder Wayne Hagin and catcher Ted Pranschke. Prospect contributed two quality pitchers, Jack Freeland and Eric Bauer, and a first baseman-pinch hitter, Tom Laspina. Mike Codiroli came from Mitty, as did Paul Jones, who had played in Quito Little

League, but by 1974 was much better known as a football player. He rushed for a still-standing West Catholic Athletic League record 367 yards against Serra as a senior in 1974, and went on to a stellar football career at Cal.

It was not a particularly good defensive team, and Mitchell made no pretenses about player development; he filled out the lineup card and took a seat in the dugout, and the team, which played practically every day after the start of summer vacation, did the rest. It was clear from the outset of the 1974 season that Post 158 had the power and the pitching to contend for a national championship. Mitchell's team easily won its league and area tournaments to advance to the state tournament in the Napa Valley community of Yountville, where Mitchell and his players were immersed for two weeks in one of America's most unique baseball climates.

Yountville, population about 3,000, is the site of the Veterans Home of California. Founded in 1884, it is the largest facility of its kind in the country. It provides residential accommodations and recreational activities for honorably discharged veterans, and on its grounds is a beautifully manicured baseball park that each year is the home of the California American Legion state tournament. In 1974, Yountville also was awarded the West Regional tournament, and the Campbell Legion team wound up spending two weeks there while winning both tournaments.

August baseball activities represented the highlight of the year for many of the veterans, and Campbell players later remembered the old soldiers — a few of whom had service records dating back to the Spanish-American War in 1898 — as the most fully engaged baseball fans they had ever met. Not only did they develop rooting interests in the various teams, they also liked to bet noisily on almost every play, and many of them were not averse to taking occasional swigs from the bottles and flasks they had smuggled into the park.

Campbell began the state tournament by outlasting Inglewood 3-2 in 15 innings, with Jones pitching the first 10 innings and Freeland finishing up, and then reached the winners-bracket final with an 8-7 victory over Rancho Cordova. Campbell led the latter game 8-0 after 3½ innings, but had to hold off a four-run rally by Rancho Cordova in the ninth. Campbell then lost to Sylmar 2-1 despite a two-hit complete game by Pete Fair, but came back in the finals to beat the same team 12-4 with Bertron and Jim Guardino hitting home runs.

It was in the regional tournament the following week that Campbell's hitters made the assembled veterans feel as if they were on an artillery range. Campbell marched through the regional with five straight wins and outscored its opponents 67-18, including a 19-9 drubbing of Hawaii in the final. That sent Campbell to its one and only American Legion World Series, in Roseburg, Ore., and Mitchell's team, which came in with a 44-11 record, was considered one of the favorites.

Post 158 started the tournament well, with Eric Bauer pitching a five-hitter and Jim Guardino driving in the game's only runs with a double as Campbell beat Cedar Rapids, Iowa, 2-0, but it was at that point that the Campbell offense ran out of ammunition, and its defensive shortcomings and its dependence on the long ball came to the fore. Rio Piedras, Puerto Rico, which went on to win the Series for the second straight year, shut Campbell out 8-0 in the second round as Post 158 stranded 14 baserunners and left the bases loaded in each of the final three innings. In an elimination game the next night, Campbell made five errors and lost 10-5 to Cheverly, Md., ending its season with a 45-13 record.

Campbell would never come close to appearing in another Legion World Series, and the program disappeared a few years later, although it was revived in 1982 and 1983. But Mitchell's 1974 team probably comes closest to the 1964 Campbell Moreland Pony League team in fantasy-baseball terms: Although its pitching and especially its defense eventually undermined it in the World Series, it was a fearsome accumulation of hitting talent.

Elsewhere in Campbell, the highlight of 1974 was the dedication of John D. Morgan Park with a July 4 community party that attracted thousands. The lot that the city originally had purchased in 1961 finally had been transformed into the community jewel that it remained 35 years later, and the original plan to name it Rincon Park was changed late in 1973 at the behest of a citizen, David Campos, whose proposal to honor the city's former police chief was enthusiastically and unanimously approved by the City Council.

The Pony League complex that had been started five years earlier had finally been completed, almost exclusively with volunteer labor, and the city had spent $800,000 to surround it with a bucolic urban oasis. In addition to a lawn that encompassed the entire plot, 13,000 small ground-cover plants and 14 varieties of trees had been planted, and an elaborate irrigation system had been installed. The grounds also included a playground, a jogging path, barbecue pits, picnic tables, and the "Beer Hill" bluff that overlooked the fence behind the right-field line of the baseball diamond.

The city and its residents used the occasion to honor Morgan, perhaps the most remarkable citizen in its history. Three years after he had suffered his stroke, John D. Morgan remained unable to speak, although he had regained some use of his limbs, and in 1973 had been able to leave his house for the first time since his stroke to attend his oldest daughter Connie's graduation ceremony at Campbell High. In 1974, he was beset by paralysis-related illnesses, including a lung ailment that had required surgery. Still, he continued on with his writing, which he accomplished by flickering his eyelids to indicate "yes" or "no" as his wife or one of his children quickly recited the alphabet. Until his death in 1980, Morgan wrote columns for the *Campbell Press*, and two books, "Messages to My Children," and "Sez Who?" Both were intended to provoke thought and perspective among his No. 1 love, young people. Each morning, he composed a message to greet his eight children at breakfast. Some of those messages included:

"If I were asked to give just one suggestion, it would be to slow down and use your five senses. I didn't and won't give advice."

"You can give without loving but you can never love without giving."

"You never stop learning or being tested. Stop learning (and you will) stop existing."

Morgan also sent a message to be read at the dedication of John D. Morgan Park: "Sorry I can't deliver this in person. I feel deeply humbled. Yes, proud to be included."

It was hoped by many in the Pony League that called John D. Morgan Park home that the league's All-Star team could celebrate the completion of the facility with a succession of postseason-tournament successes. Led by Cliff Judd, who pitched a five-hitter to beat Diablo Valley 9-4 in the sectional final, and Bob Bossi, who went 6 for 10 in that tournament, the team advanced to the divisional tournament at Santa Clara, but lost twice there and was eliminated. The second loss was a 2-1 decision against Santa Clara on a two-run single by Phil Lansford, younger — and, most thought, more talented — brother of Carney. Phil Lansford was taken by the Cleveland Indians with the 10th overall pick in the 1978 amateur draft, but unlike Carney, who became an American League batting champion and played 15 major league seasons, Phil was beset by personal issues and never advanced past Class A during five seasons in the Indians and Toronto Blue Jays organizations.

Campbell Little League's quest for a third straight District 44 championship began promisingly as pitchers Dave Favre and Jeff Melrose delivered successive shutouts, with Favre beating Sunnyvale National 4-0 on a one-hitter and Melrose following with a two-hit, 14-strikeout 5-0 mastery of Cupertino Pacific. But Campbell lost in the next round 1-0 to Santa Clara Westside despite a six-hitter by Favre. (Unlike Brett Favre, the Green Bay Packers star quarterback many years later, Favre pronounced his last name "favor." The two were not related.)

Meanwhile, Moreland Little League, which had advanced to the district finals before losing to Campbell two years earlier, in 1974 seemed to have both talent and numerical symmetry strongly in its favor. All 14 of the boys who were on Moreland's All-Star team had been born in 1962, the year of the league's World Series victory, and some dared to hope for a reprise, especially after Moreland defeated Sunnyvale Serra 3-1 to earn the league's first District 44 title since '62. The team had two overpowering pitchers, Tony Ochoa and Tim Fleury, and two other dominating players, Greg Takaki and Mike Ernst. But its Williamsport dream ended abruptly in the first round of the sectional tournament with a 4-2 loss to Branham Hills.

In retrospect, 1975 can be seen as a year of prelude in Campbell baseball, given what was to transpire the following year. The reality, though, was that for one of the rare times in Campbell baseball history up to that time, the on-field proceedings were rendered secondary, as a long-simmering dispute boiled over into near-warfare between the city of Campbell and the Campbell Moreland Pony League.

After five years of volunteer labor and more than a decade of planning, the Pony League in 1974 finally had the baseball complex it had envisioned, nestled in the midst of the newly-dedicated John D. Morgan Park. The city owned the baseball facility, at least nominally, but Pony League officials had long insisted that since the ballfield and the adjoining clubhouse had been built by the league, with donated materials and volunteer labor, it should have exclusive use of the field and clubhouse – an opinion that was not shared by many community groups, or by some Campbell city council members. Before the clubhouse was finished, jurisdictional disputes over the complex usually had been settled quietly, but after John D. Morgan Park became fully functional, the city created a new community services department. Its coordinator, Ann Cuny, proceeded on the assumption that the clubhouse was under the aegis of the city, and began to schedule events there without consulting or even telling Pony League officials.

As a result, the league twice changed the locks on the complex's doors, and in May, police were called by the instructor of a senior-citizens art class, who complained that her students were being harassed and intimidated by unknown men while they were in the clubhouse. Damage to class material also was reported. During subsequent talks between the league and the city, Councilman Norm Paul, the most vocal of the opponents to Pony League exclusivity at the park, threatened to revoke the league's year-to-year lease of the property. During the heated exchange that followed, the league's attorney accused the city of blackmail.

Soon after that, several local organizations – including baton twirlers, backgammon players, joggers and lawn bowlers – filed a class-action suit against the city, maintaining that the Pony League was being given preferential treatment. The plaintiffs were able to obtain a preliminary injunction that prohibited the city from interfering with events they planned to schedule there, and with that injunction in hand, they went to Cuny, convinced her to book their events, and then showed up *en masse* one day in what amounted to a sit-in demonstration. They set up their accouterments on the field, in the clubhouse and in the parking lot, began doing whatever it was that they had come there to do, and refused to leave – and because of the injunction, city officials could not uproot them.

Most onlookers were amused, but Pony League officials were furious. Most of the men involved in the operation of the Pony League at the time had been associated with the league for many years, going back to the days when it was subsisting at Castro Junior High. These were the men who had performed the labor that was needed to build the John D. Morgan Park complex. They were hard-bitten men who disdained compromise, and they firmly and noisily insisted that the ballpark and clubhouse they had built was theirs and theirs alone. Their intransigence inflamed the situation and turned some neutral city officials and many residents against the Pony League.

Fortunately, Campbell Moreland president Ray Knight and city manager Bob Stephens emerged as voices of reason, and by the end of June, they had hammered out a compromise that settled the dispute, although it wasn't until a few years later that the terms of the lease were changed so that only the league, and not the city, had the right to opt out each year. The league got a permanent $1-per-year lease and first call on the use of the facility; the city got the right to schedule events on given afternoons and nights, although the baseball field remained the exclusive domain of the Pony League. The city also agreed to maintain the field and the exterior of the clubhouse, while the league assumed responsibility for the upkeep of the interior of the structure. In 2009, that agreement was still in effect.

With the John D. Morgan Park skirmishing at an end, attention finally turned to the on-field goings-on. At Campbell Little League, the season was dominated by a pitcher who reminded many of Tom Davis, who had pitched Campbell to the 1970 Little League World Series final, and Ted Campbell, the man-child who had been the main architect of Moreland's 1962 World Series championship.

Campbell was 6-foot-1 and more than 200 pounds in 1962, and Keith Lindsey was at least that big in 1975 — or so it seemed to those who had to bat against him. Like Campbell and Davis, Keith was mild-mannered, and he was well-spoken and invariably polite to adults. But he had a swarthy, five-o'clock-shadow countenance that added to the intimidation factor; he looked more than old enough to drive, and it was said among players in the league that it wasn't unusual to see him tooling around town in his father Jim's car.

"He could throw *hard*," said Matt Christian, who came into the major division with Campbell Moose Lodge in 1975. "I remember one time when we played them and he hit (Moose's) Chris Gettler in the chest with his fastest fastball. He hit him so hard that the seams made an imprint on Chris' chest that you could see for the next month."

During the regular season, Keith led Campbell Plaza to the major-division championship by winning 10 games and hitting 12 home runs in a 28-game season, and in the final playoff game against Robins, he hit three more homers. His brother Kevin, one year younger and only slightly smaller, played for Doetsch Building, and during the final game of the regular season, Kevin hit a home run off Keith. Kevin was far more excitable than Keith, and he had a voice that reminded some of the yelping of an enraged Chihuahua. As he rounded the bases, Kevin screeched invective at Keith, who turned his back on his brother and put his glove in front of his face to prevent anyone from seeing his laughter.

The Lindseys' impact on Campbell youth baseball, though resounding, also was brief. Keith made the Campbell Moreland Pony League All-Star team as a 13-year-old in 1976, but Kevin never was an All-Star, and the family moved to Sparks, Nev., after the 1976 season. In 1977, Keith was a Babe Ruth League All-Star in Sparks, but neither he nor Kevin were heard from again in a baseball context.

Another Campbell Little League player of note who made his major division debut in 1975 was one of Kevin's Doetsch Building teammates, Lance Modrell, whose pedigree suggested that he could emerge as one of the league's better players. Lance's father Gary, who originally was from Ukiah, had pitched for Fresno State from 1955-58 before signing with the Boston Red Sox and beginning a professional career that got him within reach of the majors. Lance had been born in 1964 in Seattle, where Gary was pitching for the Pacific Coast League's Seattle Rainiers, Boston's top farm club. One of his teammates there was Rico Petrocelli, who became an All-Star short-stop with the Red Sox.

Lance was a fairly good athlete and had his moments in Campbell, but he played mechanically rather than instinctively, and never matched the expectations of his father, who was demanding and sometimes harsh with him. Though he was polite, Lance was painfully withdrawn, and I don't remember him ever allowing himself to enjoy any success he had. He was one of several Campbell-system players in the 1970s and early 1980s whose fathers had been professional players, and in each case, the players never were able to attain the objectives established by their fathers, and eventually became disillusioned with baseball.

The 1975 Campbell All-Star team was as physically formidable as its 1970 counterpart, and not only because of Keith Lindsey. Mark Paquin, the catcher, was considered potentially the best player Campbell had produced at that position. Bob Millar was a temperamental but extraordinary talent who could pitch with either hand, was one of the fastest players in the league even though he also was one of the largest, and was thought capable of hitting a baseball even farther than Lindsey. Paul Sargis, Bob Straight, John Murphy and Rich Alvarez were selected to the team as 11-year-olds; Alvarez, who already was a near-match for Lindsey in terms of velocity, was penciled in as the No. 2 pitcher, and manager Lou Romeo also planned to use Mark Wirth, whose *nom de guerre* was his off-speed stuff, in situations where opponents would have to adjust after seeing Lindsey and Alvarez. Roy Divittorio, although not a strong hitter, was the best defensive second basemen longtime league followers had recently seen.

Campbell's first two District 44 game went according to script. In the opener against Sunnyvale Serra, Lindsey pitched a two-hitter and struck out 14 and Alvarez went 4-for-4, hit a homer and drove in five runs as Campbell coasted 9-1. Campbell then beat Santa Clara Westside 16-3 as Sargis, Millar and Paquin all homered and Alvarez and Wirth teamed on a seven-hitter. But in the district semifinals, Cupertino American's Eric Groo kept away from Campbell's power by taking out a long-term lease on the outside corner, and his team made the most of the two hits it managed off Lindsey, winning 2-1.

Despite the presence of Mike Sullivan, Curt Aure and Ray Ybarra, the pitching threesome that had propelled Campbell to the Little League divisionals two years before, the Campbell Moreland Pony League made a quick exit from postseason play. Campbell American Legion Post 158, with many of the players from the 1974 World Series team back, again won its league, but was eliminated in the area tournament, losing twice to Redwood City. Only the Campbell Moreland Colt League squad extended its postseason beyond the Santa Clara Valley; led by Campbell High players Wes Mitchell, Mark Raust and Cliff Judd and Mitty sophomore Alex Koontz, the team won district, sectional and divisional tournaments before being eliminated from the regional final in Ukiah.

The most intriguing games involving a Campbell team in 1975 weren't even baseball games, and they were played late in August after all of the Campbell All-Star squads had put their uniforms into storage for the winter.

Pony League manager Bud Stallings, in an effort to prolong the baseball summer for some of the league's 13-year-olds, in the early 1970s began organizing an informal team known as the Shamrocks to compete against any opposition it could find. Usually the Shamrocks played Pony League or Senior League teams in practice games as those teams prepared for the postseason, but during the summer of 1975, the San Jose-Milpitas Redskins, the Northern California girls fast-pitch softball champions, issued a county-wide challenge to boys baseball teams that might be willing to face them in the softball equivalent of the Bobby Riggs-Billie Jean King tennis "battle of the sexes" two years earlier.

Stallings eagerly accepted the challenge, and the Shamrocks and Redskins were matched for two games — the first at Campbell Little League, and the second at San Jose Municipal Stadium as a preliminary to an exhibition game between a touring women's softball team, The Queen and Her Maids, and a men's softball team from San Jose. Before the first game, three skills contests were held. The Shamrocks' Gordon West won the outfield throwing contest, and Brian Cannady barely outdistanced his female foe in a footrace, but the Redskins' catcher defeated her Shamrocks counterpart, Mark Pfirrman, in a home-plate-to-second-base throw-off.

Employing a submarine pitching motion to comply with softball rules, Shamrocks pitchers Jeff Melrose, Curt Staggs and Dan Romeo shut down the softballers and led their team to a 5-1 victory in the first game. The second game, before 2,500 at Muni, was more one-sided, with the Shamrocks winning 12-4. Afterward, good sportspersonship prevailed, as the Redskins' Angel Priebe planted a kiss on the forehead of the Shamrocks' Pete Williams for the benefit of the assembled media photographers.

After the Pony League controversy and the disappointing showing of Campbell's All-Star teams, it was an upbeat ending to a difficult season. The 1976 season would end in an entirely different manner, and it would begin the four-year period during which Campbell youth baseball reached heights never scaled by any community over an equivalent period — and seldom, if ever, matched since.

1976 CAMPBELL LITTLE LEAGUE: Daydream believers

As I described in the introduction, this was the team that ultimately is the reason I wrote this book, because it changed my life as profoundly as it changed the lives of the 14 players – maybe even more so. I went from having virtually no family at all to having a hundred or so little brothers and almost as many adult role models during the three years I was directly involved with Campbell Little League. Our Williamsport odyssey was my first total immersion in a common cause, and it taught me, as it taught the kids, that even the most improbable end was possible given the proper means.

I believe the team's collective personality was the single biggest reason we were able to win 15 games in a row in single-elimination competition to reach the finals of the 1976 Little League World Series. (I use the "we" reference in this chapter, and in the chapter on the Pony League World Series titlists of 1978, because I had an official function with both teams, as the bookkeeper and statistician.) And yet, over that same 33-year period, I've never been able to put a label on that personality. Unlike the 1970 Cardiac Kids or the 1979 Clones, this team never had a nickname that widely resonated, even in Campbell. I've always called them the Daydream Believers, but only because the phrase has a personal connotation. I was and still am a devotee of the late singer and songwriter John Stewart, who wrote the song that became a No. 1 hit for the Monkees in 1967. Every time I heard Stewart perform that song in person after 1976, a vignette or a vision from that magical summer would illuminate itself in my mind. So, for lack of a better proper noun that also functions as an adjective, they've always been the Daydream Believers in my mind.

Even at that, though, this wasn't a daydreaming kind of team, although its practical application of what manager Jack Zogg taught certainly put the kids into the believers category. In 2008, I asked Dominic Costantino if he could distill his team's personality into a phrase, and maybe his answer, given after a long pause, is the best one.

"I don't know if we had one personality, really," he said. "I think that team's personality was everybody's personality."

Zogg, at the time and in retrospect, always said the No. 1 element in our success was the fact the group connected, on a lot of different levels, the day it was first assembled. There was common purpose, although I don't remember Zogg or the kids ever talking about long-range goals, even as it became apparent we had a legitimate chance to scale Everest. "I don't think going to Williamsport even occurred to us until we were right on the verge of getting there," Paul Sargis said in 2008, and that's how I remember it as well.

Obviously, the talent level was very high. Six of the kids played college baseball, although the only player on the team who became a professional team-sport athlete was John Aimonetti, and he did it in the NFL. Statistically, we did the things you would expect from a 15-1 team. Our four pitchers gave up only 18 earned runs in 97 innings for an ERA, calculated in the context of six-inning games, of 1.11. Our defense was such that we allowed only 12 unearned runs, five of them in the 10-3 loss to Japan in the World Series final. We had the long ball — 15 homers in the 16 games – but we didn't depend on it because our team batting average was .301, and Zogg, who emphasized contact hitting, always talked about the fact we had almost as many walks drawn (59) as strikeouts (64). Bobby Straight, whose .543 average was by far the highest on the team, had 25 hits (only four of them for extra bases) and drew 10 walks while striking out only four times. But this wasn't a team defined by statistics, and we played several teams, including three of our four opponents in the very first tournament, that had at least as much talent as we did.

So how did we do what we did? In no particular order of importance, here are the factors that come to mind for me:

Horizontal baseball. In 1962 when Moreland had Ted Campbell and in 1970 when Campbell Little League had Tom Davis, high-level Little League baseball was dictated by pitchers who towered over the mound and the hitters. It was a vertical game that was encased within the pitcher-batter confrontation and, to a large extent, by the fear factor therein. Just about every Williamsport-caliber team of the 1960s and early 1970s had at least one pitcher who looked older than his coaches and didn't need a breaking ball or a changeup to dominate and intimidate.

We were able to make the game more horizontal from the standpoint of involving our defense, thereby helping our pitchers keep their pitch counts lower and avoid fatigue late in games.

By 1976, the *modus operandi* of Little League offense was changing. Metal bats had come into use. Improvements in protective equipment, and wider use of the roll-in batting technique, had taken some of the fear factor out of the game, and the influence of major league batting theorists such as Charlie Lau had begun to filter down into youth baseball. No longer did most

Little League hitters simply swing the bat as hard as they could and hope they hit something; by 1976, most hitters on good teams stepped into the box with a protocol in mind, and pitchers had to be able to do more than be big and throw the ball over the plate. Our four pitchers – Rich Alvarez, Paul Sargis, John Murphy and Eddie Rodriguez – were pitchers in the tactical sense; they were mechanically sound and knew how to use one pitch to set up another, and they could locate the ball as well as generate velocity. They relied on their defense, and it almost never let them down. Even during the 10-3 loss to Japan in the World Series final, when we committed five errors, we also made some defensive plays that kept us in the game until the end. In our 15 other tournament games, our defense, in my opinion, was the one element that brought all our other assets into play. We knew we weren't going to give runs away, and our kids' understanding of the geometry of the game, enhanced by the work of manager Jack Zogg and coach John Emery before tournament play began, made us better defensively, which made our already-excellent pitchers almost unassailable. And because we had bat speed and put the ball in play offensively – another expression of horizontal baseball – we pressured opponents' defenses and exposed their weaknesses.

Quickness as opposed to speed. Aside from Bobby Straight and Paul Sargis, the shortstop and second baseman respectively and the top two hitters in our order, and Scott Freear, our center fielder, we had average team speed. But even our biggest kids had well-honed instincts for reading batted balls and the footwork to react to them, so we could keep power hitters in the lineup without sacrificing defense. And our kids understood how to take extra bases by analyzing defenses and defenders, so whatever we lacked in foot speed, we made up with instincts and baserunning expertise.

Proximity. Most of the kids lived relatively close to each other, in the neighborhood bounded by Campbell Avenue to the north, San Tomas Aquino Road to the west, Hacienda Avenue to the south and Winchester Boulevard to the east. They had grown up as playmates and schoolmates as well as teammates, so creating a team concept wasn't something that Zogg had to do when the team first assembled. It had existed long before that All-Star team did.

Intelligence. Jack was able to dispense with elementary teaching at the start of practice and implement advanced concepts, especially involving batting theory and defensive deployment, because the players were able to process and put into effect his instructions. All 14 boys were bright, some exceptionally so. If you were to apply a 1-to-10 intelligence scale, with 5 being average and 10 being extraordinary, I don't think we had a single player who would grade out lower than 7. Most were 8s or 9s, and a couple – Eddie Rodriguez comes immediately to mind – may have been 10s. Moreover, all of them were mature and self-assured enough to be able to take criticism constructively, and although I think Zogg, who tended to be a taskmaster, toned down his approach with this group, you couldn't play for Jack if you couldn't handle some pointed criticism on occasion.

Parental buy-in. All of the parents from the All-Star group, and most of the parents throughout the league, did not push individual agendas either to their kids directly or among each other. The adults supported Zogg completely and the team collectively, and partly because most of them were neighbors, they meshed socially as readily as their kids did. My sense, even in the early tournaments, was that this was a no-lose situation regardless of what happened on the field, and that took a lot of the pressure off everybody, especially the kids. Many of those parents still are friends today, just as their children are, and I think that would have been the case even if we'd never made it out of the District 44 tournament.

The kids remained kids. I think Zogg, even with his reputation as a disciplinarian, thoroughly enjoyed these kids and didn't try to repress their personalities with lock-step regimentation. Jack later talked often about the kids' looseness playing a key role in their success that summer. They were friendly, expressive, outgoing, playful kids who kept each other and us entertained with their humor and imagination, and I think their ambition had more to do with the fact they didn't want the adventure to end than with any sense of manifest destiny. I also think their personalities enabled them to stay within the moment at hand, and take each challenge as it came rather than heaping big-picture pressure on themselves.

We got lucky. In a single-elimination tournament of this magnitude and scope, you can't win 15 straight games without a few breaks, and we had more than our share in the District 44 tournament alone. We had to come from behind in six of our 13 victories before we arrived in Williamsport, and we wouldn't even have escaped the District 44 tournament had it not been for a very close umpiring call that would have ended our season if it had gone against us. During a game against Superior, Ariz., in the Western Regional in San Bernardino, we were almost helpless for four innings against the best pitcher we saw in the postseason. That pitcher lost his composure as the result of an umpire's call that went against him, and we blew him up for nine runs and won 9-2. Another umpiring decision in our favor helped us beat Bristol, Conn., in our first World Series game, a 7-0 win that very well could have been much closer than that. But luck doesn't mean anything if you don't have the expectation that you can recognize it and take advantage of it, and we always did.

Maybe some saw it as a portent that the league invited Gene Colburn and Ken Aubineau, the manager and coach of the 1970 All-Star team, to speak during the 1976 opening-day ceremonies, along with the usual coterie of city and school-district officials. But I don't remember either of them talking much about their World Series trek six years before, and in any case, talk about the postseason was usually muted when John Hanrahan and Bob Holman were around.

Hanrahan was the league president and had been involved with the league for over a decade in various capacities, even though his two children were girls who never played in the league. (The national Little League organization first permitted girls to play in 1974, the first year I was associated with Campbell Little League, but I don't recall any girls being in the program during the three years I was there.) Holman, who had been in the league since 1958, was what might be described as the league's director of operations. They were at the ballpark almost as often as I was, and it was primarily because of the two of them that the league ran smoothly, parental decorum was enforced, and the kids' welfare was valued and protected. Both John and Bob emphasized to me, and to everyone else, that the regular season and the regular-season teams were paramount, and that nothing that detracted from that would be permitted. Although it wasn't part of my job description, I kept individual statistics throughout the season, both for the managers and for my own edification. At one point, I posted them in public view. John and Bob took them down, and explained to me that the fact some kids were batting .000 should not be public knowledge, and that individual accomplishments should not be prioritized ahead of the team concept. Of course, they were right, and from then on, I simply gave the stats to the managers and let them do whatever they wanted with the information.

In due course, the regular season ended with Jack Zogg's Robins team taking the title. The usual procedure was to give the All-Star team to the manager of the championship team if he wanted it. Naturally, Jack — who had managed at least a half-dozen previous All-Star teams and had taken Campbell to the divisional round in 1966 and 1973 – didn't need any persuasion, not with the four returnees back from the 1975 elite team. Paul Sargis, John Murphy and Rich Alvarez figured to do the bulk of the pitching and would play second base, third base and occasionally the outfield when they weren't on the mound. Bobby Straight would be the shortstop, and the four of them would be the fulcrum on which the team's fate would balance. Typically, when Rich pitched, Paul played second base and John played third; when John pitched, Rich played third and Paul stayed at second; and when Paul was on the mound, Rich played third and John played second.

Eddie Rodriguez, John Aimonetti and Dominic Costantino also would be part of the team's nucleus. Eddie was a superior all-around athlete who often played shortstop during the regular season even though he was left-handed, and Jack planned to use him as a pitcher because, besides being a lefty, he relied on a motion that had more jerks and hitches than a vaudeville act in a silent movie. He had off-speed pitches and control in addition to better-than-average velocity, and thus might force in-game adjustments by teams after a turn or two through the order against Campbell's power pitchers. Dominic and John both provided the long ball; Dominic was an excellent first baseman who would play there when Eddie pitched, and John, though it didn't seem so because of his massive size, moved well in the outfield. (In 1982, he won the shot put in the CCS track meet as a senior at Blackford. Putting the shot requires mastery of footwork, and John always surprised people, including NFL scouts, when they saw how quick he was on his feet.) Scott Freear was an easy choice as well because he had both power and speed and was by far the best defensive center fielder in the league. Unlike the other All-Stars, Scott rarely played anywhere except center field during the regular season, and Jack knew from experience that Little League tournament games often were decided when infielders who had hastily been converted into outfielders misjudged fly balls or threw to the wrong bases with runners on.

Rich Okamoto had been Jack's catcher for Robins, and Jack wanted him behind the plate because Jack called all pitches and Rich had learned to think along with him in terms of pitch selection and location. Rich was a good receiver, and had the intelligence and even temperament that Jack wanted behind the plate, but he wasn't particularly mobile. Jack wanted Rich in the starting lineup primarily because of his bat, although his .182 average for the postseason was the lowest among the regulars.

In 1976, the re-entry rule had not yet been introduced in postseason play, and Jack wanted at least one more catcher because he might have to substitute for Rich late in games. Mike Walsh, though small for the position, was probably the best defensive catcher in the league, could play the outfield capably, and was a hitter who knew how to use the entire field, so his selection by the league managers also came quickly. (Mike was the only player on the team other than John Aimonetti who ever made money as an athlete. He and his brothers and I often went bowling during those years, and Mike took it seriously; before he settled into his eventual career in sales, he spent several years trying to make the Professional Bowlers Association tour.)

That left four slots to fill, and the process of doing so occupied several hours. The eight managers could nominate any players they wished, and on the first ballot, a player had to be elected unanimously. After that, seven votes were needed, then six, then five. The first 10 players were unanimous or near-unanimous choices, but picking the final four required several hours, and although I wasn't there, I heard that there was little unanimity among the managers during the latter stages of the meeting. If the decision had been made simply to base the final selections on statistics, as it often is when All-Star teams are picked, the final roster might have looked significantly different and would have required much less time to establish. But at Jack's urging, the managers ultimately decided to provide him with versatile role players he thought could be necessary to meet specific needs within games. Brian Hughes, though not a prolific hitter, was fast, bunted well and could fill in as a middle infielder. John Lawson gave Jack another good defensive catcher and a contact bat off the bench. Albert Vanegas was a superior defensive third baseman with some power. Jack liked Curt Hollars' arm strength and thought it might be put to use at some point, either as a pitcher or as an extra outfielder. This was before Little League required every player to play at least two innings in each postseason game, and Jack wanted reserves who would accept their limited roles and be good teammates – which Brian, John, Albert and Curt all readily did.

The team practiced for about three weeks before beginning District 44 play at Cupertino American against Sunnyvale National on July 23, and Jack, while characteristically loath to acknowledge publicly that he thought the team was of exceptionally high quality, talked with a glint in his eye after practices. Because most decisions involving who would start where had been made even before the All-Star team was selected, he was able to focus on defensive alignment and situational hitting, and it was apparent from watching practice that this would be an efficient team as well as a profoundly talented one. We weren't disappointed, and neither was Jack.

Against Sunnyvale Southern in a 7-0 victory, Rich Alvarez retired the first 10 batters he faced and finished with a one-hitter and 14 strikeouts, and Campbell eliminated all suspense early with a four-run first keyed by Dominic Costantino's three-run double. That sent Campbell into the second round against Cupertino Pacific, and it was at this point that Zogg made his first and perhaps most important personnel decision.

Jack's plan entering the tournament was to use righthander John Murphy as his No. 2 pitcher, and given the fact John's stuff was almost as electric as Rich's, that plan made sense. But after seeing Cupertino Pacific's first game, Jack saw that its lineup was comprised primarily of left-handed power hitters. So he shifted gears and gave lefty Eddie Rodriguez the starting assignment, and Eddie responded with a seven-inning four-hitter during which he struck out 13 and walked only two.

"God love Eddie," Jack Zogg said, smiling, in 2009. "The poor kid was petrified (between innings), but he went six shutout innings. After the sixth, when we're going to extra innings, he's looking at me and saying, 'I'm finished.' I said to him, 'Eddie, you know you can go up to nine innings, right?' He looks at me and his eyes are big as saucers. But he went back out there ... once he was on the mound, he was fine."

However, Cupertino Pacific pitcher Bret Davis matched Eddie through the regulation six innings, and it wasn't until the seventh that Campbell finally nicked Davis for the only run of the game. John Aimonetti led off with a single and Brian Hughes pinch-ran for him. Rich Okamoto walked. The next hitter bunted into a forceout at third, but Bobby Straight doubled to win the game 1-0 and move Campbell into the district semifinals at home against Sunnyvale Southern.

(Davis never forgot that game. Five or six years later, when he was at Homestead High, he pitched a particularly good game against either Prospect or Westmont, both of which had several players from the 1976 Campbell Little League team. I was covering that particular game for my paper, and I asked Bret if he remembered 1976. "Yeah," he said. "In fact, I've been waiting to pitch against Campbell ever since that game. We thought we were just as good as they were. They wound up going to Williamsport and we wound up going home, and if we'd been a little luckier, that might have been us doing everything that they did.")

The Sunnyvale Southern game was even more perilous for us than the Cupertino American contest had been. Ultimately, it was the closest we came to being eliminated from the tournament before the World Series final.

Although Alvarez limited Sunnyvale Southern to a single hit while striking out 12, his control briefly deserted him in the fourth inning and Sunnyvale Southern scored a run that held up until the bottom of the sixth. Straight led off the sixth with a walk and Alvarez singled him to second, whereupon John Murphy was asked to bunt – perhaps the first such request ever made of him in a game. He got the bunt down, but Sunnyvale Southern's pitcher made a great play and got a forceout at second base, leaving runners at first and third with one out.

Because Campbell's park contains no more than 10 feet of space between home plate and the backstop, scoring from third on a wild pitch is almost impossible under most circumstances. Impossible, that is, unless you were Bobby Straight during that 1976 postseason. A pitch got away from the catcher, but it caromed back to within a couple of feet of him, and he quickly flipped it back to the pitcher covering the plate as Bobby sprinted in. Some thought the pitcher made his swipe tag on Bobby before he slid in and hooked his toe on the left-inside corner of the plate, but the umpire ruled him safe and the game was tied 1-1 with Murphy at second.

The next batter was retired, and if the umpire's call on Bobby's slide had gone against Campbell, that would have been the end of the game, and the team photo might have wound up buried in attics or basements instead of on the cover of the 1977 Campbell telephone book. But it was only the second out, and John Lawson bounced a single into shallow right field, giving Campbell a 2-1 victory.

The championship game was against Cupertino American, and because that lineup was filled with right-handed hitters, Zogg started Murphy instead of Rodriguez. He was taken out in the fourth with Campbell trailing 2-0; Rodriguez relieved and blanked Cupertino American the rest of the way. In the fifth, Campbell scored six runs, with Mike Walsh and Scott Freear banging out two-run doubles, and the 6-2 victory gave Campbell its fifth district championship in 11 years.

As had been the case from 1968-71 when the District 44 champions reached four straight Western Regional finals and won two of them, the sense was that any team that emerged from the district had a chance to make a lengthy incursion into the postseason. Beyond that, Campbell would have a virtual home-field advantage in the sectional tournament at nearby Quito Little League, and it may have been that the team didn't have the same sense of urgency during the opening game against North Mountain View of District 11 that it had showed during the District 44 tournament. Whatever the reasons, Campbell was fortunate to escape with a 5-3 victory.

Alvarez allowed only two hits and struck out 12, but the game was tied 3-3 until the bottom of the fifth when Campbell scored the two deciding runs on singles by Lawson, Alvarez and Rodriguez. Perhaps that mild scare provided Campbell with the jolt it needed; its next game was a 17-0 rout of Pleasanton as Rodriguez pitched a two-hitter and Murphy hit two home runs. A 6-0 two-hitter by Alvarez, who was buttressed by two home runs from John Aimonetti, against San Mateo National – which had beaten Saratoga, the team that eliminated Quito in the District 12 finals – sent Campbell to the divisional tournament in Milpitas.

Concord National went down 9-3 in the first round of the four-team tournament, and Alvarez, after giving up a two-run homer in the first, no-hit Northridge of Sacramento the rest of the way and Straight hit a two-run homer as Campbell won 5-2. Of Campbell's nine wins to this point, four had been come-from-behind efforts. The next stop, and the last before the Little League World Series, would be the Western Regional in San Bernardino.

Campbell's first-round matchup was against a Rock Springs, Wyo., team that would have had a difficult time beating any of Campbell's regular-season major division teams. The final score was 14-0; John Murphy needed only one out to complete a perfect game before he hit the 18th Rock Springs batter with a pitch; he got the next out to finish his no-hitter.

Matt Christian, who played against John in Little League and Pony League and knew him fairly well, called him the most talented athlete he had ever seen. "The guy could do *anything*," Matt said. "He could master anything he tried, the very first time. He was ambidextrous ... I don't know if he ever did it in a game, but I saw him throw left-handed a few times, and he threw harder than I did right-handed."

Even for those of us who had watched him regularly for three years, though, John was considered a bit of an enigma. Though friendly and never critical of anybody except himself, he said little and sometimes seemed distant and disinterested, and he ran, threw and moved so smoothly that he seemed effortless, which led some to conclude that he wasn't putting forth total effort. But during the Williamsport experience, we got a revealing look at John's dignity and, if this is the right word to describe a 12-year-old kid, professionalism. He was courageous, too, as I found out when I had him in Legion and he played a full month with a broken hand without saying anything to me or anybody else. John's older brother Jimmy was born with a condition that limited his ability to walk and speak without enormous effort, and John always said that Jimmy was his role model. As an adult, John took up a career in physical therapy, and Jimmy was his motivation in that respect as well. (Besides that, Jimmy was also our biggest fan, and more than 30 years later, when I went to a Campbell Little League All-Star game as part of the research for this book, there was Jimmy, lighting up the surroundings with his zest for life, just as he had done during that summer of 1976.)

Campbell's next game, against Superior, Ariz., began as a crisis and ended as a catharsis.

Superior, a town of about 3,000 located 40 miles east of Phoenix, was one of the most compelling stories at the Western Regional. In 1976, Little League guidelines called for each urban league to serve a population base of about 25,000, so the Phoenix and Tucson leagues that have always dominated youth baseball in Arizona drew from a population base at least eight times as large as Superior's. Moreover, the town was and still is one of the poorest rural communities in Arizona. The copper smelter that had been Superior's primary employer went out of business in 1969, and to this day, the economic void has never been filled. In 2008, 27.8 percent of its population, including 39 percent of its residents under age 18, lived below the federal poverty line.

But Superior had overcome those obstacles to win its first (and still only) state championship, and the size and physical maturity of Superior's players, at least half of whom had visible facial hair, represented an element that the Campbell players had not seen before, even in District 44. Superior's starting pitcher, Johnny Santa Cruz, was the biggest and most ornery-looking player in that dugout, and after he and a teammate mortared solo home runs far over the outfield wall off Rich Alvarez in the first inning, we thought that a fifth come-from-behind win would come with far more difficulty than the previous four.

Luck again intervened on behalf of Campbell in the bottom of the fourth inning, when Santa Cruz, while batting, was called out on a close play and completely lost his concentration. In the top of the fifth, Campbell knocked him out with a nine-run fusillade, and won 9-2 as Alvarez ran his record to 6-0 with six complete games and 79 strikeouts in 36 innings.

On August 20, Campbell faced a team against which composure would be even more important than usual. No Nevada team had ever reached the Little League World Series at that time – and still hadn't through 2008 – but in 1976, the players and fans from Paradise Valley, near Las Vegas, seemed certain that they would become the first. Paradise Valley had won the Nevada state championship by beating a Carson City team on which the *second-best* pitcher was future major leaguer Charley Kerfeld. The No. 1 pitcher on that Carson City team was 6-foot-2 Craig Allison, whom Paradise Valley beat 11-4 even though he struck out 14 batters out of a possible 15 during his five innings of work.

Paradise Valley also menaced with its size, although not to the degree that Superior had, and its players and fans were by far the loudest and most abusive Campbell heard that entire postseason. Starting pitcher Eddie Rodriguez, perhaps unnerved by the volume and venom of the verbal onslaught coming from the Nevada dugout and rooting section, struggled and had to be relieved by Paul Sargis in the fourth as Campbell fell behind twice. But the Campbell bats eventually imposed silence on Paradise Valley. Rodriguez contributed a home run and a two-run double and Alvarez drove in four runs in an 11-5 victory.

The game that decided the regional title and the Western representative in the Little League World Series also defined Rich Alvarez, even though his three-hitter in a 6-2 victory was not the best game he pitched that summer.

Whenever his teammates and anyone else connected with Campbell baseball in the late 1970s think of Rich Alvarez, they think only secondarily of the results, incandescent as they usually were. Rich was every bit as good as Ted Campbell had been for Moreland in 1962 and Tom Davis had been for Campbell Little League in 1970, and unlike his predecessors, Rich commanded as a stylist *and* as a big kid who threw hard. His older brother Joe, a former Campbell High and West Valley pitcher, had molded Rich's mechanics, and he generated velocity with torque rather than with arm speed. His main strength was in his upper body and his legs, and he had learned to twist his body so that he almost faced third base before he committed his weight forward. Because he drove straight through the pitch even after he released the ball, his fastball had downward bite and would act almost like a slider with the proper finger pressure. If a hitter hadn't seen him before, Rich's pitches were hard to pick up out of his hand, harder to monitor in flight, and harder still to hit — and sometimes to catch. One reason Jack had three catchers on the roster was that mobility was a prerequisite for anyone catching Rich, who had occasional bouts of wildness and whose pitches had deceiving sink. Mike Walsh and John Lawson were more mobile than Rich Okamoto, although Rich did the majority of the catching throughout that postseason.

Beyond all his talent, Rich always pitched with a sunny disposition and a grin that split his cherubic face; if he had arm pain, nobody else ever knew it because he would pitch through physical discomfort to help the team. He pitched us to two national championships, yet I never remember him doing anything in the dugout or off the field to call attention to himself, and even when he played for me in Legion, his was a please-and-thank-you presence who asked me for a special consideration only once: Even though he was having arm trouble and didn't pitch at all for us during the regular season, he asked for the ball in the area tournament championship game. I gave it to him because I knew it was courage and a sense of responsibility, not ego, that had motivated him to make the request, and even though we lost, I never regretted it, because all of us owed Rich that measure of respect.

In 1976, Rich had come down with the flu early in the tournament, and by the time we were to face Hawaii for the right to make the trip to Williamsport, he was a very sick young man — sicker, I knew, than he allowed Jack and Bob to recognize. But as he was to do often in his Campbell career, he told everyone he was fine and took the mound before a capacity crowd of 7,500, by far the largest we had seen to that point. He fell behind 2-0 early against Hawaii — the sixth time we trailed in that postseason — but got stronger as the game progressed and wound up with a three-hitter, striking out 13 to give him 92 Ks in 42 tournament innings. We scored four runs in the second, with Murphy singling home two of them, and we iced the game with two more runs in the fifth on a double by Eddie Rodriguez, who was to finish as our RBI leader with 18 in 16 postseason games.

"The Hawaiian manager didn't want his kids fraternizing with any of the other players down there," Jack Zogg recalled. "The Southern California team (Santa Ana) wouldn't even talk to anybody, and the Hawaiian kids weren't as stiff as them, but John (Emery) and I both noticed that they looked really tight before the game against us. I turned to John and said, 'You know what? I think we've got these guys.'"

Eddie's father, Ed, worked at the Ford assembly plant in Milpitas, and as with many of the Campbell parents, traveling beyond the Bay Area represented a considerable financial sacrifice. He had driven down to San Bernardino, as had about 200 people from Campbell. After we beat Hawaii to earn the trip to Williamsport, Ed returned to Campbell, rented a mobile home and drove with his wife and two younger children for 60 straight hours to get to Pennsylvania. (Eddie's younger sister, Edie, was a great athlete in her own right; in the early 1980s, she became one of the first girls to play in the major division in Campbell Little League.) P.H. Kephart, whose son Tony probably was the best player in the league who wasn't chosen for the All-Star team, also rented a motor home for the trip. He brought a dozen people, including Albert Vanegas' parents, and after we beat Hawaii, P.H. and his passengers slept in the motor home and embarked directly for Williamsport the next morning.

Like a lot of the parents, I hadn't made any travel plans beyond San Bernardino, and as a typical college student, I was habitually broke. But there was no way I was going to miss this trip, and I was able to borrow enough money for the airfare and to make arrangements with two of the fathers to share a hotel room in San Bernardino. John Hanrahan, meanwhile, started working the phones as soon as he got back to Campbell, and he was able to book about 50 of us on an early-morning flight from San Jose to Pittsburgh on Tuesday morning, the same day we were scheduled to face Bristol, Conn., in the first round of the World Series. (The national organization booked and paid for only 17 people – the players, coaches and league president.) Our plan was to rent cars in Pittsburgh and drive the Pennsylvania Turnpike to Williamsport, 162 miles away, and we knew that even if everything went on schedule, making the 4 p.m. starting time would be iffy at best.

Well, the airline misplaced our baggage and the rental-car company misplaced our vehicles, and by the time we finally got out of Pittsburgh, it was about 1:30 and we were already a couple of hours behind schedule. There would be no time to find and check into our hotels before the game, and I don't know if we would have even made it in time for the start of the game if Bob Hollars, Curt's father, hadn't been a police officer. We were tooling along the Pennsylvania Turnpike at about 90 mph when a Pennsylvania state trooper stopped us about 30 miles east of Pittsburgh. Bob explained our mission to the officer, and not only were we not ticketed, the state police, upon being told of our destination, escorted us all the way into Williamsport. We got there about 15 minutes before game time, and the Kepharts and the Rodriguezes and the other motor-home drivers arrived at about the same time. We must have looked like a mob of French peasants storming the Bastille as we made our way out of the parking lot and into the ballpark, but Jack Zogg later said that our mass arrival was the single biggest factor in our 7-0 victory over Bristol.

"The fans won game No. 14," he said. "I went out to check the pitcher (Alvarez) about 20 minutes before the game, and there were no rooters in sight. You never saw such long faces. But then we saw one of the fathers coming up over the hill, and behind him were about 90 more from Campbell. From then on, there was nothing but smiles on their faces."

Besides the absence of their parents until just before the game, the kids had other factors working against them. Rich Alvarez was still sick, and some of the other players had picked up his bug. The parents had given Jack and John Emery an assortment of medicines for their kids in case of illness, and most of them were used, especially those intended to combat allergies. Several players became ill on the eastward plane flight, and once they arrived, the ones who had allergies suffered far more than usual because of the heat, the humidity and the unfamiliar accommodations. Eddie Rodriguez had the worst possible allergy for a baseball player: newly-mown grass.

The players also had been broadsided by the news that coach John Emery would not be accompanying them to Williamsport because of a family matter. John had been coaching for Zogg on the Robins team for many years, and his kindliness, enthusiasm and subtle sense of humor provided a settling influence for the players. They knew and liked Bob Holman, who had been a driving force in Campbell Little League since long before any of them were born, but the question of whether the loss of John would affect their concentration in Williamsport still lingered.

The game-time temperature that day was 93 degrees, and it must have felt like 113 to the kids because none of them had ever been exposed to Eastern humidity before. As had been the case in San Bernardino, the team was housed in a common barracks, but while the facility in San Bernardino was brand-new and relatively comfortable, the Williamsport compound was much older, had no air conditioning and was a virtual boot camp, with food to match.

Nevertheless, their cheer and their sense of adventure and fun prevailed. Keith Jackson, who was to do the play-by-play for ABC during its Wide World of Sports telecast of the championship game, spent the week in Williamsport preparing for the final, and the kids were introduced to him before their first game. At some point, he asked the kids about their interests beyond baseball, and John Lawson mentioned to him that he liked to do imitations.

John was a born performer – he later became a professional musician – and he was the best kind of humorist because he didn't impose himself on people. Most of the time, he was reserved, whimsical and wonderfully creative, and he could come up with a nickname for everything and everybody. (His nickname for me, as I remember, was "Scoop" because he knew I planned to make a career out of newspaper work.) He sensed his place in the team hierarchy and didn't try to come off as a team clown or attract undue attention to himself, and would wait quietly for the right opening. When it came, he's get this mischievous grin on his face, and he'd go into his shtick. Became he was so unassuming, his humor had greater impact. With Jackson there, he did the imitations that invariably broke up his teammates – his best were of Howard Cosell and John Wayne, but he could do almost anybody, including Jack Zogg – and from what I was told, he made such an impression that he and the rest of the ABC people made no secret thereafter of their hope that Campbell would make the World Series final.

Ernie Banks also was there, as an invited guest for the week, and was particularly pleasant and engaging with the kids, many of whom still have the autographed baseballs and posed photos with Banks that they got that week. The World Series wasn't the worldwide media whirlpool it was to become later — only the final was televised, and Lamade Stadium didn't have lights — and even though the kids understood the magnitude of what they were trying to accomplish, it was still possible for them to revel in the surroundings in Williamsport, Spartan as they were. They made friends with members of the other seven teams. Curt Hollars hung out with some of the boys from Puerto Rico, and at one point he was playing Ping-Pong with one of them in the compound. Trying to be accommodating, Curt made it a point to try to announce the score in Spanish, which amused the Puerto Rican kids no end. Finally, one of them said in precise English, "Don't worry. We know the score is 4-1."

Jack Zogg and Bob Holman, meanwhile, spent much of their free time with the two team uncles that had been assigned to the Campbell squad.

"Everybody we met back there, and in San Bernardino, was so down-to-earth, even the Hall of Famers," Jack said in 2009. "They'd do anything for you. The two uncles in Pennsylvania were especially great to us. I don't keep trophies, but I did keep one from Williamsport. The two team uncles played Bob and I in horseshoes. Now Bob really knew how to play; me, I threw the horseshoes like the horses were still in them. But we beat them, and they made up a little trophy for us with a horseshoe on it. I still have that trophy."

Amid all this, there was baseball to be played, and a decision for Zogg to make. Center fielder Scott Freear had suffered a hairline fracture of his arm while making a diving catch in the Hawaii game, and he would be out for the World Series. (Doing what he could, Scott coached first base during the games in Williamsport, and he waved runners around so vigorously that at one point, the bandage on his hand came unraveled, and he looked as if he were waving a streamer.) Mike Walsh had been doing some of the catching and Jack had been toying with the idea of making him the permanent No. 1 receiver, but after Scott's injury, Mike was the best available option in center field, especially since he had been hitting well. John Aimonetti, whose .344 average for the postseason was second only to Bobby Straight's .543, by now had become the regular starter in left field, and Dominic Costantino was at first base when Eddie Rodriguez was pitching and in right field when Alvarez, Sargis or Murphy was on the mound.

(Aimonetti, who played football at San Jose State and in 1987 was on the Kansas City Chiefs' strike-replacement team, gave up baseball after two years in Pony League, and wasn't on Campbell Moreland's Pony League World Series championship team in 1978. But he has the distinction of being one of only two big-league-athletes-to-be who appeared in that Little League World

Series. The other was Ray Ferraro, who was on the Canadian representative from Trail, British Columbia. Ferraro played for six National Hockey League teams from 1984-2002, earning the nickname "Big Ball of Hate" because of his on-ice ferocity.)

Campbell's reconfigured defense was flawless in the 7-0 win over Bristol. Dominic hit a two-run home run, his only bomb of the postseason. Rich, still woozy from his illness and working on only two days rest, wasn't at his best, walking six, but he gave up only two hits and struck out 11. While Campbell seemed impervious to the stress of the moment, Bristol was not, committing four errors, all during Campbell's two-run second inning. With the bases loaded and one out, Bristol pitcher Joey Jandreau fielded a comebacker and threw to the plate for a forceout, but the catcher's throw to first base sailed into right field, scoring the first run. Mike Walsh, who had been on second, tried to score on the overthrow, and was tagged at the plate. That apparently ended the inning, and the Bristol team left the field. But the home-plate umpire didn't see that the catcher had bobbled the throw after tagging Mike; the base umpires overruled him, and Mike's run counted. Campbell then broke the game open in the fifth with four runs, two on Costantino's homer.

Before 1976, the Little League World Series brackets had not been aligned to guarantee that U.S. and foreign teams would meet in the final. In 1970, Campbell had played Nicaragua in the semifinals before losing to Wayne, N.J. in the final, and in 1962, Moreland faced Mexico before defeating Kankakee, Ill., to win the title. But starting in 1976, the eight teams were divided into four-team brackets, with the four American teams in one group and the four foreign teams in the other. Not only did that guarantee the international-against-domestic final that ABC wanted, it also ensured a U.S. championship game – and that game would be on Thursday, August 26, between Campbell and Tuckahoe Little League of Richmond, Va., which had edged Des Moines, Iowa 4-3 in its first-round game.

Jack Zogg debated whether to send John Murphy or Eddie Rodriguez to the mound against Richmond, and didn't make his choice – John – known until it was time for him to hand in his lineup card. John had started only two games up to this point while Eddie had started four, but Jack thought John's velocity might be enhanced by the bad hitting background at Lamade Stadium. There was no batters-eye fence in center field at the time, only the grassy terraces where spectators sat, and pitched balls came out of a background that looked like confetti. Moreover, the sun was nowhere to be seen as the teams warmed up; clouds menaced everywhere, and the ballpark didn't have lights.

It was sprinkling even before the teams took the field, and as Campbell batted in the top of the first, a full-fledged thunderstorm, accompanied by lightning, descended. The umpires quickly stopped the game, and the rain increased in intensity, making it apparent to everybody that no more baseball would be played that day. As the kids waited in their dugout, they quickly sized up the possibilities that the wet knolls overlooking the outfield presented, and as soon as the game was officially postponed, they sprinted back to their barracks and came back in their bathing suits. Before anybody could stop them, they were sliding down the wet grass, and they spent the better part of an hour frolicking there before the increasingly-adjacent lightning chased them back indoors.

"Actually, I wouldn't have been surprised if they'd snuck out (and cavorted on the hill) before that," Zogg said, smiling, in 2009. "You can't pass up something like that if you're a 12-year-old kid."

Before they headed for the hill, though, they had another thing on their minds — saving the Campbell soup can.

The "can" was a cardboard soap container, about four feet high and three feet in diameter. During one of our District 44 tournament games, Campbell had a large fan contingent that was orchestrated by George Licina, a minor-division manager who had known most of the kids from their first baseball days. George was reserved and quiet most of the time, but he transformed himself into a dynamo as Campbell's unofficial cheerleader during those All-Star games. This was at a time when Krazy George Henderson, who began his cheerleading career with the San Jose Earthquakes in 1974, was establishing a national reputation with his frenzied gyrating and tambourine thumping, and George Licina, who didn't use any such props, always referred to himself as "crazy with a C."

George was one of many in the Campbell support group — before, during and after 1976 — whose loyalty to the players went far beyond their work with individual kids or even teams. One example was Ray Hirose, who was a biological uncle of Randy Nishijima and was known as Uncle Ray throughout the league. "I could go on and on, telling you all about his endless support and devotion to the kids of Campbell Little League and Pony League, particularly for the guys my age," said Randy, who played on Campbell Little League's All-Star team in 1977 and was on the Pony League world series titlists of 1979. "I still remember how he would take John Murphy to the batting cages, knowing that John did not have a dad around, like the rest of us; and how he would give kids rides to practices, and home after practices and games instead of watching them walk home. He was very close to them, as they were to him. He was everyone's 'Uncle Ray,' and he was a big part of Campbell Little League back in our time."

While George Licina was leading a "Campbell" chant at that District 44 game, some of the fans of the other team began reciprocating sarcastically by yelling "Soup." That didn't sit well with Betty Freear, Scott's mom, and Arlene Catalana, whose son Mike was an 11-year-old in the league. It was their idea to obtain the cardboard container and paint it to look like a Campbell Soup can, and the players soon adopted it as their mascot. After the victory over Hawaii in the Western Regional final, they took the can on the plane to Williamsport with them and had it in their dugout throughout the World Series. When the Richmond game was halted, they took it back to their barracks with them, and were proud to report afterward that the can and its paint job had survived the deluge virtually unscathed.

I was all too aware of the lightning as it closed in on Williamsport, too. The *Campbell Press* had commissioned me to do a first-person narrative on the Williamsport experience, and I had brought my portable typewriter, but I didn't have it with me at the ballpark because I was busy keeping the team's scorebook. So after the game was called, I went to a hotel-restaurant on the other side of the road that ran behind right field. A pay phone near the hotel was still functional, so I called the *Press* office to dictate that day's log, which I had to wing because it had been too wet to write anything down. While I was on the phone, the thunder and lightning seemed to hone in on that little booth, and I felt like a war correspondent – and a terrified war correspondent at that. The only other time during my sportswriting career when I felt such clear and present danger was 13 years later when I was covering another World Series, the major league version, and Candlestick Park was hit by the Loma Prieta Earthquake.

Fortunately, the lightning didn't hit the phone booth. I finally finished my story and went back to join the other parents at the hotel and wait for an announcement regarding the resumption of the game. I was rooming with Bob Hughes, Brian's dad, and Dan Watt, who managed the Fontanetti's team in the major division. Happily, we didn't have to venture out that evening; the restaurant and its bar were fully operational, and the parents had used our room's bathtub to ice down several cases of Rolling Rock beer. The word we were hearing was that the field was in such bad shape that the Campbell-Richmond game could not be played at least until late Friday afternoon, at the earliest, and that the Series might have to be extended into Sunday, regardless of ABC's objections. Tournament officials had brought in a helicopter to try to dry the field, but in the absence of concrete news, we had a party that night – and quite a party it was. Ralph Doetsch, the mayor of Campbell at the time, had arrived that morning and had repaired to the bar immediately after the postponement. While we were eating dinner, he passed out face-first in his mashed potatoes, and had to be helped to his room by Steve Aimonetti, John's brother and a future Stanford football player. There was a piano in the bar; Mary Campbell, John Lawson's mom, commandeered it, and we began singing along with every song she knew. When she played one song, though, the room fell silent, and I thought I heard a few sobs to accompany my own. It was "The Impossible Dream."

The game was rescheduled for the following afternoon, even though the helicopter and the other means used to dry the field were only partially successful. Jack Zogg and Richmond manager Don Roman agreed before the start of the game that they would not take the field unless both of them agreed that the playing conditions were safe. Sure enough, they were ordered to begin the game on time by the umpires, who were acting under orders from national Little League officials who were concerned about another postponement precluding ABC's scheduled telecast of the championship game the following day.

"The field was really mucky," Jack said in 2009. "They (the Little League baseball hierarchy) called down and told the umpires to get the game started. I had agreed with their coach that we were going to stick together on this ... the umpires were volunteers who did what the Williamsport people told them to do. Well, we wouldn't take the field, and finally they got blankets out and started sopping up the standing water with those. It dried up some, and after a while, it looked safe enough to play. The umpires were telling us we were the first ones ever to say no to those people upstairs."

John Murphy returned to the mound, but perhaps because of the unexpected hiatus, it was clear that he didn't have his full arsenal. He needed a bases-loaded strikeout to escape the third inning after Richmond touched him for two hits and a walk. Meanwhile, Richmond starter Brian Smith did not allow a hit through the first four innings.

With one out in the bottom of the fourth, Murphy issued a walk, and, with the count 1-and-2, threw a wild pitch to advance the runner to second. Zogg waited no longer, calling in Paul Sargis. It was a somewhat surprising move, because Paul had pitched only seven innings in two appearances during postseason play, and Eddie Rodriguez was available for the role in which Zogg had originally envisioned him — an off-speed lefthander coming in after a high-velocity righthander. But as usually was the case that summer when Jack played a hunch, it worked.

Paul struck out the first hitter, but then threw a wild pitch and the runner advanced to third. The next pitch also got past catcher Rich Okamoto, but trickled only a short distance, and Rich was able to recover the ball quickly. He relayed the ball to Paul covering the plate, and he tagged the runner out to end the inning.

In the fifth, Campbell finally broke up Smith's no-hitter as Dominic Costantino and Rich Alvarez singled, but Smith got out of the inning, leaving the game scoreless. Sargis, meanwhile, struck out the side in the bottom of the fifth, and as he prepared to lead off the top of the sixth, one thought was foremost in his mind — the fact Smith had been getting ahead of the Campbell hitters all day, usually with first-pitch fastballs. The tactical situation — a scoreless game in the top of the sixth — also seemed to call for Paul to take until a strike was called, and Paul figured Smith was aware of that too.

The first pitch to him was belt high and in the outside half of the strike zone. Paul knew upon contact that he had hit it well, but even he didn't expect to see it soar at least 20 feet over the center-field wall. Campbell led 1-0.

At that point, of course, the game was far from over, but it had been played on a precipice all day, and it was after Paul's home run that Richmond fell off the precipice. Two walks and three errors allowed Campbell to score two more runs, and Sargis retired the side in order in the bottom of the sixth, striking out two.

After he registered the final out, the scene on the field and in the stands resembled a human kaleidoscope, but it was short-lived. The kids had come to Williamsport to win the World Series and not "merely" a national championship, and awaiting them, rested and ready, was the team from Chofu, Japan. Zogg had let his players watch the Japanese team practice before their own game, and they had looked so mature and so dispassionately mechanical that after the exhilaration of the Richmond victory had faded, a hint of self-doubt crept into the players' mind for the first time since they had begun their odyssey, 15 victories, three time zones and 36 days before.

The Japanese team had lost to Taiwan — which had won four straight World Series from 1971-74 before being disqualified from the '75 event for eligibility violations — in the first round of the Far East regional, but had come back through the losers bracket to beat the Taiwanese twice and earn the trip to Williamsport. They had had two weeks to rest and practice before coming to the U.S. for the World Series. Their 5-foot-6, 155-pound pitching ace, Kiyoshi Tsumura, had thrown a perfect game in his team's first World Series outing, a 25-0 embarrassment of a bad West German team, and the No. 2 pitcher had followed with another no-hitter in the semifinals as the Japanese team beat Puerto Rico 4-0 in a game that was played on Thursday before the monsoon that had postponed the Campbell-Richmond game.

After the Richmond game, Zogg told the media that while the Japanese team deserved to be considered the favorite, he was certain that Campbell could put the ball in play — it had only 55 strikeouts up to that point, less than four per game — and that the Campbell players would be able to function as normal in front of the 40,000 spectators and the TV cameras. But although he didn't say it at the time, he knew the physical and mental fatigue had finally caught up with the Campbell players.

Unlike San Bernardino, where parents could enter the players' barracks more or less as they pleased, access to the compound in Williamsport was strictly limited, and some of the kids whose parents had not been able to travel had not seen their folks in almost two weeks. Although the flu bug had passed, many of the players were weakened by its after-effects and by the oppressive humidity, and their usual good humor was dissipated by the accumulation of tension over the previous five weeks. Watching the Japanese players practice had suggested to them that they might have to play beyond their comfort zone to win. I talked briefly with a few of the players as they got ready for the championship game, and I was not encouraged. Understandably, they were on edge to a much greater degree than I had ever seen them.

The championship game quickly went sour as Campbell committed three errors to give the Japanese five unearned runs in the second inning. Rich Alvarez threw 85 pitches in the brutal heat and gave up seven runs in $3\frac{1}{3}$ innings before Zogg lifted him in favor of Eddie Rodriguez in the fourth. Our only chance to get back into the game came in the third, when Paul led off with a single, advanced to third on two wild pitches and scored on an error. Rich and John Murphy then singled and Eddie doubled them both home to make it 5-3, but Tsumura escaped the inning with a strikeout, and Campbell didn't get another hit the rest of the way.

The final was 10-3. Campbell, which had not committed more than two errors in any previous game, finished with five miscues, and undermined itself further with four wild pitches and six passed balls. Even so, the defense that has been the team's most salient quality didn't completely disappear. Eddie, playing first base while Rich was still pitching, started a double play, and Dominic Costantino, playing right field for one of the rare times in his career, made a shoestring catch and then doubled off a baserunner. John Murphy made a couple of impressive plays at third base. Generally, aside from that decisive second inning, we didn't embarrass ourselves, and Zogg said later that many observers praised the players for the way they regained their composure after the second-inning meltdown.

Japanese manager Hidetoshi Suzuki was gracious during his postgame remarks.

"If Taiwan had made it to the Series, I believe Campbell would have beaten them," Suzuki said through an interpreter. "This was only the second game where my players could feel the pressure being exerted on them. It was a combination of being the final game and the type of opposition we were facing. Campbell was also difficult for our pitcher because each batter in the lineup was a threat."

"They were down 5-0, but still came back," Zogg said after the game. "This was typical of them. But our defense faltered. Even though we moved the ball fairly well, the shaky defense made the difference.

"The boys were disappointed that they didn't win the world championship, but after John (Emery, who had flown out from California for the title game) and I talked to them, they realized that they were the United States champs. They had thought they'd lost everything with that last game. The hardest thing they had to do after losing to Japan was go out and (congratulate) the other team, most with tears in their eyes.

"But kids have fantastic recuperative powers. They recover much faster than adults. The team was walking in tall cotton by the time we got home to that wonderful welcome."

As described in detail in the introduction to this book, the immediate aftermath of the game was emotional flat-lining, which soon gave way to an understanding of the enormity of what they had accomplished — an understanding that was still deepening more than three decades later. They went to Washington, and to Baltimore to see an Orioles game before returning home to the liberating-conqueror welcome described in this book's introduction. The team's photo was on the cover of the Campbell phone book the following year. John Lawson's humor and aplomb as the emcee of the celebratory banquet — he "interviewed" each of his teammates in his best

Howard Cosell dialect — was such that Santa Clara County Supervisor Rod Diridon, who was one of the invited guests, arranged to have John appointed to the Santa Clara County Youth Commission. At age 13, he was the youngest public official in the state. Asked later by a reporter (not me) if he had thought about a possible career in politics, John grinned. "I'd rather be an entertainer," he said. "I'm a ham."

Even if they had been inclined to do so, the kids had no time to dwell on the defeat. The team came home on a Tuesday (September 2), and most of them began junior high school the very next day. A few of the parents put together a California Youth Soccer Association age-group team, and even though most of the kids had never played soccer, more than half of them signed up and were on the pitch within two weeks, enjoying themselves and each other as much as ever.

Thirty-three years later, as Jack Zogg and I reminisced about that summer of 1976, he talked about his overriding memory of the Williamsport experience.

"You know, you try to tell people that the kids bounced right back after losing that game, and they look at you like you're crazy," he said. "They think kids are too young for competition like that, that losing a game like that will affect them for the rest of their lives. But they're so very, very wrong. I've been coaching for a long time, and there are so many times where you'll see a kid who threw a home-run pitch to lose a game walking out of the ballpark arm and arm with the guy who hit it. It hangs with the adults for a while, but it doesn't hang with the kids."

Indeed, as the boys' lives returned to normal, they gradually nudged aside the memory of that last game against Japan. But they did not forget it, and two years later, nine of them finally got the chance to expunge it ... and it was an opportunity that they fully seized.

1978 CAMPBELL MORELAND PONY LEAGUE: Unfinished business

Almost from the time the sting from the loss in the 1976 Little League World Series title game had subsided, the Campbell Little League players who had made that national championship possible began pining for the next phase of their baseball careers. All 14 of them signed up to play in Campbell Moreland Pony League (and all 14 would stay in the league through 1978), but even the marquee players from the Little League team knew they would be exploring a new frontier at John D. Morgan Park.

The most immediate and obvious consideration for them was the fact that they would be playing under "real" baseball rules, instead of the softball-like regulations that govern Little League, and on a larger diamond. They would be facing better day-to-day competition, because Campbell Moreland had only nine teams and drew the best players from three talent-laden leagues (Campbell, Moreland and Quito). Moreover, all but three of the Campbell All-Stars were the oldest boys in their families, and the three who weren't – Rich Alvarez, John Aimonetti and John Murphy – had brothers who were considerably older. Consequently, they hadn't had the benefit of having watched siblings play in Pony League. Additionally, most of them were playing for managers and coaches whom they didn't know, and who didn't know them, except by reputation.

The new Campbell Moreland arrivals, especially those who had played in Campbell Little League, also had to adjust to another reality in Pony League: The atmosphere at John D. Morgan Park was entirely different than the Little League environment to which they had become accustomed.

As often is the case in post-Little League baseball organizations, the interest and involvement levels at Campbell Moreland were minimal compared to the Little Leagues that fed it. It wasn't a matter of the facilities or the coaching being inadequate; the Pony League complex, completed in 1972 after almost a decade of volunteer effort, included a well-maintained playing field and was in the midst of a scenic municipal park. As with Campbell Little League, most of the managers and coaches had been there for many years and weren't there to coach their own kids. For the most part, they were competent baseball men; a few, like Chuck Calhoun, Bud Stallings and Al Gutierrez, were exceptional in terms of teaching the game. One of my favorite people in the league was a 71-year-old coach with the Giants, Ed Mangan, who had managed and coached at one level or another since 1922. Ed, who lived nearby with his daughter, had seen some games while strolling through the park, and had volunteered to coach. He oozed with perspective and energy, and told stories about having seen Babe Ruth and Joe DiMaggio play in person and having been persuaded to take up baseball as a boy by Hall of Fame infielder Johnny Evers, who retired in 1917.

But as most of the new players were already aware, Pony League games were usually played in relative silence, and the league's postseason record was such that the expectation to win on a high level simply had not been there before their arrival.

Campbell Moreland, it can be argued, should have won far more often in Pony League All-Star play than it had up to that point. It had won the Pony League World Series in 1964 with six of the players who had brought Moreland Little League the World Series title in 1962. Since then, the quality of the talent that was funneled into Campbell Moreland had remained high, especially since the league had a virtual monopoly on the top 13- and 14-year-old players in the Campbell area. Moreover, the path to the Pony League World Series was far less cluttered than in Little League, because only a handful of Pony League programs existed in Santa Clara County in the 1970s. Although Pony League was firmly established in the East Bay, in the Sacramento area and in parts of Southern California, the only areas near Campbell where Pony baseball was permanently entrenched were Los Gatos, Santa Cruz County, Morgan Hill, and Santa Clara. From Mountain View all the way north into San Francisco, most 13- and 14-year-olds played Babe Ruth baseball, and throughout most of the Santa Clara Valley, most former Little League players continued their careers in that organization's Senior League program. Few cities and school districts would undertake, or even allow on their property, the construction of Pony League diamonds, which are larger than Little League but smaller than regulation. The emphasis then was on multi-use facilities, and Campbell Moreland was one of the very few leagues fortunate enough to have a diamond built specifically for Pony League baseball.

Another factor that should have worked in Campbell Moreland's favor before 1978 was the fact that, unlike Little League, the leagues that hosted high-level tournaments usually were automatically seeded into them. In a year when Campbell Moreland hosted a regional tournament, as it did more often than not, it would have to win only that tournament and then the divisional to qualify for the World Series.

Yet despite those resources and advantages, Campbell Moreland never appeared in a Pony League World Series from 1965-77, and the Campbell baseball community had never perceived the league as a municipal resource to the extent that it did Campbell Little League and Gordon

Huntze's Campbell High program. One reason was that league officials had alienated many in town during their many battles with the city of Campbell and various community groups over the use of the John D. Morgan Park field and clubhouse. Another was that the league did little to promote itself or to raise money beyond what it needed to complete the ballpark. Before 1977, when new uniforms were purchased for all the league's teams, the outfits worn by the league's players looked as if they'd been rescued from their grandfathers' attics. Before 1977, Campbell Moreland rarely had social functions such as the annual pancake breakfasts and dinner-dances at Campbell Little League. The few people who showed up for Campbell Moreland games usually came only to see their own children play, and rarely socialized with other parents in the league while they were watching.

Although it took some time to enliven the environment at Campbell Moreland, it began to change in 1977 after the arrival of the Campbell Little League contingent that had forged so many friendships before and during their adventure the previous summer. Many Campbell Little League parents pitched in to help as soon as their kids arrived in Pony League – serving on the Campbell Moreland board of directors, volunteering for work parties or snack-bar duty, and creating a spectator core that hadn't existed at Campbell Moreland before by staying for multiple games and continuing to make baseball an important part of their social lives. Some liked the game environment even more than they had enjoyed Little League. At John D. Morgan Park, un-like Rosemary School or the other Little League ballparks, families could barbecue, drink beer – I don't remember any negative incidents involving parents and alcohol during games at the park in the three years I was there – and lie on blankets on Beer Hill along the right-field line. The park also had a toddlers playground right behind Beer Hill, and a number of the parents had younger kids who availed themselves of that. The parents who had come over from Quito immediately became friendly with their Campbell counterparts, and before long the Moreland contingent joined in as well.

I had the same announcing/groundskeeping/scorekeeping job at Campbell Moreland in 1977 that I had had at Campbell Little League. At the behest of several of the Campbell-turned-Campbell Moreland parents, the league had offered me $65 a week, $25 more than I had been getting in Campbell, to make the move to John D. Morgan Park. I loved the Campbell job, but beyond the fact I was paying my way through college and needed every dollar I could scrounge, I relished the idea of staying with that group of kids and parents for another two years. My setup at Campbell Moreland was even better than it had been at Campbell; the league had just installed a new public-address system, the scorers booth was almost the size of a living room and enabled me to invite more kids up during the games, and I didn't have to worry about eating on weekends because parents who were barbecuing invariably would send up burgers, ribs and beer from time to time.

At Campbell, I had been given freedom to use the PA system as I saw fit, with the proviso – one with which I agreed wholeheartedly – that the focus was never to be drawn away from the game being played. We had fun with it, both there and at the Pony League park. I played music between games, gave away Bees and Quakes tickets in trivia contests, passed along scores, highlights and league announcements, and announced the kids' names and accomplishments with all the verve I could manage. Once in a while, I'd let some of the more loquacious kids, like John Lawson with his Howard Cosell imitation, announce some of the batters. Most important, I got to know the majority of the kids in both leagues, and made many new friends among them.

My first priority was to give the parents and especially the kids the feeling that they were in a major league ballpark when I announced their names and games. I think I succeeded, and while I don't think I was the biggest reason the atmosphere at John D. Morgan Park began to change dramatically in 1977, I think I contributed to the sense among the kids and parents that this was a league where quality mattered. (By now, the parents were paying $25 per child, which seemed like a lot to me, to sign their kids up for Pony League, and I figured they ought to get as much as possible for their money.)

There was a lot of quality on the field as well that first year. The league championship was won by the Tigers, who had Mitch Morris, a former Moreland player who was the best pitcher in the league, with a 0.95 earned run average for the season. (Keith Lindsey, who had made the All-Star team as a 13-year-old in 1976, had moved out of the area.) Dave Roberson and Mark Paquin were both on the All-Star team, as was Art Gonzalez, one of Dave's teammates. Art was another kid who looked a lot older than he was, but in his case, the maturity level carried over into the way he conducted himself off the field as well. He had younger siblings for whom he already was a parental figure, and he had to juggle work as well as school and baseball.

Another kid in the league who intrigued me that year was a 13-year-old named John Gill. John hadn't particularly distinguished himself at Campbell Little League, and he was only a fair player in Campbell Moreland, but he was and still is the fastest 13-year-old I've ever seen. John obliterated two long-standing records in the junior high district track meet that year. His 16-foot, 1-inch long jump broke a record set in 1964 by almost half a foot, and his 6.5-second time in the 50-yard dash eclipsed a record set in 1958. John went on to play football and run track in high school, but I still wonder what kind of baseball player he might have become if he had been able to translate that speed into baseball productivity. The following year, we had another superior athlete whose forte wasn't baseball. Ted Ornduff wrestled at the same time he was playing baseball at Campbell Moreland during the summer of 1978, and won a national AAU championship. His family moved to Morgan Hill that fall, and he played football for Live Oak and then for Washington State. Ted went into law enforcement after college, and in 2004 won another national championship – the American weight-lifting competition for police officers and firefighters.

Rich Alvarez won the 1977 batting title with a .487 average, and was the only player on the Campbell Little League team from the previous year to be chosen as an All-Star. Rich, former

Quito All-Star Harold Sutherland and Moreland graduate Billy Roberts were the only 13-year-olds on the team; most of the other players from the Williamsport group played for Bud Stallings on the Shamrocks after the regular season, and they wound up completing a 26-game schedule that helped them prepare for what was to come in 1978.

The 1977 All-Star team easily won its first tournament, and in the regional opener against Los Gatos, Mitch Morris was cruising along with a 2-1 lead in the fifth inning when Campbell Moreland did what it had done so often in postseason play since 1964. Four errors in the inning led to 10 runs in a game Campbell Moreland eventually lost 14-2. They won only one other game in that tournament before being eliminated, and it may have been at that point that the 13-year-olds – both those on the All-Star team and on Bud's Shamrocks – determined among themselves that the 1978 postseason would not be like every other Campbell Moreland postseason since 1964.

It wasn't ... and as life-changing as the Campbell Little League national championship had been for all of us, I think Campbell Moreland's 1978 Pony League World Series title was the greater baseball achievement.

Although nine of the players who had been on the 1976 Campbell Little League national-championship team were on the 1978 Campbell Moreland Pony League All-Star team, it was a very different team in a number of respects. One, of course, was the element of expectation. The trip to Williamsport two years before had been a spontaneous joyride most of the way, but the 1978 team fully expected, and was expected, to reach the Pony League World Series, and win it. We played two fewer games and in two fewer tournaments than in 1976, but we didn't have any Rock Springs, Wyoming-type teams on which to feast. Every game was a grinder in which we faced pitchers who knew all about us and saw beating us as a career calling card.

The 12-year-old boys of 1976 were now 14-year-old young men whose lives were less serene and more complicated than they had been two years before, and sometimes it was tough for them to maintain the focus and sense of common purpose that had been so evident in 1976. The sense that all eyes in Campbell were on them was diminished as well. The 1978 team never played on live television, or in front of a larger crowd than the 2,000 or so who were at John D. Morgan Park for the final day of the team's first tournament. In 1976 we never had to come back through a losers bracket because all of the tournaments were single-elimination. The Little League World Series semifinal and final represented the only two games that came on successive days, and that was only because of a rainout. In 1978, we had to come back through the losers bracket twice, and in both cases we had to sweep doubleheaders on the last day against teams that had beaten us previously.

Our players weren't media magnets as they had been in 1976, either. Coverage outside Campbell was limited, with the wire services releasing only a five-paragraph synopsis after the Pony League

World Series final, and the *Campbell Press*, which had put out a special section after the 1976 team got home from Williamsport, had only two stories (both of which I wrote) in the edition that followed the Pony League World Series. In fact, the *Press* was not even publishing out of Campbell when we got back from the World Series in National City, Calif., and that was reflective of the fact that, beyond the baseball realm, it had been a strange, unsettling and in many ways ominous summer in the Orchard City.

In addition to my duties at Campbell Moreland Little League, I completed a 10-week journalism internship at the *Press* during that summer of 1978. It was my luck and privilege to work under the stewardship of Pat Safford, who had taken over the paper's editorship after George Vierhus retired. Pat was probably the best journalist I met in my 30 years in the business. She challenged me as no other boss ever did after I "turned pro" the following summer, and beyond the baseball, I remember that summer as a blur because we were immersed in important, ongoing stories that foretold the end of Campbell as we had known it.

- Proposition 13, which limited the tax liability of many California homeowners, passed in June, and the controversial measure was particularly popular in Campbell, where more than two-thirds of the voters and 26 of the 27 precincts were in favor. The rest of the summer was a litany of stories about panicky school officials who immediately began cutting programs and services such as sports, music, summer school and busing, and began talking about multiple school closures. By the end of the summer, the once-unthinkable concept of closing Campbell High, the symbol of Campbell's identity for almost 80 years, was unmistakably on the table.

- The federal government in 1978 made billions of dollars available to cities that would agree to build subsidized senior housing, and Campbell officials, hearing the ringing of cash registers and ignoring the fact the city already was virtually built out by 1978, pursued those projects with vigor unmatched anywhere else in Santa Clara County. Work began on the first project — Wesley Manor, a $5.8 million, 14-story architectural monstrosity on South Winchester Boulevard — that summer, and by September, plans had been finalized for several more senior housing projects, including one adjoining John D. Morgan Park that would eliminate most of its parking areas, along with the sense of tranquility that had prevailed there. Although Pat covered the issue fairly, as she did all subjects, she warned everybody who read and listened about what the "graying of Campbell" would do to a city that long had been an enclave of younger, middle-class families. Unfortunately, nobody in power heeded her. During the next decade, Campbell aged long before its time. It was inundated by retirees from outside the city who needed services that depleted municipal resources, and who contributed little to the city's economy or culture. Mostly, they complained, especially about noise. After the project next to John D. Morgan Park was built, Campbell Moreland Pony League even had to take the PA system out of the ballpark because of the insistence of seniors.

- The "Campbell loop," consisting of two one-way streets that allowed through traffic to avoid the half-mile stretch of East Campbell Avenue that constituted the downtown business district, had been finished the previous year. The idea was to make that part of East Campbell Avenue a strolling mall with no traffic, but by 1978 it was apparent that the plan was failing monumentally. The same businesses that had clamored for the loop now were beseeching the City Council to modify the plan, but by the summer of 1978, it was too late. Downtown Campbell essentially ceased to exist, and it took more than two decades to bring in the boutiques, restaurants and condominiums that created a revival in the district.

- The *Press*, under Pat's direction, in 1978 had become a high-quality journalistic product for the first time in its history. But late in my internship, the chain that owned the *Press* decided to consolidate operations, and in August, while I was on the road with the Pony League team, the office on Dillon Avenue from which the *Press* had published since 1950 had been vacated (and eventually was sold). The *Press* lasted eight more years, but it never operated out of Campbell again. Pat and the rest of the staff were moved to Los Gatos, where they worked in the building that housed the chain's paper there. The idea of operating a paper out of the town that most Campbell residents disliked and considered a high school sports rival, and was everything that Campbell wasn't – rich, pretentious and steeped in antiquity – was anathema to most of its Campbell readership, and although Pat did what she could as an absentee editor, the product began to decline steadily in quality and circulation. In 1986, it disappeared entirely after 91 years of service, and with it went another important aspect of what had been Campbell's municipal identity.

Those events all would impact Campbell's makeup and self-perception over the next decade, and the loss of such important phases of Campbell's persona would undermine the youth baseball system. In 1978, though, all that was in the future, especially from the players' perspective, and although it was inevitable that Campbell Moreland players, coaches and parents periodically thought of the postseason, the regular season was interesting and entertaining.

It was a pitchers' league, especially when Rich Alvarez was doing the pitching. Rich completed a no-hitter early in the season, and followed that up with games in which he struck out 17 and 15 of a possible 21. When he was at bat, pitchers avoided pitching to him, sometimes to a far-fetched extent. In one game, his Yankees and the Pirates were in a 1-1 tie in the eighth (first extra) inning when Rich was intentionally walked with two outs and nobody on base. Rich wasn't noted for his baserunning, but he stole second on the next pitch and scored on a single by Dominic Costantino to give the Yankees a 2-1 win.

John Murphy of the Cubs did Rich one better, authoring a perfect game. His manager, Rich Barry, was a former professional player who had spent several years in the Brooklyn Dodgers organization, and although he never made the majors, he happened to be at Yankee Stadium in 1956 when Don Larsen pitched the only perfect game in World Series history. After John's perfect game, he said he had seen only two perfect games in person in all his years in baseball — Larsen's and John's. Tom Gricius, a 13-year-old who had won three games for Campbell Little League in the 1977 postseason, also had a no-hitter, and Brett Blackwell, a 14-year-old lefthander from Moreland, had one 24-inning stretch during which he gave up no runs and two hits, walked five and struck out 32.

Billy Roberts, one of three holdover All-Stars from the previous season, won the batting title with a .430 average, with Murphy finishing second at .391 and Albert Vanegas at .349. The Mets, led by Bobby Straight, won the championship for the third time in four years

The level of excellence in the league was such that the league's board of directors, for the first time in Campbell Moreland's history, decided to choose two All-Star teams, entering the No. 2 team in preliminary tournaments while the No. 1 team prepared for the regional tournament into which it was automatically seeded by dint of being the host. The "B" team, which won its first tournament before being eliminated from the second, consisted primarily of 13-year-olds, and Steve Koontz, Joray Marrujo and Tom Gricius were among the players whose 1978 experiences would prove invaluable in postseason play a year later. But even though those 13-year-olds and others would have been welcome additions to most All-Star rosters, the "A" team was comprised entirely of 14-year-olds.

Rich Alvarez, John Murphy, Mike Walsh, Bobby Straight, Paul Sargis, Eddie Rodriguez, Albert Vanegas, Scott Freear and Dominic Costantino all had played on the 1976 Little League national championship squad. For Rich, it would be his fourth straight postseason. Four former Quito players — Steve Clinton, Harold Sutherland, Glenn Davis and Eric Crawford — joined them, as did ex-Moreland players Billy Roberts and Brett Blackwell. Bud Stallings was the manager, and Chuck Calhoun was his coach.

For the most part, Bud stayed with much the same lineup and defensive look that Jack Zogg had used in 1976, but Steve and Harold gave Bud additional options both as middle infielders and outfielders during the championship run, and both were periodic starters. Billy brought the same arm strength and range that Scott had provided in center field in 1976, but he was a much better hitter; Bud sometimes played them both in the outfield, and when that happened, the third outfielder seemingly could have fielded his position from a lounge chair. Brett emerged as the team's No. 2 pitcher, freeing Eddie Rodriguez for first-base and relief-pitching duties. Glenn was the team's backup catcher, and Eric provided late-inning speed and defense at first base and in the outfield. He was one of the best all-around athletes in the league, and expected to play a lot more than he did, but he never complained and remained a positive presence during practices and in the dugout during games.

Rich, of course, shouldered the most responsibility for the team's fate, and after the World Series was over, it was his uniform jersey that was placed on display in the youth wing of the Baseball Hall of Fame in Cooperstown, N.Y. It was a deserved honor. But although it would have been difficult, I think we could have won the World Series in 1978 if Rich had been injured or otherwise unavailable, because we had plenty of quality pitching. If anything had happened to Mike Walsh, I don't think that team would have a chapter in this book.

If the 1976 team had a weakness — and that may be overstating the case, because Rich Okamoto generally did a good job — it was the absence of a catcher who could command both the game and the pitching staff. Rich Alvarez, in particular, could make catchers (and umpires) as well as hitters look bad, because his fastball had late, abrupt movement and his breaking ball dove like a pelican snatching a fish from a pond. The passed balls and wild pitches that had been so crucial during the loss to Japan in the Little League World Series final represented a reminder, for the next two years, that if this group had designs on a world championship, its most pronounced improvement would have to be behind the plate — especially in "real" baseball, with stealing allowed and a third strike no longer an automatic out even if dropped.

Mike, of course, had been Rich Okamoto's primary backup in 1976, and he was a good enough athlete to play in the outfield, which he did in Williamsport after Scott Freear was injured. But he had always been a front-row-in-the-team-picture player, and the fact he was small (5-foot-5, 115 pounds in 1978) obscured in too many minds his technical mastery of his position. In the spring of 1978, when Mike missed the first month of the Pony League season because he was on the Campbell High frosh-soph team, he got almost no playing time. But once he returned to Pony League, he left no doubt as to his status as the best catcher in the league. Bill Walsh, his father and manager, let him call his own game and run the team on the field, and he spent as much practice time perfecting his footwork as any catcher I've ever seen, at any level. Mike was the only catcher in our league who fully understood the concept of "framing" — catching corner pitches deep within his mitt so that the umpires could get a better view of them as they bisected the strike zone. He never reached for pitches in the dirt, instead shifting so that the ball would hit his chest protector and drop at his feet, and he was the first in our league to take advantage of a new rule that allowed catchers to ask the plate umpire to ask the base umpires for help in a check-swing situation. He didn't have an extraordinarily strong throwing arm, but his quick release and his accuracy more than made up for any lack of throwing velocity.

Mike also was a student of baseball, and when he and I were watching games in which he wasn't playing, I knew not to make small talk with him because he was always focusing on what was happening before us. Completing the package was his intelligence, and the fact that even though he was easygoing and had a whimsical sense of humor that everybody liked, even a teammate could become a momentary enemy if Mike didn't feel he was exerting total effort or maintaining full concentration.

"I used to (jokingly) say that pitching to Mike sucked," said Matt Christian, who played against Mike throughout their Campbell youth baseball careers, and was his batterymate at West Valley College, "because he'd throw the ball back to me harder than I pitched it to him."

If Jack Zogg hadn't fully appreciated what Mike could do for a team, his value never was lost on the Pony League managers, who chose only one other catcher – Glenn Davis, who knew going in that his role would be strictly as a backup. This was going to be Mike's team, and Bud Stallings made Mike the team captain even though he was the smallest player on the squad. And he wasted no time demonstrating that August 1978 would be the Month of Mike.

Because we had a bye into the regional tournament at John D. Morgan Park, our first game wasn't until Wednesday, August 9, against always-strong Santa Clara. Rich started, and was in a scoreless tie when a Santa Clara batter led off the top of the third with a single. Apparently, the Santa Clara coaches had seen Rich pitch before, and they knew that because of the exaggerated torso twist that he employed, he didn't release his pitches from the stretch as quickly as some pitchers. Therefore, they reasoned, their baserunners might be able to get jumps on him, and they were certain that Campbell Moreland's little catcher couldn't possibly throw anyone out stealing.

The little catcher in question had a surprise for them. That leadoff runner tried to steal second and was thrown out by 10 feet. The next batter doubled, and attempted to steal third. Mike disposed of him too. We went on to a 4-0 victory, and Bud, whose custom was to award the game ball to the contest's most valuable player, gave that game ball to Mike.

Our next game, on Saturday, was against Diablo Valley, which had a number of future college players, including Tad Heydenfeldt, who went on to pitch for the University of Arizona. Heydenfeldt crafted a four-hitter, striking out 14, as Diablo Valley beat us 4-1 to plunk us into the losers bracket. That meant we would have to come back later that afternoon to play a very good Pittsburg team in an elimination game, and then sweep a doubleheader from Diablo Valley the following day.

We beat Pittsburg 10-0 with Paul Sargis pitching a one-hitter, and with Rich starting the first game Sunday, we felt reasonably confident that he would get us through that game and allow Bud to mix and match our pitchers in the second. The heat, though, was a scythe, and after Rich had pitched six scoreless innings – facing the minimum 18 hitters – and we had a seemingly secure 5-0 lead, he gave up a grand slam in the seventh that pulled Diablo Valley within one run.

With Mike's help, Rich navigated the final three batters and we won 5-4. In the second game – in which Diablo Valley surprisingly didn't start Heydenfeldt – we jumped their starter. John Murphy doubled home two runs in the first, and Billy Roberts' two-run double in the bottom of the fifth boosted our lead to 6-0. But Murphy, our starter, was laboring in the heat and having trouble with his arm. He needed a pickoff at second and a bases-loaded strikeout to get out of the fourth without allowing a run.

Brett Blackwell, who hadn't pitched previously in the tournament, relieved John at the start of the sixth, and Diablo Valley scored five runs against Brett before Eddie Rodriguez was called in from first base to take the mound with one out and a runner on second. In a corollary move that would soon prove fateful, Bud brought Dominic Costantino in to play first base at the time he made the pitching change.

Eddie walked the first hitter he faced, but retired the next two on a strikeout and a grounder to Paul Sargis at shortstop. We didn't score in the top of the seventh, and Eddie returned to the mound, needing three outs to win. The first out, a live-drive catch by Dominic Costantino that is described in detail during the chapter on Dominic later in this book, invigorated Eddie briefly, but a walk and an error put runners on first and second with two outs. With the count on the next hitter at 2-and-2, Mike put down the curveball sign, knowing that Eddie's deuce usually dipped below the strike zone and often spun into the dirt. Eddie threw it. The batter swung and missed, Mike excavated the pitch, and we had a 6-5 victory and a trip to Kennewick, Wash., for the West Divisional the following week.

For the tournament, Mike Walsh threw out five of nine would-be base-stealers and wasn't charged with a single passed ball while catching all 28 innings over the final two days. "He's been our unsung hero," Bud said afterward, "and I don't know where we would be without him."

With him, they were on their way to the moonscape of eastern Washington, and an experience that in some ways was right out of *National Geographic*, even for the relatively experienced travelers in our troupe.

Kennewick is one of the Tri-Cities (Pasco and Richland are the others), which in 1978 had barely enough commercial air service to get the players there in time for their divisional opener against the host team, on Wednesday, August 16. During their stay in Kennewick and environs, the players were housed by local families instead of in common barracks, as had been done in San Bernardino and Williamsport. I heard nothing to indicate that the Tri-Cities families and hosts were anything but hospitable to the kids, and they were unremittingly accommodating to the rest of us, but I do know that the players' frequent separation from their teammates, coaches and parents was uncomfortable for some of them.

Just as the Eastern humidity had proved an unpleasant revelation to the Little League players two years before, most of the Pony League players had never been in an environment as stark as the Palouse before. As had been the case two years earlier in Williamsport, the parents and camp followers were late arrivals. (Most of the parents drove the 630 miles from Campbell to Kennewick; I flew up the morning of the first game, traveling the final leg from Portland on a plane that made me wonder if I was heading for Kitty Hawk instead of Kennewick, and drove back with Steve Clinton's family in their station wagon. With Bill and Donna Clinton and I tag-teaming the driving, we drove all night after the conclusion of the final game, and got back to Campbell around 5 in the morning.) And as had been the case in Williamsport, rain was to play a role in Kennewick.

The bracket was disadvantageous; after playing the Tri-Cities team — which turned out to be fairly good, even though it had been seeded through to this tournament and was playing its first game — on Wednesday, we'd have to play again the next day, while Southwest Seattle, which we had been told was one of the best Pony League teams ever to come out of the Puget Sound area, got a bye on Thursday. Another participant in the tournament was Wilmington, a Southern California team that physically was the equivalent of the Arizona squad that had seemed so intimidating two years before in San Bernardino. Because we figured our toughest tests would come against Southwest Seattle and Wilmington, Bud held Rich back and had Paul Sargis pitch the first game against Tri-Cities. He responded with his second straight shutout, a three-hitter for a 3-0 victory, and suicide-squeezed home one of the runs. Chuck Calhoun, Bud Stallings' coach, was a career-long exponent of the squeeze bunt, and we used it so often that during the postseason banquet, the kids presented him with a T-shirt reading "Squeeze Calhoun" that he wore proudly for years afterward. Chuck, though demanding during games and practices, had a rapport with the kids and was able to see the world through their 14-year-old eyes; after we won the World Series, Chuck snuck them a couple of beers in the austere barracks in which the teams were housed.

Rich was in vintage form the following night against Wilmington, coming within a bloop single of a no-hitter as we won 1-0 to advance to the winners-bracket final against Southwest Seattle on Friday night, August 19.

Up to that point, through both tournaments, we had been doing just enough to win, but Bud knew that pitching alone could only carry us so far, especially since Southwest Seattle had been able to save its best pitcher for the game against us. Virtually everybody on the team was in the midst of a hitting malaise, and our only run in the Wilmington game had scored on a three-base outfield error and a wild pitch.

Even after that win, Bud seemed distracted by a sense of foreboding, and some of us worried that the kids were similarly pessimistic. Even our defense hadn't been particularly sharp, and we knew that if the bats weren't bestirred soon, we were headed for trouble.

We had no way of knowing, of course, that for the first time in their travels, our kids would be facing somebody they would have to pay major league ticket prices to see pitch a decade later. Mike Campbell was the Seattle Mariners' first-round draft choice in 1985 out of the University of Hawaii; he made his debut with the Mariners two years later, and spent parts of six seasons with the Mariners, San Diego Padres and Chicago Cubs. On that night under dim lights in Kennewick, we saw him, but not well, and what he didn't do to us in a 6-4 victory, we did to ourselves.

An error on what should have been a double-play ball cost us three runs in the first inning. Campbell struggled with his control in the third and fourth, enabling us to tie the game as John Murphy doubled home two runs in the third and forced home the tying run when he was hit by a pitch with the bases loaded in the fourth. Murphy, the starting pitcher, had been taken out in the second in favor of Bobby Straight, who pitched well before surrendering the three deciding runs in the top of the seventh.

I ran into Bud late that evening, and he was badly in need of encouragement, as I knew the kids were as well. I don't know whether what I said reassured him, but it was to the effect that his relationship with these players, and all of the boys he had managed over the past decade, would not be changed by the outcome of this tournament. We were scheduled to play Wilmington the following night in an elimination game, and Bud had planned a short practice for that morning. He cancelled it, instead sending the kids off to a swim party at the home of one of the host families. Everyone went except Billy Roberts, who was in a slump that had prompted Bud to consider benching him even though doing so would have weakened our outfield defense. Throughout his career, which was to include a Central Coast Section championship at Prospect High and then a state community college title at Mission College in Santa Clara, Billy tended to take adversity as a personal affront and sift through every possible solution until he found the right one. There was a batting cage near the Kennewick ballpark; Billy was in the cage for a couple of hours, and when he left, he was smiling for the first time in a couple of weeks.

That night against Wilmington, Billy came up with runners on second and third in the first inning, and singled them both home. He had another RBI single, as did Steve Clinton, in the sixth, and pitcher Paul Sargis tightroped his way through an 8-4 victory. The next day, we faced the same win-twice-or-else dilemma that had confronted us against Diablo Valley, but the kids were invigorated by the combination of the swim party, the fact we had regained our equilibrium against Wilmington, and the knowledge that even though we hadn't been able to beat Mike Campbell two days earlier, we had gotten good swings against him and were not perplexed by his velocity or his off-speed offerings.

On Sunday morning, the kids were drenched again, and this time it wasn't by swimming-pool water. A rainstorm descended early in the morning, and the possibility of a postponement had everyone, especially the local Pony League organizers, scrambling around the ballpark like Wall Street stockbrokers on Black Friday in 1929. Eventually, they brought in a helicopter to dry the field, just as Little League World Series officials had done in Williamsport in 1976, and the first game started on schedule at 2 p.m.

Southwest Seattle held Mike Campbell out of the first game, and we pummeled their other pitchers, winning 12-0 in a game that was shortened to five innings by the tournament mercy rule. Rich started the game, but was taken out in favor of Brett Blackwell after three innings so that he could start and pitch his allotted four innings in the second game. Brett, who had been hit hard by Diablo Valley in the previous tournament, was so effective that Bud decided to go with him again for the final three innings of the second game.

Mike Campbell started the second game, but he presented no mystery this time. We scored three runs off him in the first, and Billy hit a two-run homer in the third to put us up 5-1. Rich wasn't sharp in the first inning, but limited the damage to one run with the help of a fine defensive play by Eddie Rodriguez at first. His final three innings were up to his usual standards, and Brett held Southwest Seattle hitless over the final three innings. Mike Walsh, who again caught every inning in the tournament without a passed ball, even came close to a home run in the sixth when he doubled off the left-field wall. "Some of the local fans told me that of all our players," Bud said afterward, "Mike impressed them the most."

One of Bud's other changes after the Southwest Seattle loss was to insert Scott Freear in center field and move Billy Roberts to left, leaving Harold Sutherland, who had been the regular left fielder, on the bench. Scott played well in our final three wins in Kennewick, and Harold, who'd been an All-Star as a 13-year-old the previous year and certainly must have expected his status as a starter to be safe, showed himself to be as good a teammate as he was a player.

"Harold could have sat in the corner of the dugout and pouted," Bud said. "Instead, he was the loudest player on our bench, was always on top of what was going on, and was handing all the batters their helmets. He's a fantastic kid."

The celebration literally lasted only as long as it took to get the equipment packed. The 27th Pony League World Series, in National City, Calif., was to start the next day, on August 21 (although our first game wasn't until the 23rd). For most of us, it meant an all-night drive home, a day of doing laundry and then another day of travel. Fortunately, we had learned from the Williamsport experience, and had planned ahead. We already had motel reservations — we were not on a hotel budget — and getting to San Diego didn't present the same degree of difficulty (or expense) that we'd faced two years earlier in transit to San Bernardino and then Williamsport. Nor was there the first-visit apprehension that many of us had felt on our way to Williamsport. Most of us had been to San Diego before, and we assumed that National City, just to the south, would be an extension of "America's Finest City." Each day, we thought, we'd have breakfast on the lanai overlooking Mission Bay, enjoy a leisurely salt-water swim, take in SeaWorld, see the Padres, lounge around beneath palm trees in the 80-degree weather while being invigorated by the ocean air, then head for a beautiful mini-MLB ballpark to watch our team win the World Series.

Except for seeing the Padres and winning the World Series, it didn't turn out that way. From the time we arrived in National City, we were incredulous that it had been allowed to host the World Series, which usually was held at the organization's national headquarters in Washington, Pa. The team was housed in surplus Marine barracks on the nearby Camp Pendleton base, with the amenities one might expect in such a place. Our motels were ratty, and Kimball Park, which didn't even have a grass infield, looked like a recreational softball field, with no more than a few hundred seats and lights that were so bad that we might have donned miners helmets instead of caps if we'd had them. In Williamsport, the organizing committee brought in Hall of Famers like Joe DiMaggio and Ernie Banks; in National City, we got Bob Barton, a retired Padres reserve catcher who was selling insurance in the San Diego area. He spoke at the World Series banquet, which was held in a National Guard armory.

National City turned out to be an industrial port city of 45,000 that offered nothing in the way of recreation except for the fact it adjoined the Mexican border. Some of the parents made day trips to San Diego, and a few of us went to Tijuana. Harold Sutherland, Mike Walsh and I bought hats from a street peddler while the three of us were exploring Tijuana; Mike and Harold thought the hats were hilarious and wore them almost everywhere except the ballpark, but the parents and kids teased me so incessantly about my "pimp" hat that it never saw the light of day again. Mostly, the kids sat around their barracks and entertained themselves as best they could; in my conversations with them, the prevailing sentiment was along these lines: "Let's win this thing and get the hell out of here."

Five teams were in the tournament – Tampa, Fla.; Guyanboa, Puerto Rico; Joliet, Ill.; the host team, and us. We figured that Tampa would be the best of the other four teams. They had the only future major leaguer in the World Series – Lance McCullers, a burly pitcher who was with the Padres, Yankees, Rangers and Tigers from 1985-92 – and I found out later that one of the Tampa-area teams they had beaten in early-tournament play was led by Dwight Gooden. But as it turned out, we never had to face McCullers or Tampa. Joliet beat the Florida team in the first round, and it was subsequently eliminated by Puerto Rico.

We had a bye in the first round and were matched against Puerto Rico in the second. For six innings, Rich was Rich, and we took a 5-0 lead into the seventh. At that point, Rich weakened and I was somewhat surprised that Bud stayed with him, but Rich got to the finish line with a nine-strikeout four-hitter, and we won 5-1. That sent us up against Joliet in the winners-bracket final. Paul Sargis pitched the first five innings, allowing only one hit and Joliet's lone run. Bob Straight finished up, allowing only one baserunner, who was promptly gunned down by Walsh while trying to steal. Eddie Rodriguez bunted for a hit in the third – the fourth in a string of five straight hits for Eddie – and then stole second, advanced to third on an outfield fly and scored when the outfielder threw wildly. In the sixth, with the score still tied 1-1, Billy led off with a shot into the left-center field gap, and although he could have settled for an easy double, he was in triple mode from the time he left the batters box. The left fielder's hurried throw to third was wide; Billy got up and trotted home on the error for what turned out to be the winning run. We got another run in the seventh on Rich's single, a sacrifice and Billy's single, and held on to win 3-1 and advance to the finals.

Joliet beat Puerto Rico on Saturday to earn the right to face us the following day. In the previous two tournaments, we'd had to come through the losers bracket and win a doubleheader on Sunday, and Bud had been obliged to piece together a pitching rotation. This time, it was we who needed only one win in two games, and it was we who had Rich in the first game. He brought us the World Series championship on the afternoon of August 27, 1978, and he brought himself a measure of youth-baseball immortality.

The strain of the previous three weeks had taken its toll on Rich, It was hot that day, although not as hot as it had been during that Sunday doubleheader in the first tournament, and although the Joliet team didn't have anyone who represented a power threat against Rich, its hitters wielded their bats like swords, taking a lot of pitches and fouling off a lot of others to force Rich into deep counts throughout the game. He wound up throwing 117 pitches over the seven-inning distance, and walked six. Thirty years later, after managers on all levels of baseball became obsessed with pitch counts and some youth-baseball organizations began enforcing pitch limits, there would have been no way Rich would have been allowed to finish the game. Even in 1978, the only reason Bud left him in was the zero in the hit column that beamed from the scoreboard like a lighthouse beacon. He struck out 13, and only two Joliet hitters even were able to pull the ball to the left side of the infield against him.

When Rich's control wavered, Mike took control of the tempo of the game and steadied Rich. He also threw out another would-be base stealer, giving him 12 such assists in 18 attempts during the postseason. To put that in perspective, a 1:3 ratio is considered good even in major league baseball, where pitchers and catchers both throw far harder than they do in Pony League. Ivan Rodriguez, who won 10 Gold Gloves from 1992-2001 and is considered by many the best defensive catcher who ever lived, earned his niche in baseball folklore by throwing out 56 percent of the runners who tried to steal on him from 1997-99. Mike was at 67 percent for the 1978 postseason, and he was working with pitchers who were still learning the finer points of pitching out of the stretch and holding runners on base. He kept intact his string of 14 games without a passed ball, and his backup, Glenn Davis, did not catch more than a couple of innings in the entire postseason.

With Rich and Mike collaborating to keep Joliet at bay, we knew one run probably would win this game ... and Billy, who had been a terror at the plate since his batting-cage session in Kennewick, provided it in the fourth. Going to the opposite field, he banged a double to right-center field, and after Paul Sargis walked, Albert Vanegas chopped a single into left-center to bring Billy home. It was an appropriate denouement for Albert, who had sat on the bench throughout most of the 1976 Williamsport run and during the first two 1978 tournaments. But

Bud, who always had an eye for rewarding players who maintained their work habits and enthusiasm despite minimal playing time, started Albert at second base in the World Series, and Albert had four hits in nine at-bats in the tournament.

Paul went to third on Albert's single, and Scott Freear, another player who had begun the tournament trek as a reserve, brought him home with a sacrifice fly to put us up 2-0. That concluded the scoring, and all that was left was to watch Rich pursue the first championship-game no-hitter in the history of the Pony League World Series.

He was in serious trouble only once, in the sixth when the first two Joliet hitters drew walks, with the second, third and fourth spots in the batting order coming up. Rich popped up the No. 2 hitter, struck out the No. 3 hitter, and retired the No. 4 hitter on another infield pop. In the seventh, with his final tank of adrenaline kicking in, Rich retired the side in order. The last out was a routine fly ball to left fielder Billy Roberts, who let out a yelp that was audible throughout the ballpark as the team rushed to the mound to congratulate Rich.

Billy, of course, was from Moreland and hadn't been part of the 1976 Little League thrill ride. Much later, he told me that his exhilaration was such that he could barely remember the putout itself, only the gush of emotion and vindication he felt. He also was surprised that the postgame celebration was as subdued as it was; although the joy permeated the scene, most of the players took their cues from Rich and Bud and the quiet inner glow that radiated from them.

"Two things about this team come to mind immediately," said Bud, who tended to speak in terms of posterity rather than immediacy in situations like these. "They were a very composed team under pressure. At no time did they buckle when things got tough. And they were a very self-motivated group. We had virtually no behavior problems. Once I told them to do something, I seldom had to say it again.

"Another thing about this team was its determination to prove itself between the lines. There wasn't much verbal heckling, and the team was compassionate toward the teams it beat. I believe the team jelled during the first tournament when we beat Diablo Valley. Sometime during that first game (of the Sunday doubleheader we had to sweep), everything just came together and we became a tight, cohesive team."

For the postseason, Rich was 7-1 with a 1.29 ERA, and Paul was 4-0 with the two shutouts. Eddie led us with a .389 batting average, followed by Billy (.349) and Rich (.344).

Even if their home town didn't recognize the enormity of what they had done — there was no civic celebration or motorcade, as had taken place in 1976 — the players certainly did. Rich's uniform was sent to the Baseball Hall of Fame in Cooperstown, N.Y., and is still there, kept in storage much of the time but displayed in a regular rotation along with other artifacts in the

Hall's youth baseball wing. Outwardly, that distinction didn't change him; to his teammates, he remained one of the guys, and to the adults, he remained one of the kids whose élan, charm and exuberance were ingrained in our minds long after we'd forgotten all the game details. But while that title represented a springboard for most of the kids, it turned out to be a culmination for Rich Alvarez and Bud Stallings.

Most of the players on the '78 team were ticketed for Campbell High — in fact, Mike Walsh and Paul Sargis already had completed their freshman years there — and Campbell coach Gordon Huntze still smiles dreamily when he thinks of what that group might have accomplished on the high school level had Campbell not been closed in 1980. After that, Mike Walsh, Bobby Straight and Paul Sargis joined Steve Clinton, who already was at Westmont. Harold Sutherland and Eric Crawford already were in Prospect's district and spent four years there, and Billy Roberts transferred there after Campbell's closure. John Murphy, Scott Freear, Rich Alvarez and Eddie Rodriguez all started at Campbell and graduated from Blackford, joining Brett Blackwell there.

In 1982, Westmont and Prospect finished first and second respectively in the West Valley Athletic League to qualify for the Central Coast Section playoffs, and Blackford probably would have reached the postseason as well if more than two teams from each league were eligible. In the CCS semifinals, Prospect beat Barry Bonds and Serra 7-0 — in a game during which Bonds, playing center field, ignored a cutoff man and made a homeward throw that went into the stands at San Jose Muni on the fly — while Westmont defeated Mills 8-6, making the sectional championship game a veritable Campbell scrimmage. Municipal Stadium was packed that night, and they saw both a testimonial and an end to a youth baseball dynasty that could trace its roots all the way back to 1909 and Campbell High's first Interurban Athletic Union championship.

Myself, I was rooting for two weeks of rain, a cancellation of the game and the awarding of a co-championship, because I had so many friends in both dugouts. One of the benefits, in fact perhaps the only benefit, of Campbell High's closure was that some of the second-tier Campbell players who might not have gotten a chance to develop and emerge at Campbell High wound up being quality players at Prospect, Westmont, Blackford and Del Mar. Tony Kephart, always a favorite of mine even though he had never been an All-Star in Campbell, was a good example. Gordon, who also liked Tony, probably would have been hard-pressed to find playing time for him at Campbell High, but Tony started for him at Westmont. Ironically, two Prospect starters who also fit into that late-bloomer category were Gordon's twin sons, Jim and Jeff, although the Huntzes lived in Prospect's district before Campbell's closure and were unaffected by the reshuffling of boundaries.

Westmont led 7-5 going to the bottom of the seventh inning, and Prospect was down to its last strike when Harold Sutherland tied the score with a two-run, two-out single. Rob Goddard, one of the few players on either team who hadn't been weaned in the Campbell system, then singled Harold home with the winning run in Prospect's 8-7 victory. Joray Marrujo, who played on

Campbell Moreland Pony League's repeat World Series championship team in 1979, was the winning pitcher in relief.

Although I don't remember seeing him at Muni that night, I'm sure Rich Alvarez was there. At Campbell and then Blackford, he had remained a dominant pitcher, and he had never lost and never did lose the outward humility that makes him such an enduring and endearing factor to this day among those who knew him. But perhaps it was inevitable that a player who had achieved so much at such a young age might lose some of his inner fire. Gordon Huntze brought him up to the Campbell High varsity as a freshman in 1979, something I couldn't remember him ever having done with a ninth grader before.

Rich pitched two-hit shutout ball over five innings in his first outing for Campbell High, a 3-0 victory over North Salinas in the Soquel tournament. In retrospect, though, Gordon thought it might have been a mistake to elevate Rich to the varsity immediately.

"He didn't want to work hard that first year," Gordon said. "Joe (his brother) had pitched for me before, and he was a guy who worked his butt off. Rich had something (in the way of talent) going on ... I hate to say it, but he was kind of a prima donna. He was late to practice, and he didn't want to work hard in school. Finally, I called his mom and told her I'd like to sit down with them. I told them that he wasn't going to play that week, and I told them why. That made a difference, but it happened more than once while he played for me."

After Rich transferred to Blackford, he had no Huntze-like influences, and for the first time in their lives, Rich and the other former Campbell High players were surrounded by teammates and schoolmates who knew nothing about collective success and were motivated by their own self-interests, if they were motivated at all. Some, like Eddie Rodriguez and John Murphy, rose above their Blackford experiences. Rich did not. The fact he was drafted by the White Sox out of high school and was recruited by the University of Hawaii, with which he eventually signed, was the product of his youth-baseball reputation more than anything he did at Blackford. He was having arm trouble even before he graduated from high school; that summer, when he played for me in Legion, he couldn't pitch at all until our final game. He was a reserve for one season at Hawaii before breaking his collarbone in a body-surfing accident, and although he tried to come back, the production bar had been raised beyond his grasp, and he never played competitively again.

It is to Rich's immense credit that he became a success in the working world – as of 2009, he was living in Palm Desert and working for the Allstate insurance company – and for all of those who knew him in Campbell, memories of the player he was and the person he is resonate far more than any thoughts we might have about what might have been for him in baseball.

"He was really gifted," Gordon Huntze said. "He had so much ability and so much success early. It's too bad (that the latter stages of his career weren't as successful). He needed direction, probably still needed direction when he was 25, and Hawaii wasn't a good place for him at that time in his life. But mostly, I enjoyed Rich. You always think of him as a good kid."

As for Bud, I don't think he was at that Prospect-Westmont game, and a month or so later, when he died, we knew why.

I don't think he told anyone except a couple of families with whom he was particularly close, but he had been grievously ill for some time. To this day, many of the guys he coached and befriended at Campbell still feel a sense of emptiness when we talk about Bud. He enriched all of our lives, to be sure, but there was so much that we wanted him to know but never got a chance to tell him. He never got a chance to meet his kids' kids, or to see that the young men about whom he cared so much would turn out to be even better as husbands and fathers and workers and citizens than they were as baseball players.

Somewhere, he's still proud.

1979 CAMPBELL LITTLE LEAGUE: The Campbell Clones

I only wrote two stories about this most Campbell of all Campbell baseball teams during the summer of 1979. The second was a column in which I described sitting in the stands at Campbell Little League, listening to a piped-in radio broadcast of the Little League World Series championship game. My most poignant memory of the first story was the byline. I had just been hired fulltime by the *Peninsula Times Tribune* in Palo Alto, where I was to spend the next 13 years, and this was the first story I ever wrote in which the byline read "Times Tribune Staff" instead of "Special to the Times Tribune." Most of my lifetime up to that point had been devoted to attaining that "staff" designation, and now I finally had it.

As my first assignment, my boss had sent me to cover the District 11 championship game at the Palo Alto Little League complex, which I remember primarily because it had the first artificial mound I had ever seen. (It was made from some kind of rubber-type substance, and the pitchers had to wear tennis shoes while working off it.) Mountain View National won the game, over Menlo Park National, and there was much talk among the parents sitting around me about how far their team could go in the postseason. Although District 11 was far weaker than District 44, I knew a lot of the baseball operatives in Mountain View, and I was aware that it was a good baseball town, even though Campbell and Mountain View teams rarely played. The two Little Leagues there, National and North, had won four straight District 11 championships and five of the previous seven between them, and this was supposed to be the best team the city had produced up to that point.

Afterward, I talked to the Mountain View National manager, and I asked him about his team's prospects in the upcoming sectional tournament. "I think we've got a very good team," he said (and I'm paraphrasing him here, because I didn't save a copy of the story), "but our first game is against District 44, and that probably means Campbell. So we know we're going to have to play our best game to beat them. We know they've been to Williamsport twice and we respect what they've done, but we want to make sure our kids don't fear them."

Although having to play Campbell represented good reason for trepidation in the 1960s and 1970s, that may have been the only time during Campbell Little League's 1979 postseason that the word "fear" ever came up in connection with that team.

I wasn't around the league much that year and I was only vaguely familiar with the All-Star team's personnel, but I did know that anybody who feared playing Campbell hadn't seen the team photo. In 1962, Moreland Little League had 6-foot-1, 210-pound Ted Campbell. Tom Davis was not much smaller than that in 1970 when he led Campbell to the World Series final, and six years later when Campbell returned to Williamsport, its No. 1 pitcher was Rich Alvarez, who was about 5-foot-7 and built like a linebacker, and we also had John Aimonetti, who later was an NFL offensive lineman. In 1979, Campbell's best pitcher would be Rob Fraka, who was 5-foot-2 and wasn't going to have anyone at the All-Star level cowering on appearance alone.

A month later, as his team prepared to play Taiwan for the World Series championship, catcher Matt Allison described his team this way: "We're all even. No big guys. Everybody is the same." Shortstop Greg Mitchell called Campbell "a bunch of clones," and while I'm not sure it was Greg who first coined the phrase, it stuck. Matt was 5-foot, 87 pounds, and Greg was an inch shorter and the same weight. Fraka, center fielder Jim Zaccheo and left fielder David Carlson were a little bigger, but not much, and I doubt that they collectively outsized any of the 14 teams they had beaten to get to the World Series final against Taiwan, which had a lineup consisting of nobody *shorter* than 5-4.

Yet the Campbell Clones compensated for their lack of size with efficiency, quickness and effervescence that made rooters out of neutrals to a greater degree than any of their Campbell predecessors. It's doubtful that any non-Pennsylvania team in the history of the Little League World Series enjoyed the home-crowd advantage that Campbell had on Saturday, August 25, 1979, at Lamade Stadium, where it faced down the ultimate Little League fear factor and almost brought off what would have been the most monumental upset in LLWS history up to that time (and maybe since).

The Campbell Clones may have looked shapeless. But they were never spineless.

The 1979 Little League All-Star manager was Subby Agliolo, who had been one of my favorite people in my days at Campbell Little League. Subby was restrained, patient and gentle in his dealings with his players, and his demeanor never changed regardless of how well or how poorly his team was playing. Subby saw his function as a Little League manager in a far broader context than baseball; he cared not at all about padding individual stats or going to excessive lengths to win, and he wanted his kids to come away from their Little League experience with a sense that they'd done something fulfilling, regardless of their talent level. His goal, above all else, was to not be anybody's last coach; he considered any season a success when all of his players wanted to continue on in baseball.

In 1979, the word I was hearing early that summer was that Campbell was weaker in terms of talent than it had been at any time during the 1970s. There was one very good pitcher, Fraka, and a bunch of other kids who were readily taught and led but were modest in stature compared to our 1970 and 1976 teams. Subby's Doetsch Building team had won the regular-season championship, and the custom at the time was that the manager of the championship team got the All-Star team if he wanted it. From what I had heard, though, Subby was the only manager who wanted the team anyway.

Well, Subby saw something.

At age 73, Sebastian "Subby" Agliolo in 2008 lived in retirement in Spanish Springs, Nev., about 30 miles northeast of Reno. Although he hadn't coached formally since leaving Campbell in the early 1980s, he still worked with his five baseball-playing grandsons. As with most of the Campbell people with whom I reconnected while researching this book, Subby warmed to the subjects at hand – not only his stewardship of the 1979 team, but his Campbell experience in its totality – with a sense of reverence and gratefulness. Even though I hadn't seen him since he left California, we greeted each other as if it were a reunion of kindred souls, and our talk went far beyond the conventional interview process he experienced so often in the aftermath of the 1979 Little League World Series.

He hadn't changed much; he was still expansive and his voice tinged with emotion when he talked about his former players – especially David DeCarlo and Steve Tonini, who'd played on his regular-season team for three years before their shared All-Star experience. And he was still forthright as ever.

I had always thought of that 1979 Campbell team as an entity that functioned as a single seamless organism from the day it was first assembled. Turns out it didn't, and that the days before the team played its first game represented a continuous scramble.

"They gave me the team, and about a week later we voted on the kids," Subby recalled. "All the names were on the board, and it was (a) good (process) except for one name. Jack Zogg with his verbal attitude forced us to take Ray Hixson (one of Jack's Robins players) on the All-Star team. He kept saying this kid deserves it. I liked other kids better (as potential All-Star contributors) than him, and I told Zogg and the (other manages at the) meeting, 'Don't put him on there, because I'm not going to play him. I'm not going to be mean about it, but he's going on vacation (during the first couple of weeks of practice before the start of the District 44 tournament).' I had principles that I went by, and I didn't want to have a kid on vacation while 13 other kids are out there busting their asses.

"Zogg said, 'You'd be making a mistake,' and the thing that ticked me off about that, we had played Zogg in the (league) championship game, and we beat them and he was pissed. Jack took his team and went to right field (for a postgame debriefing) instead of coming over and shaking hands with us, and it made me so damn angry that I wanted to go over and confront him.

"Then, I said to Jim Martino (his Doetsch Building assistant, who was to be his All-Star coach), 'I don't know what's going on here,' and Jim said, 'I didn't want to tell you until after this game, but I can't go with you (on the All-Star expedition). My company won't (give him the time off work).' I was stunned, because the kids were supposed to report the next day. As it happened, I saw Bill Wright there; he was managing Moose (Campbell Moose Lodge, another major division sponsor) and we were pretty good friends. I said, 'I got a favor to ask. Jim isn't going to be able to coach with me; would you help me coach the All-Stars?'

"Jim helped me as long as he could (before the team advanced beyond the Bay Area tournaments) and I got everyone I possibly could get to help. Dan Watt helped; so did Ed Tonini. We were using all three fields for practice."

Subby went with nine players almost exclusively throughout his team's run to Williamsport; Hixson, Rich Sandifer, Frankie Ortiz, Tonini and Tim Farnham played hardly at all. "They knew (that the nine best players were the ones who would see almost all of the playing time)," Subby said. "Just before we had our first meeting, I told the parents, 'All I can ask is that you trust me. I'll respect the kids and I'll respect you people.' I think they did that all the way back to the World Series.

"A few years ago we had a 25th reunion at the Campbell Little League field, and I took Hixson aside and I apologized to him, and his mother too. It was on my conscience for 25 years, what I did (objecting as strenuously as he did to Hixson's selection).

"I'll be honest ... I wanted to win for the league. That league and that town meant a lot to me, and that was the only reason. I miss it still. We lived in San Jose, but Campbell was my home. I guess it's like that angel on all of our shoulders, and from '76 on, it was like the hunt. The '79 Pony League kids were in Davenport (on their way to the Pony League World Series championship) at the same time we were in Williamsport, and we talked about how we were their little brothers. I still wonder why people don't remember that stuff, that two teams from the same organization were playing for world championships at the same time. I tell people that now and they say, 'You've gotta be kidding me.'

"It was magical. You look at magic and you look at fate."

According to Subby, the convergence of talent and fate began a few days before the team's first game, when he and his wife Carol conducted an informal picnic for the players and their parents.

"Things had started to go pretty good," he said. "I tried to make sure the kids blended well, and I put them in different positions because it's not very fun for them to be playing the same positions all the time. I even put Georgie Tsamis at shortstop even though he was left-handed. Bob (Holman) came by and saw it, and he asked Zogg what the hell I was doing, and Jack said, 'Damned if I know; it's his team.' We played grab-ass at practice sometimes (to help the kids relax).

"My wife said, 'We're going to have a picnic before the games start ... just hot dogs and cokes and potato chips and stuff like that.' So we go to buy the stuff, and what do you think the price was? Nineteen dollars and 79 cents. Nineteen seventy-nine. She's got that receipt still; it was an omen. At that same time, I remember hearing a song ... I can't even tell you who it was by, but it caught my attention, and every day on my way to practice I'd put it on my car cassette player and I'd blare it. I was obsessed with it; I just wish I could remember who sang it."

And Subby, who acknowledged that he would have been happy with a district championship, established an emotional connection with his team that still glowed when he talked about it 30 years later.

"Jimmy Zaccheo ... great kid, really down to earth. He could always make you laugh, but he had a lot of spunk to him, and the other kids really looked up to him. I think a lot of it was because of his broadness ... he would listen very casually to you but he always could put it in perspective."

Zaccheo, usually the starting center fielder, came by his leadership qualities naturally; his father Myron was a longtime football coach at San Jose and Gunderson high schools. Jimmy starred in baseball and football at Blackford High before accepting a football scholarship from the University of Nevada in Reno. There, he became the first of a succession of record-breaking quarterbacks developed by UNR coach Chris Ault during the 1980s and early 1990s, when the program became an NCAA Division I-AA power before moving up to I-A in 1992. Zaccheo stayed in Reno after graduation, and in 2009 was in the construction business there.

As people observed the players disembarking from the bus in Williamsport, the thought must have gone through at least a few minds that Greg Mitchell was the batboy or a team member's little brother. (Actually, Greg, who was known as Greg Vaughn during his early childhood, was the stepbrother of Wes Mitchell, a Campbell High star of the late 1970s, who later reached Class AAA in the Cleveland Indians' organization.) Greg was the smallest and least physically imposing player on the team, but although he didn't swing the bat with the authority that had characterized 1976 shortstop Bobby Straight, Greg was Bobby's defensive equal in terms of range, hands and arm, and it was because of him that Campbell's defense became the team's *nom de guerre*.

"Greg Mitchell was the shortstop ... the smallest kid on the team, but he was our spark on defense ... it was hard to believe sometimes that a little kid could make plays like he made," Subby said of Greg, who later went on to play at Westmont High and San Jose State. "We turned six double plays in Williamsport, and that's pretty amazing for a bunch of 12-year-old kids. He had kind of a (sarcastic) mouth, but he could make you laugh. Good family. I coached his younger brother during the regular season. Terrible, what happened to him.

Jeff Mitchell, who like Greg went on to play baseball at Westmont, turned down several college opportunities and joined the Air Force after graduation. Later, he became a Sacramento County sheriff's deputy. He was fatally shot by a fleeing suspect during a traffic stop in 2006. After his murder, Westmont began conducting a preseason game in his honor. (All of the royalties from this book will be donated to a trust fund that was set up in 2006 to help Jeff's widow, Crystal, and their son Jake.)

Catcher Matt Allison already had been confronted by personal tragedy by the time the 1979 Campbell team went on the junket that was to land them in Williamsport. Kevin Allison, Matt's older brother, came close to making the 1976 Williamsport-bound All-Star team as a 12-year-old. A few months later, Kevin was found to be afflicted with aplastic anemia, a disease that results in white blood cells overwhelming the immune system. The disease was and still is incurable, although it now can be forced into remission, but Kevin still hoped to join his older brother Wade on the Cubs in the Campbell Moreland Pony League. By the start of the season, though, it was apparent that Kevin was weakening, and he died in June, a couple of days after his last appearance at John D. Morgan Park.

Matt Allison was a mischievous, outgoing kid who was a regular in my Campbell Little League scorers booth even though he was a couple of years younger than most of the other kids. After Kevin's death, though, Matt seemed to lose some of his ebullience, and during the team's progression toward Williamsport, those of us who had known him were perhaps happier for him than for anybody else on the 1979 team.

"Matt was a good kid," Subby said. "I called the pitches almost every game, but Matt controlled the pitchers. They (his 1979 pitchers) had only two pitches, but it was two different pitches for each pitcher, and Matt picked that up right away."

Rob Fraka, the focal-point pitcher on the team, was a scaled-down model of 1976's Rich Alvarez, and won seven games for Campbell in the 1979 postseason. He had not played his early Little League seasons in Campbell; his listed address was on Glencrest Way, in Branham Hills Little League's district, and he wound up graduating from Willow Glen High in central San Jose. But he apparently had received a hardship waiver to play in Campbell, because his eligibility wasn't questioned so far as I know. His fastball had neither the velocity nor the late movement that Rich Alvarez's had, but his control was slightly better, and he embraced the importance of his role.

"He was dominant, and I had faith in him," Subby said. "We had five good pitchers, and we could have thrown Mitchell if we'd had to. But the others didn't get you out by throwing the ball by you. Fraka could do that."

Of all the players on the team, Subby said he felt closest to right fielder David DeCarlo, whom he had managed for three years during the regular season. Both David and his older brother Mike went on to achieve athletic and academic success at St. Francis High in Mountain View, one of the more demanding schools in the area in both fields of endeavor, and Mike later went on to coach basketball at St. Francis. David had a son playing in Moreland Little League in 2009.

"David I loved like my son, I had him so long," Subby said. "We were really close. He always said I taught him how to pitch, and I was really proud that he did well at St. Francis. Steve Tonini I also had during the regular season, and I felt really close to him too. He was really little, but what we asked him to do, he did."

This was the last year of the single-elimination era in Little League postseason play, and Campbell narrowly escaped defeat in its very first game, a 1-0 win over Sunnyvale Serra. But as the team's winning streak lengthened — it reached 14 games before it was ended by Taiwan in the LLWS finals — Subby quickly realized that even though none of his pitchers had the size or velocity of a Rich Alvarez, his staff probably had more depth than its counterparts of three and nine years before. "George Tsamis was my lefty," he said. "We had Fraka, who was the ace of the staff, but DeCarlo, Carlson, (David) Niemeyer and Zaccheo all were good. There were no Alvarezes or (Paul) Sargises; they were all pretty much equal. In Williamsport they called us the 'clones' because almost all of our guys were the same size, maybe 5-foot-1 and 90, 95 pounds.

"There was no comparison (in terms of athletic ability) between us and the '76 team; the '76 team was better all the way around. But we just kept playing and kept winning."

After the win over Sunnyvale Serra, in which Fraka pitched a one-hitter and struck out 12, Campbell beat Cupertino Pacific 13-0, Cupertino National 4-0 and Santa Clara Homestead 9-2 to win the District 44 title. In the sectional tournament, Campbell defeated Mountain View National 8-4, Pacifica 8-4 and San Benito 10-5 to advance to the regional in Antioch. There, Campbell survived its stiffest challenge since its district opener, beating Red Bluff 4-2 in 10 innings, to advance to the final against host Antioch East.

"(Catcher) Matt Allison hurt his thumb (in the Red Bluff game) and (Tim) Farnham had done a good job for (Willow Glen Optimist manager Tony) Mimosa, so I put him in," Subby said. "We're leading by two runs, and one of their guys lays down a bunt. Farnham picks it up and nails the guy in the back of the head. You could see he was really upset ... Bill (Wright) is next to me and said to me, 'You have to get him out of there,' So I took him out and told David Carlson (who was playing left field) to put on the gear, even though he hadn't caught before. So he's catching ... around the fifth inning, man on third, a guy hits a shot to center field. Zaccheo came in and dove and made a great play on the ball, but he trapped it and the umpire called (the batter) safe."

But the runner on third never scored, because Zaccheo got to his feet immediately and pegged home, and Carlson slapped a tag on the baserunner, who wasn't sure whether the ball had been caught on the fly or not. Steve Tonini, who had gone into the outfield to replace Carlson, sized up the situation immediately and alerted Zaccheo to the possibility of a play at the plate.

"He got him," Subby said. "The crowd goes nuts. We win the game and get to the finals, and Farnham's dad (instead of being upset because his son had been taken out of the game) is out there in the parking lot handing out champagne (to other Campbell parents) and having a little party. They're on Cloud Nine. We go on and win the game (against Antioch East), and we're in the parking lot celebrating. We weren't even supposed to win a game, and we're on our way to San Bernardino (for the West Regional)."

Once they arrived there, the players and coaches were assigned to a barracks on the compound. Barracks or no, though, Subby didn't want his players to think of their upcoming challenge as a militaristic objective. He wanted a relaxed team, and he got it.

"I gave them the schedule, and I told them, when we go to meals or to practice, we will walk together, and I want you guys together when we go, no matter where we are," Subby said. "Otherwise, we left them alone. One day we were out on a knoll by the ballpark, practicing, and I look around and I see the team we're supposed to play the next day, sitting there watching us. So we just told the kids to start playing grab-ass. They were throwing balls at each other, tackling each other, and after about 15 minutes the other team just walked away, and I said, OK, let's get back to practice."

Campbell opened the regional by defeating Mount Hood, Ore., 6-0.

"That team was like a basketball team, with a lot of tall guys, but we just kicked their butts," Subby said. "Then (in the semifinals against Sunnyside of Tucson, Ariz.) we're up 8-1 and we put (a couple of the reserves) in. They made three errors and all of a sudden it's 8-6. We got them (the non-starters) out of there and David (DeCarlo) came in (to pitch) and got us out of a jam and we held on to win (9-8). Then we played Goleta Valley (the Southern California champion) in the finals and beat them good (11-3)."

In Williamsport, the field, as in 1976, was bracketed to assure a championship game involving a U.S. team against a non-U.S. team. Joining Campbell in the American bracket were Grosse Point, Mich.; North Little Rock, Ark.; and Ridgewood, N.J. The foreign bracket consisted of Sherbrooke, Quebec, Canada; Aviano Air Force Base, Italy; Santurce, Puerto Rico; and the prohibitive favorite, Pu Tzu Town of Taiwan.

Taiwan had won six of the previous eight Little League World Series, including the previous two. In 1975, Taiwan and other foreign teams had been refused entry into the postseason because of eligibility irregularities, and in 1976, Japan had knocked Taiwan off in the Far East regional to reach Williamsport, where it had beaten Campbell in the championship game. From 1969, when Taiwan won the World Series for the first time by beating Santa Clara Briarwood with Carney Lansford, through 1996, Taiwan won 17 of the 28 World Series played, and was ineligible for most of the others. Detractors, most of them in the U.S., claimed (and more than once, proved) that Taiwan grouped most of the island nation's best players onto one regular-season team, so that the team that advanced to Williamsport would in effect be a national youth team. When a U.S. team did manage to beat Taiwan in Williamsport — as Kirkland, Wash., did in 1982 and Trumbull, Conn. did in 1989 — comparisons were made between those victories and the U.S. team's gold medal in the 1980 Winter Olympic ice hockey tournament, and players such as Kirkland pitcher Cody Webster and Trumbull star Chris Drury — a future National Hockey League All-Star — became national celebrities.

In 1979, Campbell had a future major leaguer on its roster — George Tsamis, the first baseman and No. 2 pitcher — but neither he nor any of his teammates intimidated anyone with their size, as Webster and Drury and their teammates subsequently did. Mark Phillips and Greg Mitchell later played at San Jose State, and Jim Zaccheo was a record-setting quarterback at the University of Nevada, but it wasn't a team that passed the so-called "airport test." They knew relatively little had been expected of them by outsiders, and they seemed to revel in their underdog status.

Almost all of the talk in Williamsport before and during the early stages of the tournament centered on Taiwan, whose presence there had become heavily politicized, and not only because of the widespread belief that that Nationalist Chinese baseball establishment was cheating. Earlier in 1979, President Jimmy Carter had established official diplomatic relations with the Communist regime in mainland China, from which Taiwan had broken away in 1949, calling its government the true voice of the Chinese people. Before 1979, Taiwan had been politically recognized as such by the U.S., the United Nations and most nations outside the Soviet bloc, but after mainland China established diplomatic relations with the U.S., Taiwan's diplomatic recognition as China's international voice was withdrawn, and it lost its UN seat.

Its government, seeking to reclaim its lost status, tried to use the Little League World Series as a political pulpit in 1979. Several hundred flag-waving Nationalist Chinese citizens were in the stands at Lamade Stadium when the Taiwanese team played. (Most, of course, had no connection with the team itself except their shared nationality.) Calling themselves citizens of the "Republic of China," they handed out leaflets and tried to convince American fans of the legitimacy of their claim that Taiwan's government represented the interests of all Chinese. The American fans, of course, were there to watch baseball and were extremely unhappy with the introduction of politics into a baseball tournament for 12-year-olds, and the Taiwanese efforts to create sympathy for their cause backfired on them and on their nation's team. The

Taiwanese team was booed at times during its World Series games, and almost all of the neutral fans rooted hard for Taiwan's opponent.

Campbell began tournament play with an 8-5 victory over Grosse Point that served as a showcase for second baseman David Niemeyer, who had been a steady but unspectacular contributor up to that point.

As had happened with Rich Alvarez in 1976, Fraka was taken ill before the team's first game in Williamsport, and a 102-degree fever and the Eastern humidity left him far from full strength. He had a 4-0 lead after four innings as Niemeyer singled home a run in the first and hit a two-run homer in the second, but Fraka couldn't survive the fifth. He was raked for five runs before Agliolo came out to relieve him, although Rob was able to convince Subby to let him stay in the game and play left field, where he made a tumbling catch in the sixth.

Niemeyer took over on the mound and got an inning-ending strikeout, but Campbell was down 5-4. He then doubled to lead off the bottom of the fifth, and scored on Fraka's single as Campbell put together the game-deciding four-run rally. Right fielder Mark Phillips made two running catches in the final two inning to help Niemeyer finish.

In the other first-round games, Taiwan defeated Puerto Rico 3-0 as Dai Han-Chou pitched a one-hitter, and the European team, consisting as usual of dependents of American military personnel stationed overseas, won a Series game for the first time ever, beating Canada 4-3. That left Aviano with the daunting task of facing Taiwan in one semifinal, while North Little Rock defeated Ridgewood 3-1 to move into the U.S. championship game against Campbell.

"We (the coaching staff) didn't think we'd beat Little Rock," Subby said almost 30 years later. "They had a great club, and the Michigan team was pretty good too. But it seemed like we were destined to play Taiwan because they were everywhere we went. We were the last team to arrive (in Williamsport), and when we got off the bus, a lot of people were watching to see how many giants would get off. I guess we disappointed them. So we get off and a team father took us to our cabin ... a lot of different teams were there, and we passed by Taiwan. Where do you think our practice fields were? Right next to ours, and we were hitting balls to each other in the outfield. Where do you think we ate? Right next to them. They wanted to play us in the finals, and that's what happened."

Campbell earned its berth in the finals by beating North Little Rock 8-3 as George Tsamis pitched a three-hitter to earn his fourth postseason victory. He struck out only four, but seldom strayed from the strike zone and stayed away from the Arkansas hitters' kill zones. The result was a succession of ground balls and pop flies, and although Campbell made four errors in the game, none of them resulted in serious damage. Campbell staked Tsamis to a 4-0 lead after three innings, scoring twice in the first and twice in the third with David DeCarlo providing the only hits in both innings. Matt Allison walked and scored three times in the game, and Fraka, apparently feeling better, hit a game-clinching two-run homer in the fifth.

Meanwhile, Taiwan swallowed whole its European *hors d'oeuvre*, burying the Italian team 18-0 as Chao-An Chen struck out all 18 of the military dependents sent to bat against him. It was only the second perfect game in Little League World Series history, and the first since Angel Macias of Monterrey, Mexico achieved the feat in 1957. (As of 2008, three others had been thrown since 1979.)

While many thought the Taiwanese players' dispassionate precision would make them immune to the emotions of a World Series championship game, the Campbell players knew better. One reason was that many of them had made friends with their Taiwanese counterparts during their time together in Williamsport, and had found much common ground, including their middle-class backgrounds. Most of the Taiwanese players were sons of peasant farmers, and their island had just been hit by a major typhoon, so even though they didn't betray their emotions much during their stay in Williamsport, the Campbell players had gotten to know them on a different level.

Greg Mitchell, in fact, had become friends with Chao-An Chen. "He's the nicest guy on the Taiwan team, and he's a good pitcher," Greg said. "But he wasn't as good as 18 strikeouts and a perfect game. Europe just wasn't that good of a team."

The fact the Campbell players understood that their Taiwanese counterparts were not automatons helped them approach the title game with the same sense of possibility that they had brought into their 14 previous games. If they kept their composure, focused on their own responsibilities and trusted their own abilities, the Taiwanese would have to react to them, not the other way around. They felt, above all, a responsibility to play up to their standards. "I just hope we give them a good game," Rob Fraka said. "I don't care if we lose. I just want to give them a good game so they don't slaughter us."

They gave Taiwan a good game, all right. Before 40,000 live witnesses, along with a worldwide television audience that included an estimated 6 million Taiwanese who tuned in at 3 a.m. their time, Taiwan and Campbell played a game that I think players and parents who have been to the Little League World Series since 1979 can thank (or blame) for the fact the event has taken on the enormity it has three decades later.

In 1979, ABC was still telecasting the Little League World Series championship game on a tape-delay basis, although it no longer was relegated to snippets within Wide World of Sports and was being shown in its entirety. (It was on live radio, which was why so many of us assembled at Campbell Little League that day to hear it.) No other LLWS games were televised, live or otherwise, in 1979. Lamade Stadium still had no lights. Volunteer Stadium, which now adjoins Lamade Stadium, did not exist. The World Series finalists emerged from an eight-team field, not the 16-team format that came about later. Television, first ABC and later ESPN, was the catalyst for all those changes, but the previous seven championship games before 1979 had been two-hour yawns as TV entertainment because they were so one-sided in favor of the Far East. Excluding the 1975 Series, which was a four-team all-American competition from which foreign squads were excluded as part of the Taiwan backlash, the Far East had won all seven of those championships (six by Taiwan, one by Japan), and the cumulative score of those seven title games was 70-10. The closest of those games ended 7-2.

Many, including some who were in leadership positions in the Little League hierarchy, believed in 1979 that the 1975 ban on foreign teams ought to be reinstituted and made permanent. The Far East programs – including the Philippines and South Korea, both of which later similarly ran afoul of the Williamsport authorities – could not be monitored closely and operated more or less as they chose, and the question entering the 1979 event was whether American teams would ever again be able to compete with Asian teams that were bigger, faster, stronger, more experienced, more structured and seemingly impervious to mood swings. It's entirely possible that if the trend had continued much longer, the Little League World Series as network-television entertainment might have lost all legitimacy – or, alternatively, the event might have been limited permanently to American teams as a bow to U.S. xenophobia.

After the Campbell- Pu Tzu Town game of August 25, 1979, all those questions and doubts became permanently moot – because 14 undersized boys next door from Anytown, U.S.A., proved that day that the idea ought to be to play well enough to beat the Taiwanese instead of trying to legislate them out of international competition. Campbell did play well enough to win, and very nearly did, even though it didn't manage a single hit against Taiwanese pitcher Dai Han-Chou.

Even with the political backdrop, drama, emotion, intelligence, courage, resourcefulness, passion, exhilaration, tears and finally impeccable sportsmanship by both teams carried this day, and people all over the world watched and remembered. Campbell lost 2-1, but it transformed the usual six-inning Taiwanese rollover into eight innings of tumult and tension. Those who saw it got a glimpse of a future in which American teams could beat anybody. Tampa, Fla., played in the next two Little League World Series finals, and each time took the Taiwanese to the limit, losing 4-3 and 4-2. In 1982 came Cody Webster and his Kirkland team's 6-0 win over the Taiwanese, and in 1983 the Japanese team that had beaten Taiwan in the Far East tournament didn't even make the Williamsport finals, in which Marietta, Ga., beat Barahona of the Dominican Republic 3-1. Since Kirkland's breakthrough, 11 American teams have won the Little League World Series – including, as of 2008, the past four. Other nations that have won in Williamsport since 1982 include Venezuela, Curacao, Mexico, Japan and South Korea.

The era of truly competitive World Series play began that day in 1979, and the enthusiasm for the event has mushroomed ever since. That enthusiasm, and the realization by TV executives that Little League could be a ratings boon, eventually translated into a tournament-long ESPN presence, night games, a second ballpark, a 16-team field, mammoth profits for the Little League industry (though not for its member leagues), and Williamsport's status as a 12-year-old's baseball Valhalla. With that, of course, has come abuses. The win-at-all-costs mentality that prevails in 2009 has brought about flagrant and repeated violations of recruiting rules, both in the U.S. and abroad. Overemphasis and over-glamorization have squelched the fun element for the players in many cases. That having been written, most of those who have been to a Little League World Series as participants will still tell you that it's the experience of a lifetime, and the 14 players in the Campbell Little League dugout that afternoon did a lot to make it so for all the players who were to follow.

In the respects I've described, that Little League World Series title game can be compared to the NCAA basketball final five months earlier between Magic Johnson-led Michigan State and Larry Bird-led Indiana State – a game that made college basketball a television staple, and created the Magic-Bird rivalry that might well have saved the NBA as a true major league. There was one difference, though: The Campbell-Taiwan contest was a more compelling game.

Rob Fraka, by now almost completely over the illness that had befallen him earlier in the week, was matched against Dai Han-Chou, who'd pitched a one-hitter against Puerto Rico in Taiwan's Series opener. Surprisingly, it was the Taiwanese, who had not given up a run in their previous eight games, who suffered a defensive lapse that put Campbell ahead.

Matt Allison, who had drawn three walks and scored each time in the semifinal against North Little Rock, led off the game with another base on balls. After David DeCarlo hit into a forceout and Dai retired the next batter, Fraka lifted a fly ball into shallow left field. Shortstop Lu Chan-Kuen drifted back, collided with incoming left fielder Yin Ching-lung, and dropped the ball for an error. DeCarlo, running all the way with two outs, steamed into third, and when Lu's unnecessary throw home skipped past the catcher, DeCarlo scored to put Campbell ahead 1-0.

That was the extent of Campbell's offense for the day, as Dai regained his rhythm and wound up with 17 strikeouts. He allowed only one other baserunner – Allison, who walked yet again in the fifth, but didn't advance. It was apparent that the 1-0 lead would have to hold up if Campbell was to win, and Fraka, with the help of his teammates' defensive legerdemain, kept the Taiwanese at bay for four innings as the tension mounted. Phillips made three more running catches, including a shoestring effort to come up with a ball in front of him, to prevent extra-base hits, and Mitchell, at shortstop, got two forceouts at third base on plays to his right. On another play, he ranged to his left, went to his knees to absorb a dangerous ground ball and threw to Niemeyer at second for a forceout. Campbell, which most thought would be the more vulnerable team in terms of dealing with the championship-game environment, wound up with no errors in the game, to Taiwan's two (both on the first-inning play that gave Campbell its run).

In the fifth, Taiwan tied the game on a play that, had luck intervened on the behalf of Campbell, could have made the Clones world champions.

Chen Chao-An lofted a deep fly to right center that seemed to dangle in the sky as Phillips sprinted to the warning track. He got under it, braced himself against the fence, and leaped. The ball ticked off the edge of his glove and trickled over the wall for a solo home run to tie the score. But even after that disappointment, and its progressively weaker at-bats against Dai as he retired 21 of the last 22 batters he faced, Campbell would not back down.

The sixth came and went, then the seventh. Finally, in the eighth, Fraka's fatigue began to gnaw at him. He hit Lu, Taiwan's leadoff hitter, on the helmet, and was visibly concerned – partly about having allowed the potential winning run to reach first base, but mostly about whether he had injured Lu. The Taiwanese player got up quickly and jogged to first base; Fraka intercepted Lu in front of first and shook his hand in an apologetic, are-you-OK gesture. Fraka's sportsmanship softened the tension that by now had permeated the ballpark, and he settled down and retired the next two hitters. But two wild pitches advanced Lu to third, and he scored the World Series-winning run from there on a clean single up the middle by Ho Chia-mou.

Fraka was sobbing a short time later as he accepted the runner-up award, and his teammates also were wiping away tears while the Taiwanese were given their championship pennant and pins. But the friendships that had been forged during that week, and the cheerfulness that had been such an essential part of the Campbell team's makeup, soon prevailed, and before long the players from both teams were swimming and laughing together. A photographer captured a picture of Mark Phillips and Chen Chao-An thumb-wrestling. Later, as the teams watched a replay of the game, Mark was shown making one of his game-prolonging catches. He flexed his biceps, such as they were, playfully, and the Taiwanese boys were convulsed in laughter.

"They're nice guys," Mark said. "They're our friends."

"These are a loose bunch of guys," Subby Agliolo said. "They're 12-year-olds. You know how 12-year-olds are. Give them an ice cream cone after something like this, and they're OK. Thank the good Lord for making them that way."

After a trip to Hershey, Pa., to see the chocolate factory there, and then a tour of Washington, D.C., the Campbell Clones were greeted by a large contingent when they landed at San Jose International Airport three days after the championship game. As in 1976, the focus was on the national championship Campbell had won and the friends they had made in Williamsport – in the barracks, in the stands, and among the TV viewers.

"Taiwan is a good team and they deserve credit for winning it," Mark Phillips said. "But we're the U.S. champs, and you can't take that away from us."

Nobody had taken any of the impact of the Campbell saga away from Subby Agliolo 30 years later. Beyond the players themselves, the memories of 1979 ebbed and flowed in a succession of vignettes as Subby reminisced.

"One thing I remember was meeting (Hall of Fame broadcasters) Mel Allen and Red Barber when they did the (ABC telecast of the final)," Subby said. "They actually sat down and talked with some of the kids before the game, and I remember them both wanting to make sure they had the kids' names pronounced right. Even with my name ... they kept saying 'Agliolo' over and over again until they were sure they had it perfect, and I found out later they never made any mistakes during the game.

"Red Barber came up to me after the game, Mel too, and he said to me, 'Subby, we found somebody with a radar gun (which was a novelty at that time) and did you know their pitcher was throwing 80 miles an hour and your guy was throwing 68? I've never seen anything like it (the difference in velocity between two pitchers in such a close game).' Their (Taiwanese) kid was 5-foot-7, 5-8 ... just huge. When I saw the (taped) broadcast later, they showed his mother in the stands and I thought it was his wife."

In retrospect, Subby thought the fact the team was able to approach the experience as an opportunity and not a mandate played a significant role in its success. Part of that, he says, was the fact he never tried to present himself as an authority figure.

"I won't mention names, but other coaches and managers just didn't seem to want to hang around the kids that much," he said. "I like to see my kids hanging around with me, even if it's just walking around the ballpark. They were there, and I guess they respected me. Kids need discipline, crave discipline, but you have to like the kids too, and with kids like I had, you could see that they were going to be able to get through life."

George Tsamis used the experience as a springboard for the baseball career that followed. He never played again in Campbell, because his family moved to Clearwater, Fla., soon after the World Series. Tsamis' high school play earned him a scholarship from Stetson University in Deland, Fla. The Minnesota Twins selected him in the 15th round of the 1989 amateur draft, and four years later, on April 26, 1993, he became the fifth former Campbell-system player, after John Oldham, Don Hahn, Greg Gohr and Steve Davis, to play in the major leagues. (He is also the only major leaguer to actually have been born in Campbell.) Tsamis pitched in 41 games for the Twins that year, going 1-2, but he was beset by a series of shoulder injuries and never returned to the major leagues. However, he undertook a second baseball career, in minor league coaching and managing, after retiring in 1997. In 2008, he was the manager of the St. Paul Saints of the independent American Association.

As mentioned earlier, Zaccheo played college football at Nevada, and Mitchell and Phillips were baseball teammates at San Jose State. Fraka played at West Valley College after graduating from Willow Glen High; most of the others played into their high school years. But unlike their 1962 Moreland and 1976 Campbell counterparts, the Campbell Clones never reappeared again as a collective force on the national level.

Their achievements, and those of the Campbell Moreland Pony League team that repeated as World Series champion five days after the Taiwan-Campbell game, represented the apex for a youth baseball program that was the envy of every city in America. At least on the surface, there appeared to be no reason Campbell couldn't continue indefinitely as a youth baseball Parthenon as the 1980s began, and the winning didn't stop immediately.

Although the population growth of the previous four decades had slowed — and, in many neighborhoods, stopped altogether — baseball remained the pre-eminent peer pressure in and around the Orchard City into the 1980s, and while signup totals didn't approach those of the early 1970s, participation and talent levels remained high throughout the system. Campbell Little League won District 44 championships in 1980, 1983 and 1985, giving the league nine district titles over a 16-year span beginning in 1970. Although the anticipation of an almost-unbeatable Campbell High program ended when that school closed in 1980, the talent on hand was such that Prospect and Westmont, two teams stocked with ex-Campbell players, met in the Central Coast Section final in 1982. In 1984, Campbell Moreland made another trip to the Pony League World Series, and the same league reached the Colt World Series in 1987.

But beneath the surface, the erosion had begun, and by the end of the 1980s, The Last Baseball Town would soon be without deed or direction.

1979 CAMPBELL MORELAND PONY LEAGUE: The Truman Show

In a historical chronicle of almost any other baseball community, the 1979 Campbell Moreland Pony League All-Star team's saga would be a lead chapter ... and the fact that it always seemed to fall to this group to follow doesn't detract from its accomplishments.

Five days after the Campbell Little League All-Stars captured the baseball world's affection and imagination with its garrison stand against overwhelming Taiwanese force at the Little League World Series in Pennsylvania, the Campbell Moreland Pony League team accepted its opponents' unconditional surrender on a far more obscure battlefield. With its 10-3 victory over a Houston team that included Greg Swindell, who was pitching in an All-Star Game for the Cleveland Indians a decade later, and future major leaguer Rusty Richards, manager Lou Bacho's team notarized an achievement that was unprecedented even in Campbell: It defended a world championship earned by a Campbell team the previous year. But then and three decades later, the conjunction of "1979" and "Campbell baseball" provokes thoughts of Williamsport, not of Davenport, Iowa, in the minds of most Campbell baseball people who didn't have a direct connection to the Pony League champions.

Two years earlier, seven of the '79 Pony League All-Stars had been on Campbell Little League's 1977 All-Star team, which opened postseason play with six straight victories and a district championship, and given the results of subsequent tournaments, it wasn't that far removed from a return trip to Williamsport. Elsewhere, that would have been considered a seminal team. In Campbell, it was the team after the team that had won the 1976 national championship.

This group's successes were dimmed in the eyes of many by what could be called the Harry Truman Syndrome. Try though he might, Truman during his Presidency could never escape comparisons with the man he succeeded, Franklin Delano Roosevelt. But Truman, long after he left office, came to be regarded as a great President in his own right, even though he never had FDR's personal charisma or consensus-building skills. The Campbell Moreland team of 1979 similarly is best appreciated through a wide-angle lens. It had many of the assets that propelled Campbell's better-known championship teams, along with some unique attributes of its own, and it was no less spiritually congealed.

"We knew we had a good team in '79," said Randy Nishijima, who did most of the catching for the 1979 Pony League All-Stars. "In 1977 we'd won the district, which was really hard in those years, but we lost in the section final to Los Gatos. You felt lucky you played in Campbell, and there wasn't the burnout factor. Back then, you played Little League from March until July and hopefully longer, then you played basketball or soccer or whatever with your friends until baseball came around again. Now, it's (parent-organized sports) year-round, with all these travel teams and all these kids whose parents hire personal instructors for them. Back then, there was that group of neighborhood kids, and you just played when they played.

"Yeah, I think maybe some of the guys wished we had gotten a little more (recognition), but we knew that the Little League World Series was the big thing, because it was on TV. I still remember watching that game at the hotel where we were staying in Davenport. Ours was a great experience, but that was the biggest deal. We knew that."

Although it lacked the marquee allure of many of the other 11 Campbell-area teams that reached youth baseball World Series from 1960 through 1979, Campbell Moreland's toolbox was stocked just as fully.

None of the three starting pitchers – Brad Ceynowa, Tom Gricius and Joray Marrujo – could short-circuit radar guns as Rich Alvarez or Tom Davis or Ted Campbell previously had done, but all three had more than ample fastball voltage, all three could absorb extreme workloads, and all three could make the intimidation element work for them.

Ceynowa, a 6-foot-2 lefthander with a sweeping motion that made it appear as if his pitches were coming to the plate by way of first base, had played Little League baseball in Moreland, where he learned tolerance the hard way. During one three-game stretch as a 12-year-old during the 1977 regular season, he pitched three straight no-hitters – and lost two of them because of porous defense behind him. During his two years with the Mets, who were usually the team to beat in Pony League, he didn't have any such defensive-support problems, and he was utterly unflappable on the mound. He had a maturity that made many of his teammates feel that when it came time for them to work out of offices, Brad's office would still be a baseball mound somewhere.

"Brad had just incredible stuff," Randy Nishijima said of Ceynowa, who was 5-0 with 53 strikeouts in 34 tournament innings. "Nothing fazed him ... I remember one time I went out to talk to him after he'd walked the bases loaded, and all he said to me was, 'Relax, and watch this.' And he struck out the side."

Tom Gricius was about the same size as Brad, only burlier, but even though he looked intimidating, he was an even-tempered, humorously-wry kid away from the mound, and his pitching portfolio was similarly teasing and sly. Because his motion unfolded in stages, it was difficult for hitters to maintain their concentration and patience in the batters box. Unlike Ceynowa, Tom rarely pitched for strikeouts, and he was easy to play behind because he was around the plate constantly and kept the ball down, usually resulting in a succession of harmless ground balls and popups.

"Tom had a decent fastball and a good breaking pitch," Randy said, "but the hardest thing about him was his delivery ... he had a lot of movement that threw guys off. When he was really pitching well, like when he threw the no-hitter in the World Series, he was hitting spots with his breaking ball and he could throw it any time in the count. He was tough to beat when he had that working for him."

Tom also had a sense of perspective that all of his coaches — including, later in Legion ball, me — appreciated. By 1979, he had already broken both ankles, one while stepping into a gopher hole during a flag football game, and the other skateboarding. Nobody in the system during the 1970s, with the possible exception of Mike Alvarez from Campbell Little League's 1970 team, was more appreciative of the fact he was even able to play baseball at all in 1979 and beyond.

Joray Marrujo was a Moreland product who would have been on the 1978 World Series championship team had it not been for the extraordinary talent level that team had. (The league did sponsor a second All-Star team in 1978, and that squad, which included Joray and many of the 13-year-olds who were to comprise the '79 All-Star team, won its first tournament and got to the finals of the second before being eliminated.) "He was our closer," Randy said. "Low and straight and flat. You could catch him in a lawn chair."

As good as Joray was as a pitcher, he was even better as a field player. I later coached him for two years in American Legion, and I'm sometimes reminded of him when I see a Dominican or Puerto Rican player in the low minors at age 16 or 17, because Joray's game was similarly raw and utterly lacking in by-the-book tutelage. But his way worked better than any other way he could have been taught. Joray was a viper with his hands and his glove and his arm and his feet and his bat. We'd make a game, during infield, of fungoing balls as hard as we could to Joray at third base, instead of tapping the ball as is usually the custom. Joray would come up with impossible stop after impossible stop and grin fiendishly back at us.

Lou Bacho, and later I, could bat him anywhere in the lineup because he would work counts and be resourceful in terms of getting on base. He could hit a ball 400-plus feet even though he was only about 5-9 and 170. He could hit behind the runner and function in any other situation where tactical, unselfish hitting was needed. He was probably our most consistent pitcher during the Legion years, both as a starter and as a closer, and he always played the game with that toothy grin on his face. I liked Joray immensely, even though he was a quiet kid who didn't reveal much of his inner self to anybody, and in retrospect I wish I could have done more to help him steer a path beyond Campbell and baseball. He remains the best pure baseball player I have ever coached.

The 1976 Little League team's most salient positional issue had been behind the plate, and while Mike Walsh arguably was the MVP of the 1978 Pony League World Series champions, the 1979 Pony team had *two* catchers who were in Mike's class. Randy Nishijima may have been the best all-around athlete on the team and could play any position – on Bud Stallings' Shamrocks team the year before, he actually played all nine positions in one game – while adding both speed and power to the batting order. Dave Bryant, though not the all-around athlete that Randy was, had a middle linebacker's presence and was much like Dominic Costantino had been for the 1976 and 1978 teams in terms of being the team's conscience in the dugout. Dave also played two years of Legion ball for me, and I never had to worry about managing the emotions and the inventories of our pitchers because Dave could and did do a far better job of that than I ever could. Most people in the league called him Davey because his father also was named Dave, but I always called him Dave because my respect and admiration for him were such that I never was comfortable addressing him with a name that sounded childlike. In 1979, the question of whether to catch Randy or Dave was settled by the fact Dave also was the best available option at first base, and wound up playing there most of the time while Randy was behind the plate.

Campbell Moreland's infielders couldn't match some of their 1976 and 1978 counterparts in terms of offensive might, but they turned defense into a weapon. The starting infield usually consisted of Joray at third, Steve Koontz at second, Chris Gettler at shortstop and Dave Bryant at first. The most frequently-used outfielders were Tim Bottomley, Craig Trinidad and Cameron Comick, although Bobby Pogue and Dennis Gilligan were used there as well. Dan Watari and David Yates were infield backups. Con Maloney rarely played, but was perhaps the fastest player on the team, and he wound up scoring the winning run as a pinch-runner in one World Series game.

Lou Bacho was the manager.

Lou had come to the Pony League in 1977 after managing in Quito Little League. The kids generally liked him and learned from him, and Steve Clinton, who played for Lou for three years in Little League and two more in Pony League, gave Lou much of the credit for the fact he didn't have much trouble adjusting to the no-nonsense coaches, particularly Gordon Huntze and John Oldham, for whom he was to play in high school and college.

"He really took baseball to the next level for me," Steve said of Lou. "It's not often when you're 10 years old and it's raining and you can't practice outside that a coach is going to rent out a facility so you can play inside. Lou did that. He had some unorthodox ways of teaching, like he'd tie a rope to your helmet to teach you not to pull away from the ball. He was a tough guy, but at that time I think that was really good for me. Playing (at higher levels) later was a continuation of playing for him."

Dave Roberson, who later played at Mitty High and San Jose State, said of his one Pony League season with Lou: "He was tough. But I liked playing for him because he treated his players like adults and not like little kids."

I believe Lou had played in college, and from what I remember, he knew the game well and was more eager than most of the other Pony League managers and coaches to talk about its nuances, especially over a postgame beer or two. But he had his share of detractors, including some parents who had had business dealings with him (he was a masonry contractor), and while I always got along well with him, I knew he could be unpredictable and had a fierce temper. Nobody particularly wanted to contradict him when he was in a certain mood.

And he showed questionable judgment a couple of years later, when he managed another All-Star team (I don't remember which) in the Campbell system. He had T-shirts made for the kids that pictured a beer keg with the number "15" within it, a reference to a promise he had made the kids — 13- and 14-year-olds — that if they got 15 hits in a tournament game, he would buy them a keg of beer. The league leadership, apparently regarding it as a harmless promise made in jest, lightly admonished him, made him get rid of the T-shirts (one of which remained on display at Jersey's Tavern in Campbell for many years) and let him keep the All-Star team.

That incident notwithstanding, nobody ever said Lou wasn't smart. Like Joe Gagliardi, who managed Campbell Moreland to its first Pony championship in 1964, Lou had a knack for getting what he wanted with subtlety behind the scenes. A lot of what he did to make that 1979 team a winner was done individual by individual. And in 1979, he was smart enough to enlist as his coach Chuck Calhoun, who'd worked under Bud Stallings during the 1978 Pony League championship run and had played a major role in terms of keeping the 1978 team solvent during its periods of self-doubt. Chuck, a native of Oklahoma who wasn't much taller than a jockey and made his living as an exterminator, was the Pony League equivalent of Jack Zogg, winning much the same way and with much the same frequency with many of the same players. Like Zogg, he was demanding and sometimes brusque with his players, but was eminently approachable away from the field. In fact, usually he was the guy who approached you about going out for a pizza and a beer after a game. He enjoyed the social element of Campbell baseball as much as he did the baseball aspect. He and his wife Bobbie were convivial types who never missed a league social function — and we had plenty, formal and otherwise — and was universally respected and liked, even if some thought he had a bit of a Napoleonic complex. He was a bridge between Lou and the team, just as he had been for Bud, and nobody in Campbell, not even Zogg, taught 9-iron baseball better than Chuck. Given that factor, and the fact he had Lou as a beer-drinking partner,

Chuck may have enjoyed his 1979 Pony League experience even more than his time with Bud the previous year.

The genesis of the 1979 *tour de force*, as previously noted, was in 1977, when Tim Bottomley, Tom Gricius, Dave Bryant, Randy Nishijima, Cameron Comick, Craig Trinidad and Chris Gettler had been the spine of the Campbell Little League All-Star team. That team was managed by Dan Trinidad, whom I thought rivaled Jack Zogg in terms of his teaching and people skills while they both managed in Campbell Little League, and it had won the District 44 championship behind the pitching of Tom Gricius and Thomas Silvas, another superior athlete who was a national age-group champion in boxing, for which he was to give up baseball soon after. (Another player on that 1977 All-Star team, Jerry Zaro, moved to Carson City, Nev., soon after and became an all-state high school player there.)

Campbell outscored its four district opponents 23-2 – a higher level of domination than the 1976 team had attained in District 44 play – with Gricius and Silvas recording 49 strikeouts in 24 innings. In the sectionals, which Campbell hosted, it beat Oak Grove 3-2 and Mountain View National 4-1 before losing 5-3 to Los Gatos in the finals. Los Gatos then advanced to the divisional final before losing 10-5 to Hanford National; Hanford National in turn lost 4-3 to Beaverton, Ore., in the regionals at San Bernardino, and Beaverton lost in the regional final to the El Cajon team that reached the Little League World Series title game before losing 6-2 to Taiwan. Late defensive breakdowns had cost Campbell the game against Los Gatos, and it's not inconceivable that if Campbell had survived the sectional, it would have been more than competitive with any of the teams in the tournaments that followed.

The lost opportunity of 1977 may well have been on the Campbell Moreland players' minds as they began the 1979 postseason. As in 1978, Campbell Moreland hosted a regional and thus bypassed the first two tournament tiers. It won the regional relatively easily, but in the divisional tournament in Southern California, Campbell Moreland struggled to beat Garden Grove 3-2, then lost 1-0 in 10 innings to host Cypress to drop into the losers bracket.

The players, though, were well aware that their 1978 counterparts twice had come through losers brackets to advance by winning final-day doubleheaders against the teams that had previously beaten them. Campbell Moreland crushed Manhattan Beach 14-2 to earn its win-two-or-else rematch with Cypress.

"That was our first real competition," Randy Nishijima said. "They had a righthander and a lefty who were both very good; the righty was probably about Tom Gricius' size. I think we were also the first real competition that they'd faced, too, because they were *the* team down there. They were a lot cockier, spoiled. You'd see them around the ballpark in their brand-new beach cruisers. They had won so easily (in their previous tournaments) that I think we shocked them a little."

Campbell Moreland won the first game 7-1 as Brad Ceynowa struck out 13 and Joray Marrujo and Dave Bryant each hit two home runs, forcing a championship game immediately, and for about four hours, thereafter. Tom started and worked the regulation seven innings. He trailed 1-0 going to the bottom of the sixth, when Steve Koontz hit a home run to tie the game. Joray took over in the eighth and pitched five scoreless innings. In the bottom of the 12th, Randy walked, went to second on a balk and scored on Tim Bottomley's double to give Campbell Moreland a 2-1 victory and a berth in the Pony League World Series in Davenport, Iowa.

On that same day, August 18, Campbell Little League had beaten Goleta Valley 11-3 to earn its slot in Williamsport, and amid the furor over the Clones, Campbell Moreland's impending rendezvous with history was almost unnoticed, as was its arrival in the Quad Cities of Davenport, Iowa, and three cities on the Illinois side of the Mississippi River — Moline, Quincy and Rock Island. (Quirkily, Campbell Moreland had advanced to the Pony League World Series in 1978 by winning the divisional tournament in Washington's Tri-Cities, and George Tsamis, of the 1979 Little League team, reached the major leagues in 1993 with the Minnesota Twins, as in Twin Cities.)

As had been the case the previous year during the Pony League World Series in National City, the 1979 Campbell Moreland team arrived in an area that was in the midst of economic decay, caused in the Quad Cities' case by shutdowns of several key agricultural-manufacturing plants in the area. The players were to be quartered at Camp Abe Lincoln, a YMCA wilderness retreat along the river in Blue Grass, about 15 minutes from Davenport. It dates from 1858, three years before Lincoln took office as President, and after seeing the age and condition of their bunkhouse, the kids wouldn't have been surprised if Lincoln himself had come through the door to greet them.

They weren't there long, though.

"We landed, and we took the Quad Cities minor league team's bus out to Camp Abe Lincoln," Randy Nishijima said, smiling at the memory. "We got there, and it was like a ghost town. We put our bags down and started to unpack, and Grandpa Bottomley (who was not without means) comes in, takes a look around and said, 'There's no way you're staying here. You're going to a hotel.' We wound up at a hotel in town right along the river. We got ripped in the local papers ... 'California kids felt accommodations weren't up to their standards.' Later, though, the Hawaii and Houston teams stayed there too."

To an even greater degree than Williamsport had been for the 1976 Campbell Little League team, the Midwest represented culture shock for Randy's team. He says the people in the Quad Cities were friendly, but seemed to have adopted their attitudes about Californians from Frankie Avalon-Annette Funicello movies.

"They were relaxed and laid-back, so different from people here," Randy said. "But they really didn't know very much about California. They thought it was all L.A. and Hollywood and beaches. It was like, 'Wow, you guys are from California. Do you walk to the beach and do you surf all the time?' (The largest bodies of water in Campbell are the Santa Clara Valley water district's percolation ponds, in which even a waterbug can't surf.)

"While we were there, we heard about this mall ... the people there said it was the biggest mall in America. Well, we went there, and it was kind of like Westgate (a medium-sized mall by California standards, which opened in 1964 at the intersection of Saratoga, Hamilton and Campbell avenues). Valley Fair and Eastridge (both in San Jose) were both much bigger, and we told them that ... by the time we left Iowa, they were saying their mall was the biggest east of the Mississippi River."

As in National City, the surroundings and lodgings were bland, and keeping themselves occupied away from the ballpark stretched the players' and parents' creativity. Their stay in Davenport also would be much longer than had been the case in National City, because the national Pony League organization had expanded the World Series from five to eight teams while keeping the double-elimination format. Besides Campbell Moreland and the host Davenport team, the field consisted of Maui, Hawaii; Garden City, Mich.; Puerto Rico; Mexico; Houston; and Greensboro, N.C.

Beyond what Campbell Moreland was to accomplish, this World Series would have the distinction of being the first baseball event ever televised by ESPN.

The all-sports cable network, which three decades later dominated the television and sports industries, was launched on September 7 amid widespread skepticism that Americans were ready for 24-hour sports programming, and with only the NCAA as a major broadcast partner. When ESPN first went on the air — in Campbell, it did so as an adjunct to the Gill Cable sports channel, which carried many local events and employed Pat Hughes as its main play-by-play man — it had more time slots than it had live programming to fill them, so it scrambled to fill those voids with taped events. Along with portions of the Pony League World Series, which concluded a week before ESPN's debut, ESPN's original viewers watched curiosity sports such as Gaelic hurling, darts and water polo. Few people in Campbell got to watch that World Series, though, because Gill, Campbell's first cable provider, had a minimal subscriber base in 1979. Randy Nishijima said he had never seen any footage from the ESPN telecasts of the World Series, and didn't even realize its cameras were there.

Unlike the dual four-team bracket format, first introduced in the College World Series, that came into common use later in eight-team tournaments, the 1979 Pony League World Series featured a staircase-bracket format that forced teams that lost early to play almost continuously for a week to emerge in the finals. Lou Bacho had used his top three pitchers almost exclusively in the previous two tournaments, and he and the players were well aware that they would have to treat each game with single-elimination urgency. They did get one bracketing break: Houston, which loomed as a favorite, was in the opposite bracket, so Campbell wouldn't have to face the Texans until at least its third game if both team stayed in the winners bracket.

Even so, Campbell Moreland didn't have to wait long to face its first World Series crisis. Against Maui, Ceynowa, the starting pitcher, was scuffed for three runs in the top of the first inning. Campbell Moreland tied the game with single runs in each of the first three innings, with Koontz scoring the first run on an infield grounder by Marrujo, and Randy Nishijima and Dave Bryant hitting solo homers in the second and third respectively.

Brad pitched through the second and third innings without difficulty, but Joray relieved him with two on and no outs in the fourth and got out of the inning with the 3-3 tie intact. Maui took a 4-3 lead against him in the fifth, but Joray was unassailable thereafter, and Campbell tied the game in the bottom of the fifth as Tim Bottomley singled, advanced to third on two wild pitches and scored on Dave Bryant's sacrifice fly.

In the bottom of the seventh with the score still tied 4-4, Lou sifted through his inventory of spare parts, and came up with Bobby Pogue, who led off the inning with a pinch walk. Con Maloney ran for him, and two batters later, he scored the game-winning run on a single by Joray.

The 5-4 victory gave Campbell Moreland the next day off, and it was able to abbreviate its next game against Garden City. In 1978, Rich Alvarez had pitched the sixth no-hitter in Pony League World Series history, and Tom Gricius registered No. 7 as Campbell Moreland won 13-0 in a game that was called after six innings because of the tournament's 12-run mercy rule. He struck out seven and walked just two, and was unfortunate in only one respect: The game was played on Saturday, August 25, at the same time as Campbell Little League's epic struggle against Taiwan 700 miles to the east. Under different circumstances, Tom's achievement might have been trumpeted with blaring headlines, but all it got in the Bay Area papers the next day was a muted subhead.

Houston, which had beaten Mexico 9-1 to join Campbell Moreland in the winners-bracket final, had two future major leaguers at the top of its pitching rotation – Swindell and Rusty Richards, who later was Swindell's teammate at the University of Texas and pitched in three games for the Atlanta Braves in 1989-90. Neither of them started against Campbell, although Swindell did appear in relief. "I saw him later at Texas and in the major leagues, and my first thought was, 'Whoa, that guy sure changed,'" Randy said. "He was huge later, but he was maybe Dave Bryant's size then. Richards was their big stud. Swindell probably would have been the fourth pitcher for us."

Campbell Moreland didn't have much trouble solving Houston's starter, but Houston similarly had its way with Ceynowa, and Campbell Moreland trailed 8-5 when Joray Marrujo relieved Brad in the fifth. Joray had hit a three-run homer in the first inning to give his team the lead, and while blanking Houston the rest of the way, he singled home the tying and go-ahead runs in the sixth. Tom Gricius, playing center field, had three hits, including a double that scored the first two runs during the four-run burst in the sixth that gave Campbell Moreland the 9-8 victory.

The victory assured Campbell Moreland a berth in the championship game three days later, on August 30. During the interim, Mexico had beaten Michigan and Houston had eliminated Mexico, creating a Houston-Campbell Moreland rematch. This time, there was no suspense; although Richards and Swindell both pitched in relief, the outcome was decided by the time they entered. Campbell Moreland took the lead in the second on a solo home run by Randy Nishijima. In the third, Chris Gettler, Cameron Comick and Steve Koontz all walked, and Dave Bryant hit into a fielders choice to score one run. Two Houston errors brought home two more runs, Craig Trinidad's single tallied another, and Randy completed the six-run splurge with a two-run single. Brad Ceynowa and Tom Gricius combined on a seven-hitter, and Campbell Moreland won 10-3.

The victory put Campbell Moreland into the record books as the first Pony League ever to claim back-to-back World Series titles, and the feat has been achieved only twice since — by West Covina in 1981-82 and South Korea in 1988-89-90. It also remains the only time that one American city has won a national championship in Little League and a Pony League World Series in the same year. Campbell Moreland's victory was not nearly as widely-celebrated in Campbell as the Little League team's near-miss in Williamsport, partly because of the timing; by the time the team returned home, to a reception at John D. Morgan Park, the Labor Day weekend had begun and many Campbell families were out of the area. But the twin peaks made Campbell the undisputed national hub of youth baseball, and the momentum and interest generated in 1979 masked for a time the fact that the program's underpinnings had been fatally weakened.

Most of the players on the 1979 Pony League All-Star team continued their baseball careers through high school. Tom Gricius and Joray Marrujo were vital pitchers on the 1982 Westmont and Prospect teams that reached the CCS finals against each other. Joray then played at San Jose City College, although his career was ended there by off-field troubles. Bobby Pogue, Tim Bottomley and Craig Trinidad played for Westmont in that '82 title game, and Dave Bryant was Prospect's starting catcher. Dennis Gilligan played for Del Mar that same season.

Steve Koontz, whose career nearly was ended by a knee injury suffered during his junior football season at Mitty, returned to baseball as a senior and eventually played for Santa Clara. Randy

Nishijima, after playing for Campbell High during its final two seasons, finished his high school career at Blackford, played a season at West Valley College, and turned down an opportunity to walk on at Long Beach State because he wanted to focus on completing his academic work there. He got his degree in physical therapy, and in 2009 had a practice in Campbell and was coaching his sons in Campbell Little League.

Chris Gettler was the only player on the team to become a professional. Chris, who was smaller than most of his teammates in Little League and Pony League and was renowned mainly for his infield play, sprouted late in his adolescence and developed into a first-rate pitcher at Del Mar. He went on to play three seasons at Jacksonville University, where he blossomed under the tutelage of former major league pitcher Tom Bradley. In 1987, after his junior year, the Los Angeles Dodgers took him in the 44th round of the major league draft. He signed, and was sent to Great Falls in the rookie-classification Pioneer League, where he went 3-1 with a 3.74 ERA in 10 starts. In 1988, Chris began the season with Salem in the short-season Class A Northwest League, and his work there – 4-1 with five saves and a 1.53 ERA – earned him a promotion to Bakersfield in the Class A California League for nine late-season games. Arm problems ended his career at that point; he went back to college to earn his degree, and in 2009 he was working for Arrow Electronics, the same firm that employed Paul Sargis. He lived in the affluent San Ramon Valley area, and was coaching his children in baseball and soccer.

Brad Ceynowa's picture would be seen by many thousands, but not in a baseball uniform. Brad played his entire high school career at Blackford, but by 1987 he was making a handsome living as a male model. Later, he attended the California Culinary Academy, graduating in 1993, and in 2009 had returned to the Bay Area after working at high-end restaurants throughout the U.S. and Europe.

The 1979 Campbell Moreland Pony League All-Stars never really had a signature name, as the Clones and the Cardiac Kids did, and today it is almost last in line in the Campbell championship succession in terms of its players' name recognition. But 30 years after its World Series triumph, no Campbell-area baseball team that came after had matched its accomplishments, and its distinction as the last great team in the Last Baseball Town could well last at least another three decades.

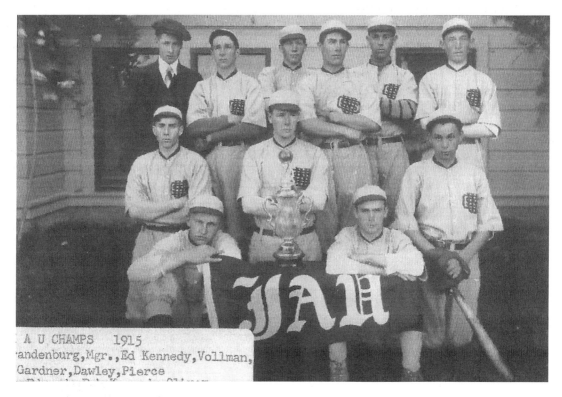

A U CHAMPS 1915
andenburg, Mgr., Ed Kennedy, Vollman,
Gardner, Dawley, Pierce

The 1915 Campbell High baseball team, winner of the Interurban Athletic Union Cup.

Billy Wilson, one of Campbell High's most successful athletes. Wilson, who graduated from Campbell in 1945, was a six-time Pro Bowl selection with the San Francisco 49ers.

The Campbell Stamps team in 1954, the first year of Campbell Little League. Craig Morton, the future NFL quarterback, is the third player from the right in the back row. His father Ken, one of the coaches, is at the far right.

Frankie Testa, shown batting in a Campbell Little League game in 1956, in 1955 was the first hitter in the first game at the league's new Rosemary School ballpark.

Laurence Hill, the superintendent of the Campbell Union High School District for more than 20 years. Hill also was the first president of Campbell Little League.

The 1958 Campbell Little League All-Stars. Joe Anderson, described by longtime Robins manager Jack Zogg as the fastest pitcher ever to play for him, is the tallest player in the photo.

The Campbell Little League women's auxiliary in 1960. Bob Holman, after whom the league's major field is named, is standing on the far left. Note the wooden scoreboard and outfield fence, and the orchards beyond them.

Thursday, May 5, 1960   Campbell, Santa Clara County, California

AT THE LITTLE LEAGUE OPENER . . . Mayor Henry A. (Whitey) Weitzel (left) in one of his first official acts since taking office tossed the first pitch last Saurday to officially open the 1960 season of the Campbell Little League. Police Chief John D. Mor- gan, official umpire for Little League is the catcher while batting is young John McMonagle, 3-year old son of Mr. and Mrs. James McMonagle, 771 Ricky Drive, Campbell. Johnny is mascot for the Italian-American Club team and his mother is president of the Little League Women's Auxil- iary. The Campbell Little League holds its annual breakfast this Sunday at the Campbell High School cafeteria. This is the major fund-raising campaign for the league.—Press photo

Campbell mayor Harvey Weitzel lobs a ball to 3-year-old John McMonagle, who later became a standout in Campbell Little League and Campbell High, during opening ceremonies in 1960. The umpire is John Morgan, the city's beloved police chief, after whom John D. Morgan Park is named.

SIXTEENTH ANNUAL · 1962

LITTLE LEAGUE

Official Program 50¢

WORLD SERIES
WILLIAMSPORT, PENNSYLVANIA

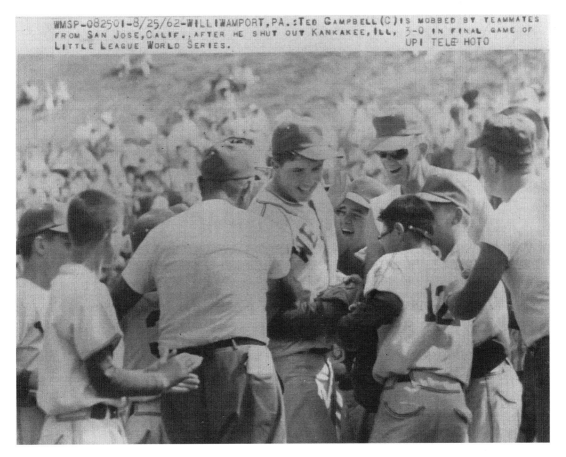

WMSP-082501-8/25/62-WILLIWAMPORT,PA.:TED CAMPBELL(C)IS MOBBED BY TEAMMATES FROM SAN JOSE,CALIF.,AFTER HE SHUT OUT KANKAKEE,ILL, 3-0 IN FINAL GAME OF LITTLE LEAGUE WORLD SERIES. UPI TELE HOTO

Moreland's Ted Campbell is congratulated by his coaches and teammates after pitching a no-hitter in the 1962 Little League World Series championship game.

The 1962 Moreland Little League All-Star team poses in front of the Capitol in Washington. Ted Campbell is noticeably taller than Charles Gubser, wearing the suit. Gubser represented the Moreland area in Congress.

Bob Miailovich poses with Willie Mays, who is signing an autograph for a young admirer, after Miailovich managed Moreland to the 1962 Little League World Series title.

Campbell Little League's current major division field as it looked when it was opened in 1963. The club-house and two lower-division fields were completed later that year.

The 1970 Campbell Little League All-Star team, which reached the World Series final before losing 2-0 to Wayne, N.J.

The 1970 Campbell Little League All-Star team during its 10-year reunion in 1980.

Jack Zogg, Steve Davis and Bob Holman (left to right) at the 1970 Little League World Series. Jack and Bob would return with the 1976 Campbell team; Davis, who was a Campbell High student at the time, reached the major leagues with the Chicago Cubs in '79

The 1973 Campbell Little League All-Star team, which beat future major league All-Star Mark Langston in the District 44 championship game.

The 1976 Campbell Little League All-Star team with Ernie Banks in Williamsport during the World Series.

Campbell players congratulate the Japanese team after losing 10-3 in the 1976 Little League World Series final.

TO BOB: YOU'RE ALL CHAMPIONS! WITH BEST WISHES,
NORM MINETA,
MEMBER OF CONGRESS

The 1976 Campbell Little League All-Stars on the steps of the Capitol building in Washington, D.C. Congressman Norm Mineta, who signed the photo at the bottom, is at the far right of the photo.

The Campbell telephone book, 1977.

The 1976 Campbell Little League All-Star team in 1986 during ceremonies in its honor.

The 1978 Campbell Moreland Pony League All-Stars after winning the regional tournament in Kennewick, Wash. Rich Alvarez, who went on to pitch a no-hitter in the Pony League World Series final, is second from the left in the front players row.

Harold Sutherland (left), Mike Walsh and Mike's sister Maureen in Tijuana during the 1978 Pony League World Series, just across the U.S.-Mexico border in National City.

Chuck Calhoun (wearing the hat) and Lou Bacho, who teamed to bring Campbell Moreland a second successive Pony League World Series title in 1979.

The Campbell Clones: Undersized but never overmatched, the 1979 Campbell Little League All-Stars became the league's third team to reach the Little League World Series during the 1970s.

Campbell Press Little League Special Edition/August 29, 1979/Page 7

ue items
msport, Pa.

If anyone thinks that finishing second in the World and first in the United States is not an outstanding accomplishment for the Campbell kids, consider this — the Little League World Series represents 32 nations and over 12,000 leagues! . . .

Some Campbellites just couldn't sit home and wait for results from Williamsport. Over 100 local residents made the trip east to follow the kids right into the Little League finale . . .

The game was televised here via a tape delay at 5 p.m. But in Taiwan the game was telecast live and more than six million fans watched their team win the World championship . . .

All three of the Campbell World Series teams have had their nicknames. In 1970, the Campbell stars were dubbed the "Cardiac Kids" because of their heartstopping victories on the road to the Series; in 1976, the Campbell team was called "Mm Mm Good" because they carried with them through the play-offs a large Campbell Soup can; and in 1979, the Campbell stars were nicknamed the "Campbell Clones" because according to shortstop Greg Vaughn, they all look so much alike . . .

In the radio pre-game show on Saturday, the broadcasters did a short interview with Campbell Mayor Norman Paul, who was in Williamsport for the final game.

During the interview Paul said, "The team looks great. Everyone is excited about the game and I know the kids will pull it off today. This team we brought is a team of miracles."

Well, Campbell didn't pull it off — they ran out of miracles against Taiwan. But not before they threw a pretty good scare into the team from the Far East, and thrilled fans across the nation. One thing's for sure — the Taiwan kids will certainly go home believing in miracles!

Greg Vaughn, a "clone."

FANCY FOOTWORK — First sacker George Tsamis was a steady Campbell starter all the way from district play through the World Series. Besides his reliable batting and fielding Tsamis picked up a couple of pitching victories along the way.

Welcome Back
Campbell
Little League
ALL-STARS

George Tsamis playing first base for the Campbell Little League All-Star team in 1979. Tsamis, who pitched for the Minnesota Twins in 1993, is the only major league player to have been born within the Campbell city limits.

P.H. Kephart - one of the good-guy parents who made Campbell youth baseball unique. P.H. managed the Campbell Moreland Colt League All-Star team in 1981.

Jeff Mitchell with his son Jake shortly before Jeff, a former Campbell youth baseball standout, was murdered in 2006 while on duty as a Sacramento County sheriffs deputy.

Ted Campbell in 1989. He's standing with Lou Silva, father of Don Silva, Campbell's personal catcher in 1962 when he led Moreland to the Little League World Series title.

PART II:
THE PEOPLE

JOHN OLDHAM: He came first

Mark Purdy, the longtime *San Jose Mercury News* sports columnist, in 2008 was serving on the San Jose Sports Hall of Fame board of directors, which is tasked with screening and selecting candidates for induction into the shrine that was made part of the main concourse at HP Pavilion when the home of the San Jose Sharks was opened in 1993.

"I'm involved with the San Jose Sports Hall of Fame board of directors," Mark wrote by way of apologizing for not responding immediately to an e-mail I'd sent him, "and we had our big banquet last night and it took up way too much of my time getting that whole thing together, putting out fires, etc. It's a lot of work, but a great event for the local sports community. John Oldham actually choked up and shed tears during his speech."

When I read Mark's e-mail, I reflected on how long I had known John – almost 30 years, going back to the early 1980s when he was head coach at San Jose City College and recruited and signed some of my American Legion players – and how rare it was for him to betray emotion. He was a quiet, restrained man who never wasted words or energy not directed at making his team or his players better, and he never concerned himself with anything that might be peripheral to that. Perhaps, I told Mark, that's one reason he was 66th in line for San Jose Sports Hall of Fame induction: He never would have said or done anything that might be construed as an attempt to take cuts in any line of recognition. And his career was more of a continuum than a crescendo, because he never played on or coached a national championship team, in Campbell or anywhere else, and his major league playing career consisted of one pinch-running appearance for the Cincinnati Redlegs in 1956.

Even at that, though, a case could be made that nobody ever did more over a longer period to bring Santa Clara Valley baseball to national prominence, and he was there at the beginning of Campbell's emergence as a premier baseball town. He first appeared on the baseball scene in the spring of 1947 as a freshman at Campbell High, and more than 60 years later at age 76, he was still immersed in the sport, as a volunteer assistant coach at Los Gatos High.

John spent 18 seasons, starting in 1966, at San Jose City, where his teams won 390 games and five conference titles. After the 1984 season, Santa Clara University coach Jerry McClain was fired by athletic director Pat Malley because he'd defied Malley's direct orders and gone to Alaska to coach in a summer league there. The Santa Clara baseball program, which as of 2008 had produced 56 players who went on to play in the major leagues, had been in decline for more than a decade with an outdated facility and diminished institutional support, and Malley, who was suffering from terminal cancer and knew his time was short, had to decide whether the program was more in need of a short-term transfusion of energy or a long-term guarantee of stability.

The two finalists were John Oldham and Alan Gallagher, the former Santa Clara star who had become known as "Dirty Al" while he was with the San Francisco Giants because of his un-bridled passion and willingness to fling himself at any task at hand, whether it be a wicked ground ball or the resurrection of a program. Al, who lived in the Fresno area at the time, took a job at the manager of the San Jose Bees, an independent team in the Class A California League, in 1984 solely to stay as close as possible to the Santa Clara situation. He and I became good friends that summer, and he told me often that the only thing he'd ever passionately wanted in baseball, besides the opportunity to play in the major leagues, was to be the head coach at Santa Clara University.

I was close to Malley as well, and in one of our last conversations before he died in early 1985, Pat told me that he came very close to hiring Al because doing so would have energized the program in the short term, brought it name recognition with recruits and media, and reflected an expression of loyalty to a loyal Santa Clara man. But he also knew that the other candidate, John Oldham, would recruit and teach well, operate in the low-key manner that Malley preferred, graduate his players and give Santa Clara's program the long-term stability it needed. So he hired Oldham, who justified Malley's foresight by taking the Broncos to four NCAA tournaments in 13 years while compiling a 433-324 record and steering a controversy-free program until his retirement following the 1997 season.

Even after that, John never really retired, serving as an assistant coach at Leigh High (where he coached his two grandsons), Westmont, West Valley College and finally Los Gatos. He also was the California League's umpiring supervisor at the time we talked late in 2008 about his Campbell roots, and it was apparent during our discussion that Campbell — where he played organized baseball for the first time, and where his coaching career began — had never been for-gotten as a force in his baseball life, distant in terms of time as it was.

"I was born in Salinas (in 1932) and we lived there, in Vallejo and Santa Cruz before we moved to Campbell in 1946, my freshman year in high school," John recalled. "It was very rural, not much of a city at all. This was long before the (Highway 17) freeway ran through Campbell, and there was only a dirt road paralleling the (Los Gatos) creek. We lived on Whiteoaks (near Campbell's southernmost boundary when Campbell was still a township and not an incorporated city), and there was a bridge across the creek but no street to take you through to San Jose-Los Gatos Road (now Bascom Avenue). So I'd walk to the street and then hitch a ride into town to get to school each day ... I can remember riding down Campbell Avenue on the running boards of cars."

John sensed that Campbell, small as it was, already was beginning to develop a sports legacy; Billy Wilson's younger brother Ernie was a senior at Campbell High at the time John was a freshman. John also remembered Bert Robinson as a local sports icon. At the time, though, sports weren't the unifying forces in the community that they were to become later, mainly because the Campbell Union High School District was so far-flung and agricultural that most area residents led relatively isolated lives.

"Our district went all the way south to the Almaden Valley and north to Cupertino in those days," John said. "When I was the athletic director at Campbell High in the early 1960s, the Los Gatos-Campbell football game each Thanksgiving was huge ... we got 10,000 at Campbell for one game (1960) while I was there, but it wasn't close to that when I was in high school. There really wasn't very much in Campbell ... I still remember the Five Spot (drive-in restaurant), and I can still see the Kopper Kettle (a doughnut shop on Winchester Road that had existed since 1931) in my mind's eye, but for anything else you had to go to San Jose.

"At least," he added jokingly, "(you had to go to San Jose) if you wanted to get into trouble. And there wasn't really time for that, at least for me. When I wasn't playing baseball, I was picking prunes and apricots and cherries. I worked at the fruit dehydrator during the summers, and there was a youth sports program at the high school, so I didn't run out of things to do too often. We had some great athletes in those days, and I think one reason was the farm aspect ... we had a lot of big, strong kids who stayed in shape because of the work they did in the orchards and on the farms."

The move to Campbell enabled John to play organized baseball for the first time, and although he'd only dabbled in the sport in the places he'd previously lived, he became an immediate standout for Campbell High. At 6-foot-3 and wiry — he weighed 193 pounds as a professional, but considerably less than that as a high school student — he was a left-handed pitcher who could generate torque with his lower body and was athletic enough to commit his motion to muscle memory without variation, thereby giving him command to go with his velocity.

By the end of his senior season, 1950, John had generated some interest from major league scouts. He had set an SCVAL record with 18 strikeouts (out of a possible 21) in one game, and his value was enhanced by a strong performance in a high school All-Star game after his senior season. He could have signed with the highest bidder at that point, because the major league baseball draft wasn't instituted until 1965. But none of the offers were substantial, and he decided to play at San Jose State, where he starred for four years under Walt Williams, the Spartans' baseball coach and a former San Jose High football coach. The program was modest in scope, then and for years thereafter, but Oldham's work maintained the interest of area scouts, and as a senior in 1954, he struck out 145 batters in 14 games, compiled a 2.72 earned run average, and pitched 12 shutout innings in a game against Cal that was declared a scoreless tie because of darkness.

"I screwed up, though," John said. "In those days there was a bonus rule where if you paid a guy a bonus that was more than $4,000, you had to keep him on the major league roster for two years (instead of apprenticing in the minors). I could have signed (for more than $4,000) after my junior year (at SJS), but I didn't want to sit and do nothing for two years, and after my senior year I didn't have any leverage at all and I signed for pretty much nothing with the Reds."

If John had signed and gone straight to a major league team after his junior season, though, he might have been able to earn more than a seat in the dugout. By 1955, only his second pro season, he was pitching for the Seattle Rainiers of the open-classification Pacific Coast League, and after a stint in the Navy in late 1955 and early 1956, he returned to Seattle late in the 1956 season. In September, Cincinnati, which hadn't had a winning season since 1944 but was in the midst of a National League pennant race with the Brooklyn Dodgers and Milwaukee Braves, called him up.

"I wasn't expecting it," he said. "I'd been in the Navy and I'd just gotten out, and it was pretty exciting. I was in awe of everything. Right after I got there, I was called in to pinch-run, and my first reaction was, 'Me?' My mouth just dropped open. We're in the middle of this pennant race and here I am in the middle of it."

The Redlegs – temporarily renamed from 1954-59, during the Communist "red scare" – were playing the Chicago Cubs before a capacity crowd of 32,559 on Sunday, September 2 at Cincinnati's Crosley Field. Ted Kluszewski, the Redlegs' 6-foot-2, 225-pound first baseman, singled home two runs to give Cincinnati a 3-1 lead with two outs in the bottom of the third inning of a game it eventually won 3-2. Kluszewski was one of the most feared sluggers in the league, but he also was one of its slowest runners, and had been bothered by a leg injury. So Oldham was sent in to run for him. He wasn't at first base long, as shortstop Roy McMillan popped out to second base to end the inning. John came out of the game, and never got into another one in the majors.

Oldham had been told by the Redlegs that he had been brought up to pitch and not to pinch-run or sit on the bullpen bench, and manager Birdie Tebbetts had him warm up during several subsequent games as the Redlegs struggled to stay in the race. (They eventually finished third, two games behind the Dodgers and one game behind the Braves.) "We were in the middle of a pennant race," John said, "and in a few games, we'd get a big lead or they'd get a big lead, and I'd get sent down to the bullpen to warm up. But every time that happened, we'd hit a home run or they'd hit a home run and the game would be close again and I'd go back into the dugout and sit down. It was pretty discouraging, because I wanted to pitch."

The Redlegs sent Oldham back to the minors in 1957, and after the 1958 season, he was taken in the Rule 5 draft by the Pittsburgh Pirates. Oldham, 26 at the time, thought the Pirates would give him the opportunity that he hadn't received from Cincinnati, but by the end of the 1959 season, he was through with professional baseball and back at Campbell High, where he joined the staff in the fall of 1959 as the school's head baseball coach.

"The Pirates had told me that even if I didn't make the big club, I'd at least be at Triple-A," he said, "but at the end of spring training, they changed their mind and sent me somewhere else. I was kind of a volatile guy back then ... I was angry and I said some things and I got off on the wrong foot, and pretty soon it became punishment time and I was released."

Oldham hooked on with the Nashville Vols, Cincinnati's affiliate in the Class AA Southern Association, but he signed as a free agent and not as Cincinnati's property. He had decided by then that his future was in teaching and coaching. So per the agreement he had reached with the Vols, he stayed with them only until the start of summer school at San Jose State, whereupon he said goodbye to professional baseball, returned to California and finished work on his education degree before joining the Campbell High faculty.

"My timing was perfect," John said. "Del Mar had just opened (in the fall of 1959) and Wade Wilson, who was the Campbell High baseball coach at the time (and one of the founders of the Campbell Pony League), had gone over to Del Mar. So they needed a baseball coach, and I applied for the job and got it."

Oldham transformed a good program into one of the best in the Bay Area; in his five years there, the Buccaneers won three league titles and finished second the other two seasons. He also taught and served as athletic director at the school, and it was during his time at Campbell that year-round competitive baseball first became the norm in the Orchard City.

"Once kids got out of Pony League, they didn't have very many (summer) options," John said. "So we started a summer program, kind of like an American Legion program except it was run directly out of the school. Craig Morton would come out mornings and take care of the field, and then I'd come out in the afternoon. I was the field supervisor, so it was a pretty good way for me to take care of the field and work with all the kids legally (without violating California Interscholastic Federation rules pertaining to coaches' off-season contact with players)."

Oldham's early summer teams played informally and did not belong to a national organization, but an American Legion program was formed in the 1970s and enjoyed considerable success, playing in the 1974 Legion World Series. It disbanded in the late 1970s but was resurrected in 1982, and in 2008 still operated under the auspices of Mitty High.

Morton in the fall of 1960 led Campbell to an unbeaten football season and set SCVAL passing records that stood for almost two decades, and both he and top receiver Jack Schraub earned scholarships to Cal. Both also played two baseball seasons for Oldham, who had several other players continue their careers beyond high school. Lonny Raymond received a baseball scholarship from Stanford after graduating in 1962. Walt Christiana, described by John as the best athlete other than Morton he coached in high school, signed a contract reportedly worth $50,000 with the Boston Red Sox out of high school. But while Christiana had a figurative gun for an arm, he also had an affinity for real guns, and his professional career was cut short after only two full seasons after he accidentally shot himself in the foot.

In 1964, when Westmont opened, Oldham moved there as baseball coach and athletic director, and was replaced at Campbell by Gordon Huntze, who remained there until the school closed in 1980 and finished the program-building process that John had started. John stayed at Westmont only two years, but he still maintained ties with the school decades later.

"My last year coaching at Westmont, I got a call from Coach Oldham," said Jason Miller, a Westmont graduate who was the head baseball coach there for seven years in the late 1990s and early 2000s, and in 2009 was a dean of students at his alma mater. "He told me he had grandsons who were playing at Leigh, but that he'd like to help out with us. 'You have me until February 20,' he said, 'and after that I'm on the Leigh side.' Of course it was great to have him come out and work with our pitchers. He gave me a lot of insight. He was old school ... he'll go out there and show the kids things, and the way he explained it to me, 'They'll listen and do things my way, and if they think they have a way that's better than mine, I'll listen to them.' He'd get up there on the mound and run through his motion, and once in a while he'd have to stop in the middle of his motion because his knee would lock up on him. But I sure learned a lot from him ... I think he's one of the most knowledgeable baseball people in the valley."

In 1966, John accepted an offer to take over the program at San Jose City College, and his high school and Campbell days were over.

But not forgotten.

"Would I have been happy if I'd spent my entire career in Campbell (instead of moving on to college coaching)?" John said in response to a question to that effect. "I think so. It was a good place with a lot of community support. The feeder program was very good even then, although I just missed having those Moreland kids (who won the 1962 Little League, 1964 Pony League and 1966 Colt League world championships), and I was fortunate to have a lot of really talented, really great kids.

"It was really a fun time, getting to work in a situation like that ... I'll always have good memories of Campbell."

DUANE KUBO: The enabler

As much as any player from Campbell youth baseball's greatest generation, Duane Kubo was an enabler ... and on a much more profound and important level, he remains an enabler more than four decades after he played competitive baseball for the last time.

Duane, at 57, in 2009 was entering his 14th year as dean of De Anza College's Intercultural/ International Studies Division, with the responsibility of guiding students through the same path of ethnic and cultural self-discovery that he navigated as a young man. Earlier in his adulthood, he had been one of the first Asian-Americans to become nationally known for translating the means and the meaning of his own voyage to the cinematic medium. The films he made in his 20s are still critically acclaimed today because they depict the realities of his teen years and his heritage honestly and through understatement rather than admonishment. It's obvious after only a few minutes of conversation with him that enlightenment is his nourishment.

By the time he had reached his 12th birthday, Duane knew more about enabling than most people ever learn, and much of that early knowledge came through baseball. Although he was the youngest and smallest player on Moreland Little League's 1962 World Series championship team, his work can be compared to that of David Eckstein, the 5-foot-6 shortstop who helped the 2002 Anaheim Angels and the 2006 St. Louis Cardinals become World Series champions. He was Moreland's No. 2 hitter, and its shortstop. Two years later, he started at second base for an even better Campbell Moreland team that went 18-0 and won the Pony League World Series ... and then, recognizing his need for broader experiences beyond baseball, he didn't linger before moving on to endeavors that were to be just as compelling and far more important.

"I still tell people my life peaked at 11," Duane said, smiling, as we lunched at the Duke of Edinburgh, a Cupertino restaurant not far from his office at De Anza. "But really, especially for me, my Little League experiences showed me that the possibilities (in life) are endless if you really want to go for it. One thing I remember ... I must have been 9 years old when I saw the

(1960) Little League World Series final on TV. It was Levittown, Pa. (against Fort Worth, Texas), and Joe Mormello pitched a perfect game for Levittown in that game. I watched every pitch, and I was just mesmerized. I'm thinking, 'We can hit that guy.' It was always in the back of my mind that something like that was possible.

"It (Moreland's brief time as a baseball citadel) was a convergence of things, really. It was the postwar period and San Jose was booming, especially west San Jose and Campbell. There was a lot of construction. Most of our sponsors were construction companies or other businesses related to building. All these housing tracts were going up, and I think that kind of econom-ic boom just lent itself to parents getting kids into different organizations and supporting them."

Unlike many of his Moreland teammates, Duane was a San Jose native and lived his entire childhood in the Moreland School District, which had been sparsely populated until the early 1950s. He says his earliest baseball memory was of the New York Giants' move to San Francisco in 1958, and when Moreland Little League was formed the following year, nei-ther he nor his friends needed much enticement to sign up. Duane says his experiences in Moreland helped shape his belief in the value and the rewards of multiculturalism. Many of the families who moved into the Moreland area in the 1950s were first-generation immigrants from all over the world, and as has been the case throughout baseball history, the sport pro-vided many newcomers with a vehicle by which they could immerse themselves in something that was quintessentially American.

"I think that's what planted the seed for a lot of people I knew," he said. "As soon as the Giants came west, the whole place went crazy and got on board. I still remember people walking around with their transistor radios pinned to their ears. Another thing was that the first and second generations (of immigrants) were embracing the culture, and that especially included baseball. Many of the coaches in our league were Italians, Slovaks, Portuguese ... they loved the game and picked up on the Giants.

"My Moreland team had all kinds of signals, not only catchers to pitchers but coaches to infield-ers and catchers. It was a very sophisticated level of playing for that time, and it started with hav-ing people who really knew the game. We had a lot of coaches who'd played pro and semipro."

Interestingly, Duane said that although most members of the future Moreland nucleus knew each other and got on well, they didn't hang around together as one group or take any sort of collective vow in terms of future success. "Some of the guys (he played with) were close, others were not," he said. "I think the Moreland district was pretty broad (geographically), so I didn't necessarily grow up with all the same guys. Some of them I did, but it wasn't like there were 10 or 12 of us from year to year.

"But I would say this: Growing up, kids used to ride bikes all over town, and we'd play just about every day after school, especially at Hathaway Park (near the intersection of San Tomas Aquino Road and Hamilton Avenue). It wasn't formal, mainly stuff like 'over the line.' But we were still developing skills, and we were very competitive. During that time period there was still a lot of land available, and it was easy for us to make our own diamonds. There were plenty of places to play, maybe unlike today."

In terms of the 1962 Little League World Series experience, Duane says the vignettes he remembers most readily had little to do with the games themselves.

"I do remember the quick turnaround (after winning the Western Regional in Vancouver, British Columbia), because we had that rainout (that postponed the regional title game), but I don't remember it being such a burden," he said. "Our first game was a pretty easy game, but the semifinals were against Monterrey (Mexico), and in some ways we were intimidated by them. I remember seeing the movie about them ("The Little Giants," first shown on TV in 1960), and I'd love to see that movie again, with Angel Macias pitching the perfect game (in the 1957 Little League World Series title game), because it was part of my motivation for wanting to see how far we could go.

"It was about the poverty in Monterrey, how they used cardboard for mitts and sticks for bats. I remember Angel Macias threw both right-handed and left-handed in the movie (as he did in reality). It wasn't the same team (in 1962), but we knew the team we played would be good. The final game wasn't easy either. The Kankakee kid (Danny Brewster) was very good. If not for Vaughn's home run (for Moreland's only earned run in a 3-0 victory), who knows?"

One of Duane's prized keepsakes from the Williamsport trip is a ball autographed by Jackie Robinson, who was the color commentator of the championship-game telecast. "We only met briefly," he said, "but it was pretty amazing. I don't recall meeting Ted Williams (who also was at the tournament), and I think I would remember it if I had. Maybe he was just part of the ceremonies.

"Certainly there was exhilaration initially (after the championship was won), but really it was just one big adventure to us. We'd gone from San Francisco to Vancouver to Williamsport to Washington and then back home, and that was a pretty big deal for an 11-year-old kid who had never been back East before. They had a lot of set activities that you go to (so there wasn't much idle time). We met the Japanese team, which I think was as interesting to them as it was to us, seeing Japanese-Americans. I was the smallest kid on our team, and people were amazed that here was a kid (on the Japanese team) who was even smaller than me. We didn't really hang with the other American teams; I mainly remember the Japanese team.

"What I remember in retrospect had more to do with this area. The demographic thing really helped (generate) support for the team — not just parents, but other people coming out to watch the games, especially after we started All-Stars. I still see people who tell me they watched some of those games, even though they didn't have any kids. Everybody loved baseball, and it generated some amount of interest and I think pride for the whole area. It was the first time any San Jose team had gone on to a national level. The buzz lasted for years, and there was no doubt in my mind two years later that we would parlay that into the Pony League team."

After Campbell Moreland Pony League's World Series conquest of 1964, a scramble ensued among local high school coaches for the services of the best players. Duane, still undersized for his age and a year younger than most of his teammates, didn't attract as much attention as some of his teammates, but by that time he knew he wanted to broaden his horizons beyond baseball. He played only one more season. After that, he decided against playing Colt League, and never played again, although he did play football and run track at Blackford High.

"I was a little burned out on baseball at 15; I'd started when I was 8," he said. "Dennis Awtrey (the basketball player) was two years older than me, and when Dennis was a junior and senior I was the basketball team manager, so we were pretty close. I see him every now and then. We didn't have soccer in west San Jose at that time; if they had, I think I would have played. We were playing in the early 1960s, but by the late 1960s there were all kinds of other things going on. We were all in the draft era, and everybody was aware of what that meant."

Duane had always loved music, and he immersed himself in the emerging Bay Area music scene as a teenager. He remembers attending a Rolling Stones concert at San Jose Civic Auditorium in December 1965, and he was closely attached to a number of San Jose-area garage bands that had strong local followings — most notably the Syndicate of Sound, which had been formed in 1964, and in 1966 had a Top Ten national hit with a song called "Little Girl" that still is heard frequently on retro radio stations. Meanwhile, his passion for self-discovery and for photography began to dovetail. An excellent student, he graduated from Blackford in 1968 and was accepted to UCLA, where cultural enablement became a lifestyle and not just an interest.

"When I went to college, all kinds of stuff was breaking out, and I wanted to try to express some of my Asian-American identity," he said. "My dad was kind of an amateur photographer; he had cameras, and even some photos from the (Japanese-American relocation) camp he was in (during World War II). I took to the visual aspect of what was going on at that time; I worked for the first Asian-American community newspaper in L.A., and I met others who were interested in the same kind of expression of Asian-American identity. Initially that came in photography, but later it was in filmmaking, and some of us got together and formed Visual Communications."

Visual Communications, which he co-founded, remains a pioneering community media arts center in Southern California. In addition to its work in film and other media, it also is active in community-enhancement projects, and Duane says today that his work with VC played a large part in the shaping of his social consciousness and conscience. Two of his most acclaimed films were "Crusin' J-Town" and "Hito Hata: Raise the Banner."

"The films I made were some of the first Asian-American films, really," he says. "Cruisin' J-Town (released in 1975) was an attempt to show how Americans of Asian descent like myself were fusing their traditional backgrounds. J-Town was a portrait of (the musical group) Hiroshima. One of the main subjects of the film had master's status on the koto (a stringed instrument that first was introduced to Japan in the 7th century and is deeply ingrained in Japanese tradition and culture). He came back to L.A. to live, and all this stuff was happening around the Asian-American identity thing. He joined (Hiroshima) and soon he was improvising koto within a Latin jazz context. Hiroshima was the group that fused all of those genres into what is now considered American. He was the first to put an electric guitar pickup on a koto, and he was in effect blacklisted in Japan because it was (seen by traditionalists as) blasphemous ... he made it something other than what traditional masters saw it as. But all of a sudden it was a new jazz instrument that was electrical.

"Raise the Banner was the first Asian-American feature length film. It was the story of Japanese Americans and the redevelopment of Little Tokyo in L.A. Whole blocks of hotels were being pulled down, and the men who were fulltime residents were literally put on the street. I wanted to make a film on what these men had contributed to America. The protagonist was given an eviction notice, just as he'd been given one to uproot his family to Utah (in 1942 as the result of President Franklin Roosevelt's Executive Order 9066, which brought about the forced relocation of hundreds of thousands of Japanese-Americans to concentration camps), so I wanted to try to draw some parallels."

Duane also taught during his filmmaking career, and used both his films and his commitment to Asian-American pride to advance numerous community projects. So his eventual move to De Anza and subsequent ascent to his dean's position was, as he put it, "pretty seamless.

"I'd always seen all of the film work I did in the context of education," he said, "and during that time I was also teaching anyway. I was pretty instrumental in (the establishment of) Asian-American studies at UCLA when I was there. Students were kind of the cannon fodder; we were the ones sitting in buildings demanding ethnic studies, so that's when the context was drawn. When almost your entire (ethnic) community resides on the West and East coasts, the people in the middle only know you through the way you're depicted in the media. We did not have control of the media, and the characterizations of Asians at that time were often wrong. We said, 'We've got to get the skills to address that.' That was the impetus to start VC.

"At De Anza, (establishing multicultural protocols and curricula) is not just focused on Asian-Americans. The same thing happens over and over, with new groups of immigrants. I've had Persian students come to me, and Pakistani students. I've gone through some of that as a third generation, and I know there are common things that people go through."

THE DEFINING MANAGERS: Gordon Huntze, Jack Zogg, Bud Stallings

Gordon Huntze's detractors — and he did have a few, despite the fact his Campbell High teams were championship contenders almost every season — attributed much of his success to the upward flow of skillful, impassioned players from the Campbell youth baseball system.

It's a premise with which Gordon, in 2009, didn't entirely disagree.

"We had some really outstanding players come to us during my coaching years," he said during an interview in his comfortable home in a West San Jose neighborhood that looks little different than it did when he bought the house in the mid-1960s. "We were fortunate ... the guys in the feeder leagues were proud of their success, and there were some really outstanding coaches who helped bring them along. There was a great tradition in Campbell (youth baseball). Those kids we had were really competitive (even before their high school years), and there weren't nearly as many outside things as there are now. It was quite an era."

The fact of the matter, though, was that the baseball energy in Campbell flowed upward just as freely as it flowed downward. Because Gordon had great respect for the Little League and Pony League programs from which his players advanced to Campbell High, he never directly involved himself with the managers and coaches there, except when specifically asked. Yet his influence on those players even before they reached high school cannot be understated, and was a major factor in Campbell's youth-baseball success, especially after Gordon's teams won back-to-back Central Coast Section championships in 1972-73. The best Campbell players' ambitions were two-pronged. They wanted to excel at their own level, of course, but always prominent in their minds was the idea that they someday might play baseball for Coach Huntze at Campbell High.

In 1978, when Campbell Moreland won the first of its two straight Pony League World Series titles, first baseman Dominic Costantino saved a game and a season by spearing a line drive with his team ahead by one run in the final inning of the regional title game. ("The Catch" is described in detail later in this book, during the chapter on Dominic.) The play was as memorable as any in Campbell's youth baseball history, but 30 years later when Dominic reflected on it, one vignette from that game's aftermath remained embedded.

"There was so much excitement after the game," said Dominic, who played for Huntze at Campbell before the school closed, and then transferred to Bellarmine Prep for his final two high school seasons, "but the thing I remember most was Coach Huntze coming up to me and saying, 'Son, I have to tell you. That was the greatest catch I've ever seen.' I'd never met Coach Huntze, but obviously I knew who he was, and here I am, an eighth-grade kid. For a man like that to say something like that to me ... I was just awed.

"I still remember when he talked to me that day ... that steel jaw ... he was almost military, kind of like my dad (a former Marine)."

Paul Sargis played for Huntze for four years, the first three at Campbell and his senior year, 1981, at Westmont. His memories of the time and the man remain vivid.

"Huntze was proud and ran a disciplined program," Paul said. "He would run us after games, either 40-yard dashes if we'd won, or foul line to foul line if we'd lost or played sloppy. Occasionally our bus driver would have to wait 30 minutes to take us back to school. Sometimes we might get off the bus and run some more when we got to school. I recall other teams' faces when we would run after beating them. I knew it was coming, though ... when I was on Campbell Plaza (in Little League), our practice field was at Campbell High and those high school players would do seemingly endless laps around the whole grass field, including ours.

"(Huntze) was a very motivating speaker. He was not afraid to show emotion, even an occasional tear. He was most effective when we got a smile out of him when we did something well. He had a (fictitious) 'Grandma Beck' that apparently played baseball ... he would often refer to her prowess when a kid booted a ball or did something like that. He'd remind them that 'Grandma Beck' could have made that play. He could be intimidating. If a kid misplayed a ground ball, he would fungo him another (harder) and so on and so on even from the grass.

"Speaking of the grass, Coach Huntze spent hours on his infield grass. It was the best infield in our league. I would be interested to know if he even let the school groundskeepers touch it. As a drivers-ed teacher he once had me and three other kids driving and made a route to the district yard on Camden Avenue to negotiate a deal for some more infield dirt or a new mower or something.

"I learned more individual mechanics from Huntze than was popular in the day. Footwork, positions and movement in turning double plays, relay-throw positions, crow hop, infield set position. I teach it now and it has lasted. I think Huntze got a lot of feedback from (his former) players who went far, like Wes Mitchell, and cared to learn what the pros were doing and taught us thusly. Bud (Stallings) was also very good at this. (They were) probably the best two coaches I have ever played for, for many reasons: teaching, motivating, team building, leading, winning."

Dozens of Campbell youth baseball graduates who played for Campbell High or Westmont over Huntze's 30-year coaching career echo many of those sentiments, and virtually all of them take issue with the assertion that Gordon won simply because he inherited ready-made teams. For one thing, they point out, Huntze's Campbell High program didn't always get all the Campbell-system talent. In 1974, for example, Del Mar had no less than four players — Kevin and Kelly Linnane, Steve Esau, and Kent Ohmann — who had been starters on the 1970 Campbell team that reached the Little League World Series, and the Dons' first baseman that year was Steve Picone, who went on to play at San Jose State. Del Mar's WVAL record that year was 1-17, and even in 1975, when the four ex-Campbell Little League players were seniors and a fifth '70 squad member, Gerry Ford, had been added, the Dons finished tied for third with Campbell, which was in the midst of a down year (by Campbell standards) and had only one 1970 Little League All-Star, Rickey Roth. Moreover, even in the late 1980s and early 1990s after Campbell's youth baseball program began to decline precipitously in scope and quality, Westmont — which had never made the postseason before Huntze's arrival — stayed good, getting to the Central Coast Section playoffs four times in his first five seasons there and six times overall before his retirement after the 1992 season.

In 2009, he was spending much of his time hunting and immersing himself in his family, which stood as a testament to the wisdom of Gordon and his wife, Kay. All four of their children had chosen careers in public service, and all had done well. His oldest son, Dave, is a teacher in Redding; his daughter, Debbie, is the highly successful women's softball coach at San Jose City College; and his twin sons, Jim and Jeff, both are fire captains, in Daly City and Contra Costa County respectively. Although all three of his sons played baseball in the Campbell system, and Jim and Jeff both played against him for Prospect against Westmont, Gordon made it a priority to allow his kids to have baseball experiences that were distinct from his. They always gave their best effort, they got better as they progressed in the system, and they always played with smiles on their faces, and Gordon and Kay took the most pride in those elements.

Gordon won about 600 games as a high school coach — he never kept track and doesn't know the exact number — but his reputation and influence in the developmental leagues were based on far more than his win total, or even the back-to-back CCS titles he won at Campbell High in 1972 and 1973. It was he, more than anybody else, who shaped and defined the way baseball was played in Campbell during the years when the system had a national-championship contender almost every year. Because he treated the Little League and Pony League managers and coaches so respectfully, they were eager to implement both his teaching techniques and his passion for winning while playing the game the right way.

"I think I coached at a pretty good time and I got out at a pretty good time," he said. "When I first started coaching, all the schools in our league were pretty close together ... the kids all knew each other and they had rivalries among themselves, and that helped make them better. At the end (after the WVAL was dissolved and its schools became part of the Blossom Valley super league) we were busing all over to play teams we didn't even know, and we got away from some of those rivalries.

"And the kids I had (at Campbell and in his early Westmont years) were really committed. Their parents were responsible, and they knew where their kids were and what they were doing when they weren't playing baseball. I think it's kind of gotten away from that now."

Gordon was born and raised in Oakland, and played baseball at Fremont High and what is now Laney College there before transferring to San Jose State and playing there in 1961 and 1962. Much later, when soccer began to emerge as an athletic alternative to youth baseball in Campbell and elsewhere, Gordon was one of the few baseball men who wasn't surprised. He had moon-lighted as a soccer player during his two baseball off-seasons at San Jose State, long before soccer became fashionable or even identifiable on the American sports scene.

"(SJS soccer coach) Julie Menendez kind of recruited me out of a (physical education) tech-nique class," he said, laughing. "I could always kick real well, and he told me, 'I need a goalie. Would you come out?' I played almost all the time as a senior. Julie had a great program later on (he remains the only American to be a head Olympic coach in two sports, soccer and boxing) but back then the program was just forming, and when we'd play a Stanford or a Cal, we'd just get our butts kicked. I remember yelling at my fullbacks, 'Hey, I can use a little *help* back here!' a lot of the time."

After graduating from San Jose State, Huntze was ready to accept a job in Covelo, a small com-munity in Mendocino County, when a friend alerted him to an opening on the staff at Campbell High. Preferring to start his career in a growing urban area, Huntze applied for the job and got it. He served as an assistant football and baseball coach, working under John Oldham in the latter capacity. He took over as head coach in 1965 after Oldham left to start the program at Westmont, and he won a league championship, Campbell's fourth in six seasons, his first year.

"I was fortunate in that I had a pretty good group, with Don Hahn and a couple of very good pitchers," he said. "John was responsible for a lot that had gone on (in terms of building Campbell into a winning program), and that first year, I pretty much just sat in the dugout and said, 'Go play, guys.' We beat Westmont a couple of times that first year, and afterward he (jokingly) said to me, 'I don't know if I should have left.' But I did kind of pattern the program after what he'd done.

"One thing he did that I continued was having the frosh-soph and the varsity practice together as one unit. We began teaching the kids (a Campbell High style of play) as freshmen, and by the time the kids got to be juniors and seniors, they had a pretty good idea of what we wanted to do and could really help the coaches by helping the younger kids. We'd work all our fundamentals together, an hour or an hour and a half each day, before we broke into team groups. It really worked out well for us.

"Another thing I remember we kept was having the kids always wear their hard hats (batting helmets, which didn't become mandatory until the mid-1960s) all the time, even in the field, during practice. We didn't even use the soft hats except as part of the uniforms during games. I can still remember spray-painting those helmets."

Like Oldham, Gordon believed that maintaining a quality baseball plant was essential to creating a proprietary sense among the players. While many of the high school ballparks in the WVAL, especially Del Mar's, were eyesores and represented a safety hazard to players, Campbell High's infield resembled a putting green, and infielders could count on true hops because their practice day usually ended with them using rake and hoe to manicure the dirt surrounding their positions. Around 1970, Campbell High became the first prep program in the area to have its own batting cage, which was built by Huntze and parent volunteers beyond the high screen that overlooked the short left-field corner.

"I think that (high-quality facility) really created a lot of pride in the program," Gordon said. "We'd play on the road and the kids would comment, 'Coach, it doesn't look like those guys care very much about their field.' Every week, we'd have two or three of them assigned to the infield grass, and we'd cut that thing every other day. Some of the parents asked me about the possibility of building the batting cage. I told them that anything they could do would be appreciated, so they scrounged up the materials and got a welder and we climbed up there and installed it.

"Was I a stickler about our field? Yeah, I was, both at Campbell and later at Westmont. A couple of times at Westmont, somebody spray-painted (obscenities) across the backstop, and the district maintenance people thought I'd done it, just to get the backstop painted. And at Campbell, it was kind of a unique park because it was out away from the main school grounds. I'd sometimes see (non-students) out there on a Saturday or a Sunday and I'd feel like they'd broken into my house. I'd tell them to get off and most of the time they'd do it, but a couple of times they wouldn't, so I went in the dugout and got one of the big sprinklers we had and fired that baby up. They got the message then."

Gordon also was an early believer in the concept of using psychological factors to his advantage, and the short left-field porch at Campbell High was one of his original props. Because the contours of the school's property made it impossible to extend the left field foul line beyond about 230 feet from home plate, a high screen (eventually replaced by the batting cage) was built atop the left-field wall as it jutted out toward left-center. This created a Fenway Park-like effect among opposing hitters, whose eyes widened as they pondered the possibility of lofting balls over that screen. They were pitched accordingly, and the result usually was a torrent of harmless popups and grounders to the second baseman. Meanwhile, Gordon taught his hitters to ignore the screen and concentrate on hitting balls to the left-center field gap, which usually was vacated because opposing left fielders would be in the left-field corner in front of the screen.

"From that corner, it jutted almost straight out, to about 330 in straightaway left," Gordon said. "Guys would come to that field and think they could hit every pitch out, so they'd try to pull it. For us, I always thought line drives were the way to go, and the way the park was shaped was perfect for guys to hit the ball in the gaps and run forever."

Gordon began his coaching and teaching career a year after Moreland Little League won the 1962 Little League World Series. He never coached anybody on that team — most attended Blackford, and some didn't play high school baseball — but he did sense that the accomplishment fueled community-wide enthusiasm for baseball in Campbell.

"To me, right from the start, it was pretty obvious to me that these kids really enjoyed playing baseball," he said, "and they did a lot of it on their own, on sandlots and playgrounds and in the street. When I became the coach and started making contacts with some of the Little League and Pony League managers and coaches, I was thinking, 'Geez, these guys teach some really good fundamentals. They're really competitive and they take a lot of pride in what they're doing.' They invited me to talk about some things a couple of times, and it was always a real good experience for me, but I liked what they were doing and it was working well (in terms of producing players who were ready for high school baseball by the time they arrived at Campbell High)."

In addition to the fact the Campbell system provided Gordon with experienced, motivated, well-schooled players, he also appreciated the pre-high school managers and coaches because their skills and commitment meant he didn't have to run a year-round program at the expense of his family. Gordon always fervently believed that while the months during which school was in session belonged to his players and to baseball — and no coach in the area outworked Gordon during those months — his summers belonged to Kay and the four kids. As soon as school vacation began, the Huntzes were in the family truck and on their way to a summer of immersion in the outdoor life that all of them loved.

"I didn't get much of a chance to participate much with my kids during the school year," he said. "Kay just did a fantastic job with them ... she was the one taking them to practices and all the other things they had going on. High school ball pretty much consumed me for nine months. The summers, I took off, and those summers were great family time."

Huntze never had a losing season during his 16 years as Campbell High's last varsity baseball coach, and one reason his players exuded passion was that they saw it in their coach. Another reason was the fact he never shied away from high expectations. Still another was the fact that when fatigue set in — as if often did in the WVAL, which usually had three league games scheduled per week — the players' conditioning would take over.

"I had kids say to me, 'Coach, I didn't know I was going out for track,'" he said, laughing. "I used to be a stickler about having guys run, and I used to run them a lot after losses. Then one day one of the kids asked me why we only ran after losses, so we started doing that (running after wins) because I didn't want to use running just as punishment. The idea was that every kid who came out for the team knew that there was going to be running involved. I had a reputation as a disciplinarian, and there was nothing wrong with that. The kids picked up on that, and they worked hard.

"I guess I was young and dumb then, but every year, I really felt that, hey, if we don't finish first or second in the league, we're not doing our job. It wasn't being cocky; it was just that I thought we had the best team every year. We tried to do everything with a purpose, which was getting ready to win the league. The first week of practice, the kids never put a glove on. We played catch bare-handed because I wanted the kids to learn to have soft hands and use both hands, and because I didn't want to wear out their arms so early, before we even played a game."

Gordon's teams, from the time he took over, usually closed fast and finished high in the standings. In 1972 and 1973, the Campbell High program reached its zenith, winning back-to-back CCS titles and compiling a combined record of 48-11, and both teams closed their seasons with 10-game winning streaks. The Buccaneers also made the CCS playoffs in 1977 and in 1980, the school's last season, and in 1978 lost a playoff game with Leigh after tying the Longhorns and Del Mar for the league championship. Campbell probably would have been an annual playoff participant in the 1970s under the system that was implemented by the CCS in the late 1980s. In the 1970s and early 1980s, the WVAL was unquestionably the section's strongest league, but until 1979, only the league champion advanced to the CCS playoffs.

"We had a little success, and I think a lot of the kids were kind of looking forward to coming to Campbell High to play," he said. "The fact we had a feeder program was a real plus, and I think it worked well both ways. We were pretty good every year, but that league was just so hard to win and the schools were so close together that every game was like a rivalry game. There were great coaches too — Joe Winstead at Los Gatos, Hal Kolstad at Leigh, Fred Rasmussen at Branham — and even some of the teams that weren't contenders had some talent and could beat you if you overlooked them. There just wasn't a team in the league where you could say, 'Well, OK, we shouldn't have any trouble beating them.'"

While Gordon maintained his high standards and strict demeanor throughout his coaching career, both at Campbell High and later at Westmont, he says he also saw the need to evolve in terms of seeing matters through his players' eyes. And while he always felt that a certain distance between player and coach was not only necessary but desirable, he understood, even early in his career, that he needed to be accessible and willing to help his players beyond the baseball realm.

"One of my first years, it might have even been my first year, I had a player knock on my door and tell me, 'Coach, I'm going to have to quit baseball,'" he recalled. "I asked him why, and he said, 'My girlfriend is pregnant.' It happened again a few years later, around '73. You know, kids are going to be kids sometimes and do things they regret, but you can't turn your back on them. Fortunately in both cases the families were really supportive of the kids, and we were able to work things out without them having to drop off the team. I didn't try to get that close to my kids early in my career, and I tended to try to treat all of them the same. Well, you get older and maybe wiser, and later on I found out that maybe you can't always treat every player the same way. Sometimes it sometimes worked better to put my arm around a kid and talk to him and ask him what's wrong rather than yelling at him."

Gordon has stayed in touch with many of his former players, especially after Westmont in 2006 began holding an annual alumni game to honor Jeff Mitchell. Jeff, a former Campbell Little League, Pony-Colt League and Westmont player, was the younger brother of Greg Mitchell, the starting shortstop on Campbell Little League's 1979 national championship team. After graduating from Westmont, where he was a standout outfielder, in 1986, Jeff went into the military and then into law enforcement, and by 2006 was a deputy sheriff in Sacramento County. He was murdered that fall during a traffic stop. His killer has never been apprehended. (All of the royalties from the sale of this book will be donated to a trust fund set up to financially assist Jeff's widow and two children.)

Asked what he hoped above all that his players would take from their experience in his program, Gordon paused for several moments before answering.

"I think just the fact the competitiveness we had on the team ... I wanted them to be able to succeed when they stepped out of sports," he said. "That's what's so great about sports ... it teaches you to compete. I had a few kids I came down hard on at times, and I thought at the time that they probably hated me. Then five or 10 years later they go out of their way to come see you and tell you how much you helped them. That's the ultimate for a coach. It isn't just what you see of them walking down the street; it's inside. Campbell just seemed like a huge family to me, and it was different at Westmont (after Campbell High closed). We still had great kids and great parents and we had some very good teams, but Campbell was special. I don't know if after that we had the same kind of thing, playing baseball (for baseball's sake) and having the family feeling.

"It hurt me when they shut down Campbell High. It hurt a lot. I mean, this is the Campbell Union High School District and there's not going to be a Campbell High? They said the campus was in bad shape and all that, but look at it now (as the refurbished Campbell Community Center). The baseball diamond is gone now (it has been grassed over to accommodate soccer) but sometimes I walk my dog over there and it's like I can still see this player or that player, or this game or that game."

Gordon coached at Westmont from 1981 through 1992, and taught there two more years before retiring from the district in 1994. Since then, he has indulged his passion for hunting and immersed himself in his family, which now includes six grandchildren, all ages 7 to 10. He also helped his daughter Debbie during the early stages of her softball coaching tenure at San Jose City College. Through 2008, Debbie's teams had registered 16 straight winning seasons, and 92 percent of her players graduated.

"All four of the kids have had success," he said. "The grandkids love to come around, and they're all into sports. Deb's oldest daughter Kayla is 10, and she just got her black belt in karate. I didn't realize how much dedication that involved ... we went to a couple of their contests and you want to talk about dedication? This little girl did it, and she's the sweetest kid you'd ever want to meet besides.

"My wife and I are really blessed. I feel really fortunate to have been able to coach for so long and to be able to do it when I did it. I only thought about leaving (to go into college coaching) once ... West Valley came and talked to me about going over there. I kind of weighed it, and I realized I really enjoyed the high school atmosphere and that being a college coach would mean I'd have to take even more time away from my own kids, which I didn't want to do. I just felt like I could do more on the high school level. What's going to happen to these kids after they graduate, because so few actually go on to play beyond that? On the high school level, you can teach them so many other things."

Huntze's indirect influence was the one overriding constant during the Campbell youth baseball phenomenon of the 1960s and 1970s. On the Little League and Pony League levels, the directional element, as might be expected, was far more of a variable because nobody in the Campbell system at that time was a professional teacher-coach, although many had extensive playing experience. Of all the yardsticks that can be used to quantify just how good Campbell's teams were when the program was at its peak in the late 1970s, perhaps the most revealing is the fact Campbell won four national championships from 1976-79 with four managers who had nothing in common except for the success they engendered and the type of proactive baseball they taught.

Bud Stallings, Jack Zogg, Lou Bacho and Subby Agliolo all knew each other, but they were not friends or even frequent acquaintances, and if their spectrum of coaching and communication techniques were to be mapped, one would be in Seattle, one in Maine, one in Florida and one in San Diego.

All, of course, had no lack of talent with which to work, but even at that, the four teams they managed to national championships were comprised of different players with different skills and different motivational buttons that needed to be pushed. Like Huntze, Stallings, Zogg and Bacho all preferred precision and speed over brute force, and emphasized pitching, smart base-running, and defense. Each was able to establish a way of playing the game that worked with the available talent, and their collective skills and approaches all became elements in what became "the Campbell way" of playing baseball.

The 1976 Campbell Little League team was managed by Jack Zogg, who had first come to the league in 1958 and managed the Robins team in the major division from 1959-80. He went to Oak Grove Little League in southeast San Jose after that, and managed in the major division there until 1992. In 2005, he returned as a farm-division manager in Oak Grove, working with his grandson, and was still doing so at age 75 in 2009.

During the 1980s, when I covered Stanford football, I became good friends with Otto Kofler, a Stanford assistant coach whose son Matt was an NFL quarterback for four seasons. I still think Otto, who died in 1994, is the best football coach I've ever met (and I differentiate between true football coaches and the sweat-sock CEOs who run most college and NFL teams), and in retrospect, I think one of the reasons I liked and admired him so much was that he reminded me a great deal of Jack Zogg.

Otto was in his 50s when I knew him and had been a high school coach much of his career. He was a tobacco-chewing, boot-wearing, George Strait-listening guy who was strictly moleskin and leather-helmet when it came to the effort and structure he demanded. You played hard for him all the time, or you heard about it in terms and language that never were misunderstood. But more than any of the other Stanford coaches, the kids loved Otto. He had been an English teacher as well as a high school coach, and he embraced the Socratic method of teaching: Instead of lecturing, he asked questions that initiated dialogue and prompted self-evaluation, and the result was that the players would come to conclusions on which they would act more readily because they thought the answers represented their own thinking. Otto also made the game simple to play by distilling information in such a way that his instructions were easily followed, and though he was sometimes gruff with the kids, he also was able to convey the sense that he was on their side and genuinely liked and cared about them.

Jack was the same way in his baseball milieu. One of his early pupils was Kent Ohmann, the third baseman on the 1970 Campbell Little League All-Star team, which reached the World Series finals before losing to Wayne, N.J.

"I probably learned more from him than from any coach I ever had," Kent says now. "He was a perfectionist. We had to have the perfect infield-outfield before games; if any of us dropped a ball, we had to do the whole thing over from the beginning. But when I think of him now, I think of (singer-comedian) Dean Martin. You might have made the worst error of your life, and you might be thinking this is the end of the world and you're choking back tears. Mr. Zogg would give you a little smile and let you know it was no big deal."

"I remember the whole time I was in Campbell Little League, you'd look at him and you'd say to yourself, 'That guy knows more about baseball than anybody in the world,'" said Matt Christian, who played for Campbell Moose Lodge from 1975-77. "Campbell was our baseball world then, and he was the guru of it."

As Jack, John Emery and I talked over breakfast in March 2009, I was reminded that another trait that Jack and Otto had shared was the fact both of them coached and taught in a way that transcended eras. Otto had never been one of those aging coaches who pined for the good old days, and Jack, in his 37th year as a Little League manager, was enjoying his 8- and 9-year-olds at Oak Grove for the same reasons that had first motivated him when he first came to Campbell Little League 51 years before.

"I enjoy it in a different way," he said. "The idea is, you're still showing somebody ways to do things. I've had times (with his current kids) where I've said, 'OK, you go to right field and you go to center field,' and they'd just stand there. You look at them, and one of them would finally say, 'Coach, where's center field?'" But the satisfactions are still the same when you see them learning how to do things and playing the game better."

Jack, more than many baseball men, could always identify with the occasional blank look, because he was almost as new to baseball as his players when he first came to Campbell Little League in 1958.

Jack was born in Oakmont, Pa., a suburb of Pittsburgh, and had moved to El Cajon, Calif., in 1946, at age 12. After graduating from high school, he had served in the Navy, and had moved to the San Jose area after being discharged in 1955. Although he was a baseball fan, particularly of the Brooklyn Dodgers, he played almost no baseball as a kid. In 1958, he was working as the manager of a Mayfair supermarket owned by his brother-in-law when he had a conversation with Pete Vassar, who was managing the Campbell Stamps team in Campbell Little League.

"He asked me if I knew anything about baseball," Jack recalled. "I said, 'Well, everybody knows *something* about baseball,' and he said that he needed a hand. Bob Holman and myself helped him out that first year, and after they made the cuts, they needed somebody to manage one of the minor league teams. So that was how I started. The next year, the Robins team opened up. That was how easy it was."

In the early years, Jack says, much of his sense of fulfillment was being part of the building process of a new organization in which shared goals prevailed. In 1958, Jack was hired by Santa Clara County as a surveyor, and he was heavily involved in baseball-related construction throughout

Campbell. Besides the renovation of the Rosemary School complex in 1963, when the permanent clubhouse and three new fields were built, Jack and John Emery (who was a bricklayer and masonry contractor) helped Campbell Moreland Pony League build both of its home facilities, first at Castro Middle School and then at John D. Morgan Park. When he first joined the league in 1958, the major division had only four teams, and usually, all of the managers and coaches lent a hand with the All-Star teams and with any other projects that had to be undertaken.

"Working together like that, you made friends that lasted a lifetime," Jack says. "I worked with Pete Mesa (a Campbell coach and parent) as a construction surveyor, and his oldest son was a bridge engineer ... I worked with him on the San Tomas Expressway project. Great guy. We got almost everything done (at Rosemary School) in that one year (1963). I still remember building the Little League clubhouse ... the only thing that went wrong was after we finished it, there were a few heavy moms in the lot, and we found out that they couldn't get through the bathroom doors. So we just widened them. We got things done because everybody pitched in."

John Emery also had been a major manager in the 1960s before leaving the league for a couple of years. He returned in 1971 to join Jack as a Robins coach, and the two of them worked together for a decade. John was Jack's coach with the national championship All-Star team in 1976 before he had to leave the team before the World Series because of a family matter. The two of them complemented each other ideally – Jack as the taskmaster, John as the facilitator. By the time they first teamed up, both of them had absorbed the nuances of Little League baseball, and both had come to the conclusion that it was best defined and taught as a game of speed, preparation and technique, not of size and power. They also came to understand that baseball, while never easy to play, is essentially simple and should be taught as such – and that while winning was important, friendships and long-term bonds were the truest long-term rewards, both for them and for the players.

It was a formula that made Robins a title contender almost every season, and made Jack and John exemplars to hundreds of boys, and many other Campbell managers and coaches, over the years. Both of them can remember almost every kid who played for them, and many others throughout the league as well.

"You know how they say with twins, one of them knows what the other will do before they do it?" Jack says. "Well, that's how we were. I'd start to give a sign and I'd look at John and he'd already be giving the sign. We thought the same on almost everything. And we had so many great kids, so many great families. You know, really, when you're talking about any kind of success, the playing of the game is a snap (for the coaches). The kids do all the work. Don't tell anyone this, but John and I didn't score a single run during that run in '76. Those kids *worked*. You'd call it something in baseball terminology, but really it was the kids wanting to take more and more ground balls, more batting practice, more outfield flies.

"What was the best thing I did as a coach? Probably putting together the coaching staff. I think one of the biggest things is just being able to bring yourself down to what the kids know and then expand on that. John works defenses as well as I do, so he'd work with the pitchers and I'd work with the defense, or the other way around. The batting part was pretty simple. John would throw batting practice until his arm got tired, then I'd throw batting practice until my arm got tired. (Jack and John both firmly believed that pitching machines did not properly simulate live pitching, and never used them.) We'd work through every situation. Pitching is simple too ... up and in, down and away, change speeds. You have four pitches (with which, ideally, each hitter should be retired) and you try to pitch to contact. After a week, you usually have a pretty good idea of what you have, and if the team is good, the idea is to not screw it up. You also have to get them to understand that dropping a ball or making a bad throw once in a while is part of baseball. The only thing you don't want to see is them not knowing what to do after that. Mental errors will always hurt you a lot more than physical errors."

Going into the 1976 All-Star tournament, Jack knew that the team had enough talent, cohesion and motivation to play deep into August. Hitting and pitching plainly were not going to be issues with the team, so he spent much of his practice time working on defense, implanting the idea that playing defense in baseball is not unlike playing defense in football. The entire field must be covered, regardless of the situation, and Jack and John focused on going through every possible backup situation and getting players acclimated to multiple positions.

"There were 10 players on that team who were going to be the main guys ... they were the ones the managers picked unanimously," Jack said. "With the other four boys, you're looking for something that's a little different in their abilities. Every boy we had, all 14 of them, could play at least two or three positions. Some could pitch; some could run the bases. They knew they had a role to play, and we tried to prepare them to play those roles. When the situation came up, they were there."

Jack and John also tried to maintain an informal level of communication with the kids away from the field, so that the team would remain relaxed.

"I won $1.40 from them once," he said, laughing. "I bet them one dime each that I couldn't do 25 pushups. Well, I get down and do three pushups, and they're asking when I'm gonna do the other 22. 'I didn't say anything about doing 25 at once,' I said. 'I just said I'd do 25.' I think I did the last one at the party after we got home from Williamsport."

Then as now, Little League generally was a station-to-station enterprise, but not with Jack. His kids knew how to handle the bat, they knew where they were supposed to be and what they were supposed to do, and they applied pressure with their speed and their opportunism.

Even so, nobody was sure how well Jack's approach would work with the All-Star team in 1976, because at first glance, it didn't look like his kind of team. Bobby Straight and Paul Sargis were the only guys on the team who had exceptional speed, and they were also the only guys who brandished their bats as swords; most of the rest of the central players were ax-wielding types without exceptional speed or range, and because so many honors teams tend to look better in the team photo than they do playing together, nobody was sure how the shortstop-and-pitcher types would take to unfamiliar defensive assignments and Jack's demand for continuous collectivism.

Paul Sargis remembers an early practice that was spent exclusively on defensive zoning, a concept that had never occurred to him or anyone else on the team. "I thought all we were going to do was hit and scrimmage and compete for positions," Paul said. "But not only did he know, and teach us, where all of us were supposed to be in every situation that could come up, he also showed us how to communicate with each other so we always had the whole field covered and there was never any confusion. We did stuff like that every practice, not the typical things, and we did that stuff until we got it right. We weren't sure how to take it at first, but the farther we got, the more we admired him — and we still do."

Campbell committed five errors and gave up six unearned runs in its 10-3 loss to Japan in the Little League World Series title game that year. Before that, we played and won 15 games, and we gave up only 12 unearned runs — a remarkable level of efficiency at any level, let alone Little League. Our pitching, already good, was made virtually unassailable by the fact we gave away almost no outs. Beyond that, we made plays on grounders and flies that would have been hits had Jack not taught his defenders to anticipate the ball off the bat and to always have their feet moving and their equilibrium established.

Two years after Jack took Campbell to the Little League World Series title game, we won a Pony League title with an equally remarkable manager and man — a man the kids revered, almost without exception, yet hardly knew.

Maybe Tom T. Hall knew him, or somebody like him, because the country-music balladeer did a song in 1972 that to this day brings Bud Stallings back to life for me. It was called "Old Dogs, Children and Watermelon Wine," and it describes Hall's meeting with an older gentleman in a Miami bar during one of his tours. (Bud was not an old man in 1978, maybe 45, but he always seemed much, much older, and it wasn't long afterward that his old man's body failed him.) The man in Hall's song was telling Hall how he'd come to distrust people in general, and he went on to describe the mental alcoves that sheltered him.

"Ever had a taste of watermelon wine? he asked,
"He told me all about it, though I didn't answer back,
"Only three things in this world that's worth a solitary dime,
"That's old dogs, children and watermelon wine.

"He said, 'Women think about they-selves, when menfolk ain't around.
"And friends are hard to find when they discover that you're down.
"He said, 'I tried it all when I was young and in my natural prime;
"Now it's old dogs and children and watermelon wine.
"Old dogs still love you, even when you make mistakes,
"God bless little children, while they're still too young to hate,
"When he turned away, I grabbed my pen and copied down that line,
"'Bout old dogs, children, and watermelon wine."

Bud had coached in the Pony League for six years before I moved to the Pony League in 1977, but he had spent almost his entire lifetime involved with baseball in some capacity. He began managing in 1953, in his hometown of Lynn, Mass., where he coached high school and Little League. After moving to California in 1961, he settled in Los Altos and led the Babe Ruth All-Star team there to a state title in 1964. He moved to Campbell in 1971 and began managing in Campbell Moreland that same year.

The Pony League atmosphere at John D. Morgan Park had been sedentary in the years before our arrival, and that suited Bud just fine because he had about as much use for adults, particularly noisy ones, as Joe McCarthy had for Communists. He rarely made an effort to socialize with the parents; he much preferred to be around the players. Bud had no off-season. During the autumn, he helped organize and run Campbell Moreland's fall-ball league and winter clinics, and after the regular season was over, he organized the Shamrocks, a group of 13-year-olds who would play against any and all comers — including, as previously chronicled, any girls softball teams that thought themselves capable of competing with boys. His constant companion was his dog, Sandy, a creature of indeterminate breed and age who seemed as negatively disposed to the adult public as Bud sometimes was.

I'd met Bud a few times at the Campbell Little League field during the early stages of our 1976 Williamsport run, and we got to know each other better in Williamsport. He was a sportswriter for the *San Jose Mercury News*, which sent him to cover the World Series. Beyond his coverage assignment, his interest was in finding players for the winter league program he always organized and ran at the Pony League field, and scouting players he might want to draft for his Pony League team. He sought me out for my insights, such as they were, and that element of trust was something I always appreciated. He knew that I had a lot of friendships among the kids, and knowing me would enable him to better know them. He also took an interest in me because I was majoring in journalism at San Jose State, and planned to become a sportswriter myself. In fact, I had him peruse some of my college work, and his suggestions were invaluable.

We became closer friends during my three years at the Pony League field, and I liked to watch his team practice because he went to extraordinary lengths to make his practices worth his players' attention. He had all kinds of unusual drills, most of them designed to imprint basics while capturing his players' imagination and keep them in a fun mode, and when he was around the kids, he took on the sort of little-kid demeanor that amused them and amazed me because he was so much the opposite around most adults. One of his practice twists was to make his infielders use a Ping Pong paddle instead of a glove, even in pregame warmups, and he sometimes let them go through infield sessions without using a ball, serving the dual purpose of letting the kids show off their athleticism while also giving them the opportunity to anticipate situations requiring difficult plays. I used both of those tactics later when I went into coaching, and he taught me a lot about making the game fun and the players fully engaged, especially during practice.

Bud was extremely close to most of his players, many of whom told me later that he went out of his way to help them through any off-field problems they might be having. Many of them remember tooling around town with him in his dune buggy, with the personalized license plate "3ON2OUT." (Later, after his Campbell Moreland All-Star team won the 1978 Pony League World Series, his *Mercury News* colleagues bought him a new plate, "CM UNO.") Even some of the kids who had been moody or diffident in Little League played with smiles on their faces when they were on Bud's team.

If he ever doubted just how much of an impact he had on these very impressionable 13- and 14-year-old lives, I think I may have imbedded it in him as the result of a situation that still makes me think of the "watermelon wine" reference in the Tom T. Hall song.

We were in Kennewick, Wash., for the 1978 Pony League West Regional, and in the winners-bracket final, as previously described, we'd just been beaten by future major league pitcher Mike Campbell and Southwest Seattle. Even before that, we'd been disjointed, and we hadn't been playing up to our capabilities, collectively or individually. We had a more talented, more versatile and more pitching-rich team than we'd had two years earlier when we'd gone to Williamsport, and we fully expected to win the Pony League World Series. We were supposed to dominate, and not only had we not done that, we hadn't looked anything like a team on the cusp of winning a world championship.

Bud was even quieter than usual during this time, and the players were beginning to take their cues from him. After the Mike Campbell game, I went out with some of the parents and others who had traveled north with the team, and while none of them badmouthed or blamed Bud specifically for the team's showing, the mood was one of extreme frustration. I knew the kids were as frustrated as their parents, and our chances of coming back through the losers bracket were not promising at all if that state of mind persisted.

On my way back to my motel room, I spotted Bud sitting alone in the bar adjoining the coffee shop, and even though I'd had a few cocktails with the parents, Bud looked so forlorn that I decided to go in and have a word with him. He wasn't eating; he was staring into space, and in front of him was a glass of wine.

Now, Bud's sobriety was total so far as any of us knew; I'd never even seen him take a drink with a meal, let alone wander up to "Beer Hill," the grassy embankment that paralleled the right-field line just beyond the first-base dugout at John D. Morgan Park. (Alcohol was forbidden within the ballpark horseshoe itself, but was allowed everywhere else in the park.) But there Bud was, and although the light was dim, there was no mistaking the depression that enveloped his face.

"I'm letting them down," he said, looking up at me. "These kids deserve so much and I don't know if I can get them there. We're playing badly and I don't know what to do and I'm afraid they'll hate me for letting them down. Maybe I should just quit and turn the club over to Chuck (Calhoun, his coach)."

"Bud," I said, "you know if there's anyone who knows these kids as well as you do, it's me, and I'm telling you this – these kids want to win for you as much as they want to win for themselves. They respect you and they trust you. I think what you have to do is just relax and trust them and have some fun with this."

"You think so?" Bud said. "You think they still believe in me?"

"Yeah," I said. "You've always said baseball should be fun, right? Well, it needs to be fun again for you too, and we're gonna beat (Mike) Campbell the next time we play them because all he throws is a fastball and that plays right into our hands."

Bud finished his glass of wine, and smiled, seemingly for the first time in a month, before heading off to bed. The next morning, one of the host parents in Kennewick had organized a pool party; Bud had a short practice scheduled, but he cancelled it and let the kids go to the party early. By the time they got back, the fog of discouragement had dissipated. The kids told me he gave them a talk to the effect that they should play as if they had everything to gain and nothing to lose, not the other way around as we had been doing. We blasted our next opponent, and then swept a doubleheader from the Seattle team to win the regional and advance to National City, Calif., and the Pony League World Series, which we won in a canter.

I didn't see much of Bud after that. Although I filled in from time to time in the Campbell Moreland Pony League booth the following season, 1979, I got my first fulltime newspaper job in July and I wasn't able to spend much time at the field during the remainder of the summer. But I do know Bud stayed close to a lot of the guys, and his virtual year-round involvement with the Pony League continued. In fact, he offered me the job of business manager of the 1979 team if he were to be voted in as its manager. It didn't happen, but I appreciated the fact that he would entrust a job as important as that – I would have been responsible for all the team's logistical needs, including travel – to a 22-year-old kid.

Early in 1982, I talked to Bud for a piece I was doing for *Baseball America* about Rich Alvarez, and he sounded a little more detached than usual, though no less enthusiastic as he described his relationship with Rich, who had played for him in Pony League as well as on that '78 All-Star team. I didn't think much of it at the time, although I did wonder why he hadn't been out to see the Legion team I had put together for a run at one last national championship for Campbell.

Early in July, I got a phone call during the early afternoon from Janine Crawford, whose son Eric had been a reserve on the '78 Pony League team and had remained friendly with Bud even though he'd played little during that postseason. Janine, like her son, was a very proud and poised individual who didn't often give voice or face to her emotions, but this day, she was overcome.

Bud, she managed to say after an interminable pause, had died.

We had a game that evening, a very important game against the San Mateo Legion team led by Barry Bonds and Gregg Jefferies, and I wondered what we should do. I didn't feel like playing the game under the circumstances, but soon after my conversation with Janine, I got several calls from players who had heard the news. All of them said they wanted to play that night and they wanted to play for Bud.

We did. We won, and afterward, we talked about Bud and what he had meant to all of us. I wish that there had been a public memorial service of some kind, but it turned out Bud has specified in his will that no funeral or any other kind of service be held. Bud apparently had been suffering from an illness he had known for some time would be fatal — he was only about 50 when he died — and I guess he wanted all of us to remember him in our own individual, private way, rather than in terms that might be etched on a monument.

We still do. But there should be a monument. And the current Campbell baseball generation should do what should have been done a quarter of a century ago — name that Pony League ballpark Bud Stallings Field.

JIM SAEGER: A top hat and a half-century of tales

He is the only man ever who conceivably could have coached a boy, his son *and* his grandson in the Campbell youth baseball system, yet Jim Saeger never has sought a high profile during the 46 years he has been involved with Quito Little League.

That low profile only changes when he takes the field wearing a top hat.

When he's not helping to tend to Quito's fields at Rolling Hills Junior High (one of which is named after him), assisting one of Quito's baseball coaches by coordinating a practice or by working individually with players, or simply watching kids play, Jim serves as an umpire for Bay Area Vintage Base Ball. The league is one of several throughout the country that plays games under the rules of the 1880s, before the conjunction of the Base and Ball in contemporary advertising and newspaper stories. Former major league pitcher Jim Bouton, best known today as the author of the groundbreaking baseball book *Ball Four*, was one of the founders of the Vintage Baseball movement, and in 2009 its Bay Area chapter included teams such as the San Jose Dukes, the Santa Clara Stogies and the New Almaden Quicksilvers. (Quicksilver, or mercury, mining was widespread in the south Santa Clara Valley before the turn of the 20th century.) The teams play with 1886 rules, equipment and uniforms. A walk is awarded after seven balls. Hitters are allowed to designate the zone to which they want the pitches thrown. A foul ball isn't counted as a strike. The ball is softer, players wear gloves that look better suited for gardening than for catching line drives, and the bats are much larger, resembling miniature tree stumps in weight and circumference.

BAVBB plays many of its games at Hamann Park, near the San Jose-Campbell border. Jim became aware of the league through Steve Gazay, a former Quito president who was one of the league's founders, and the top hat is part of the formal outfit of the sort that umpires routinely wore in the 1880s and now don for BAVBB games.

"It's a really interesting concept," Jim said. "It's a lot of fun, taking yourself back to the baseball that was played in the beginning. And I've gotten more than my 15 minutes of fame out of it. I even got my picture in the *Wall Street Journal* (accompanying a story about Vintage Baseball)."

The "15 minutes of fame" represents 15 more minutes of fame than Jim ever sought at Quito, from the time he began coaching there in 1963. Not only has he never coached a future major leaguer or an All-Star team, he never has even managed or coached in Quito's major baseball division. He has spent 30 or so years as a manager or coach in the league's developmental programs, where winning is secondary and skill mastery is the main priority. His most visible role at Quito was as a major division manager in the Quito girls softball program, which won a Senior World Series title in 1987 and was among the top Little League-affiliated softball organizations in the Santa Clara Valley before its demise in the mid-1990s.

"The longevity of it has paid off tremendously for me," Jim says. "Just when kids come up to you and talk about what a fun time they had playing for me. We always did OK, and sometimes we won championships, but that was always a bonus, icing on the cake. Those 12 bright, shining faces … just eager to learn how to play the game and have fun. That's what always kept me going."

In conversation with Jim, it's hard to imagine him even raising his voice to any of his players. He has a soft, measured, reassuring aura, and the closest thing to invective that you'll ever hear from him is that he doesn't care for something. He's gray-bearded without looking like a period piece, and he's firm and direct without being stern or intimidating. While it's difficult to envision some of the hard-nosed, autocratic Little League managers of the 1960s and 1970s being effective amid 21st-century cynicism and hypersensitivity, it's easy to see why the approach that Jim used in the 1960s still works now. He taught simple basics through repetition and patience, and he tried to open windows of improvement for players without throwing them through those windows.

In those respects, Jim personifies the five-decade continuum of Quito Little League in ways that have nothing to do with chronology. During the west Santa Clara Valley's frenetic-growth period, Quito usually had as many players and teams as Campbell. It produced two major leaguers, Doug Capilla and Dan Gladden (although neither can be called Campbell-system products because both played most of their youth careers elsewhere), and it rarely lacked for conscientious, knowledgeable managers and coaches. In other ways, though, Quito was the antithesis of Campbell Little League, especially during the latter league's peak period. Campbell youth baseball was never a single formal organization; it was more of a synergism and a collection of philosophies, and Quito's approach represented the idea that Campbell Little League's way of doing things wasn't the only right way.

The closest Quito has come to national or even regional prominence from a competitive standpoint was the presence of several of its players on Campbell Moreland Pony League's World

Series championships in 1978 and 1979. (The '78 team had four Quito players – Harold Sutherland, Steve Clinton, Eric Crawford and Glenn Davis.) None of the league's baseball All-Star teams has ever advanced as far as the divisional (Northern California championship) level of the national Little League tournament. Unlike Campbell, which has always had a built-in identity as "Campbell's league," Quito serves children in five different cities – Campbell, San Jose, Los Gatos, Monte Sereno and Saratoga – and never has been claimed as its own by any municipality. Most of Campbell's players come from middle-class backgrounds where economic disparities were never an issue, while Quito's district includes some of the richest and poorest neighborhoods in the Santa Clara Valley. And while Campbell has been playing at the same park since 1955 and has usually thrived financially, Quito twice has had to uproot its entire program and play anywhere it could while building brand-new facilities from scratch.

"We weren't like Campbell in that we didn't have that name recognition like Campbell did," Jim says. "It always kind of hurt us a little bit in getting sponsors. Downtown Campbell always seemed to back 'its' Little League, and the same was true with Los Gatos and Saratoga. And I know Campbell never had to move lock, stock and barrel like we had to do, twice."

Yet Quito not only has survived for almost half a century, it has established credibility of a sort that isn't measured in terms of Williamsport trips or college and professional players produced or money generated. Moreland, Campbell's other next-door neighbor, in 1962 had become the first and still only Northern California team to win a Little League World Series, but after that, Moreland diminished in stature while Campbell blossomed. The result was an often-adversarial relationship between Campbell and Moreland, and when parents and players from the two leagues were thrust together, strain and sometimes outright hostility often prevailed. That was one reason Campbell Moreland Pony League never reached a World Series between 1965 and 1977, even though it had the talent to do so more often than not, and usually had a relatively uncluttered path to the World Series because it was seeded into many late-stage tournaments that it hosted.

Quito, on the other hand, was content to define success on its own terms and did not try to out-Campbell Campbell. In 1976, Campbell went to the Little League World Series title game, and Quito's All-Star team also had an abundance of talent and chemistry, losing in the District 12 finals to a Saratoga team that advanced to the semifinals of the same divisional tournament that Campbell won on its way to Williamsport. (Quito finally won its first district title in 1978, beating Saratoga in the finals.) It would have been understandable if Quito families had arrived at Campbell Moreland with a certain degree of envy or even jealousy of the Campbell people. Yet from the first day of the 1977 Pony League season, there was little sense of a "Campbell faction" or a "Quito faction" among players or parents. Both groups thought of their involvement with Pony League as a collective endeavor – an attitude eventually adopted by most of the Moreland contingent as well – and the result was a level of harmony throughout the league that contributed mightily to Campbell Moreland's World Series titles in 1978 and 1979.

From Jim's perspective, Quito people generally admired and respected Campbell's success without being envious of it – something that seldom was true in Moreland.

"Not only me, but as far as Quito itself is concerned, there's still the kids-come-first attitude," he says, "and as far as the board members and the managers and the coaches have been concerned, it's been that way since the first year I was here (1963). Quito never really had this 'we're going to Williamsport' attitude; for us it was more of a pipe dream. Our program was never set up for that. A few years, we would play three games a week, but mostly it was two (while Campbell played three), and managers in Quito were discouraged from practicing more than one day a week. From my (correct) understanding, most Campbell teams had either a game or a practice almost every day of the week. We played on Sundays for a while, like Campbell did, but that was only because our field-space situation was such that it was the only way we could accommodate all the kids we had."

Jim said Quito, even before his arrival, had a mandatory-innings rule that guaranteed that each player would have a fair opportunity to participate in each game. In 1963, the national Little League organization did not have any such rule, and it wasn't until the 1970s that Campbell and other area Little Leagues began imposing similar participation mandates.

"From when I started in 1963, we had a mandatory two-inning (per game) rule, and that was kind of a pioneering attitude, I think," Jim says. "At the major level, they may not have had the rule where every kid had to play in every game, but I know we did at the lower divisions. It was a mandatory four innings a week, and they had to play in every game. In fact, there was a period during the 1970s where we upped that to three innings a game or half the innings a team played in a week, because not every game went six innings (because of darkness)."

Beyond the fact Quito was anxious to establish that kids of all talent levels would be valued, Jim says there was an emphasis on inclusion throughout the league community that helped minimize the effects of the economic disparities between league families.

"It always was interesting to me as a coach, and coming from a small town and a low-income family ... some (Quito) kids had parents who were lawyers, doctors, CEOs, but it was a good cohesive mix of people," Jim says. "There was no snobbery or anything like that I ever noticed, nothing like 'we live over here and we have this really fancy house.' People just blended in very well, and there was no problem with different economic circumstances. I remember going to end-of-year parties in mansions with huge swimming pools ... all the kids were there and everybody had a good time and it didn't matter whether one little guy had parents who were out of work or on welfare. There was no distinction ... everybody was treated fairly."

Above all, Jim wanted his players to be eager to play the game, and that stems from his childhood in rural Wisconsin. Some of Little League's critics maintain that the program is too regimented and that baseball is more fun when kids themselves are organizing it, but Jim says his personal experience tells him that laissez-faire youth baseball has more than its share of drawbacks.

"I always liked baseball," he said, "and I would have given anything at that (Little League) age to have played baseball on a real team. But we had never even heard of Little League. We played sandlot baseball, and don't believe anybody who tells you what a glorious thing that was. On a good day there would maybe be 10 or so of us, so you played with five kids on a team at the most. The ages would range from probably 7 or 8 up to 15 or 16, and the older kids pretty much dominated the game ... they played the positions they wanted to and batted when they wanted to. There was a lot of arguing ... no structure to it at all. The only organized baseball we had then was American Legion, and you had to be at least 13 or so to play that.

"I just dreamed of being able to play on a team, to have a regular team and play other teams, but that never came about. When I settled in this area after I got out of the Navy in 1960, I was able to purchase a home in the Quito area. I heard a lot about Moreland after they won the World Series in 1962, and I thought about how I might like to get involved in a program like that. Just after I moved into my home, I was driving by Quito School (the league's original base) and saw kids out there playing and found out there was a league in the area. So I went down and started talking to people and said I'd like to help out. My oldest son was born in February of 1963, and I started in Quito as a coach in March. I got a team called the Colts, in what was called the C League, a beginning league with kids 8, 9, 10 years old. All they got was a T-shirt with Colts in script on it. They played in jeans and tennis shoes.

"In the middle of the season, the manager left, so I took over as manager, and I stayed on as manager of the Colts for maybe 10 years, until my two sons moved up out of that division. I moved up (with them) into the minor division. We had like 400 kids in the league then, and I had C league teams with 16, 17, 18 kids on them ... everything in the Quito area was brand-new then. There were a lot of little baseball players out there. There was no competition for players ... no soccer, no basketball, no (competitive) swimming, no video games or computers. There were still a lot of orchards out there; it was on the outskirts (of Campbell)."

Unlike Campbell and Moreland, which throughout their histories have concentrated their resources on pre-teen baseball, Quito officials were quick to embrace the idea of their league broadening its service scope. By the late 1970s, Quito had programs accommodating players up to age 18, including a Big League team that included Doug Capilla, a Westmont High graduate who spent most of his childhood in his native Hawaii.

Jim coached his own two sons in Quito's Senior Minor program, and helped construct a new Pony League-sized diamond for that league on the Westmont campus. In 1980, Jim was among the founders of Quito's new girls softball program. At the time, Campbell had a softball league that was affiliated with the national Bobby Sox organization, but the dissatisfaction of his daughter, who played Bobby Sox, prompted him to look at the then-new softball arm that Little League Baseball had recently started.

"My daughter played in (now-defunct) Bobby Sox, which I did not care for," Jim says, "and at the end of the softball season, I met another lady who was also very unhappy with Bobby Sox. So we decided to start a fall softball program. She got me the phone numbers of all the girls in Bobby Sox, and I sat down and called every one of them. I told them, 'Quito will have a fall ball program; it'll be fun and instructional and recreational.' Surprisingly, we were able to put together five or six teams, and we pulled enough girls that the following year we were able to have four major division softball teams. At the same time, some of the (baseball) guys started a fall baseball program, and that was new for the area also.

"By that time, I'd gotten into the softball. I *loved* softball. I managed a major team, and it was a kick. The girls were fun. You'd get maybe one-third of the girls that were really into it, and maybe one-third of them were in it just as a social thing. But the girls who were into it were so much fun to coach and teach. I loved it. We've lost half of the flags they gave us for winning sectional and regional tournaments during those years, but at the time, we'd have flags lined up all around our field. It was that perfect storm ... some really good coaches and managers, and we had talented girls who were really into it."

At the time Quito started its softball program, Sunnyvale Metro was the only other area Little League that already had done so, and Quito began to play an interlocking regular-season schedule with Metro. At first, Metro, which was a regular participant in the various softball World Series that Little League sponsored, pummeled Quito teams with impunity, but in 1987 Quito knocked Metro out of an early tournament and went on to win the Senior League World Series in Kalamazoo, Mich. They returned to the same event in 1991, and made deep postseason runs almost as frequently as their Campbell Little League baseball counterparts, but by the mid-1990s, the softball league was abandoned in the aftermath of a crisis that almost led to the demise of Quito Little League itself.

According to Jim, Quito began in the late 1950s, although it didn't become a Williamsport-sanctioned Little League affiliate until about 1961. The league began at Quito School and took its name from the school, although some early accounts refer to it as "Quito-Saratoga." But it wasn't long before Quito faced its first crisis. In 1965, it was forced to move from Quito School as the result of a jurisdictional clash with that school's principal. Fortunately for Quito, it found a seemingly-permanent haven at San Tomas School at the intersection of Hacienda and Abbott avenues. At the same time, the elderly owner of a nearby orchard deeded his land to the school district, permitting Quito to expand its complex onto that property.

Eventually, though, the Campbell district closed San Tomas School, and while it didn't dispose of the property – now the site of Jack Fischer Park – immediately, Quito officials knew that their days on the San Tomas property were numbered. Eventually, they reached an agreement with the school district to move the entire operation to Rolling Hills Middle School, but that plan initially was thwarted by Rolling Hills neighbors who didn't fancy the idea of hundreds of children roaming the school grounds on weekends as well as during the school week. (Some years earlier, Rolling Hills neighbors had forced the Campbell Bobby Sox program, which was playing at Rolling Hills, to relocate to the former Campbell Grammar School grounds.)

"The school district wanted to accommodate the league as much as they could," Jim says, "so they said, 'We'll just move you to Rolling Hills.' But as soon as the people near Rolling Hills found out they were going to move the whole Little League onto that property, they hired a lawyer. After a period of negotiation, the district did talk the neighbors into agreeing to let them build just a major field, away from where the houses were."

But the Quito softball program was left with no place to play, forcing the league to drop it, and the league cut back its lower baseball levels so that it could shoehorn all of its games onto the one permanent field and the handful of temporary locations it could obtain. With its reservoir of players drying up and its scheduling and developmental capabilities limited, Quito appeared to be on the brink of oblivion.

Fortunately, the NIMBY attitude of the neighbors softened.

"A few years later – I don't know the circumstances – the school district just said to go ahead and put another field in," Jim said. "Gradually we put more in to the point where we are now."

Over a five-year period, the league enlisted corporate and individual donations totaling over $1 million, and by 2009, Quito's Rolling Hills facility was comparable to any in west Santa Clara County. It houses three well-maintained fields, batting cages and a snack bar, and most important, the arrangement is permanent. According to Jim, Quito's signup numbers are beginning to creep upward for the first time in years, and the league is finally out of survival mode.

As for Jim, he hasn't managed a team in several years, but he helps out any manager who asks, and he helps tend the fields and serves as an advisory board member. He says he'll stay on at Quito as long as he feels he is contributing, and one reason he wants to stay is that he senses that Quito's tribulations haven't changed its priorities.

Because of people like Jim, Quito is and always has been an integral part of Campbell's baseball synergy. It could never be Campbell Little League, in terms of national recognition and college and professional players emerging. But Campbell Little League could never be Quito, either, and most of the kids and parents who were involved with Quito in the 1960s and 1970s justifiably feel that even though Quito never came close to sending a team to Williamsport, it was still part of the special something that was Campbell baseball in the days when Campbell baseball meant so much to so many people.

And after almost a half-century of service to that Campbell baseball community, Jim Saeger is still standing – wearing his top hat.

JIMMY SHOCKLEY: DEATH ON A DIAMOND

The best day of Campbell's century of youth baseball? That depends on whom you ask, and with thousands of participants and 14 World Series appearances, you could literally get thousands of answers.

The worst day in Campbell's youth baseball history? Nobody can dispute that it was May 5, 1973 – the day that a young life ended on Quito Little League's San Tomas School ballfield.

The boy's name was Paul James Shockley, and everybody who knew him referred to him as Jimmy. He was 12 years old, and he lived with his parents, sister and brother on Harriet Drive in southernmost Campbell, not far from Westmont High. In 1973, Jimmy played in Quito Little League's minor division, and all one needs to know now in terms of his love of baseball is the fact he was happy to play in the minor division during his last Little League season. Most 12-year-olds who don't make it to the majors for their last season wind up moving on from baseball to something else, but Jimmy loved the game so much that he cared only about playing it, regardless of the level. He was a Boy Scout, and was a sixth-grader at Forest Hill Elementary School, where he was an excellent student by all accounts. He also had a way of befriending and encouraging younger boys, such as Dave Roberson, who knew him well even though he was two years younger than Jimmy.

"I'm picturing his face right now as we speak," Dave said in 2009. "We weren't best buds or anything like that, but we were friends. We did a few sleepovers. He was on the first team I ever played on in Little League. He was kind of quiet, but very friendly and nice, and his brother Jerry (one year younger) was the same way. The Shockleys lived near us ... there were quite a few of the kids on our street who were in Quito at the time, and we'd go over there (to San Tomas School) and play all the time (during off-seasons or at times when the field wasn't being used for Quito Little League games)."

The Boy Scout and Little League emblems are embedded in Jimmy's tombstone at Los Gatos Memorial Park, a few miles from the hospital where he died on that spring day in 1973. His school photo, showing a shy smile and shining, inquisitive eyes that to this day seem to extend friendship, also is encased in the tombstone. Jim Saeger, who had been Jimmy's coach when he was a 10-year-old and stayed in touch with his family for many years after 1973, visits the gravesite often. When he does, he envisions this same boy on what may have been the happiest day of his life.

"Jimmy and my son Wes were good friends (as well as teammates) that year," Jim said. "Jimmy was 10; Wes was 8. Jimmy was a good little player, not outstanding ... put everything he had into it. Nice family. Good kid, very respectful. They lived around the corner from us. That year that Jimmy played on my team, we won the championship. The season was divided into two halves, and if one team didn't win both halves, there was a playoff. We won one of the halves, I don't even remember which, and then we won the playoff. I can still see it as if it were today ... Jimmy and the other kids on the team riding their bikes around the neighborhood just wired on the thrill of this victory. Those kids were just so excited, riding their little Stingray bikes all over the neighborhood, and running through our house and then saying they were all going to the Shockleys.

"That is a very vivid, very wonderful memory."

Dave Roberson, on the other hand, has an equally indelible but far less joyous lingering memory of Jimmy. Dave was in the major division as a 10-year-old in 1973, but his team's schedule was parallel to that of Jimmy's minor division team, so all of their games that year were played at the same time on adjoining fields. Consequently, Dave saw as much of Jimmy that season as he did of his own teammates. Dave didn't see the actual accident that took Jimmy's life, but he was in the midst of the confusion that followed, and he got first-person accounts from others who actually saw what happened.

"(One of Jimmy's teammates) was warming up with a bat just before the start of their game," Dave recalled. "He was outside the dugout, swinging a bat, and Jimmy was standing near him. The kid was left-handed, and when he swung the bat, apparently Jimmy wasn't expecting him to be swinging left-handed. (The swing) hit Jimmy in the back of the head, right at the base of the spine. There was a big commotion; some people were trying to get him into a car and take him to the hospital, which was only about three blocks away. I remember people running back and forth between the snack bar and the field."

Jim Saeger wasn't at the park at the time the accident occurred; his team was scheduled to play later in the day. When he arrived, one of the other managers in the league told him what had happened.

"The thing about it ... they always say that when you're dealing with an injury like this, don't move the person," Jim said. "Mel Peyton had told me that they'd taken him to the hospital. I've always wondered (what might have happened) if they hadn't had to wait for the ambulance and gotten him straight to an emergency room, because the hospital was so close."

Chances are that it wouldn't have made much difference. Jimmy never regained consciousness, and was pronounced dead a short time later at Los Gatos Community Hospital. Because criminal activity or gross negligence were not considered to be factors in Jimmy's death, no autopsy or coroner's inquest was performed, and details regarding the actual cause of death were never made public. Two generations later, an incident such as this might have precipitated a media frenzy and perhaps a public outcry for more answers regarding what had happened, but in 1973 the local newspapers, amazingly, virtually ignored the story.

Three days after Jimmy's death, on May 8, the *San Jose Mercury* ran a seven-paragraph story on Page 62 regarding the incident. Jimmy's father Jerry was quoted in the story as saying that the accident occurred because Jimmy "wasn't expecting the bat to swing in his direction." Jimmy had not been wearing a helmet at the time he was struck, but Jerry Shockley said a helmet probably would not have made any difference because his son was hit at the base of his neck, below the area protected by helmets. The *Campbell Press* carried only a short obituary notice, and the *Los Gatos Times-Observer* did nothing other than re-run the *Mercury* story, even though Jimmy died in Los Gatos and played in a league that included many Los Gatos residents who knew Jimmy.

In the years after Jimmy's death, some Quito people told me they had heard that Jimmy was chewing gum at the time the bat struck him, and that the trauma resulted in the gum being lodged in his throat, halting his breathing. If that was true, delaying his transportation to the hospital might have been a fatal mistake, even though moving him immediately might have caused or worsened paralysis. I also was told that a doctor, whose son was playing at the time, was at the ballpark and quickly tended to Jimmy, so it wasn't as if he wasn't given immediate medical attention as he lay motionless on the ground. In any case, everybody who mentioned the tragedy to me in later years said the general opinion was that even if mistakes were made in the immediate aftermath of Jimmy's accident, it's unlikely that anything done at the scene could have prevented the ultimate result.

The waiting for news, in any case, was almost as bad as the final news itself. Even some of those who were at the park that day didn't find out until the following day that Jimmy had died.

"I happened to be at Quito the day it occurred," said Steve Clinton, a 9-year-old Quito Little League player at the time. "My only memory is of ambulances and sirens after it happened. Everyone who was not at that particular field, including myself, was wondering what happened. It was the following day I learned he died."

A service was held at the Darling-Fischer funeral parlor in downtown Campbell three days after Jimmy's death, and he was buried that same day at Los Gatos Memorial Park. Jim Saeger was one of the pallbearers. Thirty-six years later, Jimmy's tombstone is the only public reminder of a young man who lived so richly.

In 1973, the Campbell Union School District and the City of Campbell were collaborating on a project to install swings, teeter-totters and other playground equipment on elementary-school grounds and work cooperatively to maintain them. Forest Hill, Jimmy's school, had just completed such an installation at the time Jimmy died, and it was decided immediately thereafter that the mini-playground should be named in his honor. A month after Jimmy's death, about 300 people showed up for the dedication ceremony, including Dean Chamberlin, Campbell's mayor. At the same time, Quito Little League began giving a Jimmy Shockley Award to the team in each division that exhibited the best sportsmanship during the course of the season.

By 2009, Forest Hill School was still there, on McCoy Avenue, but the playground equipment, which fell into disrepair in the years after Jimmy's death, was long gone. So was the sign that designated the enclosure as Jimmy Shockley Park. The memorial fund that had been set up in Jimmy's memory disappeared long ago, and Jim Saeger says the Jimmy Shockley Award faded away after the league was forced to move out of its San Tomas School headquarters in the mid-1990s and lost much of its membership in the process.

Jimmy's death wasn't the only tragedy to befall Campbell youth baseball, or Quito, over the years. On June 29, 1960, John Ezzie, a manager in Campbell Moreland Pony League, died at age 49 of a heart attack at Campbell High during his team's game there. In 1977, Kevin Allison, who had come close to making the Campbell All-Star team that reached the 1976 Little League World Series final, died on June 23, a month before his 13th birthday, of aplastic anemia, a condition where bone marrow does not produce sufficient new cells to replenish existing blood cells. (Kevin's younger brother Matt was the catcher on Campbell's 1979 national-championship squad, and his older brother Wade had made the 1975 All-Star team.) And the Quito community was broadsided again in the early 1980s when Nicole Stevenson, a 12-year-old girl who played in the league's softball program, died of an apparent brain aneurysm during a pool party after her team won a championship.

Statistically, a death such as Jimmy's was and still is an aberration of overwhelming proportions, given the fact millions of children play youth baseball. After five Little League players died within a two-month period during the 1961 season – including one California boy, in Temple City – the national organization moved rapidly to introduce improved equipment and more stringent regulations regarding its use. After that, about one Little League fatality per year was reported, and Jimmy's was the only one reported for 1973. (Some of the subsequent fatalities were attributed to the advent of metal bats throughout amateur baseball in the mid-1970s, but Jimmy was hit with a wood bat.) Later, a study by the University of North Carolina determined that 13 children had died nationally in baseball-related accidents during Little League games from 1987-96. Based on that number, and on the infrequency of non-fatal injuries in Little League and other youth baseball organization, the report deemed baseball as one of the safest recreational outlets available to American kids.

Jimmy's death prompted much shock and sadness throughout Campbell, but it didn't lead to much outrage, or condemnation of Little League baseball as unsafe. Baseball went on as before, and most likely, that's the way Jimmy would have wanted it.

But Jim Saeger thinks more could have been done to tell future generations about Jimmy – not how he died, but how he lived.

And he's right.

KENT OHMANN: The grownup amongst us

I didn't meet Kent Ohmann until a year after the 1970 Campbell Little League All-Star team on which he played etched its Cardiac Kids nickname into the Campbell youth baseball narrative. I never saw the 1970 team play in person, having been packed away to summer camp while Kent and his teammates were making their way to Williamsport. And yet today, I can see the totality of the Campbell youth baseball experience as clearly through his eyes as through anyone else's.

The main reason for that, I think, is because Kent, unlike the other former Campbell players who are prominent in this book, was an immediate contemporary of mine, having graduated from Del Mar High with me in 1975, and I had a vantage point that didn't involve baseball from which to think highly of him.

Today, Del Mar is decidedly multicultural, with all the connotations, both positive and negative, that adjective evokes. It inherited much of the enrollment of two troubled schools, Camden and Blackford, when they were closed in 1980 and 1991 respectively, and that permanently perfo-rated the societal cocoon in which it functioned when Kent and I went there. In the early 1970s, most of Del Mar's students came from upper-middle-class households, and like many such high schools then and now, it had a clearly delineated social strata within which non-conformists, newcomers and those who didn't think the naming of the homecoming queen was of importance were not welcome. Most of the athletes tended to walk among their fellow students as if they were the anointed among the heathens, although I never could figure out how they attained their sense of self-righteousness because Del Mar rarely was any good at anything except basketball. It was also a party school of bacchanal proportions, and both Kent and I knew people whose subsequent lives went unfulfilled – and in a few cases were cut short – because of their penchant for self-destruction.

Kent was different, and in some ways, I looked up to him even though at 5-foot-6, he was a half-foot shorter than I was. I saw him play for four years in high school, and beyond the fact he played the game the way it was supposed to be played, he was a genuinely good guy at a place and a time that it wasn't fashionable to be a genuinely good guy.

Although he was one of the school's more prominent athletes, partly because of his Little League World Series involvement, he went out of his way to mix with people throughout the school without imposing himself on them, and he listened a lot more than he spoke. His sense of self-confidence and manifest destiny never crossed over into conceit, and although he was a kid of few words, the way he chose and conveyed those words gave me the sense that he was a grownup amongst us. He also was a guy, I thought then, who would never lose his way, and when we arranged to meet in 2009 to watch his son Jakob play for Gavilan College's baseball team, it was with both eagerness and with a certain degree of apprehension. We had been friendly in high school, and I was looking forward to seeing him again solely because of that, along with the fact that I was eager to make him part of this book because of the role he had played in Campbell's youth baseball history. But I also worried a little as I made the 30-mile drive down U.S. 101 south to Gilroy. At age 52, had the grownup amongst us kids evolved into an exemplar among adults as well? Images from one's youth can be blurred by idealism and yellowed by age, and while I didn't expect any of the subjects of this book to be exactly as I knew them 30 or more years ago, I hoped that the reasons that I thought so highly of them so long ago would still be readily identifiable.

It didn't take long for my apprehension to dissipate. Kent's brownish-blond hair was almost entirely gray, and his hands, which had been his most salient tools of trade as a baseball player, had the fissures and bends of implements earnestly used over a long period. But otherwise, he still looked to be in good enough shape to take the field with players half his age. He had the same sense of understatement and equilibrium, the same welcoming expression, the same gentle sense of humor, and the same Point-A-to-Point B way of talking that I had remembered.

Our conversation lasted throughout the first game of a doubleheader and well into the second. Good baseball blends into good conversation rather than interrupting it, and I liked Gavilan's team, especially in terms of its mastery of the nuances that had characterized so many of the Campbell championship teams, and its apparent sense of shared purpose. Jakob Ohmann is a 6-foot-1 catcher who plays so low that he seems to lather himself over the ground, the way Pittsburgh Pirates great Manny Sanguillen used to do when Kent and I were teenagers. He had been an all-league catcher at Palma High in Salinas the season before, and had played on a Watsonville team, the Aggies, that had reached the Senior Babe Ruth World Series that summer. He moved, threw and orchestrated his pitchers with skill and aplomb, and my impression was that with a couple of years of upper-body weight training and natural maturity, Jakob had a chance to play on the NCAA Division I level. Kent and his wife Fiaau, who were celebrating their 22nd wedding anniversary that day, have three children, and all three of them are community-college athletes. His younger daughter Jade plays softball for Cabrillo College in Aptos, and his oldest daughter Jazmin, after attending the University of Hawaii for three years, had come back home and joined the women's soccer team at Foothill College in Los Altos Hills, earning first-team all-league honors the previous fall as the Owls won the Coast Conference championship.

The Ohmanns live in Aromas, a town of 2,700 that is nestled in the coastal California mountains near where Santa Cruz, San Benito and Santa Clara counties adjoin. John Steinbeck, a Salinas native, mentioned Aromas in some of his writings, and he would recognize it if he were alive today. Kent has been in the real estate business for 30 years, mostly within an hour's drive of Aromas, and he and Fiaau own and operate Prunedale Properties in northern Monterey County. The area their business serves, once exclusively rural, during the 1990s became popular among homebuyers who work in the San Jose and Salinas areas, and even though he has had to endure some downturns – "We didn't sell a single property for seven months after the (1989) Loma Prieta earthquake," he says – he has lived comfortably and has been able to send all three of his children to private high schools. "So far, so good," he says. "We've raised three kids in a small-town environment. We've been blessed."

Living and working in a small town represents the completion of a cycle for Kent. Even though Campbell had long since ceased to be anything like Aromas by the time Kent was born, his family had been there since the 1930s, and his father Art owned one of the last vestiges of small-town life in the Campbell area – the Ohmann and Beutel service station on the corner of Hamilton and Meridian avenues, about a half-mile east of the Campbell city limits. Art Ohmann was known for many miles around as a mechanic one could trust, and the size of his clientele became evident to Kent when he began working there as a child. "You knew everybody, because everybody brought their car in there," he says. "You washed all the windows of every car – front, side and back – and you checked every car's oil and water. Now people blow out their engines because they never get their oil level checked. I was lucky during the big gas shortage (in 1973, when both of us first got our drivers licenses) ... I never had to wait in line for gas.

"Campbell was a good place to grow up in ... I still remember the cherry and prune orchards and sitting in those trees before they tore them all down when they extended Campbell Avenue all the way through to Leigh Avenue. It still felt like a small town, and of course we had baseball.

"I remember being with Pete Cirivilleri (a mutual friend of ours, and later Kent's teammate at Del Mar) at the Sprouse-Reitz store and seeing the signup notice and wanting to play. I guess (the baseball seed was planted) listening to Giants games on the radio and going to see Willie Mays play. My mom (who in 2009 was still living, at age 92) hardly even let me ride my bike across the street then, but I signed up, and it just turned into something that I did well and liked. We had great coaching ... the coaches really took an interest in us. My first coach in minors was Cliff Judd, who already had kids playing in high school. I remember I couldn't even hold the ball right; I was gripping it with all five fingers, and he was real patient teaching me to throw it right."

The following year, 1968, Kent was drafted by Jack Zogg, and he played for Zogg's Robins major division team for three years. Small as he was, his instincts, footwork, manual dexterity and ability to throw from any angle made him a natural third baseman, and he flourished under Zogg's tutelage.

"I think probably the only time I ever said anything to another manager about a player was with Kent in 1970 (during the Campbell Little League World Series run)," Zogg said in 2009. "Kent wasn't playing a whole lot in the early games, and I mentioned to Ron (manager Ron Colburn) that I thought he had a pretty good little third baseman there. Finally, he started putting him in. Kent was a good, good boy, and his family was just great."

As described in earlier chapters, Kent was one of three 11-year-olds to make the Campbell Little League All-Star team in 1969, and he was the Cardiac Kids' most frequently-used third baseman the following year as they made their way to the Little League World Series championship game. As he gained experience, he came to know his position so well that it earned him his first nickname. "(One of his coaches) used to get mad at me because he'd tell me to move in or move over for a certain hitter. Well, I had it in my mind what the guy was going to do, and I didn't want to give it away. So he started calling me 'Iceman.'"

Almost four decades later, his most vivid memories of the Cardiac Kids are of the friendships that were forged and the sense, especially during the final two tournaments, that so much already had been achieved that no defeat could diminish those accomplishments. Even then, he thought of that summer of 1970 as a base camp and not as a summit. It was the second of his string of six straight All-Star team berths, ending as a 16-year-old in Colt League in 1974, and he says some of the games he played after 1970 were just as important in his mind as the one that was observed by 40,000 people at Lamade Stadium in Williamsport.

"Maybe it (the cohesion among the 1970 group) started the night that Ron Colburn threw a croquet mallet through a plate-glass window," he said, smiling. "But really, after '70, after we all really knew each other, we could look each other in the eyes and know what we had to do and that we could do it. That was Campbell ... we expected to win. We didn't win any more championships, but we won a lot more than we lost, and we always thought we could make it to the Pony World Series or the Colt World Series. It wasn't like we had to pull together for this tournament or that tournament. It was just playing baseball."

At Del Mar, Kent played four seasons – two on the frosh-soph, two on the varsity – for Gary Cunningham, who joined the faculty in 1971, our freshman year. When he retired in 2008 after 20 seasons at Bellarmine Prep in San Jose, Gary was known for a coaching portfolio that included more than 800 high school victories and three Central Coast Section titles. But at Del Mar, where he became varsity coach in 1974 and stayed six years, Gary inherited a program that was laughed at. Gary, who was built like the warning on an iodine-bottle label and probably could have made a career in stand-up comedy if his life passions hadn't been teaching and baseball, changed that dynamic. At first, he did so by making Del Mar the program that was laughed *with*.

Gary more than once arrived at the field for Del Mar's first game of a season wearing not his baseball uniform, but a tuxedo. He once had Carol Doda, a famed San Francisco stripper who in profile resembled a camel lying on its side, throw out the ceremonial first pitch. At a time when high school uniforms looked little different than they had at the turn of the century, and were replaced only when they bordered on the unusable, Gary bought flashy two-toned double-knits and outfitted his team in gold sanitary stockings. People stayed in the stands during blowouts just to hear Gary verbally joust with the umpires; he had a funny comeback line for everything they said to him, and his shrill, staccato voice could be heard halfway across the Del Mar campus. ("You're out of the game!" an umpire would yell at him. *"I'm* out of the game? You've been out of the game for six innings, Blue!" Gary would rejoin.) Before Gary got to Del Mar, high school baseball games were sedentary affairs usually played in library-like silence. Gary hooked up an improvised public-address system, put the most eccentric Del Mar student he knew — me — in charge of it, and told me to play the loudest rock music I could find and to let lack of propriety be my guide. (Except for the lack of propriety, announcing those games was ideal training for my Campbell Little League and Campbell Moreland Pony League days.) Before long, people were coming out to the games just to see what the hell might happen next, and the players reveled in being part of the show, even when they were losing.

Gary's antics didn't win him many games at first — the 1974 Dons, despite having Kent, Kelly and Kevin Linnane, and Steve Esau from the Cardiac Kids, went 1-17 in league — but Gary promoted shamelessly and taught, cajoled and scheduled relentlessly. In 1975, Kent's senior season, Gerry Ford was added to the varsity to give Del Mar five former Cardiac Kids. (Another senior on that team, Keith Ferguson, became an NFL official, and in 2009 was the back judge in Super Bowl XLIII.) The Dons finished third in the WVAL and posted the program's first winning record in more than a decade, and in 1978 the Dons won the league championship — the high school baseball equivalent of the Tampa Bay Rays making the World Series three decades later.

"That first year was a real lesson in humility," Kent says. "We'd done pretty well (under Cunningham) on the frosh-soph level, but some of the seniors were already experimenting with illegal substances. (Actually, by that time, most of them were doing a lot more than experimenting.) Some of them were pretty good athletes, but they didn't care about it like some of the younger guys. That's one season I've always tried to block out, but I was able to stay positive. I never really thought of it that way, but yeah, it did feel good being part of that (the beginning of Del Mar's turnaround his senior year)

"Gary was a great, great guy, and some of the stuff he came up with ... I saw the three-ball walk the other day, and I hadn't seen that since Gary did it in high school. (With a runner on first base, the defensive team pretends that a third ball to a batter is the fourth, and when the unsuspecting batter trots to first base, the runner on first jogs to second and is surreptitiously approached and tagged out.) A guy (on the other team) would be stealing, and Gary would have somebody on the bench crack a couple of bats together and then the catcher would throw a popup. The runner would think the batter had hit (a popup) and he'd run back to first. We pulled the hidden-ball trick a few times. We had all kinds of trick plays, and you'd be surprised how often they worked. He sure made it fun, and the guy really knew his baseball."

Kent also played for the semipro team that Gary organized each fall. It was called the Rainbows because its uniform combinations were incoherent even by Gary's standards, and it was comprised partly of Del Mar players and partly of former high school and college players (including Gary) from around the area. "One of the teams we played had (former San Francisco Giants) Jim Ray Hart and Ken Henderson," he says. "I'd grown up watching those guys play, and it was pretty interesting playing against them, especially since I was still just a kid."

Kent was no stranger to playing in unfamiliar environments, but even his Williamsport experience didn't prepare him for his first road doubleheader against a team that was murderous in the life-without-parole sense. One of the teams in the Rainbows' league was a squad comprised of inmates from Soledad State Prison, and it played all of its games at home because nobody, least of all the California Department of Corrections, wanted to find out what kind of a road team it was.

"In one game, their leadoff hitter was a guy who'd murdered a bunch of people in the '60s, and our pitcher hit him with a pitch," Kent recalled. "I'm a 16-year-old kid, and I'm thinking, 'Oh my God, suppose he slides into me.' We always figured that if we won the first game, we probably ought to let them win the second. The umpires were prisoners too, so there weren't a lot of arguments, and some of the guys watching the game down the lines looked like bullets wouldn't bother them much.

"Most of us didn't say anything to them, but the Linnane twins were always chirping. They would talk to them, ask them what they were in for. We'd tell them, 'Geez, *shut up*. You want to get us killed?' They (the Linnanes) were quite the characters ... still are."

After graduating from Del Mar, Kent attended San Jose City College, and played against Dave Righetti and Dave Stieb, who appeared in nine major league All-Star Games between them, during the Jaguars' winter-league season. In retrospect, he thinks he could have played well at the community college level, and perhaps beyond. But he couldn't sustain the single-mindedness that had propelled him throughout his career, and his stay at City was brief.

"I got my priorities a little mixed up," he says now. "I started drinking when I shouldn't have been. I was more concerned with partying the night before than I was about the fact we had a game the next day. I think about not putting out 100 percent (for the only time in his career), and I've tried to relate to players I've coached since because of that."

Kent left school, took a job at Westinghouse, and began studying for his real estate license, which he earned in 1979. While he was making a success out of his real estate business, he also began to coach in the Santa Clara-Santa Cruz-San Benito tri-county area, especially after Jakob began playing. Like many former Campbell players, he felt the lessons he had learned in baseball would be applicable to the next baseball generation, and he has tried to instill in his players the sense that he had – that baseball was to be played for the moment and for the sake of learning of and from it. He says he was hands-on while working with Jakob to a much greater degree than his father had been with him, but that he always was conscious of not being hands-around. Apparently he has succeeded, because Jakob plays with obvious verve that cannot be imprinted and must instead be inspired.

And watching Gavilan and City College of San Francisco play that afternoon, Kent's eyes never left the field as we talked. He was probing, anticipating, thinking, absorbing, immersing himself in the game, still part of it even after all those years.

Yep, I thought. This remains the Kent of whom I thought so highly so long ago. He's still a Campbell guy. And even among adults, he's still the grownup amongst us.

MARK PAQUIN: Enduring

Mark was probably the first kid with whom I became friends when I first got involved with Campbell Little League, even before I became the scorekeeper there. As with a lot of the Campbell players, we lost track of each other after he graduated from high school, but I thought of him occasionally. I remembered how close we had been and all the good qualities he had. I also re-membered how it seemed as if the one thing Mark never had going for him was luck, so I wasn't sure what to expect when we talked for the first time in more than 20 years.

It turned out that Mark's life, at age 45, hadn't turned out as he had once hoped. He was working as a chef in San Jose, and had a job he liked and at which he was accomplished, but he'd had some serious health and personal issues, and he'd needed to reaffirm his sense of self-worth many times as an adult. Our discussions that summer, and in the fall after I moved back to Campbell, may have been part of that process. I hoped so, because Mark was always someone who had so much to offer, and so much willingness to offer it, on and off the baseball diamond.

If somebody had asked me when I left Campbell which kid I had seen there had the best chance of playing major league baseball, I probably would have mentioned Mark. He was big, smart, athletic and quick on his feet. He could hit for both power and average, his teammates respected and took their cues from him, and as a catcher who never had wanted to play anywhere else, he was position-specific and cared passionately about his role as a pitching enabler. "I looked up to him," said Randy Nishijima, who was a year behind Mark in school and was his teammate at Campbell High and Blackford. "I still don't think I've ever seen anybody who was better than him at blocking balls. I learned a lot about catching from him. He was *the* catcher when I was growing up."

I still think he could have gone far in baseball if it hadn't been for the Campbell closure, which hit him harder than most and forced him to finish up at Blackford, which until its own closure in 1991 was known as a school where sidetracking pressures were difficult for a lot of kids to withstand. I was pleasantly surprised in the spring of 2008, before I moved back to Campbell, when he tracked me down via e-mail and we arranged to talk on the telephone. That conversation, and several others in the following weeks, represented one of the seeds from which the idea for this book sprouted.

Through all his difficulties, I was happy to see that Mark had endured ... and I couldn't help but think that Campbell baseball has continued to be a pillar for him, long after his playing career ended.

Mark had a warmth and an inquisitive mind that made it easy for him to make friends across many age and personality spectrums, and he was the kind of kid who seemed to gravitate toward the smaller and less talented kids on his team. You knew you could depend on him when something really mattered, and what he felt, he felt deeply. One particularly vivid memory I have of him involved an incident in 1977 when he was playing Pony League baseball and I was the announcer at John D. Morgan Park. While I was in the booth, Mark and a couple of his friends took my car — a Fiat sedan that was shaped like a shoebox and wasn't much heavier, or much faster for that matter — and lifted it over one of the parking barriers so that it was dangling on its frame, immovable.

Mark, of course, meant nothing malicious by it and thought I would consider it a humorous prank, and I probably would have reacted that way if I hadn't been in a hurry to leave the park after the final game on that particular day. It took me an hour to dislodge the car, and I was so visibly and audibly furious that he didn't want to risk acknowledging his involvement, and I didn't find out that he was the primary perpetrator until he approached me the next day. When he came to me to apologize, he was almost in tears; the thought of one of his friends feeling betrayed seemed devastating to him, and he was so profuse in his apology that I felt guilty about publicly expressing any anger at all, especially since I'd just about forgotten the entire incident by the time Mark talked to me.

At the same time, Mark had a bit of a Machiavellian streak, and in high school he hung with a tough crowd and had more than a few brushes with trouble. There was some pent-up frustration involved with that, partly because injuries had plagued him throughout his high school career, and for reasons both within and beyond his control, nothing had come easily for him in his adult life. I wish I'd known during the 1980s and 1990s what he was going through, because I would have found a way to help him, and I told him that in 2008 during our conversation at a pizza joint near his apartment on San Jose's southeast side.

But he wanted no pity, and he was in good humor. The first thing he laughingly did was lower his head so I could see his bald spot. He was a little overweight, but not to the extent that you couldn't tell he'd once been an exceptional athlete. He looked older than 45, but unremarkably so; the only sign of his bouts with illness was a portable IV kit, hidden under an armband, that was part of his treatment for a staph infection that nearly proved fatal because, typical of Mark's luck, it had initially been misdiagnosed. He had catcher's fingers, but they were bent by arthritis, not by fastballs in the dirt.

The eyes still probed and his mannerisms and conversation still were measured in terms of insight. He'd pulled his life together and seemed to have come to grips with his sadness, anger and disappointments. This was the same Mark I'd known, and as I'd sensed in our phone conversations, the talk of long summer days and baseball in Campbell brought back much of the sense of élan I'd seen so often in him as a kid.

Our on-field success in Campbell notwithstanding, Mark wasn't the only kid in the program whose baseball and life ambitions hadn't worked out as planned. Ours were imperfect kids in an imperfect community in an imperfect world, and I knew that several of his contemporaries had made complete shambles of their lives, under less trying circumstances than Mark had encountered. I was glad to see that he reflected on his baseball days with fondness tinged with only a little regret.

"I can still close my eyes and remember those days, those games, just being on a baseball field," he said. "You know what I liked most of all? Having that brand-new baseball, right out of the box, in my hand just before the first pitch of a game. The way it felt, even the way it smelled. I can still feel that.

"It was fun because you were friends with most of the guys you were playing with and even with the guys you were playing against. Everybody got along … there were a few assholes, but the main guys were people you respected, guys who made you better because they were so good themselves. And all our parents were friends … some still are, in fact. My parents are good friends with Brian Hughes' parents and some of the other parents from back then. You'd get to the ballpark for a 10 a.m. game and you'd wind up staying the whole day because you had friends on the other teams and the parents had friends who had kids on the other teams. Pony League was even funner because it was in the middle of a city park (John D. Morgan Park) and you had Beer Hill where all the parents hung out.

"You know, I wish things had gone different for me in baseball. Sam Piraro (at the time the coach at Mission College, and later the longtime coach at San Jose State) talked to me, and I could have played college baseball. The only reason I didn't was because I wasn't into it; I had a girlfriend and I was more into her and with hanging out with my friends and partying.

"I did some stupid things. I remember one night some of us were partying on Bonny Doon (a notorious party beach north of Santa Cruz) and this guy comes up to us and asks if he can have a beer. We're like, yeah, whatever, but then he started to hang around with us and we told him to leave. He came back with like a dozen other guys … they were bikers; they belonged to a gang called the Hell's Jokers or something like that, and we had a huge fight. The cops broke it up and I wound up in the hospital, chained to my bed. One of the cops told us that several guys in that gang had guns and knives. He told us to get the hell out of there as soon as the hospital released us, and never come back. I was like, 'Yes, sir, officer.' We were lucky we didn't get ourselves killed that night.

"I just didn't have the ambition to play baseball anymore. But I still miss it a lot. I coached for a long time after that, in Pony League, Colt League, Palomino. I was a players' coach because I wanted my guys to know that baseball is supposed to be fun. I'd blow up at them once in a while, but it was unexpected and they knew I meant it because I didn't do it very often. I think even with everything I went through, I'm a good guy … I'd never steal from anyone or intentionally hurt anyone. I work hard. I do the best I can, and I keep my word. I guess maybe some people might think I failed because I didn't go as far in baseball as maybe I could have, but I don't feel like a failure. Every day's still an adventure for me … you never know what will happen."

As with many of the Campbell players, Mark kept track of many of his former teammates and opponents, several of whom are now dead – Jeff Baxter, an All-Star teammate when Mark was 12; Jon Middlekauff, an introspective kid who loved music far more than baseball even though (or maybe because) his father Pete once played at Stanford and in the Minnesota Twins organization; Todd Phillips, one of the most talented athletes in the league who had to deal with more than his share of personal demons; and Todd Boyd, another of my favorites and a kid with an appetite for self-improvement that enabled him to outwork far more talented players and become a very good high school player even though he had never come close to making any All-Star teams in Campbell. Todd, who was one of Mark's teammates in Little League, died in a construction accident at the age of 21.

"I think Campbell was hard on some guys, in some ways," Mark said. "But I don't think you were ever really alone if you played in that league or if you were involved with Campbell baseball in some way. I know it helped me get through some tough times. I know my life would be way different if I hadn't grown up in Campbell and played baseball there."

PAUL SARGIS: Two generations

Before the first of several visits, in June 2008, I hadn't seen Paul since his wedding day, 20 years before. I don't remember much about the ceremony, but I do remember a private moment we'd had a couple of nights before. "It means a lot to me that you're going to be at my wedding," he said, "because you were a very big part of my growing up."

Maybe more than any of the Campbell kids, Paul had always had a knack, one I appreciated more than most because I was a journalist, of getting from conversational Point A to Point B via the straight line. Communicating just the right way was always important to him, even as a 10-year-old. (The first time I'd talked with him was the result of my having misspelled his name in a story.) Even though he had a hint of a rebellious streak during his teen years, he relished structure and assembled his game the same way he assembled his vocabulary – painstakingly, to the point of occasionally demanding more from himself than he could give. That frustration delayed his entrance into college baseball (at Sonoma State, a Division II program) for two years after he graduated from high school; as he put it, "I needed to learn a little bit more about what it took to be an adult."

Something else that Paul said as we sat in a sports bar/restaurant a few miles from his South San Jose home made me remember why I liked him so much. He mentioned that I had taken him to a Marx Brothers festival when he was a kid, and while I only vaguely remember the occasion, it did occur to me that perhaps the reason I'd invited Paul was that with his puckish sense of humor, he'd appreciate the Marx Brothers more than any of the other kids – and I guess he did, if he still remembered that night more than 30 years later.

As we talked, and before that as I watched him conduct his Little League All-Star team's practice, it was apparent that he had put Campbell both ahead of him and behind him.

"The whole thing was kind of magical, something I didn't really appreciate until I was older," he said, echoing the sentiments of many who were immersed in that summer of 1976. "For us to win 15 in a row in single elimination, some magical things have to happen to you, and I think all of us learned a lot about ourselves and each other that summer.

"Now, though, I think I've started to let it go a little. I'm 45 years old, for crying out loud, and that was something that happened when I was 12. Besides, I've had to let it go because I've had to let a lot of people go. Tony Kephart's dad died two years ago; Harold Sutherland's mom died about the same time, and it was right after that my dad died. All of cancer. (The same disease also had claimed Bill Clinton, father of 1978 Pony League All-Star Steve Clinton, and Bob Straight, father of Bobby, around the same time.) It was the people who mean the most to me now, and we've lost a lot of them."

One reason Paul finds no need to mourn the community we all lost is because of the community he has found.

The Almaden Valley, where Paul lives with his wife Dina and their three children – Andrea, 15; Erik, 12; and Julia, 8 – was developed in the early 1970s virtually as an autonomous community. Most of the people who live there are affluent, but not gaudily rich, and many adult lives revolve around youth activities, sometimes to an extent that Paul finds troubling. "I know a lot of parents have their kids in private (baseball) tutoring and spend all kinds of money on batting cages and stuff like that," he said. "I'm not going to do that with Erik because I don't think that kind of teaching replaces the basic fundamentals, and because I think it takes a lot of the fun out of it for the kids.

"We had good coaching in Campbell, but it was mostly dads who happened to love baseball. Most of us learned baseball by playing baseball, and I think that's kind of been lost now."

It was evident during our conversation that Paul's impact on the Almaden Valley has been substantial, and not because he once played in a Little League World Series – an experience he says he rarely brings up, except on the infrequent occasions he is asked. At least a half-dozen people came by our table and engaged Paul in conversation, mostly about baseball but also about families and jobs and golf scores. At practice, he bantered easily with his son and with the other players, making points firmly but also with a sense that he still is able to see the world through 12-year-old eyes.

He's a comfortable man living a comfortable life – he works for Arrow Electronics in Santa Clara – in a comfortable community. You knew from the time you met Paul, back then, that he had a chance to do something really important with his life, and while he's not a millionaire and he hasn't cured any diseases, perhaps the biggest impact Campbell had on him was to implant the idea that family and loyalty and trust represent currency that is never devalued.

"Baseball was a really important part of my life," he said, "but one thing I've tried to do with my kids is to encourage them to get involved with as many things as possible. Erik played soccer and he's going to play Pop Warner football, and a couple of years ago he got involved with the saxophone and he's gotten pretty good at it. I want baseball to be important to him, but the more things he has that are important to him, the better off I think he'll be."

Paul's parents, Ray and June, were unceasingly and instinctively kind and gentle people who were among my first adoptive "parents" in Campbell, but they were also strict with Paul, who yanked at his leash from time to time. I think Paul felt a little distance in his relationship with his parents, much as he loved them and much as he knew they loved him. I didn't see that distance between Paul and his children, which tells me that how he would raise kids had occurred to him long before he and Dina actually started their family.

"While you're trying to teach them, you find out that they're teaching you too," he said.

A day after our first conversation, Paul's All-Star team played its first game — a game of rising tension that seemed to fuel his team's efficiency and confidence rather than undermine it. His team won 7-6 on a walk-off hit in the bottom of the sixth and final inning. Afterward, the team and parents descended on the same restaurant at which we had talked the previous day, and both Paul and I felt as if we had been transported back a generation. The kids were wolfing down pizza and sandwiches and badgering their parents for quarters to feed into the video games. Pitchers of beer crowded the empty pizza platters off the tables as Paul and the parents revisited and reenacted the central plays and players of the game.

"Yeah, it kind of feels like that, doesn't it?" Paul said, grinning. "God, I love baseball and what it can do for people. I don't think I'll ever lose that. Campbell was a long time ago, but you still get the same feeling. And with Erik, I'm glad that as an 11-year-old (this conversation occurred before his 12th birthday), he can still come watch his father play, and sit in a dugout and see how ex-college and ex-pro players approach the game. Not many kids that age can say that."

The next day, Paul played in an over-30 league game (he was 45) and it was apparent that while his athletic skills had been dulled somewhat by age, they hadn't eroded — nor had his competitive instincts. The tableau I liked most, though, happened before the game — watching Paul warming up by playing catch with Erik.

It reminded me of something else that had happened while I watched Paul pitching batting practice to Erik's team. Paul had unintentionally low-bridged one of Erik's teammates with a high-inside pitch, and as the kid settled back into the batters box after dusting himself off, Erik grinned and said to him, "Way to take evasive action."

I had to laugh, because one of the things that had made Paul engaging as a kid was his ability to say something clever and creative about an occurrence that to most people would seem mundane. Yeah, I thought, that's *exactly* what Paul would have said to some teammate during a long-forgotten summer day more than 30 years ago.

The continuum was continuing, and six months later, Paul and Erik were again in a celebratory milieu – this time in a burger-and-beer joint in Atherton after their Almaden Valley Pop Warner team – Paul was an assistant coach, Erik a starting defensive tackle and tight end in his first season of organized football – flattened San Francisco 31-6 at nearby Woodside High to earn a trip to the national semifinals early the following month in Orlando, Fla.

As kids and parents swirled around the table where the eight coaches were sitting, one might have expected Paul to maintain a certain emotional distance. After all, he had achieved more in athletics before he graduated from high school than all of the parents and boys in the room could expect to achieve in their collective lifetimes. But he exuded the same exuberance as all of the other dads; he was a proud father and coach caught up in the now and not the then.

"One thing I'd thought about was watching the Japanese team (that beat Campbell 10-3 in the 1976 Little League World Series final) take infield," he said. "They used two balls and they moved so quickly they made your head spin. I think that intimidated us. Last week when we played Douglas (a strong Northern Nevada team in a regional semifinal game, won 14-0 by Almaden), we knew they would make a big production out of taking the field and that they'd be talking a lot and be loud. What I tried to tell our guys was that what they did before the game or what talking they did, didn't matter … you can't let those things affect the way you play. Same thing with San Francisco … that was kind of an unfamiliar thing for us, playing against inner-city kids, and we talked about the same thing.

"In Campbell, guys like John Murphy and Rich Alvarez and Bobby Straight were humble and they were team-oriented, but they also *knew* they were good, so they didn't have to say it. The kids we have on this team are kind of the same way. We have a lot of weapons and a lot of different guys who can beat you, but I think they understand that it isn't what they do individually that's going to matter to them when they're older. It's what they do together that will be remembered.

"Hey, maybe they'll get their own (team) picture on the telephone book, like we did."

For Erik, it was his first season of football while many of his teammates had been playing together for several years, and he was tentative at times because he didn't have his teammates' reservoir of football instincts and often reacted mechanically to on-field situations. I asked Paul whether Erik had had to battle discouragement as he learned a sport that is so exacting from the standpoints of pain, exhaustion and the subjugation of individual goals – and that his father never played except for one season of freshman football at Campbell High.

"He *loves* it," Paul said. "Every day when I get home, he's waiting there in uniform and it's him telling me, 'Dad, hurry up or we're going to be late for practice.' Before, it was always the other way around. That's exciting to me. He likes baseball and soccer and playing the saxophone and all the other things he does, but this is the first thing I think he's really become passionate about. It's a lot like me about baseball when I was his age, and that's what makes this experience so exciting for me. I really couldn't appreciate what I went through at the time because I was so young, so maybe it makes me appreciate this that much more.

"When I was a kid, there were some parents who were go-out-after-the-game parents, but my parents were go-home-after-the-game parents. When I'd go out after games with some of the other kids and their parents, it would be like Christmas when they'd give us quarters and we'd play games and hang out together for hours. That's still something I remember, and I'm glad Erik is able to experience the same thing, doing something big-time with guys he likes and guys he'll be friends with and remember long after this is over."

As it turned out, it was far from over. The Almaden Mustangs went to Orlando and defeated Hawaii 10-6 in the national semifinal on December 9, and three days later, they defeated Memorial Park, Ill., 30-6 to win the Pop Warner Pee Wee national championship. The Mustangs finished with the same season record, 15-1, as Paul's 1976 Campbell All-Star team had compiled.

When I heard the final score – Mark Paquin called me to pass along the news – I thought about the fact that Erik Sargis had been polite but reserved around me after his father introduced us, and on the occasions our paths crossed afterward. I thought one reason was that Erik, though appreciative of his father's athletic feats, was understandably tired of hearing about them and was anxious to carve a niche of his own.

Well, I thought, now father and son are athletic peers ... and I was sure Paul, having been too young in 1976 and even in 1978 to fully grasp the enormity of what his teams had accomplished, felt even better about that than Erik did.

STEVE CLINTON: Quality of life

At age 44, Steve Clinton's life has been a litany of voyages, but the only destination he ever intended was full quality of life.

Maybe that's why Joshua Clinton has had seven years of quality life even though he'll never realize it.

As with most of the other leverage players from Campbell's baseball era of good feeling, I hadn't seen Steve in many years at the time I visited he and his family at their home in Pleasanton just before Christmas in 2008. I knew, of course, that the Pony League World Series title he'd helped Campbell Moreland earn in 1978 had been prelude rather than denouement. He'd gone on to play baseball at San Jose State and Santa Clara, earning a law degree from the latter institution, and I knew from previous correspondence that he'd gone on to become an attorney and felt blessed and bulwarked by his wife Carol and their four children.

At the time I first became friends with the Clinton family, it made me homesick for a place I'd never been. Bill and Donna Clinton were from Nebraska, and from them and from their children I gleaned a sense of Midwest values: pride, hard work, the importance of family and faith and community, the belief that all people are entitled to respect and consideration until they prove undeserving of it, friendliness without motive, love without conditions. I was thrilled that Donna Clinton was there when I arrived, because she and Bill (who had died of cancer three years earlier) had been supporters and exemplars as well as friends in my Campbell days, and I had always been grateful to them for that. Bill and Donna had moved to Santa Rosa upon Bill's retirement from the personnel department at the Veterans Administration in Palo Alto, and when I visited the Clintons, Donna had just moved to nearby Dublin, within a dozen or so miles of Steve, his younger brother Mike and his older sister Cathy and their families.

I expected that same sense of inner tranquility in this new Clinton household; I didn't expect to be floored with the spontaneous effusion with which Steve's children greeted me almost as soon as I'd stepped inside the door.

Avery, 8, was grinning so broadly that I couldn't help thinking her braces might have blinded me if we had been in broad daylight, and I also couldn't help thinking, during dinner and conversation afterward, that this kid could give warmth lessons on Walton's Mountain. She had been told that I was a writer, and she eagerly read to her dad and I a seven-page composition she had written. Actually, she performed it, because she'd created intricate, believable characters that she'd fully fleshed out in her mind before she picked up pencil and paper. I was amazed at her ability, at her age, to capture dialogue and commit it to the written word, something I never quite mastered as a writer. Amelia, 4, and Nathan, 3, also showed none of the wariness that kids usually display when they're introduced to adults. Like most children their age, they were bundles of endless energy as they careened around the house, but they clearly understood what was expected of them from the standpoint of restraint. Their parents were affectionate and calm and attentive with them, and they responded in the same way.

Then, there was Joshua. Like his siblings, he seemed to have an ear-to-ear grin permanently affixed to his face, and he seemed to radiate as Steve and Carol hugged him. But what the body certainly felt, the eyes and the mind couldn't comprehend as he sat in his wheelchair.

Joshua was born with the most acute form of microcephaly, a neuro-developmental disorder in which the circumference of the head is more than two standard deviations smaller than average for the person's age and sex. What it means in layman's terms is simple and stark: The child's brain size is in proportion to his/her head size, and thus is too small to function in any meaningful way. Relatively little is known about microcephaly's causes, although cases like Joshua's are considered genetic in nature. Some children develop the disorder as they grow older, and in those cases the condition can be addressed to some degree through surgery and other treatments. In Joshua's case, the only treatment is love, which the Clinton family has in no small supply.

"He's going to be 3 months old for the rest of his life," Steve said. "We don't know why it happened; it just did, and obviously when something like that happens, it's traumatic. But we feel so fortunate to have him. He gives us so much. Kids with (his form of) microcephaly usually don't live anywhere near as long as Joshua has. He has to be fed through his stomach, but he's actually very healthy for a guy his age. We have a wonderful nurse who comes every day, and I can't tell you how phenomenal Carol is with him. He's really an exceptional little guy, just like the rest of our children. Every single day, he teaches us something."

How long Joshua will live, of course, is out of his parents' control to a large degree. It's a finality that people without Steve's background would be hard-pressed to accept. But throughout his life, Steve has never yearned for a destination or an outcome. The savoring of life, he believes, is in the voyage, and he has embarked on more voyages, both in the passport and in the rite-of-passage senses, than just about anyone I know.

As an adolescent, Steve was so skinny that he seemingly could have taken a shower in the barrel of a .22. But his frame was streamlined for speed and helped make his throwing arm a whip, and while Bobby Straight stormed the shortstop position, Steve glided through it. Like Bobby and Paul Sargis, his batting swing married quickness with power. He had huge hands for a kid his size – he was maybe 5-foot-8 as a 14-year-old, and is about 6-1 now – and in 1978 All-Star play he made a seamless transition to second base and complemented Bobby in such a way that with those two and outfielders Billy Roberts and Scott Freear, the spine of our defense virtually was a no-fly zone, which made our already-strong pitching even better and may have been the single biggest reason we won the World Series that year. While playing American Legion ball for me in 1982, he played shortstop and Harold Sutherland moved in as his collaborator at second base, and with relatively fragile pitching, we wouldn't have gone 22-8 that year if not for the stability they provided.

As good as he was in baseball, though, Steve found in football an even more rewarding outlet for the cerebral and adrenal aspects of his personality. At Westmont High, he became probably the best quarterback in school history, and led the Warriors to successive Central Coast Section playoff appearances, although he couldn't play in the postseason as a senior because of a neck injury he'd suffered late in the regular season. He says now that if it hadn't been for the injury, he might have sought to play football in college rather than accepting the baseball scholarship he was given by San Jose State after leading Westmont to the Central Coast Section championship game, which it lost to Prospect. He played shortstop for Westmont that year; Bobby, who'd transferred to Westmont after Campbell High closed, played third.

"To tell you the truth, I would have preferred to play football," Steve says. "I was a quarterback all four years at Westmont, and I thoroughly enjoyed it. It's an entirely different mentality from baseball … one game a week, and it's a war. The adrenaline is pumping, and it's such an exciting sport. But once you start thinking about stepping up (to the college level), you start coming across guys who are 6-4 and 250 and are just as fast as me. And I'd had two surgeries after having my disc dislodged (his senior football season), and I'd lost some arm strength. So maybe it's a good thing I didn't try it."

At San Jose State, Steve was the only freshman on the varsity squad, and he played regularly both at shortstop and second base. From a baseball standpoint, Steve says his experience at San Jose State was fruitful and he would have had no qualms about returning. But academically, he had higher aspirations, and he decided to place himself back in the recruiting process by transferring to San Jose City College and playing for John Oldham.

"He had a lot of really great things to teach me," Steve says of his season with Oldham. "As far as I'm concerned, not only was he a great coach, but he was just a quality person. He wasn't high profile and he never thought of himself, just us."

With most baseball players, the main motivation to transfer from a four-year program to a community college is to gain eligibility for the major league draft. Under MLB rules, once a player attends a class at a four-year school as a freshman, he doesn't become draft-eligible again until his junior season ends or he turns 21, whichever comes first, and the only way around that rule is to play on the community college level. Draft eligibility wasn't Steve's reason for leaving San Jose State, of course, but the Cleveland Indians must have thought it was, because they chose him in the 33rd round of the 1984 draft.

"It was such an honor to be drafted," he said, "but I knew that unless they made me a phenomenal offer, it wasn't going to happen. Being a professional takes a lot ... you really have to love the game. I liked it, but I'd lost a little in my throwing arm (because of his football injury) and I knew I wasn't going to be going to the major leagues anytime soon. I never thought that baseball was what I was going to be doing with my life, and they only offered me a baseball hat and a little bit of money, maybe a thousand dollars."

That same summer, Santa Clara fired coach Jerry McClain, who had recruited and signed Steve, and hired John Oldham as his replacement. Steve played his final two college seasons for the Broncos, at which point he was ready for a new voyage, this time in the literal sense.

"I think I probably read too many Ernest Hemingway novels," he said, laughing. "I had my business degree from Santa Clara, but reading about all his travels and his being an expatriate, I wanted to see what the world was like. So (throughout his) four or five years after college, I'd get out my backpack and buy a plane ticket and just take off for a couple of months. Bob (Straight) came with me on my first and last trips. We spent two months in Europe on the first trip, and later he and I went to South America. I went to the Pacific and Asia for 3½ months another time, and after that I saw the Middle East, Egypt and Israel. I wound up visiting 36 countries in all, and I've been to every continent except Antarctica."

During his travels, he also spent time in Washington, D.C., and became familiar with American University there. Eventually, he enrolled in American's MBA program, and in 1995 he returned home, finished up his MBA work at San Jose State, and entered Santa Clara's law school. When he hadn't been traveling, he had worked for Farmers Insurance, and after he got his law degree and passed the bar exam, he became a trial attorney for Farmers.

"I did that (trial work) for a year and a half, maybe two years, and then I kind of reassessed myself again," Steve says. "I'd had some success in going to trial, but I knew a couple of people who'd done corporate transactional work and I thought I might like that. I made a smooth transition in 1999, and since that time I've never really looked back."

Steve's bio on the website of his law firm, Palo Alto-based Nixon Peabody, reads thusly:

"Mr. Clinton represents a broad range of companies from privately held start-up companies to publicly traded corporations. He has extensive experience in all aspects of corporate transactions and assists clients with the negotiation and consummation of mergers, stock sales, asset acquisitions and other reorganizations. Mr. Clinton regularly assists with cross-border transactions. Mr. Clinton advises public clients in the preparation of reporting documents and registration statements filed with the SEC under the Securities Act of 1933 and the Securities Exchange Act of 1934 as well as other SEC compliance matters. Mr. Clinton represents clients in equity financings, convertible debt offerings, and venture capital transactions. His practice also consists of representing emerging growth companies in all aspects of business and corporate transactions, including entity formation, entity governance and business planning issues."

Steve says his broad spectrum of clients makes his job a succession of unique challenges that bring with them a broad spectrum of unique rewards.

"It's really an emerging field (of law practice) in Silicon Valley," he says. "There are so many things going on, so many smart people walking in with ideas and stuff that can change the world. In terms of places to practice, this is one of the best in the world."

As he built his career, his personal life also began to coalesce. He met Carol while both were working at Farmers, and they dated for more than three years before marrying and settling in Campbell to began raising their family. Early in 2008, they bought a bigger home in Pleasanton, a south Alameda County community that in many ways is a larger, East Bay equivalent of Campbell: A onetime agricultural hamlet that's now a suburban enclave.

"I really hadn't planned that (career) path for myself," Steve says, "but it's funny how life faces you in different directions. Nowadays it's so much different; you're supposed to have this one goal and keep striving toward it, but really it's the road that you travel that's the most important part, and enjoying that road when you're traveling it. You never know where you're going to wind up, no matter what your goals are, so you'd better enjoy it.

"It hasn't always been smooth, but for the most part I've enjoyed it, and I think the good feeling you have about your life goes back to your friendships. And for me, that goes back to Campbell. Guys like Bob, Paul Sargis, Harold Sutherland, Steve Koontz ... those are guys I grew up playing with, those are guys who were at my wedding, guys who are still my best friends to this day.

"At a young age, I really didn't think in terms of goals. I've always been more of a day-to-day person. I wish I could say I had more vision back then, but this was back in the day before you were in second grade and you started thinking about going to Harvard. I wanted to enjoy the experience, whatever it was, and again I think that started with Campbell."

Steve had played in Quito Little League, which during his time there had an array of talent that was just as rich and almost as deep as that of Campbell Little League. He acknowledges now that he was more that a trifle apprehensive about meeting and playing with the kids who'd been to the Little League World Series the year before; at the same time, he was confident that he and the other Quito graduates would not be overwhelmed by their better-known counterparts across town.

"Quito was very competitive," Steve says. "My 12-year-old year, we went to the District 12 finals where we played Saratoga. I pitched a two-hitter, but one of those hits was a home run, and Jeff Arrillaga beat us 1-0. (Arrillaga later starred in football and baseball at Saratoga High and went on to play four years of football at Stanford.) Even now I sometimes joke with Bob and Paul about how Quito really was better than Campbell, but we never got a chance to prove it.

"I was excited, because I knew the caliber of play with the Campbell, Moreland and Quito guys was going to be exceptional. We followed what Campbell had done (the previous summer), and it was such a huge deal for everybody, them being on Wide World of Sports and having their picture on the Campbell phone book. I guess none of us knew how well everything was going to mesh, but I can't think of a single experience (during the transitional phase) where I was made to feel uncomfortable. So yes, it seemed like everybody meshed together right away, and not only did we mesh, we formed those relationships that we still have today. I don't even remember the games that much, but I remember the fun we had together after the games. And I think one of the intangible things we had, had nothing to do with the kids. That's where you saw the melding of Campbell and Moreland and Quito.

"It was like all the parents had known each other a long time, and there were no issues between them that I can remember. It's easier to do that within a team; as a team you usually wind up bonding at the end of the day because you're together so much. But when you're sitting there watching your kids play, maybe you start thinking your kid ought to be playing more or he ought to be playing a different position. But you talk to the (1970s) parents now, and all they have are these great memories. Maybe that (the parents' harmony) was the biggest intangible we had."

Likewise, Steve always felt that the biggest intangible he had in his favor was his own family. It occurred to me, as we talked, that a lot of the Campbell guys had waited until they were in their late 20s or early 30s before they started families. They took their lives in stages, and after having had their fun during the previous stages, they were now ready for the most important stage of all. And they were prepared for parenthood because their parents had prepared them.

290

"I know I wouldn't have been the person or the athlete I was without my parents," Steve says. "If I were to write a book, I'd write about how much I think of my dad and mom. I would say I was an OK athlete who wanted to get better because my dad would come home at 5 each day and the first thing he'd say to me is, 'Let's go outside and play catch.' He motivated me and he always made baseball a lot of fun. My parents always said they wanted me to get a good experience out of everything I did. 'Do your best. That's all we expect, first or last, as long as you have a good time and try your best.'

"And I think that's pretty much the way things have turned out ... at this point in my life, it's time for me to be my dad."

DOMINIC COSTANTINO: The heart and soul

As during his playing days, now almost a quarter-century distant, Dominic Costantino's passion to excel and to meet his own expectations seethes largely within. In that respect, he was Campbell's answer to Lou Gehrig, who happily tacked in relative anonymity behind Babe Ruth's flamboyant tsunami, and whose inner quest for professionalism and self-maximization wasn't as appreciated in his time to the degree that it was celebrated later.

Like Gehrig, Dominic was a left-handed hitting first baseman with a scythelike power swing, and like Gehrig, Dominic's presence was one of poise and not noise. Also like Gehrig, Dominic worked harder at his perceived weaknesses than at his obvious strengths. One of the reasons he never was able to realize his goal of playing professional baseball was that his game was painted in earth hues rather than in pastels. He was and still is understated, and watches and listens a lot more than he talks … yet when he does express himself, it's in an eloquent and thoughtful way, and it's in a way that matters.

All of which makes it appropriate that even though he was a player without conscious flair, he made the defensive play that maybe mattered more than any other single play in the history of Campbell youth baseball. For San Francisco 49er fans, it was Dwight Clark who made "The Catch," the play that sent the 49ers to Super Bowl XVI. Those who were in Campbell at the time would beg to differ; in our eyes, it was Dominic who made The Catch that made Campbell Moreland's 1978 Pony League World Series conquest possible, and he did it four years before the other guy.

In 1978, expectations for the Campbell Moreland Pony League All-Star team were broadened to the extent that anything short of a world championship would have been deemed inadequate, especially by the players themselves. The fiber of the 1976 Campbell Little League national championship team had been enriched, in Pony League, by the addition of players from Quito and Moreland little leagues who contributed their talents, their ambition and their focus on the greater good. Yet Campbell Moreland almost never made it out of its first tournament.

Diablo Valley came in with a coterie of talented athletes who physically dwarfed their Campbell counterparts and, like almost every team that played Campbell during that era, was intent on establishing its own niche by taking out the Bay Area's most visible program. On a Saturday afternoon, Campbell ran afoul of San Ramon Valley pitcher Tad Heydenfeldt, who already looked like the college pitcher he would eventually become at the University of Arizona, and lost 4-1. That meant that Campbell would have to come back to beat Pittsburg, another East Bay team, later that same afternoon, then come back and sweep a Sunday doubleheader from Diablo Valley to win the tournament and advance to the regional. In temperatures that approached 100 degrees on both days, running that gamut seemed like a virtual impossibility.

As described in the previous chapter on the team, Campbell Moreland easily beat Pittsburg 10-0, then edged Diablo Valley 5-4 to force a deciding game, and moved ahead 6-0 in that contest before Diablo Valley rallied to score five unanswered runs. In the bottom of the seventh, Diablo Valley's leadoff man smoked a line drive to the right of Dominic, who hadn't started the game and had taken over at first base when Eddie Rodriguez was switched to the mound in the sixth inning.

The percussion of ball against bat said but one thing: Double, tying run in scoring position and winning run at the plate with nobody out.

"I remember there were a *lot* of people there, for Campbell Moreland and John D. Morgan Park," Dominic said in 2008, his voice beginning to lilt as he recalled the moment. "There weren't very many stands, just the ones between third and first, but out on Beer Hill and down the left-field line and even in the outfield, it was just wall to wall out there and everybody was rooting for us and giving us standing ovations. I know we were maybe feeling some pressure because we had to win twice and we'd been embarrassed by that team the day before. We were past our best and second-best pitchers (Rich Alvarez and Brett Blackwell), and not that our third or fourth pitchers were bad, but as a team we really had to win it (collectively) instead of putting all the weight on Rich's shoulders.

"I think I was playing in a little bit, but as a first baseman I always kind of slid off the bag and wasn't holding the (foul) line. I kind of moved to my right before the batter hit the ball … I guess it really looked like I went a long way. I felt like this was a big strong kid and I think he may have gone that way once before. You know how a base-stealer reads the pitcher to try to get a good jump? Well, I was trying to get a jump on the batter. I remember going one or two steps to my right and then going almost vertical."

If Dominic had been right-handed, with the glove on his left hand, it would have been impossible for him to get to the ball, and as it was, nothing short of perfect timing and full extension would have sufficed. Dominic was completely parallel to the ground and about two feet off it when the line drive snow-coned in the webbing of his glove. There was a second or two of stunned silence, after which the 2,000 or so spectators – most of them Campbell supporters – unleashed a volley of sound that eclipsed anything we had heard during the Little League World Series two years before. Even though the out was only the first of the inning, it was a game- and tournament-winner, because Diablo Valley got runners to second and third with two outs before Eddie Rodriguez got the final strikeout to preserve Campbell's 6-5 victory. Without Dominic's play, Campbell Moreland would have been fortunate to escape that inning with a tie, and even if it had, its chances in extra innings would have been remote because its pitchers were exhausted, both in terms of energy and in terms of eligibility under tournament rules.

"It was maybe the biggest (athletic) thing of my life, looking back," he said. "I was part of a lot of great teams that did a lot of heroic stuff, but I always prided myself as a really good first baseman, so it meant a lot that I was able to help us win a game with my defense."

He played a year of Legion ball for me, then moved on to San Jose City College and then Cal Poly San Luis Obispo, a top-tier NCAA Division II program then and a competitive D-I entry now. I went down there during his senior year to see him play and spend a weekend with Dominic and his roommate Mike Briare, a frequent youth-baseball opponent from Los Gatos and one of Dominic's Bellarmine teammates. Dominic was in the midst of a season that would end with him making first-team All-California Collegiate Athletic Association (the toughest league in Division II), and we talked at length then about Dominic's yearning to prove he could play professionally, and what his chances of being drafted by a major league organization after Cal Poly's season might be. Like Bobby Straight, he knew his physical stature might work against him – he was solidly built and perfectly proportioned for a first baseman, but even with a left-handed swing that oozed with power, he didn't look like a guy who could hit a ball 450 feet – and he was hopeful that some of the scouts who had seen him play often would be able to sell their decision-making bosses on his intangible qualities.

As it turned out, he was overlooked in the draft, and no team expressed interest in signing him as a free agent. It wasn't easy for him to let go; he played a season in a new league in Ecuador before acknowledging that the time to move on to the next phase of his life was at hand.

It wasn't that Dominic had nothing else going for him besides baseball. Always a strong student, he graduated from Cal Poly with a business degree, and went on to two successful careers. He began as a computer-components salesman, eventually forming his own company, and then switched to real estate.

He also found a way to replace baseball in his life — by running triathlons. "I completed the Hawaii Kona Half Ironman in 2003 and in 2004 I ran the San Diego Marathon," he said. "I am not fast, but I always finish."

You didn't compromise when Dominic was around, just as Dominic didn't compromise when his father was around, or even when his father wasn't around. "Jobber John" Costantino was perhaps the most vivid of all the parental personalities when Dominic played in Campbell. He'd been a Marine captain and had served multiple tours of duty in Vietnam, and I wasn't the only person who initially was intimidated by him. Every sentence had the impact of a barked order that you didn't dare disobey or question, and even when he said something that was tongue-in-cheek funny, which was fairly often, there was always that foreboding growl lurking.

Early in my tenure as announcer at Campbell Little League, I routinely called Jobber's son "Dom," which seemed logical to me since that was what his manager called him and what I called him in casual conversation. John called me aside one day — the first time I'd met him — and told me, succinctly, that he wanted his son to be called by his correct name. And when John made a suggestion, you did well to follow it, which I did.

Brusque and opinionated as John was, he never interfered with Dominic's career or the way any of Dominic's managers and coaches ran their teams; in fact, he bulwarked their authority rather than undermining it. He always said that baseball was a game and not the most important thing in any kid's life, and even after we began our journey to Williamsport in 1976, John maintained his military sense of chain of command and dispassionate decorum. He was there at all our stops, of course, and it's hard to envision him today without his loud Hawaiian shirt, holding a beer in one hand and holding court with the other. But you didn't really know what John was thinking or feeling, because he usually kept his emotions under wraps.

Then came the Western Regional championship game in San Bernardino, in which we beat Pearl City, Hawaii, 6-2, to earn the trip to Williamsport. I was sitting in the first row of the stands, keeping the team scorebook, and as it happened, John was sitting right next to me. After the final out was recorded and our group erupted into celebration and noise, I looked over at John. He didn't say anything, but the toughest man I'd ever met up to that point in my life had tears running down his cheeks and was not making any attempt to hide it. We looked at each other, and impulsively hugged and danced around like a couple of hyperthyroid debutantes.

Jack Zogg's favorite Jobber anecdote happened in Williamsport, where Joe DiMaggio was among the invited guests during the week of the Little League World Series. DiMaggio had thrown out the ceremonial first pitch of the Campbell-Bristol first-round game, and Jack hoped to retrieve it to give to an uncle who was a Yankees fan.

"I told John about it, and he said, 'Don't worry; I'll get it for you,'" Jack said in 2009. "So he walks after DiMaggio and says in that booming voice of his, 'Hey, you guinea, come here!' I'm saying, 'Oh, *nooooooo*' ... you don't just yell at Joe DiMaggio. DiMaggio turns around, and it turns out both of them are from Martinez ... before you know it, they're standing there just chirping away like two old paisanos. And I got the ball."

I learned that night in San Bernardino, and later when John and I became closer friends, that there was limitless depth beyond the tough veneer. So it was with Dominic as well. Never a great all-around athlete, he made himself into a college-level player (and later a triathlete) because of what was inside. And quiet as he was, he had a Gobi-like sense of dry humor. So maybe I shouldn't have been surprised many years later, at his wedding, when the Dominic Costantino who had always seemed so hyper-serious decided that his wedding song would be "I Got Friends in Low Places."

With his father serving multiple tours of duty as a Marine in Vietnam, and with two younger siblings, Dominic had to assume home responsibilities at a very early age. But Campbell being the way Campbell was, Dominic doesn't remember that time in terms of tedium.

"I always worked, from a young age," he says now. "At 12 I had a paper route and a lot of re-sponsibilities. My folks didn't have a lot of money, and I had to get myself to games a lot (rather than rely on his parents for transportation). But I think it taught me responsibility. I don't want to say I'm a risk taker, but I try things, like running triathlons. I always push myself, and I have to always be challenged. When I didn't make the (1980) Colt League All-Star team, I kind of became like that 14th man on a 14-man roster, but I was able to excel my way back up in college. Learn about it, do the research and try to do it better than anybody else ... that's what I learned growing up.

"All of us lived really close to each other ... I remember walking to John Murphy's house, and Eddie Rodriguez's, and John Aimonetti was right around the corner from me. I remember play-ing kickball at Rosemary School when we were really little, but mostly I remember just playing baseball all the time. We played on the minor league field (at Campbell Little League) because it had higher fences, and being lefthanded, if I hit the ball over the major league fence it would go bouncing into Hamilton Avenue and we might never get it back. Kids have so many options now ... electronics, other sports, 200 channels on TV. God, I sound like my dad now, but it's true. You know how you always have to tell kids to go outside and play? Well, *nobody* ever had to tell us that.

"I hope it happened that way for other kids, because it was really neat and I felt really fortunate to have been part of that whole thing. When you grow up and play with guys as much as we played together, you become each others' best coaches. I was so fortunate to have had great coaches my whole life, but I knew that if something was wrong with my swing, even as good as our coaches were, they didn't know me as well as the other guys knew me."

Dominic lives with his second wife, Laura, and daughter Ashley in Hollister, a rural community about 40 miles south of San Jose. After a previous career in the electronics industry, he is now a prominent Realtor, working for Intero, the largest real estate marketing firm in the area, and he may branch out — literally — from that. "I recently planted a Malbec wine vineyard and plan to have my first harvest in 2010," he said, "and I may even get into the wine business."

Like many of his Campbell teammates, he is firmly entrenched in the present, but he still keeps in touch with his baseball friends, and the baseball accomplishments and memories from Campbell still warm and invigorate him.

"One thing I remember about Williamsport was Joe DiMaggio sitting in our dugout during one of our games, just talking to us," he says. "I mean, Joe DiMaggio … can you get any bigger than that if you're a 12-year-old kid? I hit a home run in Williamsport (in Campbell's 7-0 first-round win over Bristol, Conn.) and Richard threw a gem, and we were both brought upstairs to the press box and got interviewed by Keith Jackson. I've still got a picture of us … I'm like, wow, I'm being *interviewed*, and by *Keith Jackson*. After the series, all the teams went to Washington and toured the White House, and I've still got a flag they gave us that had been flown (atop) the White House.

"The other thing I remember was the humidity in Williamsport. None of us had ever experienced it before, and it just hit us like a ton of bricks. I remember chasing fireflies, too. Big as your hand.

"It was all part of a journey. We spent so much time together, going back almost as far as I can remember. Being a part of that Bellarmine (football) team was very neat, but it all comes back to the (Campbell) guys … I never got as close to the Bellarmine guys because we were together only two years and I wasn't in the trenches with them until I was a junior in high school. I grew up with Campbell and those guys were my best friends … we were together 24 hours a day, 365 days a year. It was a long time ago — it was pre-skateboard even — but sometimes it doesn't seem like it was that long ago at all."

Asked about the legacy he would like to have attached to his name, Dominic smiled and, characteristically, thought for a long time before answering.

"I think the thing I remember most was after it (the Williamsport trip) was all over," he said. "Do you remember the other great things that were happening in 1976? It was an Olympic year, and I heard someplace that if the Bay Area had been a nation it would have finished sixth in the medal count. It was the year of (Olympic decathlon champion and San Jose resident) Bruce Jenner …

there were all these great track athletes and swimmers, and we were right there on the banquet circuit with them. A bunch of 12-year-olds, and we were part of that circuit and people were recognizing us the same way they did the Olympic athletes.

"After the banquet circuit, we were just starting junior high (at Castro) and can you believe they placed our team photo on the *cover* of the Campbell phone book? That certainly did not hurt our popularity in school. Rich (Alvarez) had a rock-star type of status at Castro.

"I think another thing (for which he'd like to be remembered) that I was the captain, at least once, on every single team I ever played on. But most of all, we had this bond. Any one of those guys could call, and I would do anything for them. And isn't that the thing everybody would want to remember?

"You know, whenever this book comes out, I'd like to make a point to pick a day on the calendar where all of us can get together. I stay in touch with some of the guys, but I need to talk with them more. Scott Freear (the starting center fielder on the 1976 Williamsport team) was my best friend … we lost touch for a while, but I saw him in Santa Cruz a couple of years ago and he's the same happy-go-lucky Scott. He's driving a truck now (after many years as a bartender).

"Steve Clinton is my lawyer, Bobby (Straight) and I were business partners a few years back, and I still talk often with Paul Sargis. But I wonder how some of the other guys are, what they're doing. Geez, we were so together then."

BOBBY STRAIGHT: The teeth

When I think about the kids who reflected the heart and soul of Campbell in the late 1970s, a lot of names come to mind — and, of course, that was one of the primary reasons we won. Ask about who represented our teeth, and there's only one answer: Our shortstop, Bobby Straight.

All of Bobby's teams — regular season and postseason, Little League, Pony League, Colt League, high school, college — won, and a lot of them won on a sublime scale. I saw them all, and it always seemed to me that the biggest reason was that he wouldn't let them lose. As long as I've known him, Bobby's build doesn't even begin to suggest the extent of his quickness, physical strength and endurance. He also had, and has, and a disarming way of redirecting praise away from himself, so the baseball layman probably isn't going to appreciate him until he's on the field with or against him.

But I have now watched him play in four different decades, from age 10 in 1974 to age 44 in 2008, and seeing him this most recent time was like a drive down a country lane where the landmarks reassure with their familiarity and their grace.

Bobby, Paul Sargis, Harold Sutherland and Tony Kephart play on a San Jose-based over-30 team — each, of course, is in his mid-40s — in a national age-group league. A lot of former college and pro players, and even occasional ex-major leaguers, participate, and the games are recreational only in the sense that guys from opposing teams have been known to meet afterward for pizza and beer. During the games, the outcomes matter a lot, as much as they did when these players were much younger, and while the speed and the arm strength of many of the players have eroded, the baseball instincts and passion and self-demand for playing the game correctly have not. At one point in the game I saw, an outfielder on the Indians (Paul and Bobby's team) laid out parallel to the ground in an attempt to make a diving catch, which he barely missed. When he came back to the dugout, somebody in the stands asked him, presumably in jest, "Why did you even try to make that play? Aren't you too old to be doing that?" The player shrugged, then said, "I dunno. It's in my blood, I guess."

Paul Sargis almost hit a home run in the game — the ball landed just in front of the left-field wall — and still played with the same sleekness that I'd always remembered. Bobby never was sleek, and he now plays second base instead of shortstop as his only concession to his age. But to hold to the country-lane metaphor, all the same brooks and meadows and farmhouses and ponds that were there the first time I drove through Bobby's game have changed not one scintilla in 34 years.

Although not a power hitter by inclination, Bobby always could stay inside of the ball and get the sweet spot of his bat on pitches that handcuffed lesser hitters, and he did that twice for resounding singles in this game. In the field, he ranged far to his left to spear a well-hit one-hopper, pirouetted and threw to second to start a double play. He then side-sprinted almost behind second base, with the same economical footwork he had always had, to corral a wicked grounder and get a force play at second, and he completed that inning by venturing into shallow left-center field to spear a pop fly that was out of the other defenders' range. And on the bases, he skulked and pounced just as he had 34 years before.

Afterward, I told Bobby that his play that day had reminded me almost startlingly of his days in Campbell and later at San Jose State, where, in an exhibition game against the San Francisco Giants, he once got a hit against Vida Blue, who won 209 games in the major leagues and was a six-time All-Star. He smiled. "I don't think the instincts really go away," he said. "You're just a little slower, that's all. I love playing in this league ... it's serious baseball. A guy from Long Island started it about 20 years ago, and now it's huge and there are a lot of guys here who know how to play, and love the game."

In 1976, he was the No. 2 hitter on Campbell's All-Star team. This was a period when pitchers' size and power dictated Little League to a much greater extent than they do now, and to hit .250 over a deep postseason run was more than respectable. Bobby hit .543 (our next-best hitter finished at .344) over 16 games in that postseason, in addition to congealing our infield to such an extent that it enabled our pitchers to work to contact rather than risking control by trying to overpower the opponents' hitters. It was much the same in Pony League in 1978 when we won the World Series, and he was one of the few players on our Colt League team in 1980 who met expectations as we were making an unexpectedly early exit at the Western Regional in Garden Grove.

Bobby came up to the Campbell High varsity as a freshman, along with Rich Alvarez, and he started and starred as a sophomore on the last Campbell High team, in 1980. After being reassigned to Westmont upon Campbell's closure, he led the Warriors to the CCS championship game against Prospect in 1982. This was the game in which both teams had so many Campbell-system players that it resembled an intrasquad game; Prospect had beaten Barry Bonds' Serra team to reach the finals, and Westmont had survived a regional encounter with Alisal and Gordon Dillard (who starred as a pitcher at Oklahoma State and later had brief major league stints with Baltimore and Philadelphia) to get to the semifinals, where the Warriors beat Mills of Millbrae to set up the showdown with Prospect.

Bobby then played four years at San Jose State, and while he had a quality career there, he was an early victim of the combine mentality that then was starting to permeate major league teams' player-evaluation process. I have no doubt that Bobby would have found a way to succeed at any level — today, Boston Red Sox second baseman Dustin Pedroia, the American League MVP in 2008 even though he is only 5-foot-9 and 180 pounds, reminds me a lot of Bobby — but the scouts and cross-checkers, as too often is their wont, saw only a commodity. They deemed him too slow, too small, or too much a victim of his own success, in terms of expectations that he could continue to get better as a professional. So he wasn't drafted, and he drifted out of baseball, working a number of jobs. He was in the hospitality industry for a while and also did work for a beer distributor, and later on, he had gotten into website design. In 2008, he was working for Interactive Identity, headquartered in San Jose.

I told him it seemed a shame to me that there was no place in the baseball industry for a man of his baseball knowledge and integrity, not to mention his accomplishments.

"Well, it's funny that you mention that, because I'm doing some coaching now," he said. "I live in Morgan Hill (a onetime rural hamlet south of San Jose that has evolved into a bedroom community for Silicon Valley) and one of the guys on this team got the job as the first baseball coach at Sobrato (Morgan Hill's second high school, opened in the fall of 2004). He asked me if I was interesting in helping out, and I've been an assistant coach there for the past couple of years."

In 2008, the second season during which Sobrato had its full complement of four grades, the Bulldogs won the Santa Teresa Athletic League title and advanced to the CCS playoffs. For the 2009 season, they were to move up to the Mount Hamilton Athletic League, the top tier of the 24-team Blossom Valley super league that covers the southern, eastern and western segments of the Santa Clara Valley. (Westmont, Leigh and Branham, all of which were in the now-defunct West Valley Athletic League, also were in the MHAL for baseball in 2009.)

If Bobby had a shortcoming as a young player — and whether this was even a shortcoming could be debated — it was the fact he found lack of effort and commitment instantly and irretrievably unacceptable, and he never hesitated to speak his mind to teammates he didn't think wanted to excel and win as intensely as he did. So I asked him whether he'd been able to make the adjustment in terms of having patience with high school players whose backgrounds don't give them the same frame of reference that he had.

"Actually, yeah, I think I've learned to be pretty patient with them," he said. "As long as they try. I'm not patient with anybody who isn't trying. We had a couple of guys this (past) season who were two of our best players, but it was like they took everything for granted. They were just satisfied with being as good as they were, and they were dragging the other players down. Finally we wound up kicking them off, and from the time we did that, we were a better team."

Better team.

It was Bobby Straight's two-word baseball manifesto … and it remains his two-word Campbell legacy.

MATT CHRISTIAN: Persistence

It was an odd coupling, their joint listing as the two pitchers who completed no-hit games during Campbell Little League's 1976 regular season.

Rich Alvarez was the face and force of Campbell youth baseball when Campbell youth baseball was the face and force of American youth baseball. His arm was the trebuchet that flung us to a Little League national championship and a Pony League World Series title, and his reputation still radiated long after the effervescence had faded from his fastball. Matt Christian, on the other hand, never made a first-tier All-Star team in Campbell, and in terms of pitching velocity, his arm was more like a Slinky than a trebuchet. Rich was on the Campbell High varsity as a freshman. Matt didn't play baseball, or anything else, his first two years in high school. After high school, when Rich was drafted by the Chicago White Sox and turned down their offer to accept a baseball scholarship from the University of Hawaii, he was a major-party nominee. Matt was always an independent-party candidate for whose name you had to thoroughly search the ballot.

Yet in terms of the intangible elements that made Campbell youth baseball what it was, Matt ultimately won the election, implausible as that might have seemed to anyone who saw them both pitch in 1976.

Rich, who is a year older than Matt, pitched only his freshman season, 1983, at Hawaii before he suffered a broken collarbone in a bodysurfing accident. He never played competitively again. In 1987, four years after Rich's career ended, Matt was still pitching, as a senior for a San Jose State team that might have made the NCAA tournament had it not been for a season-ending seven-game losing streak. Rich left Hawaii soon after his injury, and switched jobs several times; as of 2009, he was living in Palm Desert and working for the Allstate insurance company. Matt left San Jose State with a sociology degree and a career plan, and after 20 years in Santa Clara County law enforcement, he has transformed that plan into reality with security.

Rich Alvarez is rightly remembered as the force that made so many things possible for Campbell youth baseball (and as a class act throughout that time and afterward). Matt Christian remembers Campbell youth baseball as the force that made so many things possible for him.

"Nice ... sure, I remember that no-hitter," Matt said, smiling, as we ate lunch at a golf-club restaurant in Hollister, where he lives in an upscale neighborhood with his wife Susan and their two sons, Ryan, 14, and Nick, 9. "Jack Larva (a Campbell Moose Lodge teammate) saved that game (a 9-0 win over Bruener's) for me with a diving catch. I think maybe that was the only way (in 1976) that you could have compared me with Rich; he was so great. Even in college I never threw hard at all.

"I never considered myself more than an average player, but I think I reached most of my potential. I think loving baseball was what did that, and what made me love baseball was Campbell. Those were good times. I think I played real well there and was one of the better players by the time I was 12, but it's hard to be one of the best players when you're playing against some of the best players in the country at the time.

"Everything about that league was great. One thing I remember was the (major division) uniforms. They weren't like the one-year uniforms you see now; they were woolen, and they kept them for a lot of years, but they were so beautiful. Every year, before the season, you'd get your uniform and it would be all pressed and starched. I remember sleeping in mine the night before Opening Day.

"I remember on a Little League Saturday, you'd get to the field at 8 in the morning, even if you weren't playing the first game (which started at 10). I'd ride my bike over there ... it was three, three and a half miles from my house (on McBain Avenue in easternmost Campbell), but in those days Campbell afforded you the luxury of riding down Hamilton Avenue (then and still one of the busiest thoroughfares in town) without having to worry about it. You'd go down there and watch your buddies play, and you'd stay all day. It was our own little cocoon, just the safety of it. The announcing made it feel like a big-league atmosphere, and we were able to read about all the games later (in the *Campbell Press*) too. For us, that was baseball ... not many games were on TV, and there was no ESPN (which started in 1979). Our baseball was Campbell.

"Another thing I remember was that there was no jealousy, ever. What I've seen now, coaching my kids, is that everybody is worrying about everybody else; you hear somebody saying about somebody else, 'Well, he's not that good,' and you'll hear coaches talking about other people in front of the kids. Maybe I don't remember it now, being older, but I don't think it was there in Campbell. Whatever was going on with the adults, they kept it away from us. We had no clue what was going on (behind the scenes) and we didn't care. Our thing was to have fun and play baseball, and they provided that."

Matt as a preteen was oversized, though certainly not overweight, and his coordination never quite paralleled his size as a Little League player. But he was amiable, earnest, and eager to learn, and when you talked to him, the conversation usually took the form of him asking questions. As an adult, it's easy to see what being a good listener has done for him. He exudes a sense of reason that accentuates his 6-foot-4 presence and makes him a natural moderator — a skill that he has put to full use over 18 years in the San Jose Police Department, in which he is a patrol sergeant.

Like most Campbell kids of his generation, he was afforded few luxuries and fewer shortcuts. He was the fourth of Jack and Marge Christian's eight children; Jack was a fireman who hardly ever missed a game, and sometimes parked his fire truck beyond the right-field fence on Hamilton Avenue and sat atop it while Matt's team played. Jack, who died in 2008, was a lot like John D. Morgan, the beloved Campbell police chief after whom the city's main park is named. Jack was an animated but sensitive man who knew relatively little about baseball and acknowledged as much, but he was unswerving in his loyalty and support, not only with his own children but with everyone in the Campbell baseball community. I particularly remember a situation during Matt's junior year at Mitty High, when Paul Balbas, also a junior at Mitty and a friend of Matt's since their Little League days, was cut from the Mitty varsity baseball squad.

I always thought that the friendship between Matt and Paul, with whom I also had a strong friendship, was one of the best things that ever happened to both of them. They tapped each others' best qualities; Paul, who never met a conversation he didn't want to enter and would try just about anything, helped make Matt more outgoing, and Matt's good sense and ability to take multiple looks into any situation helped make Paul more contemplative and less impulsive. I knew how much making that Mitty team had meant to Paul, who was skilled but somewhat overlooked during his time in Campbell, and I had seen how hard he had worked to achieve that goal. But after he told me he had missed the cut at Mitty, I wasn't prepared for his level of discouragement, which far exceeded any I'd seen in him during the six years I'd known him. I later found out that Jack also had called him later that night, and succeeded in getting Paul to commit himself to accepting a spot on the JV team and taking another shot at the varsity the following year. (He did, and made the varsity as a senior and played well alongside Matt, who was the Monarchs' best pitcher that year.)

"I don't know how he ever knew Paul got cut," Matt said in 2009. "Darlene (Paul's mom) said that to me when she heard my dad had died. My dad cared about people. There were several times where he called the family together and said there would be somebody living with us for a while that was having a hard time.

"Another thing I remember … sometimes when there weren't any Little League games going on, my dad would pile all of us in our station wagon and take us over to the (Rosemary School) field. We lived across the street from the Farnhams (including Tim, who was on the 1979 Campbell Little League national championship team) … Tim had six brothers and sisters, so there would always be a court full or a street full of Christians and Farnhams. He'd have six kinds of soda and a couple of beers for himself, and we'd just go over there and he'd spend the whole day pitching lob ball to us. The Balbas kids lived around the corner, we'd have all my brothers, and sometimes John Murphy and Kenny Vaughn and Greg and Cameron Comick and some of the other kids in the neighborhood would come over and play. I remember that as much as I do the games. He made sure everyone played, and it was good baseball. We played the right way, even though it was just pickup.

"My parents were the biggest reason I kept playing ... they always supported me and always told me that doing my best was most important. I could never thank them enough for it. My dad never pushed me. I think the only one of us that my dad pushed a little was my (youngest) brother Jeff. Jeff was a really good athlete; he was the only Christian ever to make an All-Star team in Campbell, and he played Division I college basketball on a full scholarship (at the University of San Francisco from 1987-90). But he never pressured any of us. We played because we liked it."

Matt says the instruction and encouragement of his Little League and Pony League coaches served as his bridge over the turbulent baseball waters into which he waded between the end of his Pony League career and his 1987 season as a pitcher for, and inveterate student of, San Jose State coach Sam Piraro.

He says his love for baseball first was nurtured by his farm-league manager, Don Bernard. Starting with his 10-year-old season in 1975, Matt played three seasons for the Campbell Moose Lodge major division team, managed by Rick Rixman and coached by Al Aiken. Both were relatively young and, like many of the league's coaches and managers at the time, did not have their own children on their teams. Matt's Moose teammates included John Aimonetti, the starting left fielder for the 1976 national champions, and Chris Gettler, a velvet-handed infielder who later played for Jacksonville University, was drafted by the Los Angeles Dodgers and played in their minor league system in 1987 and 1988.

"I just remember their coaching technique was disciplined," Matt said of Rixman and Aiken. "They taught us the way baseball should be played, and it was to win the game. They taught us you had to compete as a team. There was no one person they were trying to showcase. If it took Chris bunting to get the go-ahead run into scoring position, that's what he did, even though Chris was the best hitter on our team. It wasn't about you; it was about trying to win and trying to compete with the best players around.

"Al was an excellent pitching coach. Stuff he talked about with me was stuff I later taught when I was the pitching coach at Mitty. Balance, release point ... he knew what he was talking about, and what he taught me about pitching was what got me to the level I was at as a 12-year-old."

By 1977, the year after Campbell's All-Star team went to the Little League World Series final for the second of three times in the 1970s, Matt had emerged as one of the best pitchers in the league. To his surprise, he wasn't chosen for the All-Star team, which repeated as District 44 champion before losing to Los Gatos in the first round of the sectional tournament. His disappointment, Matt says, was acute at the time, but it was assuaged and his confidence bolstered by his two Pony League seasons on Bud Stallings' Yankees.

"Your feelings get hurt when you don't make an All-Star team when you think you might have deserved it," Matt said. "It was a bummer that day, but I didn't think much of it. Bud came up to me the next day, and he must have known what it's like to not make a team. He told me not to let this get me down, that I would still play a lot of baseball, and that he ran this team for 13-year-olds called the Shamrocks after the Pony League season and he was hoping I would play for the Shamrocks after my first Pony League year.

"He told me some of the same things I tell my kids ... you have to be persistent because sometimes guys blossom late."

Bud drafted Matt, who played for the Yankees during his two Pony League seasons and enjoyed it for more reasons that he expected.

"His antics and his passion for the game were great," Matt said, "and he knew, really knew, baseball. Those were two of my greatest years ever. Dave Bryant (the catcher on the 1979 Pony League team that won Campbell Moreland's second straight World Series) was on that team; so was Dominic (Costantino) my first year. We never won the championship, but we were right in it both years. And I loved some of the stuff Bud did during practice. He'd have a kid slide into second base into a guy's hand, and (the fielder) would have a rubber hand (concealed under his baseball sleeve) and he'd pull it out and it would look like the kid's hand was broken. Everybody would gasp until they saw the hand lying on the ground. We did the no-ball infield, and he had some trick plays that really were good trick plays. One would be where a guy would be stealing (with Matt's team in the field) and somebody on our bench would clank two bats together to make it sound like the batter had hit the ball. If the kid who was stealing wasn't watching the ball, he'd think it had been popped up and he'd start running back to first."

In 1978, Campbell Moreland began selecting a second All-Star team that would play in early-round Pony League tournaments, and Matt made that No. 2 team in 1979. As had been the case two years earlier, he was disappointed that he hadn't been chosen for the first team, but even though it cost him a chance to play for a World Series championship winner, he thinks in retrospect that being on the No. 2 team had more long-term benefits for him than a berth as a seldom-used player on the top team could have provided. With Matt as the No. 1 pitcher, that B team unexpectedly won its first two tournaments, earning a slot in the regional tournament into which the Campbell Moreland A team was automatically seeded as the host.

"We lost the game before the one we would have played (the A team) in," Matt recalled. "It was actually one of my better-pitched games. I had a no-hitter through seven innings and the other guy had a one-hitter; I couldn't pitch any more (because of Pony League rules limiting pitchers to a given number of innings per calendar week) and we lost it in the eighth. Bud told me that I could have been on the first team, but I wouldn't have played much. 'You want to play,' he said, 'and I voted to have you on the second team as the No. 1 pitcher because I think that will be the most fun for you and because it'll make the second team better.'

"Sometimes (in retrospect) it surprises me that I was so persistent in baseball; those were two pretty big letdowns (not making either the Little League All-Star team or the Pony League first team), but Bud was right. It was a great experience. Dan Murphy (John's older brother) was the coach (of the second Pony All-Star team), and he was another guy who was an excellent coach and didn't have an agenda (superseding team goals)."

After that summer of 1979, Matt began as a freshman at Mitty, a Catholic school in west San Jose that was attended by many top Campbell baseball players after its opening in 1967. Even though he'd pitched so well in Pony League, Matt didn't play sports at all during his first two years at Mitty.

"I don't really know why," he said. "I kick myself for it now ... I don't think I would have been a standout, but I think I would have been a little better than I wound up being. I think part of it was (lack of) confidence, and only knowing a few people at school. I also had an early birthday, in October, so I was a few months younger than most of the other guys in my grade. And the passion for sports wasn't really there at Mitty. We were getting beaten up by Earl Koberlein (of Bellarmine and later Stanford) in basketball and Barry Bonds (of Serra) in baseball, and St. Francis had great teams in everything. But that's my biggest regret in sports, not playing those first two years.

"Finally I started playing basketball after school and I beat up on a couple of seniors who were varsity starters, so I figured I might as well go out as a junior."

Matt played varsity basketball and baseball his final two years at Mitty. He did well, but didn't attract any recruiting attention, especially since he was only a 6-footer at the time he graduated in 1983. Bill Hutton, who was to make Mitty a Central Coast Section baseball powerhouse, was in the program by then, but only as the freshman coach, and Mitty continued to lag behind West Catholic Athletic League rivals Serra, Bellarmine and St. Francis. Matt enjoyed and respected his varsity baseball coaches, but he says now he was always yearning to learn more about the subtleties of high-level pitching than they were equipped to teach him. Upon graduation, he planned to go either into teaching or police work, but he hadn't decided on a definite direction and didn't have much money, so he enrolled at the nearest community college, West Valley College in Saratoga.

"Working at Taco Bravo (a local fast-food restaurant) wasn't going to pay for a four-year school," Matt says. "I was working at a moving company (as well) to make a little money, but I didn't know what I wanted to do for sure, so I went to West Valley. Back then, books were more expensive than tuition at junior colleges. I saw that they were having baseball tryouts, and I figured, what the heck. So I introduced myself to the coach (Steve Bordi) and got into the (baseball players') class and played winter ball. They had some pretty good players there. Dave Wright was the pitching coach; he'd played in the Yankees' minor league system, and I learned a lot from him."

Matt began to blossom at West Valley, especially after he began the belated growth spurt that eventually elevated him to 6-foot-4, and gained the coordination he hadn't had as a boy. But despite West Valley's proximity to the Campbell baseball talent lode, the program usually was a bottom feeder under Bordi, who did few of the things that characterized the much stronger programs at San Jose City College under John Oldham, Santa Clara's Mission College under Sam Piraro, and Cupertino's De Anza College under former major leaguer Eddie Bressoud.

"Bordi ... was Bordi," Matt said. "In hindsight I wished I'd played for Oldham or for Sam. The story I love about him (Bordi) was that once we'd start practice, he'd go down in the creek (that ran behind the outfield) and spend 30 minutes looking for (lost) baseballs in there. If he'd find five or six, that was just the greatest thing.

"I'm sure if I saw him today we'd shake hands and there'd be no hard feelings, but I had some run-ins with him. He was the only coach I ever had a problem with. My sophomore year, I was voted the team captain by my teammates. I was throwing the ball pretty well, but in my first three starts I went 0-3; I lost one game by one run and the other by two. The next game, I got blown out, and he kind of confronted me in front of everyone. He said I was the team captain and should be doing better. It was the first time any coach had ever questioned my integrity or my will to win. I always gave 100 percent; that's the way I was taught. I began to wonder what I was doing out there. I stuck it out and played the rest of the season, but that was the end of my relationship with Bordi."

By the time he graduated from West Valley, Matt had attained not only his full height but also a full complement of athletic attributes that he hadn't had in high school or before. Under the right circumstances, he thinks, he could have played basketball at a four-year college, but his first priority remained baseball. As a pitcher, he had mastered his mechanics to the point where he could locate his pitches almost anywhere he wanted, even though he still had below-average velocity. He enrolled as a student at San Jose State, and as he had done at West Valley, he went to San Jose State coach Gene Menges, introduced himself and requested and was granted permission to try out for the team as a non-scholarship player.

"I went out for winter ball," he said, "and I was a little over my head at first as far as the talent and how hard those guys threw."

The cornerstone player in the program at the time was Anthony Telford, from Silver Creek High in east San Jose. During his high school years, most scouts and recruiters lost interest in Telford as soon as they saw he was only 6-foot and 175 pounds, but San Jose State eagerly recruited him, and Telford – who as a 16-year-old had beaten Campbell Moreland's Colt League All-Star team while pitching for a San Jose Police Athletic League squad – had a 92 mph fastball by the time Matt got to San Jose State. By 1987, he was throwing even harder than that, and the Baltimore Orioles took him in the third round of that year's major league draft. Telford reached the majors in 1990, and despite persistent arm trouble, he had a strong nine-year career in The Show, twice finishing in the National League's top five in pitching appearances while with the Montreal Expos.

"I saw him pitch a no-hitter at Fresno State that first year," Matt said. "Here's a guy throwing 92 with a curve that wouldn't stop. I was redshirted that year, and I didn't really do much except work on things, but I could throw strikes all day long, and Gene started having me throw batting practice before games. He brought me on two road trips, and one of them was Fresno. Anthony was a great guy, a great teammate. He had been an All-American as a freshman, but he treated everyone the same, and I'm sure that if I saw him today, we'd give each other a big hug.

"There wasn't much coaching going on there, although Red Walsh (the pitching coach, and the grandfather of future Olympic volleyball player Kerri Walsh) was there, and he was a good baseball guy. Very old school, always with that big chaw of tobacco in his cheek. The next year (1986), which was Gene's last year before he retired, I should have made the team, and didn't, and I still don't know why. They wound up having a JV team, and I wound up pitching for it … it was as miserable as baseball got for me, except for that time with Bordi. We played JC teams and traveled around a little bit; we weren't very good, and there were a couple of guys recruited by Menges that didn't make the varsity team, and I thought he did a bad recruiting job on those guys, because they couldn't play."

Matt did earn promotion to the varsity for a two-game stint at midseason, and I saw his debut, on April 22, 1986, at Santa Clara. It didn't go well. It was a midweek non-conference game, and although Telford started, it was only as a two-inning tuneup for that weekend's Pacific Coast Athletic Association series. San Jose State was trailing 3-0 when Menges brought Matt in to start the third. The first four batters reached base, on a walk, a double and two singles, and all four of them scored before Matt retired the side. After getting through the fourth without giving up a run, he was lifted after giving up two hits and a walk to start the fifth. He was relieved by Bobby Straight, who was a regular infielder as a senior that year and pitched only in mop-up situations. He didn't fare much better than Matt, and Santa Clara eventually won the game 20-6.

Menges retired after that season, and was replaced by Piraro, a former SJS player who had been an assistant under Menges before leaving in 1980 to start the baseball program at Mission. Sam won a state community college title in his second season, 1981, and captured another in 1983 with a team that included Billy Roberts, the starting center fielder on Campbell Moreland's 1978 Pony League World Series championship club. Bobby Pogue, a member of the team that gave Campbell Moreland a second straight Pony League title the following year, also played for Sam at Mission, as did several other former Campbell players.

In 2009, Sam was still at San Jose State, and entered the season with 949 career wins — 654 of them as San Jose State's head coach, even though the SJS program was chronically underfunded and usually was comprised of late-blooming and overachieving types who hadn't been recruited by more prominent baseball schools. In 2000, Sam took the Spartans to the College World Series in Omaha, Neb., for the first time in the history of the program.

Unlike Menges, Sam took to Matt from the start, and even offered him the team captaincy for his senior season. Sam brought a businesslike approach to the program and rewarded those who worked hardest, and during that 1987 season, Matt finally regained the baseball *joie de vivre* he had not felt since his days in the Campbell youth baseball system. It's an exhilaration he still felt more than 20 years later, and largely because of Sam, Matt became imbued with a desire to coach that he still has.

"He was a legend already, with those state championships at Mission," Matt says now. "Right after he got the job, he made a point to call me and tell me he was looking forward to having me next year. He called me in (after practice had started) and wanted to make me the team captain. I declined it. I said, 'To be honest, coach, I'd like to lead by example, and I know I'm not going to play (regularly). I'll always give 100 percent, but I'd rather be led as a player by somebody who can lead by example.' But it was an honor, and if you find a picture of Sam from that season, you'll probably find me standing next to him because I spent all the time I could picking his brain and seeing how he ran a game. I loved learning the finer points of baseball. The first practice that year, we were out there at 1:30 and we knew exactly what we would be doing, right down to the minute. I'd never been at a practice like that before. Everything was written out, and there were groups (for every drill); you were never just standing around shagging. It was just awesome to watch him work."

Matt pitched in 15 games that season, all but one in relief. He worked $26\,{}^2\!/_3$ innings and struck out 20 while walking only five. He went 2-0, and although his ERA was 7.09, it was bloated by one bad outing in a game that already was out of hand, and Piraro didn't hesitate to use him in close games when linkage between the starter and the late-inning specialists was needed. In one game, on February 21 against Cal Poly, Telford pitched 12 scoreless innings before being relieved by Matt, who held the Mustangs without a run for two more innings before San Jose State scored in the bottom of the 14th to win 1-0.

The Spartans, who had finished with a losing record in five of the previous six seasons, got off to a 15-4 start. Although they couldn't sustain that early burst, they were 8-7 in the PCAA and still in contention for an NCAA berth before losing their final six conference games in Orange County against Cal State Fullerton and UC Irvine. They finished 8-13 in the PCAA and 31-28 overall.

"I think we were borderline as far as getting a national ranking (after the 15-4 start)," Matt said, "but we kind of got big heads and got away from playing baseball the way Piraro wanted us to play. We got greedy. We stopped bunting guys over and putting in effort to win by doing the little things. That last trip was a doozy. But we had a good team, especially the pitching. Anthony and Dan Archibald were our two studs, and I didn't feel hurt because I wasn't pitching that much.

"I'm still proud that I played for San Jose State and that I played for Sam in his first year. When they went to Omaha, I felt like I was part of it, and even though they lost their first two games there, it was incredible. just them getting there. Just to say I was part of that program ... it's like bragging about being part of Campbell."

Matt graduated from SJS that summer with a degree in sociology and a minor in history.

"I was all set to get my teaching credential and go join the teachers world," he says. "Bill (Hutton, by then the head coach at Mitty) had asked me to come coach for him when I was finished at San Jose State, and I did that for three years. I was the freshman coach in '88 and the varsity pitching coach in '89 and '90. I was a substitute (public-school) teacher for a year, and that was a mistake because subs aren't teachers. They're babysitters, and that soured me on teaching in a hurry. But I loved the coaching part. I got a job with the (Santa Clara County) probation department ... I was there three years (before joining the San Jose Police Department) and it worked out well because I got off work at 3 and went straight over to Mitty to coach."

Growing up, Matt had a dual interest in teaching and in police work, and his brief experience as a substitute teacher swung him toward law enforcement. He hasn't regretted it, and has been both effective and versatile during his police career, working in all sections of the city and in the detective and plainclothes divisions as well as on patrol. He is proud of the SJPD's level of professionalism and of the fact that San Jose has a reputation as one of the safest large cities in the country. According to FBI crime statistics, San Jose, with a population of 934,553 in 2007, had 405 reported violent crimes. San Francisco, with 200,000 fewer people, had more than twice as many, 874. Oakland, with a population of 396,553, had 1,918 violent crimes, almost five times as many as San Jose, during the same period.

"It (joining the SJPD) was the best move I ever could have made," Matt says. "I have my own team (of subordinates) now, and they're great to work with. I tell people that the most effective weapon you'll ever have on you will always be your mouth, and the competitiveness you have as an athlete comes into play a lot. You want to make things work (without having to resort to extreme measures). But the negative is that I've seen enough to know that it will never be the same for my kids as it was for me. My kids will never ride their bikes to Little League every day like I did. Things I've seen have soured me from ever living that dream again. That's not gonna happen. The sad truth is that (the) Campbell (experience of his youth) is gone."

Both of his boys are enthusiastic athletes, and Nick, the youngest, already is wondering aloud about the relative academic merits of schools like Duke and Stanford. Matt coaches them in both baseball and basketball, although he follows the example of his own father from the standpoint of enhancing his sons' athletic experiences rather than trying to manipulate them. He still has a yearning to coach – partly because of Ryan and Nick, but mostly because he feels he's in a position to do for kids what was done for him by people like Rick Rixman, Al Aiken, Bud Stallings, Sam Piraro and Bill Hutton.

"We made CCS (at Mitty) for the first time in a while when I was there (as Hutton's pitching coach in 1990)," Matt says, "and I remember after Mitty won CCS for the first time (in 1997), I asked Bill, 'What feels better? The chase, or the feeling after winning the whole thing?' For me, I think it would be the chase, building a program from scratch. It's like I've been funneled toward coaching from the time I was 9 years old. Bud once told my dad that I would be a coach someday, and I wish I could sit here and be talking to you from the perspective of having been a high school coach like Bill, but I'm not. You have to make choices, and my choices have worked out really well, but it's still in the back of my mind that I want to do that. Maybe if I can retire early enough, I can find a school or a place that needs a coach, and I can enjoy coaching my kids and other people's kids. I think I'd do a pretty good job, just because of the coaches and the experiences I had.

"I was pretty persistent to end up where I did with baseball, and I feel pretty good about myself staying in it as long as I did. (The rewards) depend on what you're looking to get out of it. I got out of it the personality. Who I am is very much from baseball, working hard, having the family I did and the people who influenced me. I enjoy watching my sons, and I coached my little guy last year, but I'm taking this year off. He'll be in the (Hollister Little League) majors next year, and I don't know if I want to mess with that. Even here (in an environment that's far more rural than Campbell) I see so many parents getting upset at coaches ... they take it so seriously instead of trying to build a team or build the league. And it's pretty much that way everywhere now. Everyone's out for No. 1.

"But I know one thing – there's always a smile on my face when I think about Campbell. I'll always have that."

DAVE ROBERSON: On again

Of all the young ballplayers with whom I developed friendships in Campbell during the years when the road to most national championships went through there, Dave's relationship with baseball probably was the most tempestuous.

So in 2008, when we got together for the first time in at least 20 years, I wasn't surprised when he described to me the emotional extent of his reconciliation with baseball, with his 10-year-old son Harrison as the conduit. The love is on again.

"I'm more into baseball now than I ever was," Dave said. "I took my family (his wife Shelly, Harrison, and 5-year-old twins Hailey and Spencer) on an awesome trip over the summer ... we saw games at Yankee Stadium and Shea Stadium (both in their final seasons of operation). We went to Fenway Park and Cooperstown, and we even saw some games in the Cape Cod League (a summer college league). My law firm represents the Oakland A's, and one of the partners is married to (owner) Lew Wolff's daughter. We've had season tickets for years, and Harrison plays in Moreland Little League and on a travel team.

"I thought I was done with baseball when my (playing) career ended, but it's turned out to be just the opposite."

When I first met Dave in 1977, he was a 14-year-old catcher playing for the Dodgers in the Campbell Moreland Pony League. He was a moody kid who sometimes seemed as if he were trying to reach adulthood before adulthood was ready to accept him. He stormed and remonstrated as the result of poor play, either by himself or by his teammates, and at the slightest hint that an adult was reacting to him in a condescending manner, he'd withdraw behind a veil of suspicion. His parents were strict with him and he chafed at authority, and many in the league mistook his intensity for selfishness.

But once I got to know him, it was obvious that his brooding veneer obscured a wickedly delightful sense of humor, and our early conversations revealed him to be one of the most intelligent and eclectic kids I was to meet in Campbell. In retrospect, I think it was because he grasped the totality of the game so well that he found more ways than most to find fault with himself. He could play, too. Dave hit for both power and average, and he thrived in his helmsman position behind the plate. He was as good as any of the Campbell-system catchers of the late 1970s — Mike Walsh, Mark Paquin, John Lawson, Randy Nishijima and Dave Bryant among them — who would go on to excel at the high school level and beyond, and he understood the intricacies of the game better than some of the coaches in the league. He also pitched, and at one point in 1977 he threw back-to-back no-hitters.

Dave's parents weren't well off, but they sacrificed financially to send him to Mitty, where he thrived and matured both on and off the field. During a West Catholic Athletic League playoff game against Barry Bonds and Serra High at Santa Clara University's Buck Shaw Stadium his senior year, Dave hit a ball over the scoreboard beyond the left-field wall — a poke of well over 400 feet. Dave says Bonds, who usually was as aloof in his high school days as he was during his record-breaking major league career, sought him out after the game, shook his hand and congratulated him on the distance his homer had traveled.

After high school, Dave attended San Jose State and graduated in 1986 with a degree in political science. He already had switched career objectives several times by the time he graduated. He was keenly interested in aeronautics when I first met him — his middle name is Scott, after the Mercury astronaut Scott Carpenter, who, like Dave's father, had served in the Navy — and at one point he also expressed to me a vision of himself as an FBI agent. In the late 1990s, he went back to school to study building inspection technology, earning certification in almost a dozen phases of structural analysis, and he went to law school after that, graduating from Lincoln Law School in 2003.

By 2008, Dave had combined his mastery of inspection technology with his knowledge of law, and he had the financial wherewithal to indulge the baseball passion that his son's participation in youth baseball had rekindled within him. He was an associate in the San Jose law firm of Rossi, Hamerslough, Reischl and Chuck, and he was one of only two practicing attorneys in the country who specialized in building-inspection law. "My clients are inspectors themselves," he said.

Harrison (or "H") Roberson, at age 10, in 2008 played both in Moreland Little League and on a travel team, the Peninsula Youth Baseball Blaze. My visit with Dave and his family was at the Twin Creeks sports complex in Sunnyvale, and it represented another baseball first for me — the first baseball game I'd ever viewed in person in the month of December.

The weather was ideal, and watching the game and seeing the hundreds of parents and uniformed kids teeming around the 10 Twin Creeks diamonds — which throughout most of the year are occupied by softball players – another thought occurred to me. I had seen, in Campbell, the state-of-the-art youth baseball program of the 1970s. Now, three decades later, perhaps I was seeing the next level of youth baseball evolution, the type of program that already supplements and very well could supplant Little League as the 21st century progresses.

I arrived at Field 9 just after the start of the 10-and-under game between the Blaze, Harrison Roberson's team, and a squad named TABU – an acronym, I was told, for Try And Beat Us. As I greeted Dave, who was sitting in the bleachers keeping the Blaze's scorebook, one of Harrison's teammates, Andrew Caselman, executed a perfect fadeaway slide to evade a tag at home plate. I was impressed. Even as a high school coach, I had found that kids master proper sliding techniques grudgingly and gradually, if at all. Now, here I was watching this 10-year-old kid comfortably executing a type of slide that entangles players even on the major league level.

I have always disliked Little League rules because they are almost identical to those of softball, a sport I despise; the only real difference is that the pitchers are allowed to throw overhand. Before travel-team baseball, Little League players who advanced beyond that level had to learn the niceties of real baseball from scratch at age 13. These kids I was watching now were three years younger, yet were already playing real baseball, not the Little League/softball version. They were not yet past the stage where they could play instinctively and not mechanically, but they were reinforcing my long-held belief that preteens are quite capable of playing real baseball, and that at least the advanced players should be taught to do so, if they wish.

The manager of Harrison's team, Mike Taylor, is a former Menlo College player, and like all of the other coaches in PYB, he had been hired by the league itself and did not have a child on the team. In fact, Dave told me, parents are not allowed to manage or coach in the PYB. The kids were being taught by baseball people, not by dads and moms with a nepotistic agenda, as so often is the case in modern Little League.

"We pay $275 for a quarter year, and tournaments run about $100 or $110 (compared to Little League signup fees of about $100 for a season)," Dave said. "It's expensive. But it's quality practices, quality coaching, quality experience, baseball people teaching baseball. Harrison will wind up playing something like 60 baseball games this year, plus soccer, tennis, golf and skiing, and I've not seen any sign that he's burned out on it at all. They say kids like to succeed to please their parents, but they enjoy getting better for themselves too, and that's what I see with Harrison."

In addition to his Little League and PYB games, Harrison worked out regularly with a Campbell-based company run by former major leaguer Jason Hardtke that provides aspiring players with individual instruction. He has taken up switch-hitting, and his batting instructor was Nattie George, a former Cal State Fullerton player who spent several years in the minor leagues. Although Harrison plays several positions, he has gravitated, like his father, toward catching, and his catching instructor was Jason Orr, like Dave a former San Jose State receiver.

As the game continued, Dave and I reminisced about the latter stages of his baseball career, and its aftermath.

"I played for Pete Petrinovich (another no-nonsense coach of the type who always seemed to bring out the best in Dave) at Mitty," he said, "and he was tough, but I think he liked me and appreciated what I did, and that made it a good experience. I played two years at San Jose State after that, and all I remember is that (SJS head coach Gene) Menges hardly said a word to me during that time. The only guy he talked to much was Mark Langston."

Langston, the Spartans' No. 1 pitcher and a graduate of Buchser (now Santa Clara) High, was a second-round pick of the Seattle Mariners in the 1981 amateur draft, and went on to win 179 major league games over a 16-year major league career.

Dave didn't return to the SJS program after his sophomore season, although he remained in school and got his degree in political science. (In 2004, he would dabble in real-world politics, running unsuccessfully for a seat on the Moreland school district board of trustees.) While he continued to play amateur baseball into his 20s, he was casting around for new and more rewarding challenges. He took up ice hockey – "it was something new to try, something completely different," he said – and played it competitively for almost a decade. Then, he turned to triathlon competition, and in 1994 was ranked as the No. 1 triathlete in the country in the 30-34 age group. He finished the Hawaii Ironman World Triathlon Championships, the sport's most grueling test, three times, and completed eight 26-mile marathons.

It was also through the triathlon community that he met his wife Shelly.

"When I married him, I didn't even know he'd played baseball," said Shelly, who played softball and swam at Cal before taking up triathlon competition. "He'd just kind of put that part of his life aside." She grinned. "Now, it's exploding like a mushroom cloud. It turns out I married Winter Guy in *Fever Pitch*."

From the standpoint of vibrant, adventurous personalities meshing, theirs is a perfect marriage. The family owns property at Lake Tahoe, and Harrison says his favorite sport might be skiing. "We have Sharks and A's season tickets, and three Labradors," Dave says. "We ski, golf, play tennis. I love watching my kids try new things and seeing their satisfaction when they get better at them. Sports are great for kids because team building never stops, especially when you get into the business world.

"I don't really remember what my sense (of the bigger life picture) was in Campbell, but I'm pretty sure it was much different than any other place, especially with the combination of the three Little Leagues (Campbell, Quito and Moreland) in Pony League. I just don't remember any bad experiences there, and maybe what I remember most was that just about all the guys I played with were great guys. I wasn't even in Campbell Little League, but when guys like Rich Alvarez and Bobby Straight came over to the Pony League, it was like they were saying, 'You're one of us now.' They were really good guys, really humble guys, even after all that they'd done.

"When I was at Castro Junior High, we had a baseball team there with guys like Mitch Morris, Tim Fleury and Garth Setoguchi (all of whom were Pony League All-Stars along with Dave in 1977). We went two whole years without losing a game. With that group, the Campbell guys and the Quito guys, we were playing some really high-level baseball there, and I have some great memories of those times and that ballpark.

"This year I went over to the Pony field to see some of the kids who'd been on that Moreland team (that reached the Little League West Regional in 2007). When I played there, the park around the baseball field was pretty barren, because the trees that had been planted (when John D. Morgan Park opened in 1974) hadn't started to grow yet. Now they're huge, and I remember just looking around and thinking to myself, 'What a beautiful place to grow up playing baseball.'"

As he reflected, Dave seemed also to be thinking about his late father, Robby, who was as much of a fixture at John D. Morgan Park as the backstop during Pony League games – usually with a beer in his hand, a smile on his face and a kind word on his lips.

"Beer Hill," he said, smiling. "You know, I think that might have been my dad's favorite place on this earth."

PART III:
REQUIEM FOR A DYNASTY

THE LONG GOODBYE: The start of Campbell's decline

By the spring of 1982, it was apparent to me that Campbell youth baseball as we had known it was going the way of Top 40 radio. It wasn't spontaneous combustion, nor was it the result of any one situation, and it didn't happen overnight, as the Campbell system added two more World Series appearances, for a total of 14 since 1960, during the 1980s. But even before the two-national-championship 1979 season, the smoldering already had begun.

I've already outlined the impact of several trends that actually began in 1978, and contributed, at least indirectly, to the end of Campbell youth baseball's sublimity. That was the year that Proposition 13, which ultimately brought about the closure of Campbell High and the end of its destination baseball program, was passed by California voters. It also was the year that Campbell began building federally-subsidized senior housing far out of proportion to its acreage and population, thereby prematurely graying and unnecessarily crowding a city that already was virtually built out. Although the *Campbell Press* wasn't officially euthanized until 1986, it moved out of Campbell for good in 1978, leaving Campbell without a locally-owned, locally-operated paper. The Campbell Loop also had sounded the death knell for Campbell's modest downtown area, which had been decaying for the better part of two decades anyway. Campbell lost much of its civic identity because of those events. Many people stopped caring about Campbell to the extent that they had cared in the past, and it was therefore inevitable that the indifference would filter down to the youth baseball program.

It didn't have to happen as quickly as it did, though.

In 1978, the baseball system still was populated and controlled by the altruists, like John Hanrahan, Bob Holman, Jack Zogg, John Emery, Bud Stallings, Jim Saeger and many others who have been profiled in this book. By the mid-1980s, almost all of them were gone, replaced by poacher parents who imposed their personal agendas on the leagues. Many of them knew little about baseball or kids, and as with many youth baseball leagues in the 1980s, people who had baseball backgrounds but had no children in the league found that the rewards of working with kids were not worth the interference and ignorance they had to endure. So they left, and they weren't replaced.

"You know who was the backbone of Campbell Little League?" Subby Agliolo asked rhetorically as we talked in 2008. "Bob Holman (after whom the Rosemary School complex is now named). He was a father to that league, and I don't care what anybody says. He'd be there every day, setting up things, designating people. He was a magnet and people came to him because they knew he was out there for the kids ... his own kids had gone through Campbell long before that. Bob didn't (officially) run the league, but really he did. He ran it with his soul, and whatever happened, you knew Bob would be in the middle of it. And maybe you (argued) with him, but you respected him, and he listened to you."

Holman – whose grandson Joe was playing baseball for Westmont High in 2009 – had been with the league since shortly after its founding, and while some were initially perplexed by his outward gruffness, most soon saw his sense of loyalty and fairness, and his humor. Because of that, he rarely had to rule by edict; instead, he was a facilitator who helped people figure out what needed to be done and how to do it. In my case, if I did something with which he disagreed, he never admonished me. He instead mentioned subtly that my way might not have been the best way, and brought up alternatives. I considered him the Campbell equivalent of Atticus Finch, and because he was almost always right, I usually wound up taking him up on his suggestions without his having to make them directives.

Although I never heard all of the details relating to Bob's departure from Campbell, I know that it was in protest of the league's direction, particularly its decision to drop teams in the late 1970s and early 1980s when signups began to decrease from their 1972 peak of more than 500. Like many of the league's longtime members, Bob believed in smaller rosters that would afford all players more field time, and he thought that shrinking team sizes was preferable to shrinking the size of the league.

In 1976, Holman had joined Jack Zogg as a coach just before the team left for Williamsport in 1976, replacing John Emery, who was unable to continue with the team because of a family issue. Bob was still in the league three years later when Campbell made its third Little League World Series of the 1970s, but even then, the circumstances that eventually were to sidetrack the league were beginning to manifest themselves, according to Subby Agilolo.

"We stayed good for a couple of more years (after the 1979 World Series appearance) ... Jim Phillips (father of Mark, a member of the 1979 team) had the team a couple of years later and did pretty well and would have done better if they hadn't had a guy thrown out at the plate when he shouldn't have tried to score," Subby said. "But really, I think the biggest problem was that you had a lot of really experienced guys leaving within a few years of that. (Major division managers)

Tony Mimosa, Lou Romeo, Dan Watt, Jack, myself. Bill Wright stayed maybe a year longer. I heard Phillips and Bob (Holman) had a big row, and Bob said, 'That's it, I quit,' and the league was never quite the same after that."

For Jack Zogg, who had been the Robins manager since 1959, the end of his Campbell tenure came in 1980, just one year after Campbell Little League, with Subby managing, reached the World Series for the third time that decade. Jack went to Oak Grove Little League, near his home, and managed his sons Ricky and Steven during a 12-year stint in the southeast San Jose league. He coached an American Legion team for a time after that; in 2009, he was entering his third season coaching 8- , 9- and 10-year-olds, including his grandson, in Oak Grove's farm division.

Jack said his departure wasn't prompted by any specific incident, but an important consideration was a desire to keep intact his memories of Campbell as it had been.

"I really loved the camaraderie there (during the 1960s and 1970s)," Jack said. "You had everyone in the organization pulling in the same direction. The people of Campbell were the biggest thing. They did not have tunnel vision. At different places you go, all they see is their boy and their team, but in Campbell, good play was applauded by everyone.

"I think at the time (he left) we felt it was getting kind of goofy. We'd worked pretty darn hard to get the league where it was, and people were coming in and making changes. Instead of pulling in the opposite direction, I thought it was best that I go coach somewhere else. Things weren't the same. John and I spent a lot of time pouring cement and laying bricks and painting by flashlight out there over the years. (By 1980) you almost had to beg people to come out for the work parties, but they always had people who had an opinion on something. There were a lot more cliques, and I just decided that wasn't why I was out there.

"They forgot that in order to get to the tournament, you have to play a season. If you forget to play the season, you shouldn't be out there, and I'm very serious about that."

John Emery left Campbell Little League at the same time as Jack, with whom he had coached the Robins team for a decade, and he had managed or coached in the league since the early 1960s. John came back as a coach in 1985, but left for good in 1990.

"They (the board of directors) told us that we all had to umpire minor division games," John said. "They said, 'If you don't, you can't coach.' You know, I was out there to volunteer; I was there because I wanted to be. All they had to do was ask me if I would umpire some games ... it would have been simple. But if it comes down to that (issuing orders), I walk. It was their attitude ... with volunteers, you don't treat people that way."

Infighting, lack of managerial continuity at all levels, inept leadership, and overemphasis on winning at the expense of the regular season — all brought about primarily by the carpetbagger parents — were the primary reasons that Campbell began losing signup numbers in the early 1980s, undermining the foundation of the system. Campbell still had talent and its reputation working for it in 1985, when Campbell Little League's All-Star team won the District 44 championship for the 10th time in 20 seasons, but it has captured only one district title since, in 1995. Overzealous conduct by parents who wouldn't have dared to make spectacles of themselves during the Holman/Hanrahan years became common, starting in the early 1980s. One individual, the father of one of Campbell's more prominent players in the early 1980s, was out of control to the point where he damaged the experience for players, coaches and parents alike. And because he got away with his behavior, it was imitated by other parents who weren't happy with some aspect of the league.

"I had his kid," Subby said, "and I almost killed that son of a bitch (the father) one day. I was in center field (within shouting range of parents sitting beyond the outfield fence) and he starts yelling at me, telling me I'd better teach his kid how to hit. He threatened me. I hated him. The league hated him. He was the kind of guy who could ruin a league, and eventually he did."

The turnover in the adult leadership of Campbell Little League also extended into the Campbell Moreland organization, although the aging of the older men who had been involved with the Pony-Colt program for decades probably had more to do with that league's decline than did meddlesome parents. The league was further hurt by the construction of senior housing around John D. Morgan Park — an undertaking that might have been Campbell's most ill-considered building project ever, because the new senior housing was bordered not only by the park, but by Campbell Junior High. Beyond the constant clashes with the new neighbors over noise, parking because an acute problem. Fewer parents attended the games, and most of those who did come did not arrive before their own kids' games or stay after they were concluded, as had become the custom in the late 1970s.

Despite these problems, Campbell still had players who had come up through the system while it was still intact, and were determined to uphold Campbell's baseball tradition. For a time, that countered, at least to some extent, the fact the system was turning away from the egalitarian, altruistic principles that had guided decision-making in the 1960s and 1970s.

Jason Miller, who came up through Campbell Little League and the Campbell Moreland Pony-Colt system, was an All-Star as a Little Leaguer in 1983 and as a Pony Leaguer in 1985. In 1987, he played on the last (as of this writing) Campbell team to reach a World Series. His Campbell Moreland Colt League squad reached the finals of the World Series in Lafayette, Ind., that summer before losing 7-6 in the championship game to Marietta, Ga.

"I can remember when the guys on the '79 teams would come back to the Campbell Little League field to umpire," said Jason, who in 2009 was in his fifth year as dean of students at Westmont High, from which he had graduated, and where he was the baseball coach for seven years before going into administration. "As younger kids in the minors and majors, we looked up to those guys. There was a tradition. We wanted to do better than the group before us. My older brother played on the 1980 (Little League) All-Star team, with Greg Gohr, Troy Buckley, Craig Middlekauff and those guys, and the word always was that the 1980 team was better than the '79 team. We wanted to be better than that team."

Greg Gohr's older brother Mark played at Campbell Little League when I was working there, and his family was part of the group that spent entire weekends watching and supporting players throughout the league. Mark was never an All-Star, but he was a solid player and one of the most polite, well-spoken kids I've ever been around, and my memories of Greg as a kid are along similar lines. After I left Campbell, Greg's skills and growth accelerated, and he was an All-Star by the time he was 12, and thereafter. But his parents, fearing he would damage his arm, would not let him pitch more than occasionally in the Campbell or Campbell Moreland systems. He didn't take up pitching in earnest until he began high school at Bellarmine Prep, where he dominated the West Catholic Athletic League, which had supplanted the West Valley Athletic League as the Central Coast Section's best. Greg got a scholarship to Santa Clara University, and I still remember a day during the summer of 1989 when I was covering a Giants game for the *Peninsula Times Tribune* at Candlestick Park and I got a call in the press box.

The call was from Jeff Moorad, whose name I didn't recognize; he was in the sports-representation firm headed by Leigh Steinberg, one of the few agents who was known for his credibility and honesty. Jeff, of course, later became a familiar name in the baseball industry, first as an agent and then as a co-owner of the Arizona Diamondbacks and San Diego Padres. He told me he was representing the Gohr family, that Greg had just been chosen by the Detroit Tigers in the first round of the amateur draft – the first Campbell-area player ever to go in the first round – and that the family wanted me to be the first in the media to know. He put Greg on the phone; I hadn't talked to him in a few years, but I remember his excitement, and he wanted me to convey in the paper the degree to which playing in Campbell had made this day possible for him. Unfortunately, the *Times Tribune* was out of existence and I was out of work by April 7, 1993, so I wasn't at the Oakland Coliseum that day to see Greg pitch for the Tigers against the Oakland A's, thereby becoming the fourth Campbell-developed player (after John Oldham, Don Hahn and Steve Davis) to reach the major leagues.

Greg's 1980 Little League All-Star team repeated as District 44 champions, although it lost in the sectional tournament. Jason Miller's 1983 team won another district title.

"Our year, it was neat," Jason said. "I don't know if kids do this anymore, but we'd get together with all the guys we thought would be on the All-Star team; we'd go to one guy's house and we'd stay up until the (All-Star selection) meeting was over, around 11 at night. The coaches would call us and tell us, and we'd be together when we all found out.

"We were a close group of guys. I remember Mr. Holman always chasing us off the field when we were playing there and they had to get the field ready ... we couldn't get enough baseball. We had more guys join us in Pony, and even after we didn't make the World Series in Pony, our goal was to make it in Colt, and we did. We knew a couple of guys who'd been on the 1984 Pony team (that reached the World Series, the last of four Campbell Pony teams to do so), and they were telling us how it was the greatest thing to be able to play in a World Series. That's what we shot for. We had goals. If you were a (top-flight) baseball player in Campbell, your family planned vacations around baseball. You might be playing in a World Series in the first part of August, so you didn't go on vacation until the end of August.

"I know there were some problems with some of the parents when I was playing, but we didn't really pay too much attention to the politics. I know with my parents, if I'd ever complain about my manager or something like that, they'd say, 'You know what? Deal with it.' We played for our town, and we played for each other. All we wanted was to be able to play baseball all summer."

For me, the first tangible sign that Campbell baseball was headed in the wrong direction came in 1980, when the kids saw for themselves that Campbell youth baseball had ceased to be a meritocracy.

Most of us thought that year's Colt League All-Star team would be stronger at its level than any of Campbell's four national-championship teams over the previous four years. Most of the centerpiece players from the 1976 Williamsport squad and the 1978 Pony League world champions were still around, and we had added important players who hadn't been in the Little League or Pony programs, or were second-tier players who improved because of the competition they faced on a day-to-day-basis. Most people connected with the Colt League (for 15- and 16-year-olds), in which I coached that year and again in 1981, thought the managers could go to one of the local pizza joints, order their food and beer, and have the All-Star team picked by the time it arrived.

The manager of that All-Star team was Bill Walsh (no relation or resemblance to his better-known namesake), who had three sons in the Campbell program and had managed all three of them at one time or another. I was probably closest to John, the oldest, who in 1981 was drafted by the Chicago White Sox out of Westmont in the 36th round of the major league draft, and played a couple of seasons in their organization. I was also good friends with Mike, a year younger than John, who had been a reserve catcher on the 1976 Little League team, and in 1978 arguably was the MVP on our Pony League World Series title winners. Jim, a year younger than Mike, was a feisty but athletically limited second baseman; everybody admired the full commitment he brought, but he could play only that one position, didn't hit much, and was a quiet kid who kept to himself and wasn't going to add much to the personality texture of any team that was looking to win a world championship. (I personally thought the sport in which Jim, who was exceptionally strong for his size and age, had the best chance to carve himself a niche was wrestling, and if I remember right, he took up that sport and subsequently did very well at it.)

Bill Walsh and I were friends; in fact, I probably spent more time at the Walshes in 1978 and 1979 than I did in any other Campbell household. He was a good guy and a good father, although he was occasionally prone to exaggerating his own importance, and nobody among the volunteer parents contributed more to the upkeep of our various ballparks. I remember just before the start of my first season as the Pony League operations director, in 1977, there was a mini-panic because the new scoreboard at John D. Morgan Park had been delivered late and had to be wired on impossibly short notice. Bill spent the entire night before Opening Day wiring it, and it worked perfectly. I always thought he was one of the altruists. I didn't think he would ever intentionally do anything to harm the league or the kids in it, and even in the situation I'm about to describe, I think he honestly felt he was doing the right thing.

He was a decent baseball man, though not on the level of a Bud Stallings or a Chuck Calhoun when all of them were in the Pony League. Most of the kids who played for him seemed to like him and sensed that he did care about them, and they usually responded well to him. I knew he was like most dads when it came to being proud of his offspring, but I also knew – or thought I knew – that he was about Campbell first and he wouldn't use his managerial position to put Jim on that Colt League All-Star team, as he had the right to do under league rules.

A few days before the All-Star meeting, Bill told me he intended to do just that. I wasn't that much older than his sons, and I was as reluctant as they to contradict him on anything, but I told him flatly that putting Jim on the team would be seen only in terms of nepotism, especially if it resulted in one of the foundation players from the 1976 and 1978 teams being omitted. Bill took that as an implication that Jim wasn't good enough to be an All-Star. He said he didn't have a true second baseman available to him elsewhere in the league – a contention that may have been true, but also was inconsequential because we had several guys who could play second base as a second position better than Jim could as a first position – and that he could justify taking Jim purely on that basis. A few days later, he did ... and one of the players who didn't make the team as a result was Dominic Costantino, who'd been central to the two championship teams and by 1980 was as much patriarch as teammate on the field and on the road.

The response was immediate, and if Bill thought the players and parents would trust his judgment on the question of Jim's selection, he was wrong.

Lest anybody think that I'm blaming the downfall of Campbell youth baseball on one player or on one father-manager, I'm not. Jim was a good player, although I think he'd be the first to tell you that he wasn't among the top 15 players in the Colt League that year. If the league had selected a second All-Star team, as the Pony League had started doing in 1978, and Jim had made that second team, I don't think there would have been a murmur of protest. Even if Jim had been voted onto the first All-Star team, and that team had been managed by somebody other than Bill, I doubt anybody would have had a serious problem with it. After all, the rosters of several highly-successful Campbell All-Star teams had been completed on the basis of specific needs rather than statistics or overall ability, and taking role players to fill the final roster spots had almost always worked out well for us.

The difference this time was in perception. In the past, as long as I'd been involved with Campbell baseball, it hadn't mattered who had parented whom when it came to rewarding players with selection to an All-Star team. Since I first came into the Campbell baseball system in 1974, there had never been a situation where a manager-father had taken his own son when better alternatives obviously existed. (In fact, of the seven Campbell teams that reached World Series championship games in Little League and Pony League from 1962-79, only one – the 1970 Campbell Little League squad – was managed by a father with a son on the team, and in that case, Gene Colburn's son Ron was perhaps the team's best player.) Bill could rationalize the choice, and did, but the way it looked was that nepotism had motivated him when he added Jim to the team, and the other players didn't like it because nepotism had never been an overriding consideration in Campbell youth baseball before.

In any case, Jim was the starting second baseman on the 1980 Colt League team from the start of practice, and while his teammates seemed to make an effort to accommodate and incorporate him, the team never had the *joie de vivre* that characterized the Little League and Pony League champions on which many of them had played. Again, that wasn't Jim's fault, or even Bill's fault; it was up to all the players to perform with whatever roster the league managers had given them, and they didn't. We won our first tournament, which we hosted, but had to come through the losers bracket to win the next tournament, at Leland High in San Jose, to earn a trip to the West Regional in Garden Grove. We lost our first game, and I remember commenting to Billy Roberts after the game to the effect that getting through a tournament the hard way was not something that had daunted Campbell teams in the past.

"Yeah," he said, "but we're going to have to do it the *real* hard way."

The implication, though Billy may not have meant it that way, was that they'd have to do it with three infielders and eight hitters. They couldn't. We lost again and our season was over, although, again, that wasn't Jim's fault, because just about everybody on the team played poorly, and Jim was doing his best under difficult circumstances. We mourned not so much the loss of the game and of the possibility of winning another World Series, but of something bigger, something that had always been more important to us than all-encompassing on-field success.

That something never existed in Campbell youth baseball again, at least not as a continuum.

The 1981 Colt League team, which included many of the players from the 1979 Pony League World Series championship team, pulled off a comeback for the ages after losing to Santa Cruz and slugger Glenallen Hill, later a major leaguer, in the first round of a sectional tournament at Harvey West Park. Trailing 9-2 with two outs and a runner on base in the bottom of the seventh and final inning of the next night's elimination game, we rallied against Los Altos (led by Mark Leonard, who played six major league seasons) and won the game 10-9, and we beat Santa Cruz the next day before they eliminated us in the tournament final. But from the standpoint of Campbell supremacy, everybody knew that was little more than a vapor trail – the next-to-last, as it turned out.

By the spring of 1982, most of the former Campbell High players had migrated to four other Campbell Union High School District campuses – Prospect, Westmont, Blackford and Del Mar – and Westmont and Prospect went on to face each other in the CCS championship game. Prospect, which had beaten Serra with Barry Bonds and Gregg Jefferies in the semifinals, scored three runs in the bottom of the seventh inning to win 8-7 in one of the three or four best baseball games I've seen at any level. With Prospect down 7-5 in the bottom of the seventh and final inning, two outs and Harold Sutherland down to his last strike, Harold delivered a bases-loaded single to tie the game, and Rob Goddard's gapper to left-center gave Prospect its first and (as of 2009) only outright CCS boys team title in the school's 41-year history.

As I made the rounds of both teams' postgame parties that night – they were interchangeable, since almost all of the kids had been friends for years, as had their parents – I talked to Ed Boffy, the Prospect coach, at length. Ed wasn't the official head coach; that designation belonged to Jim Kuhn, a Prospect faculty member whose function was supplementary at best. Gordon Huntze remembered the night of the CCS title game. "Everyone was excited," Gordon said. "Before the game, I wanted to say hello to Jim and wish him good luck. I asked one of his players where the coach was, and he pointed out to the right field corner. There was Kuhn, off away from everyone else, eating sunflower seeds."

Ed had handled all the operational responsibilities throughout Prospect's season, and had been responsible for creating a viable blend from what had been an incongruous mix of tenured Prospect players and Campbell High refugees. I'd previously known Ed, who had played and coached in the Moreland Little League system, and we'd become friendly as Prospect's season metamorphosed. We both knew that Campbell baseball was headed for a possibly-permanent downturn, and as we talked that night, we both gave voice to the same idea: Why don't we try to outfit this ship for one final Campbell baseball voyage?

At the time, Campbell had not had a viable program for 17- and 18-year-olds since the demise of the Campbell American Legion team, which had operated for several years in the 1970s and had reached the Legion World Series in 1974. The Campbell Moreland Pony League organization had a couple of teams in that age group, but the play was little more than recreational, the scheduling was loose at best, and the postseason possibilities were dubious. The Palomino World Series, to us, sounded more like a horse race than a baseball event. Ed and I also knew that the Campbell talent pool included a number of players who likely would be recruited by colleges and scouted by professional teams, and both of us were anxious to provide them with visibility beyond the limited scope of high school baseball.

I had thought for some time about the possibility of restarting the American Legion program in Campbell, mainly because of my familiarity with the Palo Alto American Legion program, which was one of the best in the state. The Palo Alto manager was Tom Dunton, the universally-admired Stanford pitching coach, and the program had produced a number of future major leaguers. (Bob Melvin, who in 2009 was managing the Arizona Diamondbacks, was on the 1982 team.) I knew Tom well from having covered Stanford baseball for the *Times Tribune*, and I also knew George Sanborn, a longtime Palo Alto baseball paragon who served as the Palo Alto Legion program's navigator and fund-raiser. Although Legion ball had once been very big on the San Francisco Peninsula, and still was the primary age-group outlet in the East Bay and the northern San Joaquin Valley, it was virtually dead in Santa Clara County south of Palo Alto, and Tom and George felt that reviving it in a high-profile baseball area like Campbell might have a domino effect elsewhere. (It did; by our second year a five-team league had formed, and that league still operates.)

Tom and George walked me through the organizational maze, and they used some of their contacts to help us put together a schedule in addition to playing us themselves. We weren't able to recruit all of the mainstay Campbell players — Bobby Straight had already made commitments elsewhere, and Paul Sargis wanted a summer off from baseball — but we knew we could get enough of them to put together a formidable team. I promised them that I would get them seen by recruiters and scouts, and it was a promise I knew I could keep because of the baseball ties I'd established as a sportswriter. We were only able to raise a few thousand dollars, paltry compared to the budgets of programs like Palo Alto, but we completed a year's worth of organizational work in just three weeks, and we had a team on the field when the Legion season started. Ed ran the team on the field, with help from Scott Lavender, a friend of Ed's who'd been a pitcher at St. Mary's College in Moraga. I coached first base, trouble-shot with individual players, headed up the refreshment and morale committees, and handled the paperwork and finances.

It was a combination that worked well for the next two years, and that Legion team became two things to me: My way of saying thank you to the Campbell guys and helping them extend their careers, and the most rewarding on-field experience I had during my years in Campbell, because I really was on the field with the kids I liked and admired so much. I think our mutual respect deepened and our friendships were cemented during those two years, especially since all of the guys were adults for all intents and purposes, and were treated by us as such.

Those were fun summers, our last together. We knew we represented Campbell's last shot at winning a national championship for a long time, maybe ever, and even though we were knocked out in the regional tournament both years, we went 44-15 and played against at least 14 future major leaguers – Mark Leonard from Cupertino, Eric Johnson and Mike Myers from Danville, Mike Macfarlane from Stockton, Greg Jefferies, Scott Chiamparino and Barry Bonds from San Mateo, Bill Haselman from Saratoga, Tony Scruggs from Palo Alto, Mike Dalton from Mountain View, Paul Faries and Chip Hale from Lafayette (the latter by way of Cupertino), and Matt Williams and Charley Kerfeld from Carson City. The two teams that eliminated us, Lafayette in 1982 and San Mateo in 1983, both went on to finish second in the Legion World Series. I kept my promise to the kids that I would provide them with the showcase they needed to extend their baseball careers. We had a total of 24 players during those two seasons, and all but four of them played at least one year at a junior college or a four-year school.

John Murphy, who'd been the No. 3 pitcher and one of the biggest bats on the 1976 and 1978 national championship teams, could and did play almost every position for us. (He wound up playing tight end for San Jose State's football team, and might have reached the NFL, as his Little League and SJS teammate John Aimonetti did, had it not been for a series of injuries.) John was a big, hulking kid, and yet he was so graceful and his game contained so little waste motion that even those of us who had watched him since his Little League years had to fight the temptation to mistake his efficiency and smoothness for indifference. He didn't engage in small talk and he didn't express emotion a lot, and before he actually played for me, I didn't know him as well as I did some of the other kids, and I didn't see the depth of the individual.

That summer, though, John and I talked a lot about where he'd been and where he was going. I knew that his father was out of the picture, and that he felt a strong responsibility for his older brother Jimmy, who suffered from a neuromuscular disorder his entire life but was one of our most rabid fans through the Campbell years. I found out for the first time that becoming a therapist, or otherwise working with the physically challenged, was a passion that superseded his desire to become a professional baseball or football player. And although I'd known it before, I came to understand more completely the depth of John's loyalty to those around him. He played the final month of the season with a broken hand about which he never told me until after the season was over, and I still don't know how he was able to mask the pain he must have felt.

Steve Koontz, one of our infielders and a member of the 1979 Pony League World Series championship team, had been the MVP of the powerful West Catholic Athletic League as a sophomore at Mitty High before blowing out his knee playing football as a junior. When it came time to assemble our Legion team, I didn't even think of asking Steve, because he'd missed his entire junior baseball season, and it had been my understanding that he wouldn't be able to play that summer either. He called me and asked for the opportunity to play, even though he still was moving at half-speed at best, and of course I was more than happy to oblige him, just because I knew how important baseball and competition were to him, and he never asked for anything he wasn't willing to earn. He never regained his old speed, which had matched that of any player in the Campbell system, but he worked hard on honing his baseball instincts and using anticipation to cover for his loss of mobility. Steve wound up having a good season for us in 1982 and a great season the following year, and went on to play at Santa Clara.

Billy Roberts was another strong/silent type most of the time, but he had a sense of playful mischief about him that I always liked, and our relationship was such that I think I was able to help him in ways others couldn't, especially during the year he played for our Legion team.

Billy and Bobby Pogue gave us two outfielders whose range almost made the third outfielder superfluous, and he had great speed and could hit for both average and power. Like Steve, Billy was built low to the ground, and while his straight-ahead speed was well above average, he was a human Maserati when it came to cornering. But during the early years of our friendship, which began when he was 13, he sometimes seemed hamstrung by insecurity and self-doubt. He had come from Moreland Little League and thus felt like something of an outsider among the guys who'd been through the Williamsport experience. He knew he didn't fit the lean-and-lanky outfielder prototype, and at times he seemed to think that nothing he could do would enable him to get the acknowledgement he deserved. He probably spent more time in the announcers booth with me than any other kid during my two years at Campbell Moreland Pony League, and I think he got a lot out of the fact I appreciated and admired him both as a player and a person. He later played on a state junior college championship team at Mission College, and he was one of the few Campbell guys with whom I kept in constant touch after he graduated from college. (In fact, he proved to be the truest possible friend in the 1990s when my career was at its nadir.) He went very successfully into sales, public relations and even body-building, and I got a great deal of satisfaction out of seeing his once-reserved personality become a garrulous one while staying a giving one.

As with Billy, I think Bobby Pogue was one of those guys who played with more verve and less self-consciousness for me than he had been for any of his other coaches, and for a lot of the same reasons. Bobby came out of Quito Little League and was considered a supporting-cast complement to the likes of fellow Quito players Steve Clinton and Harold Sutherland. He was slight and physically unimposing. He didn't run all that well or hit the long ball, and while he was as smart and mature and conscientious as anybody in the system, he seemed to withdraw into a shell of introspection when some of his other coaches admonished him or did something to draw negative attention to him.

But Bobby could play – he'd proved that by making the 1979 Pony League World Series championship team – and as I got to know him during those Legion years, I could see how intelligent and observant he was, how important it was for him to voice his thoughts just the right way, and how much baseball meant to him as a means of self-expression. He seemed to sense that I appreciated him, and he responded by being one of the best and most dependable players we had during the two-year Legion run. Although he was a natural center fielder, he played a lot of second base for us as well and made the No. 2 spot in the batting order his fiefdom. I know he hit at least .400 during his two years with us, and I'd be willing to bet that he didn't strike out more than a dozen times during those two years.

The 1983 season was my last in Campbell. I'd already moved out of town by then, and my newspaper bosses made it clear that I would lose the San Francisco 49ers beat if I wasn't available from the start of preseason practice onward. The Legion postseason begins in August while the 49ers assembled for preseason training camp in July, and it was obvious by 1983 that commuting back and forth between Rocklin and Campbell wasn't going to work for the team, for the paper or for me.

I don't recall us carrying more than 18 or so players at any one time, and in retrospect, I shouldn't have been surprised by our inability to make a real advance on another national championship, simply because we didn't have the pitching depth we needed for post-season Legion play. Despite the satisfaction of being on the field with the kids, it was a tough experience organizationally. On more than one occasion, because guys had to work or had other commitments, I wasn't sure we'd be able to field a nine-player team by game time. Our uniforms, especially the first year, left a lot to be desired, because we were operating on a piggy-bank budget. (I was able to buy the 1970s Legion uniforms from Wayne Mitchell, who'd run the previous version of the program, before the second season. He'd kept them in good-as-new condition, and they helped us convey the class that Campbell represented to all of us.) Several of the non-Legion teams we'd scheduled failed to show up, often without explanation, and the result was a number of gaps in our schedule.

In our first year, 1982, we got to the finals of the Area 3 tournament in Palo Alto, against a Lafayette team led by Ron DeLucchi, who shortly thereafter was a first-round draft pick of the Pittsburgh Pirates and remains one of the best Legion-age players I've ever seen, even though he never made it past Class A as a pro. Our pitching was worn to a nub, and the other coaches and I were trying to decide what to do when Rich Alvarez approached us.

Rich's achievements, of course, require no recapitulation at this point, but he was one of the few Campbell players, maybe the only one, who was exploited to some degree by his managers and coaches during his Campbell experience. Whatever the league innings-pitched maximum for a given week was, you could be sure Rich would pitch that number of innings. He also had an older brother, Joe, who'd been a top pitcher at Campbell High and West Valley College, and seemingly was more ambitious for Rich than Rich was for himself. Rich was a burly, durable, enthusiastic kid who never complained about any workload assigned to him, but by the end of his senior high school season, Rich simply wasn't able to throw with his former velocity or movement anymore, and we had him on the roster primarily as a third baseman and No. 3 hitter. I know his arm was hurting throughout the season, but he was the kind of kid who always had a smile on his face, and he asked nothing more from baseball than the opportunity to play it as long as he could as well as he could.

Rich was being recruited by the University of Hawaii, and just before the area tournament, Hawaii coach Les Murakami called and told me he was interested enough in Rich as a position player and possible DH to come to the mainland to see him play in person. He also hoped to see him pitch, even though Rich hadn't been on the mound at all for us. Ed Boffy usually gave me the final call on most personnel decisions, including those involving our lineups, and I'd been trying to decide what to do in terms of pitching Rich in the tournament, but we didn't use him through our first five games leading up to the title game against Lafayette.

After we'd reached the finals, Rich approached us and said his arm felt fine and that he wanted the ball. I never did find out if Murakami had spoken to him about pitching, but for me the deciding factor was that the most successful and probably the best pitcher in Campbell youth baseball history — and one of the most courageous players I'd ever known — wanted the ball for a championship game. Under the circumstances, and after talking to the other coaches, I decided that I owed it to Rich to give it to him.

He didn't get past the fifth inning in a game we lost, but his stuff was as live as it had been in years, and his main problem was his inability to establish rhythm after not having taken the mound since the end of the high school season. Based on that outing and the potential it represented, Murakami signed him, although he spent only one season in Honolulu, mainly because he broke his collarbone bodysurfing over there and never fully recovered his pitching skills after that. We stayed in touch for several years after he left baseball — my fondest memory is of going with Rich and Billy, both of whom were huge USC football fans, to a Stanford-USC game at Stanford Stadium and partying before, during and afterward — and neither his personality nor his appreciation for baseball ever changed. Unlike a lot of guys who have stardom and notoriety thrust upon them early in their baseball careers, Rich always was grateful for what he did get out of baseball, and he was able to be a productive citizen even after baseball no longer was the focal point of his life.

Great as Rich was, though, he wasn't the best player I ever coached ... and his baseball life, truncated though it was, had a better ending than those of the two players I had who were even more talented.

The *best* player I ever coached was Joray Marrujo, although the sad reality is that if Joray had played anywhere other than Campbell, he probably wouldn't have made it as far as Legion, or even high school baseball.

Off the field, Joray's life was as unordered as his baseball skills were incandescent. His father was not in the picture, and his mother, though pleasant enough, never imposed any structure on him. School never interested him much, although he somehow managed to keep his grades good enough to stay eligible in high school. And although he never did anything — as in *not one thing* — to dishonor the game of baseball or any of the Campbell-system teams for which he played, he had a problem, away from the field, with being a follower and with controlling his temper when he felt like he had been disrespected. A lot of the Campbell guys, our catcher and team leader Dave Bryant in particular, monitored and mentored him while he was in the system, and from my perspective, he was never anything but a pleasure to coach. But we couldn't tether him 24 hours a day, and he was in trouble from the time he was a freshman in high school. At Prospect, where he was the nexus of the CCS title team in 1982, he was scheduled to pitch against Wilcox in a quarterfinal game on a Saturday night. He got arrested the night before after getting involved in a fight of some kind, but his coaches and some of the Prospect parents bailed him out in time for the game, in which he pitched Prospect to a victory. Although he had two great Legion seasons, and went on to play briefly for San Jose City College, eventually his other problems overrode his baseball talent, and after he left City, he disappeared from our sight entirely.

Then there was Brent Hahn, who played for me in 1983 when he was 16, a year or two younger than any of our other players. Brent's situation, in one way, was even sadder than Joray's, because while most of Joray's later problems were problems he created himself, most of Brent's were created for him.

Brent was the son of Don Hahn, the first Campbell player to carve out a major league career of any length; he had played from 1969-75 with four teams, and in 1973 with the New York Mets, became known as Willie Mays' late-inning defensive replacement during the latter's final major league season. As an ex-major leaguer, Don's was a voice one couldn't ignore in Campbell baseball circles.

Don was convinced early on – correctly, I think – that Brent, a 6-foot-3, 210-pound lefthanded-hitting catcher who was probably the fastest player on our team, had the opportunity to take baseball even farther than he, Don, had taken it. But Don wasn't content to guide Brent. Brent was less Don's son than he was his marionette, and his efforts to control every aspect of Brent's baseball life represent, in my opinion, the biggest reason he never came close to fulfilling his potential in college and professional baseball.

Before I relate my personal experience with Don, in fairness, I here insert Gordon Huntze's far more impartial remembrances of the Hahns. Don had played for Gordon in 1965, Don's last year at Campbell High and Gordon's first as head coach there, and Brent played for him at Westmont.

"Brent was tough," Gordon said. "He'd be the kind of guy that, if he was on first, you knew he wasn't going to be staying there. I never had to give him the steal sign, and if he was on first and there was a routine single to the outfield, you better watch out because you knew he would round second and just keep flying.

"I remember Don called me (before Brent came to Westmont) and said, 'I want him to play for you.' My first response was no, because we had a senior catcher and something would have to

happen there. I told him he has to have residency, and he said. 'We can do that. I'll rent an apartment (in the Westmont district). He's *got* to be down there.' So I said, OK, (if he establishes residency), we'll do that. Sure enough, within a week, Brent was enrolled as a student at Westmont
High School.

"I hadn't seen him play, but I remember talking to guys at the (Campbell) Little League park
(where he'd been an All-Star in 1978, before moving out of the Campbell area) and they talked
about how he'd hit balls across the street (Hamilton Avenue). I called the kid (who had been
penciled in as the starting catcher) and I told him it was pretty obvious that Brent had a lot of
ability and can help our team (most) as a catcher. I told him I knew he had worked hard and done
a great job, and that if he didn't catch, he would still be our DH and that I would still get him in
there (on defense). He said, 'Yeah, I know he's good,' and that he would do it.

"Brent got in there as a sophomore and led the league in hitting, so nobody could say I favored
the kid. You could play him anywhere you wanted, he was that good. I think what really hurt
Brent was that Don put a lot of pressure on him. He never had any time to himself. Don developed him, but he also burned him out.

"But one thing I have to say about Don: He worked with me (as an assistant), and he helped me
a lot. And he helped every one of the kids on our team with something. He had a lot of knowledge. You don't play next to Willie Mays and not learn something."

Brent played for us after his sophomore season at Westmont, and I knew that he'd already
changed high schools once and that Don had shopped him among a number of summer
programs in the area. Don had a number of expectations related to Brent playing for us, and
he didn't hesitate to remind me of them at every opportunity. One was that Brent would be
catching every game, and I told him that wasn't going to happen because Dave Bryant was
our catcher and he was a positional and directional rock for us. Ed and I eventually decided
that the two of them would split time at first base and catcher, something Dave was willing
to do for the good of the team. I don't think Brent really had a problem with it either, but
Don did.

Don was and remains easily the worst example of parental interference I've come across in sports,
but we dealt with him as best we could for half a season. I saw Brent in my own selfish terms;
with him, I thought, we had not only the possibility but perhaps even the expectation of giving
Campbell a last national championship. He really *was* that good. And because baseball is perhaps
the most nepotistic of all sports, the Hahn name would get our other players scouted and recruited. That did happen, even though Brent was only with us for the first half of our season. At
that point, he simply stopped showing up and his father stopped answering his phone. He didn't
even bother to turn in his uniform.

We later found out that Don had taken Brent up to Eureka, a dreary fishing town on the Pacific coast about 100 miles south of the Oregon border, to play for a semipro team, the Crabs, that had a lot of college players and scheduled accordingly. I liked Brent personally and didn't want to impede his baseball progress, so I left the situation at that, and while the guys were sorry to lose Brent, they certainly didn't mourn the loss of Don.

The Hahns' departure actually invigorated our team, which went on an eight-game winning streak after they left. Because of the pitching dearth that I mentioned earlier, the San Mateo team that beat us in the area tournament probably would have done so regardless of whether we had kept Brent or not, because with two major leaguers-to-be (Gregg Jefferies and Scott Chiamparino) and a roster full of major-college recruits, they were better than us, and proved it decisively every time we played them. As for Brent, the same scenario that had impacted our team kept recurring.

After he graduated from high school, Arizona State gave Brent a full baseball scholarship – rare in that sport, because NCAA Division I schools are allowed to give only 11.7 scholarships and usually divide them among their players – and once the Hahns arrived in Tempe, Don immediately got the idea that he knew more about coaching and about baseball in general than Jim Brock, who finished his career with 1,100 victories, two national championships and 12 College World Series appearances. As a result, Brent's stay at ASU was short; after he left school, he was taken by the Minnesota Twins in the sixth round of the 1986 supplemental draft, but didn't sign. At a Santa Clara function the following summer, I ran into Broncos coach John Oldham, who knew I'd had Brent in Legion but wasn't sure about the circumstances surrounding his departure from our team.

John had just taken over the Santa Clara program, which had been a national powerhouse for many years but had foundered since the death of longtime coach Sal Taormina in 1979, and he told me that Don had been in contact with him about a possible transfer by Brent to Santa Clara. (In those days, and until the rule was changed in 2008, baseball players could transfer from one NCAA Division I program to another without having to sit out a redshirt year.) John, of course, knew of Brent's talent, and was willing, as Brock had been, to invest a full scholarship to bring Brent to Santa Clara. He also knew about Don, and asked me if he thought having Brent on the field was worth having to put up with Don off it. I told him that for me, the answer had been no, but that Brent was so talented that I probably would have co-existed with Don for the remainder of that season had Don not made that decision for me.

John signed Brent, with the predictable result. Brent left Santa Clara after that one season, ending his college career, and I heard that he and his dad shortly thereafter had an acrimonious parting of the ways and that he, Brent, had gone up to Oregon and put baseball behind him. I did see him play again in 1990, when he was attempting a comeback with the Salinas Packers, an independent team in the Class A California League, and what I saw was wreckage. He was out of shape and the skills at which I had once marveled were eroded almost to the point of non-existence. (He finished that season with a .221 batting average and not a single home run in 123 games.) I arrived at the Salinas park hopeful that Brent might at last be able to maximize the limitless potential I had once seen. I left angrier at Don, who wasn't there, than I had ever been.

Two decades later, Don resurfaced again, this time in a different state with a different son and much the same result.

I was living in Nevada and running the NevadaPrep.com website, which covered high school sports in Northern Nevada, and early in the 2002 baseball season I went to Reno to see Galena High, which was considered talented enough to beat the top Las Vegas teams and become the first Northern Nevada team since 1979 to win a large-school state title. Six players on that Galena team went on to perform at the Division I level. One, Billy Paganetti, would have been a first-round draft choice as a senior had he not let it be known he intended to accept a scholarship offer from Stanford. He pitched only briefly in college, first for Stanford and then for the University of Nevada, before injuries ended his career.

The name Dustin Hahn in the Galena scorebook naturally caught my eye, and when I sat in the bleachers, I saw Don (who apparently didn't recognize me, which was just as well) sitting not a dozen feet away from me. After I got home, I did some legwork on the Internet and it turned out that Dustin had been one of the top players in the CCS the season before as a junior at St. Francis High in Mountain View.

Well, Chris Bradford, the St. Francis coach, was one of my best baseball friends when I covered and coached baseball in the Bay Area, so just for the heck of it I gave him a call. It turned out that Dustin had abruptly left St. Francis near the end of his junior season, after denying to Chris' face widespread rumors that his dad was shopping him around and that he was planning to transfer. It also turned out that Dustin had been academically ineligible at St. Francis — which also would have made him ineligible in Nevada, as I understood it.

There was more. Dustin apparently had become friendly with Billy Paganetti and some of the other Galena players during the Area Code Games in Fresno that summer. Billy's father is Bill Paganetti, who is a part-owner of the Peppermill hotel-casino and one of the wealthiest men in Nevada, and Bill had provided Dustin with transportation on his private airplane from San Jose to Fresno and then from Fresno to Reno. That would be a violation of NCAA recruiting rules, let alone those governing high school sports.

The Hahns and Galena weren't penalized, because Nevada Interscholastic Activities Association executive director Jerry Hughes said he couldn't prove that Bill Paganetti provided Dustin with the airplane transportation with the specific intent of helping Galena recruit him. According to Hughes, Bill Paganetti was under the impression that what he did wasn't any different than providing Dustin with ground transportation to a local game would have been, and for a guy who owned jets, it probably wasn't. (The Peppermill had been one of NevadaPrep.com's early advertisers; I had talked to Bill Paganetti a few times, and thought and still think him honorable.) As for his academic ineligibility at St. Francis, Hughes ruled that Dustin was academically eligible when he began playing for Galena, and that his St. Francis ineligibility wasn't retroactive.

So Dustin was allowed to play for Galena that season. He played well, and Galena made it to the 4A state finals before losing. But the episode probably cost Dustin a lot of money. Don had been quoted in the Reno paper as saying Dustin wouldn't sign with a major league organization out of high school for anything less than third-round money. By now, every scout assigned to Northern Nevada – many of whom were based in Northern California – knew of Don's history and of the controversy involving his transfer to Galena, and all of them crossed Dustin off their high-priority list after Don threw down the money gauntlet. Dustin was drafted by the Orioles in the 21st round and was offered a tiny fraction of what he had expected. As a result, he went to LSU for a year before washing out there. He then played for Sacramento City College for a year before being drafted by the Colorado Rockies, for whom he played a couple of years in the minor leagues before being released.

Would either or both of Don Hahn's sons have reached the major leagues had it not been for their father? I think it's quite possible, especially in Brent's case. But Don did more than undermine his sons' baseball futures. He also had a large role in undermining Campbell youth baseball, and while he was far from being the only self-absorbed parent in Campbell youth baseball's declining years, he was the one who had the most influence because of his status as a former major league player – a status he chose to use in a bullying and selfish way.

That was his prerogative, of course, and even he wasn't as bad as some other parents who marred Campbell's baseball landscape in the early 1980s. Another father, whose son is still employed in the baseball industry and who played in the league in the late 1970s and early 1980s, started fights because of the way he treated his own kid and other players in Campbell Little League. Don never made a spectacle of himself in that manner, at least to my knowledge, and he was gone from Campbell by the time the program completely lost its bearings. But he had been there since Brent made the Campbell Little League All-Star team in 1978, and I think he was a major reason that winning leaped to the top of the priority list, ahead of the priorities that had defined Campbell baseball for so long, after the dual national championships of 1979.

When winning became the most important element in Campbell baseball, the winning stopped. And it hasn't resumed since. Campbell Little League, which reached the divisional round (in effect, the Northern California finals) five times between 1966 and 1979, has been that far only once since, in 1995. The only Campbell-area Little League to advance beyond the divisional level since 1979 has been Moreland, which in 2007 got to the Western Regional, the last step prior to Williamsport, before being eliminated in the round-robin phase of that tournament.

During the 1980s, the Campbell system lost almost all of the people whose altruism had guided and empowered the league for so long. Those were people who had been involved long before or long after, and sometimes long before *and* long after, their children were done playing baseball. While some of them left because of their disgust over the direction the program was taking, it may well have been that some of them simply lost their enthusiasm for the sort of thankless work that was needed to make the leagues what they had been.

Regardless of their reasons for leaving, the fact is that they left, and to this day they have never truly been replaced — although there are still those who carry on, hoping, in their own ways, to reignite the torch.

NOW: Campbell baseball today, and those who carry on

Jason Miller

If there is true linkage remaining between the Campbell in which he grew up, the Campbell that he now serves as an educator, and the Campbell that will be populated by the kids with whom he now interacts, Jason Miller represents it.

Jason is dean of students at Westmont High, which inherited many of Campbell High's students and some of its identity when it closed in 1980. Before moving into administration, he was the baseball coach at Westmont for seven years, during which he restored relevance to a program that had nosedived after Gordon Huntze retired from coaching in 1992. Jason also is a product of the Campbell youth baseball system, having been an All-Star in Campbell Little League and Campbell Moreland Pony League, and then a player on the 1987 Colt All-Star team that remains the last Campbell team to appear in a World Series. He played for Gordon Huntze at Westmont, and then spent a season in the West Valley College program, which had been revitalized when Steve Bordi retired and Mike Perez replaced him as head coach.

My visit to Westmont to interview him was the first time I had been there since the 1980s, and aside from the lights that towered over the football field, it didn't look much different. The first six Campbell Union High School District campuses that were built after Campbell High were virtual replicas of each other, built from a cookie-cutter design from which there was little deviation. All seven schools (including Prospect, which had a slightly different look than its CUHSD counterparts) also were named after the street on which they were located, all seven had alliterative nicknames (Camden Cougars, Del Mar Dons, etc.), and all seven had 3-foot-deep swimming pools. I graduated from Del Mar, and walking down the halls of the Westmont campus that day, I couldn't help thinking that it was 1975 and I was between classes at Del Mar and I'd better hurry or I would be late to Mr. Ferrie's English lit class. (Richard Ferrie, by far the best and most influential of my Del Mar teachers, later taught at Westmont for many years.)

Like most American public high schools, Westmont looks more institutional than inspirational. But the kids seemed to intermingle more freely than I had expected, and weren't walking around with the glazed, let's-get-it-over-with expression I had come to associate with government schools, especially after running a high school sports-based Internet site in Nevada over the previous 10 years. The 45-year-old campus was maintained in such a way that I had the feeling that people cared about this place. Jason, having graduated from Westmont, certainly does, and even though I had never met him, I got the impression during our conversation that if I were a Westmont student and I found myself in this office, I would find authority without authoritarianism, and someone who might listen and not just hear. Jason was a Campbell guy, all right, just as the players I'd coached and with whom I'd become friends in Campbell remained Campbell guys long after they ceased being Campbell baseball players.

Jason suffered a career-ending shoulder injury during his year at West Valley, and he went on to graduate from Sacramento State with plans to enter the educational field. We talked at some length about his experiences in the Campbell baseball system, including that 1987 Colt World Series. "Maybe the thing I remember most," he said, "was the final game against Marietta (Ga.). It's a 6-6 game (that Campbell Moreland eventually lost 7-6) and I'm at the plate with a runner on third and the squeeze is on. Marietta's pitcher was Marc Pisciotta, who later pitched in the majors (from 1997 to 1999 with the Cubs and Royals). He's a 16-year-old, but he's 6-6 and he was throwing 94, 95 (mph). We're playing at night so we're not seeing the ball that well anyway, and I square around a little early and he throws one high and tight on me. That's the only time I've ever had my life flash before me."

As described in an earlier chapter, Jason's memories of Campbell baseball are of an experience that enriched his childhood, even though the system already had sustained the fissures that eventually broke it apart. Like many who were there then and are still there now, Jason believes elements of Campbell's youth baseball past can be resurrected, although he is a realist in terms of the difficulty of doing so in the current baseball and societal environment.

"I think one thing that's happened is that (Little League All-Star play) is so watered down," he said. "When I was growing up, they only had the 12-year-old All-Star team in Little League, and to make that 12-year-old team was something we *lived* for. We live in Morgan Hill, and I tell my wife that I compare Morgan Hill a lot to the way Campbell was; it was like a small town, and there wasn't much to do except play baseball and football. But now they have All-Star teams starting when kids are 6 years old, and the expectations for those kids start so early because of that. You also have the club (travel) teams. For me it was, you play for your hometown team and that was it. Now it's whether to do away with the school season and play with traveling teams people are trying to put together."

Jason said baseball interest appears to be rekindling at Westmont, where a total of 70 kids had tried out for the school's two 2009 teams. Because the freshman class was thought to be one of the school's most talented in years, there was even talk about putting together a freshman team — something that even Campbell High never did.

"I think what hurt Campbell (when the youth program declined, starting in the 1980s) was partly numbers," he said. "The kids just lost interest. Even now, looking at our sports programs here, there are just so many other things going on. Back in the '80s, before the Internet, I remember we'd be playing wiffle ball in the street and the parents would call us in for dinner, and as soon as we were finished, we were right back out there again. Every time I asked Coach Huntze about what his secret (for success) was, he'd always say, 'That's easy. It was the youth programs.' They were the ones that locked it in. Now there's so many other things going on, and it's too bad.

"Now it seems like most parents think their kids are going to be the next Barry Bonds, and as a kid, I don't remember any of us ever having that impression. I grew up a Dodger fan so I had Ron Cey and Steve Garvey and those guys (as baseball role models), but my parents never said that when you grow up, I think you should be a professional baseball player. Now, parents have such unreasonable expectations, starting when their kid makes a 7-year-old All-Star team. I'll have kids come up to me and say 'I want to play for Stanford.' That's fine, but you have to be realistic. I have a cousin who played high school ball in Brentwood (an East Bay community) and then played at Sac (Sacramento) City. I'd seen him play last year at West Valley, and I thought he would be a good guy for a program like UC Davis or Sac State. But he wound up going to Oregon State (which won the College World Series in 2006 and 2007) and he got cut. Your expectations have to be realistic.

"It's changed a lot. Coach Huntze never said it to me, but I know part of the reason he decided to retire was because of the changes that were happening. When I was playing and Coach Huntze ran us halfway to death after a loss, my parents would say, 'Well, he's the coach, and maybe (the team) deserved it.' Now you have parents ... Johnny comes home and tells mom and dad that the coach ran them to death after a loss, and the next day they're calling the school and asking what's going on. But now (in Campbell) you're starting to get the second generation (after the 1970s) coming through, and what I'm seeing is an attempt to refocus."

Jason knows from experience that wholesale refocusing of a sports program is possible, because he became an expert on that subject early in his coaching stint at Westmont.

After he graduated from Sacramento State — he later took a year off from coaching and teaching, and returned there to get his masters degree — Jason applied for the frosh-soph job, and to his surprise, he was instead offered the varsity position, even though he was only 24. Huntze had left five years earlier, and Jason found a program in ruins. The West Valley Athletic League had disbanded, and its four remaining schools had joined the new Blossom Valley Athletic League, which now consists of 24 schools. Each year, the BVAL is broken down into A, B and C divisions on a sport-by-sport basis, and Westmont's baseball program was in the bottom tier when Jason took the job.

"I had kind of lost touch with the way the program was run," Jason said. "I was surprised. Instead of playing Los Gatos and Branham and the other big baseball schools (that had been in the WVAL when he was in high school), I get our schedule and I see we're playing people like San Jose and James Lick (schools in central San Jose that struggle even to field teams in most sports). We go to some of those places and I couldn't believe what I was seeing – no scoreboards, guys tripping over gopher holes on the field. Well, we won that league and got moved up to the second tier, and by the third year we were in the Mount Hamilton (A) league. We ended up coming in second-to-last that year, but we stayed up, and the following year we came in third. I left that year to get my masters, and we got dropped down again during that year. When I came back, we were in the Santa Teresa (B) league, and we won it and got bumped back up again. My last year, we ended up second to Leland (in the Mount Hamilton league)."

In 2009, the Warriors, under third-year coach Tony Pianto, remained in the top-tier league, joined by Branham, Leigh, Live Oak, Sobrato (with assistant coach Bobby Straight), Pioneer and Santa Teresa. Branham and Leigh were longtime powerhouses in the WVAL years, and both had fierce rivalries with Campbell High in the 1960s and 1970s. But they do not have a similar history with Westmont, and the other schools are relatively unfamiliar from a Campbell perspective. One factor that once characterized WVAL baseball was the fact the schools were all in close proximity and had players who had competed against each other for years – and made each other better doing so. Now, the passion must come from the playing, not the team being played.

In addition to his administrative duties at Westmont, Jason still maintains close ties to the program, and is instrumental in organizing the Greg Mitchell Memorial Alumni Game, played each year to honor Jeff Mitchell, a former Westmont and Campbell Little League player who was murdered in 2006 while on duty as a Sacramento County sheriff's deputy.

Does he sense that today's Campbell players are aware of, and draw from, the experiences and achievements of his day and the days before his day?

"It's hard to say," he said. "Every once in a while I'll come across somebody who will say 'I was at the Pony field and I saw your picture on the wall there. I didn't know you played in a World Series.' But I don't know if they're into it as much as before. There's so many All-Star teams and parents are always asking how much money they have to shell out so their kids can play on travel teams. We never had that. And it seemed like the parents (of his playing era) were very close, more than they are now.

"But I'd like to think that baseball can be exciting in Campbell again. There's just so much tradition here."

Randy Nishijima

Because he was there during the halcyon days of Campbell baseball and is still there now, as a coach and father, Randy Nishijima often finds himself searching for a concrete answer to a nebulous question: To what degree should what Campbell did three decades ago matter now?

"Jeff Nelson (who played Little League and Pony League at the same time Randy did) is on the board and was a manager in the league," said Randy, who played on the 1979 Campbell Moreland Pony League world championship team, and in 2008 managed his 10-year-old son Brandon during regular-season and All-Star play. "Jeff and I came up together, and he's a really good coach and he's gone back to teaching the game we played it back then — not only the physical side but the mental side. I always pick him for my coach, and it's kind of neat when parents see what we're doing and ask us to draft their kids.

"But you know, it's hard to say whether things can be the way they were. It's hard to imagine, say, how Mr. Zogg would do with all the rules and the different attitudes you see now. A lot of parents are brand-new to the area and they're seeing certain families and people controlling things, and they don't like it. When Irene (former Campbell Little League president Irene Ydens) came into the league as president, a couple of cliques that for some reason didn't like her did everything in the world to try to sabotage her.

"It's not the same as it was before (in the 1970s). I've seen some people run for the board to have the right to do whatever they want (instead of trying to do what's right for the league as a whole). We had people run for the board not because they want to be on the board themselves, but because they want to shoot somebody else down. It got very nasty."

The major division at Campbell Little League in 2009 had only five teams, down from eight when Randy played in the league, and was doing something that would have been unthinkable 30 years before: It played an interlocking regular-season schedule with two neighboring leagues,

Moreland and Santa Clara Westside. (Ironically, Santa Clara Westside's president in 2009, Tim Farnham, was on Campbell's 1979 Little League national championship team.) Like most long-standing youth baseball leagues, the organization is struggling with declining signup numbers attributable to a number of factors already discussed in this book: Competition with travel teams, other sports and non-athletic activities, the disintegration of the family unit, the increased transiency of the population, and a city that aged before its time.

Just before the publication of this book, I attended a Campbell Little League board meeting, and was impressed both by the turnout and by the sense of fellowship and commitment that seemed to prevail. Of course, the season hadn't started yet, and parental harping doesn't start in earnest until the season does. Randy says it's far more difficult than it once was to attract and keep qualified managers, coaches and umpires, partly because parents tended to care either too much or not enough about their kids' baseball endeavors.

"I'm sure some of that went on back then," Randy said, "but as players, we never felt the tensions that the kids seem to feel now. All the kids play at least the minimum (weekly) requirement of innings, but now if you only play kids the minimum, even if it's a safety issue, you hear from parents because they think their kids should be playing shortstop or pitching and playing all the time.

"Back then we just pretty much played, but now you see the kids going along with what their parents say. It's almost like they live through their kids, because they're always pushing them. What's strange is that the guys who were superstars when they were playing are the ones who sit back and let everything go. There's a rift between them and the other parents, and a lot of times the kids are being told, 'You don't want to do this,' or 'You don't want to play for this person.'"

In those respects, Campbell's youth baseball program is hardly unique, and some think that not even a total rededication to the principles that guided the program in the 1960s and 1970s would enable Campbell to reclaim the youth-baseball prominence it once had. Randy says he doesn't dwell on the subject much, even when he's questioned on the subject by newcomers ... but that doesn't mean his memories, or his sense that baseball can be an important component of a complete childhood, have diminished.

Randy was primarily a catcher, but he was one of the best athletes in the league, and he played every other position except pitcher during his baseball career, which continued through high school (two years at Campbell and the final two at Blackford) and ended with a season at West Valley. A left-handed hitter who controlled the bat deftly and understood the strike zone as well as any of his contemporaries, he also ran well enough to be a leadoff hitter, and had some power as well.

He also was driven by self-demands that at times made it appear as if he wasn't playing with the sort of youthful zest that characterized some of his teammates, but he was self-sacrificing and, away from the field, one of the most congenial and sensitive young men in the league. And although he was close with his age-group teammates, he also was in the same grade as most of the 1976 Little League All-Stars, and very well might have been among them for postseason purposes if his birthday hadn't fallen on September 3, three days after the Little League age cutoff at the time.

He also played a part in the game that, to many, represents the essence of Campbell's youth baseball heritage – in 1981, when Campbell trailed a powerful Los Altos team 9-2 with two outs in the seventh and final inning of a Colt League regional tournament game at Santa Cruz's Harvey West Park. Randy kept Campbell alive with a double that was followed by doubles by teammates Craig Trinidad and Tim Bottomley, and after six runs had poured across the plate, Randy came up again. He hit an infield grounder that was misplayed and then thrown away, allowing the tying and winning runs to score and giving Campbell a 10-9 victory.

"You never want to think it's over," Randy says now, "but it was such a shock to even be in that position in the first place, with all the talent we had on that team. We had two aces, one lefty and one righty (Brad Ceynowa and Tom Gricius) … you might remember Tom threw a no-hitter when we beat Michigan 13-0 in the Pony League World Series (in 1979). We had Dave Bryant. We had Joray Marrujo and Steve Koontz and a bunch of other guys who could run, and we had the mix of Campbell and Moreland and Quito guys. So we really weren't believing everything that had happened (resulting in the 9-2 deficit). But after the doubles you could see a little glimmer. You keep hearing and talking about the game never being over until the last man is out, and we kept that last out going for a while.

"How did we do it? I guess it was just kind of a Campbell thing. We knew we had this history behind us, and you see it even now. If you're from Campbell, you're still going to have that target on your back (against other teams)."

The Hughes family

As close as I was to many of the kids during the years when Campbell was still Campbell in the baseball sense, the parents were my influences. I learned a lot about being a grownup from them, and at the same time, they accepted me as one of them, despite the fact I wasn't much older than their kids. More than anybody else I'd met to that point in my life, they appreciated me for who I was and what I'd helped bring to their kids, and in turn my appreciation for them deepened, especially after I left Campbell.

During the summer of 2008, I watched one of the Campbell All-Star teams – I can't even keep track of how many there are, now that Little League postseason play is conducted in single-age subdivisions – play at Cupertino American, once one of our biggest rivals, and the site of two of our District 44 victories in 1976. Seeing the railbirds who were perched along the fence along the first-base line was like driving through the gate of an antebellum plantation. And maybe in another time and place, Bob and Pat Hughes would have been the personification of gracious Southern living.

Bob was an electrician – now he's retired and likes watching the kids and betting the ponies in his spare time – who never lost the gently flowing accent of his South Carolina youth, and the thing that always struck me about him was the fact he never lost his sense of humor or his dignity, even if he was upset about something. His suggestions carried force, yet people respected him so much that he hardly ever had to raise his voice, and he had a smile for me on this day, just as he had every day in Campbell during that time so long ago. He didn't look much older than he did in 1976, either, and as we exchanged greetings and remembrances, it was apparent that the sand in his hourglass of time still filtered without grating. Just as he had watched his son Brian play on this field – Brian was on the 1976 Little League World Series team – in the 1970s, he was watching Brian's son Justin now. And as with Brian, he was there to acknowledge and support and enjoy himself in the process.

"We still go to a lot of the games at Campbell," he said, "and you've still got a majority of good people involved. You get some people all hot and bothered and they make a lot more of a scene than they did back then, but I don't see that as the biggest difference. Back then, it was *competitive* ... every team had good players and every team could beat you and challenge you. You didn't hear the whining, especially from the parents, that you do now. You went out there and *earned* it, and I think just having that competition every day made all of our kids back then better players.

"But as much as everything has changed, you know, it's still the same game, the same game Brian played and the same game I played as a kid. Maybe people forget that sometimes. There were a lot of arguments and a lot of fussin' and fightin' this year, and nobody's going to win those kinds of fights."

When her son was playing, Pat Hughes was more conscious than most mothers of being the supportive influence and not the interfering one. She was the consummate team mom, and seemed to know the other kids as well as, or even better than, some of their own parents knew them. She generally kept her opinions to herself until she had enough information to draw an unassailable conclusion, and I found out this day that nothing had changed.

"I think my grandson is having a good experience and I think Brian is having a good experience (coaching him)," she said. "The thing that bothers me about what's happened in Campbell, and I think just about everywhere else, is that it seems to me that parents are afraid to have their children have to deal with not getting something they want.

"Back when Brian made that (1976) All-Star team, that was a very big achievement for him ... he was surprised he made it, and to tell you the truth, so were we. That was when there was only the one All-Star team, not the 8-year-old and 9 and 10 and 11 All-Star teams they have now. It's like every kid *has* to be on an All-Star team ... the other day, one parent who was upset that her kid didn't make any All-Star teams was complaining that now her kid wasn't going to be an All-Star until he was at least 12. And my thought was, *how is that bad?* All-Stars used to be a special thing. Now it's expected, and I think that kind of sucks. The parents here now seem to be afraid to expose their kids to the possibility of failure, and they think not making an All-Star team is failure. That's maybe the biggest thing that's changed."

Bob and Pat discussed one situation that troubled both of them. John Aimonetti, who had been the starting left fielder on the 1976 Williamsport team and who later went on to play football for San Jose State and the Kansas City Chiefs, was one of the managers in the five-team major division during the recently completed regular season. He'd had a running, antagonistic discourse with several of the parents throughout the season, and during the final game of the year, from what I'd been told, that antagonism degenerated into a series of shouting matches. A few days later, John — who had been designated as one of the All-Star managers — pulled both himself and his son Nico out of the league, a move that only served to escalate tension. A roster spot on the All-Star team had been left open for Nico, even though he was strictly a weekday player because he was obliged to spend weekends with his mother, who lives outside the area. After John disassociated himself with the league he had helped bring to international baseball prominence, another player was added as a replacement for Nico – only two days before the start of the District 44 tournament.

"Back then, there were parents who were having trouble, and there were a few divorces," Pat Hughes said. "But it always seemed to be about the kids, everything that happened in Campbell. I don't know what the situation with John was, but it affected a lot of people in a way it shouldn't have. It's supposed to be about the kids."

The Hughes family, and so many others in those years, always were about the kids, and even as we talked, their eyes and their thoughts were directed on the game in front of us. If this had been a wrestling meet, Cupertino American would have had to forfeit the top five or six weight classes, because the Campbell team was huge – especially a kid named Garrett Runyon, one of the four pitchers Campbell used as a result of Little League's latest national absurdity, the 85-pitch maximum. Campbell's first pitcher, a left-hander named Pierce Urban, seemed almost able to physically touch the hitter during his follow-through, but his primary weapon was his off-speed assortment. Runyon, on the other hand, was so big that he almost seemed to blot out the center-field wall. Even so, Campbell had a tough time with Cupertino American, finally winning 6-3 after a fourth pitcher marooned the tying run on base in the sixth inning with a strikeout.

One of the sidebars to this game that surprised me was the proliferation of coaches, official or otherwise, who seemed to swarm around the Campbell players. I counted five who seemed to have some in-game function, and the 12 players didn't seem to know to whom they should be listening at any one time. I couldn't help but think that if Jack Zogg and John Emery were running this team, most if not all of the five dugout-committee members would be sitting in the stands.

I couldn't see this Campbell team going very far in tournament play, if for no other reason that size does not have the impact it once did as the postseason progresses. The old Campbell teams could find ways to manufacture runs with speed, batsmanship and daring. This team was strictly station to station, both in terms of advancing runners and in terms of understanding the geometry of defense. As I've written, particularly in the chapter about the Campbell system's defining managers, there once was a Campbell way of playing baseball, but it wasn't evident on this day, just as it hadn't been in 1995 when I saw the only Campbell Little League team that has advanced as far as the divisional level since 1979. That 1995 Campbell team was one of the biggest Little League teams I've ever seen, but it lost the game I saw, at Branham Hills against one of the Palo Alto teams, because it was too big to play small ball in a low-scoring game.

Judging from some of the comments I heard in the stands that day in the summer of 2008, you *knew* that at some point, somebody would beat those big kids and the fingers of accusation — both index and middle — would soon be extended throughout what's left of the Campbell baseball community. That didn't happen in the Campbell I knew, at least not for public consumption, and that day, I couldn't help but feel for the kids of today. I wished their baseball lives weren't parental minefields.

Paul Balbas

Reflecting on my Campbell jobs and the games I monitored more than 30 years ago, I tend to think of those spring and summer afternoons as a non-stop succession of enlightening vignettes – the baseball, the kids, the fellowship, the funny things that happened, the sense that I was doing a job in a way that augmented and supported what the kids, their parents and the managers and coaches were trying to do. In retrospect, I think of those days as a time when hundreds of us were involved in something that was going to remain special long after it was over, and I regained that sense when I saw the sons and the grandsons of my old Campbell friends cavorting in their own baseball landscape.

The reality, of course, is that baseball isn't always riveting, especially if you see a great deal of it. On Saturdays back in the 1970s, I'd be at Campbell Little League or Campbell Moreland Pony League from 8 or 9 in the morning until at least 6 at night, emerging only between games to line and water and drag the infield. Some of those games were one-sided, or dreary for one reason or another, and some of the teams did not include many players or coaches or parents I knew well. There were times that it was out-and-out boring, and more than once during some of those filibusters, I remember thinking that I hoped Paul would wander by and climb up to the booth and keep me company – because with him around, the boredom wafted out the window like the smoke from the barbecues beyond the outfield wall at Rosemary School, or from Beer Hill at John D. Morgan Park.

Paul, whom I'd first met when he was 11, could and still can work a room like nobody I've ever met, of any age. He's still the only person I've ever known who was the personification of the adjective "garrulous." As a kid, he struck up conversations, even with adults, without a hint of self-consciousness, and even at that age. he had a gift for finding and mining even the tiniest nugget of absurdity. I figured if I could find a way to plug him in, he'd light up the entire city for a month, and beyond that, he was bright and funny and inquisitive and articulate and, above all, entertainingly impulsive. If he felt like saying or doing something, he did it, and although I knew some others found him annoying at times, I never did, because I knew there was no malice attached to anything he did and because you couldn't buy the entertainment he always provided for free. I also knew that whatever happened to him as and after he grew up, this kid was going to have himself an eventful life.

When I saw him in 2008, it was for the first time since his days as a student at Cal Poly San Luis Obispo, from which he graduated with a business degree and a minor in political science. He had to wait to finalize our meeting, which was over dinner at a Japanese restaurant in Cupertino and wound up lasting three hours, because he didn't know whether the adult-league ice hockey team on which he played had a game that night. He told me about his job litany during his working life, and I wasn't surprised. He'd run a car wash, he'd toured with Metallica and several other big-name heavy-metal bands — "This was when bands were still thought of as punk, before they became heavy metal," he said — and he'd traveled extensively, with his itineraries ranging from the Belgian Grand Prix to the battlefield at Gettysburg. He'd been broke, he'd subsided in menial service jobs, and he'd been a distributor of a line of LCDs in which the traffic numbered in the millions of units. Now, he wanted to write and publish children's poetry. "I'd rather be paid more for what I'm doing now (as a sales rep for a Silicon Valley electronics firm)," he said, smiling, "but I'd rather be paid *nothing* for doing what I'm doing. I've always been that way. I'm always kind of looking for something more, something different."

His main focus, though, is his two children — Ian, 13, and Clarissa, 9. Ian, who had just completed his final year in Campbell Little League, is a left-handed pitcher who, according to Paul, has mastered a knuckle-curve and has learned to get hitters out with motion, movement and legerdemain even though he can't throw very hard yet. The problem, Paul says, is that bigger players with more conventional skills always seem to get more attention than Ian — a situation to which Paul is attuned because as a baseball player, he never really established an identity in Campbell.

Ian is a third-generation Campbell Little League player; Paul's uncle, Frankie Testa, in 1955 had been the first player ever to bat in a game at the Rosemary School complex. Paul could run as well as any player in his age group, and he developed into an efficient defensive player both as a center fielder and as a second baseman. But he was never considered an All-Star level player until he was 14, when he made the second All-Star team in Pony League. His parents sent him to a private high school — Archbishop Mitty High in San Jose — and it was there that Paul, and later his younger brother Jim, were able to independently apply what they had learned competing in Campbell. Paul was cut from the varsity as a junior, but stuck with baseball and was a major contributor as a senior, and Jim made it to the varsity as a sophomore — enabling he and Paul to play on the same team together for the first time — and was an all-league caliber player by his final season.

Paul thought about trying out for the baseball team at Cal Poly as a walk-on, but decided against it after his father, Frank, convinced him that playing baseball, working part time and studying full time would be too much for him to handle.

Although Paul shrugged off the suggestion by me that he might subconsciously be superimposing his own long-ago baseball ambitions on Ian, he said he'd considered that and was being very careful to let Ian have a distinct baseball experience of his own. And he was honest about his overzealous behavior at a couple of his kids' athletic events, which to me meant he had considered the possibility that he, Paul, was trying too hard.

When Paul arrived this day at the Tri-Cities Little League field in Cupertino, the Campbell 9-10 All-Star team was playing a team from Sunnyvale Serra Little League, a familiar Campbell punching bag in the old days. Randy Nishijima, the manager of the Campbell team, also had been Ian's manager during the regular season.

Even as a kid, Randy was tough-minded, ambitious and not very forgiving of himself when he didn't play up to his very high standards. Paul and Randy were the same age and had known each other well since Little League, and part of Paul's frustration in the aftermath of Ian's season had been with Randy. They hadn't had a confrontation, and Paul had taken the attitude that it was now time for Ian to move onto "real baseball" at the Pony League level and beyond. But it was Paul's opinion that Campbell had become like any other youth baseball league in terms of kids like his, with unconventional but obvious skills, being sidetracked in favor of the home run hitters and the power pitchers and the kids whose parents had influence.

When he came into the Tri-Cities park, I was sitting with Bob Hughes and Jim Phillips, two of the most prominent parents of Campbell's halcyon era. Bob had been a board member, a coach and a volunteer – not to mention a profound raconteur – since before I was involved with the league, and Jim, *after* sending three sons through the league, served as its president. In fact, Jim may have been the only Campbell parent to travel to Williamsport for the Little League World Series in both 1976 and 1979. He went in 1976 even though he didn't have a son on the team; in 1979, his son Mark was on the Campbell squad that took Taiwan into extra innings before losing in the title game.

"You know," Paul said later over dinner, "even when I was a little kid, Bob Hughes and Jim Phillips were the greatest guys ... they treated me and all of us with respect even though we were just kids. That's I think what I remember most about those days, the respect everyone had for each other. And it was a league where you got what you earned. I wasn't that good a player in Little League or even in Pony League, but because you were playing against all those great players every day, you were challenged to get better. Putting as much effort as I did into getting better and then getting rewarded by making that second Pony All-Star team was something

I was able to take with me to Mitty, and I think I was still getting better when I graduated from high school.

"I wish Ian could have had the same kind of experience in Little League as I had ... back then, everybody competed, but everybody was friends and so were our parents. But I don't think anything like that will ever happen again, at Campbell or anywhere else. Things have just changed so much. I don't think it's about the kids very much anymore. I think it's about the egos and the individuals and the parents."

EPILOGUE: Final thoughts

It's February 23, 2009, as I begin the final chapter of this book — a project I began about six months ago, while I was still living in Nevada. I've interviewed and corresponded with dozens of people, and spent countless hours sifting through old books and newspapers and my own memories. Beyond the times and places and people and achievements, I intended to draw dual conclusions. First, what, exactly, did Campbell's youth baseball do? (Yeah, we won a lot and we won for a long time, but what did we *do*, in the making-life-better sense?) Second, and I write this as a Campbell resident for the first time since 1982, what can be done now? What *should* be done?

As I've indicated throughout the book, I don't think Campbell's tradition of winning and winning the right way was the result of any master plan. There were exemplars who set the tone from the very beginning, and the work that first made baseball important in Campbell many decades ago represented a heritage that was handed down and enriched through the 1960s and 1970s after formal youth baseball provided a mechanism by which excellence could be quantified. There was continuity, with good baseball men and good people staying involved whether they had kids playing or not. There was a community-wide commitment to provide good facilities, mainly through volunteerism, and there was a sense of community-wide accomplishment when Campbell teams did well. There also was a sense that even though All-Star championships were important, the regular season and the experiences of every 14th player on each 14-kid roster were more important still. If those are the elements that the readers sensed as they read this book, then I will have made the points I set out to make. Above all, Campbell in its glory years had talented, imaginative, joyous, giving kids in whom the community took and still should take justifiable pride, whether they were all-conquering All-Stars or not.

I think the youth baseball system here, beyond the championships, did a great deal to make Campbell a desirable place to live, and judging from the comments of the former players I have profiled, playing here and being part of something larger that worked so well helped them establish the credos by which they have lived their adult lives. Many of the friendships they made during the time they played baseball still exist, decades later. Not everyone from our system went on to success as an adult, but I think most of the kids who played here were introduced to the concept of altruism, and walked away feeling good about their experience. I think most of the kids who played here sensed that they were cared about and that they could make friendships that would last a lifetime, and when you're able to achieve that *and* win to the degree that Campbell did ... well, you could write a book about it.

I've also pointed out that the loss of Campbell's baseball identity was part of a much larger municipal loss that filtered down to the baseball program. The closing of Campbell High, the foolhardy decision on the part of city officials in the late 1970s and early 1980s to actively seek federally-subsided senior housing, and the slow asphyxiation of the *Campbell Press* all entered the equation. So did the proliferation of video games, skateboards, cable television, soccer, and individual sports like golf, tennis and swimming. Another factor, here and nationally, has been the deterioration of the traditional family unit. While a few Campbell players I knew in the 1970s came from single-parent households, far more kids in Campbell and elsewhere did by the end of the 1980s, and the result was that kids who still played baseball often did so while one parent was at work and the other was living many miles away. Much later, the travel-team movement thinned the traditional youth-baseball leagues even more, and could very well threaten the existence of many of them as the 21st century progresses.

Maybe, given these factors, Campbell could not have maintained its youth baseball supremacy even if the program had continued under the same type of management that had existed in the 1960s and 1970s. By the early 1980s, newer, larger, more prosperous communities already had caught up with us in terms of talent and resources, and I think Campbell did well to stay good for almost a decade after the two-national-championship culmination in 1979. Campbell changed in the 1980s and 1990s, and the changes are not reversible. It still offers a very high quality of life, but it's a different kind of life, built around the dollars spent by outsiders and the needs and interests of a much older populace than the one that existed before 1980.

Can Campbell turn back the clock? I've raised that question with almost everyone I've interviewed or otherwise communicated during the course of piecing together this book. After considering their opinions, and my own coaching and journalistic experiences after I left Campbell, I think it's possible, and I think the people now involved with youth baseball here generally have the right motives. But the only way I see it happening is if doing so were to become the municipal will – and I don't think Campbell has a municipal will anymore, at least with respect to youth baseball.

By municipal will, I don't mean government involvement with youth baseball, because that never has and never will happen in Campbell.

Aside from its upkeep of the Campbell Pony field at John D. Morgan Park, the participation of some city employees who volunteer their free time, and the police- and fire-department sponsorship of two of the teams in Campbell Little League, the city has never been directly involved with the Campbell youth baseball program. The mayor and the city council members dutifully showed up on Opening Day at Rosemary School and John D. Morgan Park in the 1960s and 1970s, and some of them used to travel to World Series sites from time to time if it meant they could get their pictures taken doing so. Otherwise, we hardly ever saw or heard from the local politicians, and that seemed to be the way most people preferred it, although I never understood why the city didn't do more than it did to promote the program or use it to project an image of Campbell as a well-run, family-friendly city. Moreover, Campbell has been largely apolitical since its annexation wars with San Jose ended in the early 1960s, and as I mentioned earlier, the population is far older than it was 30 years ago. Even if city officials were inclined to invest public money and manpower in the youth baseball program today, their constituents, many of whom are far past the age where they are interested in financing anything involving kids, probably would react the same way they did in 1978 when Proposition 13 passed by a 2-to-1 margin among city voters. So any attempt to revamp youth baseball in Campbell would have to be a volunteer/corporate effort.

That having been written, the population numbers support the idea that Campbell can become a baseball town again.

It's true that the median age of the city's residents is far higher than it was in 1980, and that Campbell does not attract as many young, home-buying families as it once did. Only 28 percent of Campbell's households include children younger than 18; in Pleasanton and Morgan Hill, two cities that have been compared to Campbell as it was in the 1960s and 1970s, the percentages are 40.8 and 44 respectively.

But it isn't as if Campbell has gone the way of Virginia City after its silver mines played out, either. It had about 30,000 people when I left; it has about 40,000 now, and there are still 7,300 students enrolled in the Campbell Union School District. And while some people think changes in Campbell's ethnic makeup over the past 30 years preclude baseball excellence, census statistics don't support that theory at all.

According to the 2000 census, and I don't think these numbers have changed much since then, Campbell's population was 73 percent white, 14 percent Asian, and 13 percent Hispanic – not very much different than it was in 1980. As of 2007, the median income for a Campbell household was $89,285, and only 4.8 percent of Campbell residents lived below the federal poverty line. Campbell is not wealthy, at least by Bay Area standards, but it is hardly destitute, either. There are enough kids here, there is enough money to maintain the facilities and keep the kids in high-quality equipment, and from the standpoint of team- and consensus-building, the ethnic makeup is just about what it was during Campbell's glory years.

The first priority, then, has to be getting signup totals back up to where they were in the 1960s and 1970s. Obviously there's a problem when Campbell Little League, which had 32 teams through the early and mid-1970s, had 22 in 2009 despite Campbell's population increase over the past 30 years. And Campbell has had downturns in its signup numbers before. In 1977, the year after it went to the Little League World Series for the second time, only 280 children signed up – little more than half of the peak total of the early 1970s. (This was after the national economy went through a severe recession from 1973-75, and reflected the fact that Campbell essentially was built out and no longer had many young homebuyers settling in the city.) Eventually the signup numbers began to increase again, especially after the league started a tee-ball program for 6- and 7-year-olds in 1979, and they stayed fairly constant until the league's internal difficulties and some of the other elements discussed previously began to manifest themselves in the late 1980s and early 1990s.

Certainly there is more competition for names on the dotted line than there was 30 years ago, and baseball isn't the right sport for every kid, but in the generic sense, baseball is more popular in this country than it has ever been. It is not dying on any age level, or in any demographic sphere except perhaps in the most poverty-stricken inner cities. Presented well, it has a great deal to offer to kids in terms of fun, healthy recreation, and confidence-building as well as skill development. In Campbell's case, it also has heritage, and while what happened 30 and 40 years ago largely is abstract to kids today, you can't tell me that it doesn't mean *something* to a kid to play in a system that has been to 14 World Series, including four Little League World Series.

Quite a few Little Leagues against which Campbell, Moreland and Quito competed in the 1960s and 1970s no longer exist, and the leagues that have faded or failed are the leagues that haven't marketed themselves or their product very well. You can't just post signup announcements. You have to get into the schools, into the grocery stores, into the skate parks, and onto the Internet, and as in any marketplace, you have to convince potential buyers that you have a product they can't find anywhere else. You have to have incentives, perhaps in concert with local merchants. You have to make the case to kids and their parents that the existing leagues can offer more than a uniform and a schedule, and that playing Little League baseball represents an experience that the travel leagues, and other sports and activities, can't duplicate. If I were running a youth baseball league today, marketing of that sort is where I would start.

The next step is to put emphasis on growing the league from the bottom up, not from the top down. Everybody wants to manage or coach All-Stars, but it's the youngest kids who will ultimately determine the success of your league – in terms of the skills they develop, and in terms of whether they have fun playing and want to continue. The youngest kids are afterthoughts in too many leagues, but they need the best coaching and support, and if it were up to me, I'd follow up on an example I saw in Nevada.

Reno High has a baseball program that is comparable in many ways — including its level of success — to Gordon Huntze's powerhouse at Campbell High, and I became good friends with Pete Savage, the Reno coach, during my years in Nevada. Pete, whose brother John is the head coach at UCLA, is practically evangelical when it comes to insisting that his players give back to the game, and he *requires* all of the players in his program to serve as Little League coaches. Beyond the fact this helps Pete implant the idea of wanting to be a Reno Husky in young minds, it also gives his players a sense that they're doing something generationally important. And from what Pete tells me, the children bond with their teenage coaches more readily than they do with adults, and are receptive to anything that the players have to teach them.

According to Pete, many of his former players found they enjoyed coaching so much that they stayed involved with youth baseball after their own playing days were over. You have to have parents prominently involved, of course, but as I've mentioned many times, one of the keys to our success in Campbell was the fact that many of the best managers, coaches and overseers were not parents themselves, or stayed involved after their children had moved on from the leagues with which their parents were associated.

Why can't a Little League-high school link be established in Campbell? I bet the baseball coaches at Westmont, Prospect and Del Mar — and maybe at some of the nearby private schools, like Mitty — would love the idea if it were broached to them. I think you could even get Mark O'Brien at Santa Clara University and Sam Piraro at San Jose State to invest their time and their players as well, if asked. I've known both of them for many years, and I know both understand well the value of infrastructure of the type I'm proposing.

In terms of mentoring, Campbell has another asset other leagues don't have — its heritage. A lot of the guys from the 1960s and 1970s are still in the Campbell area, and even if they don't have kids of their own or aren't in a position to commit to a full season of coaching, I'm sure a lot of them would gladly help on a one-time or short-term basis if asked ... and they have Campbell-specific credibility you can't find anywhere else.

Just as better coaching begets better players, better coaching of coaches begets better leadership. Many leagues have skill-development clinics and camps for players, and I think the same emphasis should be placed on developing the expertise and teaching skills of the adults. In addition to former players, I'd try to enlist the help of educational and personnel professionals to try to accomplish this. It isn't always possible, of course, to have an experienced and knowledgeable baseball person in charge of every Little League team, but since I left Campbell, I've been around leagues where kids know more about the game than the adults who are purportedly running the team. That doesn't have to be the case anywhere, and it certainly shouldn't be the case in a system with Campbell's history.

Once they're settled and confident, the managers also have to have the unwavering support of the league administration. A familiar refrain among many youth-baseball managers and coaches who get out is that they believe their league's board of directors will undermine them whenever there is a dispute with a parent, even if the parent's complaint turns out to be unfounded.

I've never understood why youth baseball leagues don't actively seek out large corporate sponsors to underwrite their entire operation, instead of (or in addition to) gathering small team sponsorships on a piecemeal basis. If you, as a league, were able to obtain a naming corporate sponsor in addition to the smaller team endowments, you might be able to offer your product free of charge to the parents. And when you get rid of signup fees, you'll also get rid of a major parental rationale for interfering with the operation of the league and its teams: "I paid a hundred bucks for my kid to play, and for that kind of money, I have the right to say anything I want." It may well be that parents also would be more willing to put in time on work parties and in snack bars if they hadn't already had to write a check to sign their kids up.

I think the next question that Campbell's baseball community has to answer is whether Little League remains the best developmental vehicle by which to serve Campbell's youth-baseball population.

As I mentioned at the top of this epilogue, it's February 23 as I write this. It's raining, and has been raining almost non-stop for the past week. There was a time, very early in Campbell's formal youth baseball history, that the season didn't begin until early June, and when I was there, it usually started the second week of April. This coming season, the first games will be played on March 14, less than three weeks away, and more than a month before the Campbell Pony League begins play.

That's ridiculous. Even the major leagues with their 162-game regular season don't start that early.

Even in mild climates such as that of Northern California, teams are not going to have sufficient practice and bonding time, and it will be difficult to have the fields anywhere near suitable condition by March 14. (In fact, Santa Clara Westside had to hold its opening-day games at Campbell Little League because the Westside fields weren't yet playable.) In many parts of the country, the weather is such that it's ludicrous to even think about playing baseball before May, and that means the regular season has to be squeezed into a six- or seven-week period.

I managed a farm-division team during my last spring in Nevada, and our schedule consisted of exactly 10 games, even though we had more than enough facilities and teams to accommodate a schedule of 20 games or more. But the weather made it impossible to play before the end of April, and we had to be done by the end of May because of the various postseason tournaments, which are superfluous in the part of Nevada where I lived. So we played our 10 games, and just as the kids were getting to the point where they could sense their own improvement and we were getting to the point where we knew all the kids' names on sight, the season was over.

That's ridiculous as well.

There is only one reason for that convoluted calendar – the fact Little League Baseball, Inc., cares far more about the Little League World Series and the other postseason tournaments, and particularly about the income it can accrue from them, than it does about its rank-and-file leagues and players. There were issues, even in the 1970s, in terms of the boys being secondary to the business during Campbell's Williamsport experiences, but the marketing carnivores had not yet made Little League baseball a full-blown industry. The World Series was still a baseball tournament, not a media event or a TV rating bonanza. The only Little League World Series game that was televised in 1962, 1970, 1976 or 1979 was the final. Now, every game is on ESPN, along with most of the regional finals, and when you tune in to watch, it might as well be the Home Shopping Network, so shameless is the exploitation and profiteering.

The national organization in Williamsport couldn't care less about some 8-year-old in Winnemucca, Nevada (or Campbell, California, for that matter) who will never play in a Little League World Series but just wants to play a reasonable number of games in decent weather with teammates he likes and with coaches from whom he is learning. Baseball is a summer game and youth baseball is supposed to provide kids with summer recreation.

Of course, Little League baseball has been a fixture in this town for more than half a century now, and moving in a new direction undoubtedly would meet with opposition. Still, if I were the Campbell baseball czar, I would look hard at divorcing Little League and its ravenous business arm.

With what would I replace it? Again, another concept that I saw in my baseball travels comes to mind.

In 1990, the Cincinnati Reds were in the midst of a season that ultimately would end in them sweeping the heavily-favored Oakland A's in the World Series. I was covering major league baseball for the *Times Tribune* at the time, and one aspect about the Reds' dominance that caught my attention was that they had an unusually large contingent of players who had grown up in or near Cincinnati. I did a piece on those players, and when I was interviewing each of them, I asked about Cincinnati's youth baseball system. It turned out, much to my surprise, that Cincinnati had almost no Little League baseball at all. Instead, every one of the Reds' Cincinnati-born players, and a number of other Cincinnati natives throughout the major leagues, first took up baseball in Hamilton County's Knothole program.

The Knothole system, I learned, was heavily subsidized by the Reds, the county government, the city of Cincinnati, and prominent Cincinnati-area businesses – so much so, in fact, that it didn't have to charge parents. It was Cincinnati-specific, and wasn't affiliated with a national organization, although the concept has since spread to other metropolitan areas, and is incorporated to some extent in Major League Baseball's RBI program, which is designed to revitalize baseball in the inner cities. Players were grouped by ability levels, rather than by age as is done in most conventional youth baseball programs. The Reds' organization ran clinics for the kids and extensive training programs for the coaches and parents, and as is the case now with some of the better travel-team programs in the Bay Area, managers and coaches with baseball backgrounds are hired and paid by the Knothole organization. It wasn't a high-pressure program, the Reds players told me, but it enabled each of them to develop their skills and stoke their passion as their physical growth and coordination dictated. And none of them thought much about wanting to play in a youth baseball World Series, because simply winning a city Knothole championship as kids was a memory they cherished.

Of course, Campbell isn't Cincinnati, and if a Knothole-like system were to be set up here, it would have to obtain all of its sponsorship money from the private sector, because there's no way that city or county government would invest in such an operation in Campbell. It's also doubtful that Campbell could go it alone with such a baseball structure; the city just isn't big enough.

But the same Williamsport-related issues that undermine Little League baseball in Campbell also exist elsewhere in the Santa Clara Valley, and it wouldn't surprise me if the same grumblings about starting the season in mid-March can also be heard in Sunnyvale and Cupertino and Santa Clara and Los Gatos and San Jose and elsewhere in Santa Clara County. If enough Little League leaders got on board, you could create a regional organization that would be similar in scope to the Knothole program in Cincinnati. In fact, there's already an organization – the travel-ball association in which Dave Roberson's son plays – that operates much the same way as the Knothole program. I wrote earlier, in Dave's chapter, that I think setups like that represent at least a part of the future of youth baseball. Ideally, maybe you could find some way to knit the Knothole and travel-ball concepts and have them work in concert. The Knothole program would prevail during the regular season, and once, and not until, the regular season ends, All-Star teams could enter the already-existing travel-ball postseason system. This also could be done without the Little Leagues in the area seceding from their national organization, although the Little League people – both here and in Williamsport – should know that the travel-ball movement is not going away and that, in the absence of a working arrangement with which both sides can live, travel ball can do far more to harm Little League than Little League can do to harm travel ball.

Losing the carrot that is the Little League World Series would be detrimental, you say? Well, my response would be to the effect that only a handful of Little Leagues actually enter a season with the idea that their teams should, or even can, make it to Williamsport. That wasn't the ambition at the start of Campbell Little League's 1970, 1976 or 1979 postseasons, but because of their success, winning became the No. 1 priority at Campbell Little League in the 1980s, and when that happened, the winning stopped and has never resumed. The chances of any one team getting to Williamsport in a given year are almost too astronomical to calculate. The odds against winning the World Series are off the charts. Northern California is, and has been for many decades, one of the most productive talent incubators in the world. How many Northern California teams have actually *won* a Little League World Series? One — Moreland in 1962, when the scope of Little League was far smaller than it is now.

The way the mainstream youth baseball system works now, each league is obliged to sacrifice the best interests of hundreds of children so that a handful of All-Stars can play in the postseason — which, for the vast majority of them, consists of one tournament or two at the most. That's patently wrong, and if baseball is to become fashionable in Campbell again, the youngest and least experienced players must again become the No. 1 priority.

If I were running a contemporary Little League, I would tell the national organization this: We will start the season when the weather, facilities, extent of our athletic pool, and wishes of the parents — in that order of importance — dictate we should. We will not telescope the regular season to extend the postseason. We will not have All-Star teams for every age level, because the regular season must have its importance restored, and the All-Star teams we do field will not begin play until after our regular season is over. And that regular season will end when we want it to end, not when Williamsport wants it to end.

If Little League Baseball, Inc., could accommodate those needs within the context of its own selfish agenda, the problem is solved. If not, I look elsewhere.

Of course, what I'm suggesting here is fairly radical, and would require the subjugation of multiple parental egos, along with the widespread acceptance of a shared goal — to make Campbell a place where baseball for children, *all of the children*, is a community priority. The reality is that altruism on such a lofty plane and on such a wide scale is highly unlikely, here or anywhere else. Campbell is not what it was as a city, and it's probably not realistic to expect it to become what it was as a baseball program either.

So maybe the best perspective to have is to acknowledge Campbell's baseball past without feeling a need to resurrect it. Most of the people with whom I reconnected while writing this book have done that; they happily relive those days at Rosemary School and San Tomas School and John D. Morgan Park and Campbell High and Williamsport and Kennewick and Davenport, but they think of those days and those places and those people as foundation and not fortress.

It is with these last four paragraphs that my story of The Last Baseball Town will end, and I wish to end it with an image that for me will always be indelible.

Now that I've moved back to Campbell, I'll occasionally go over to Rosemary School or John D. Morgan Park or Campbell High (oops, the *Campbell Community Center*) when nobody else is there.

If I use my imagination, I can transport myself mentally back to those wondrous years, and I can recreate some of the bat-ball-and-glove sounds, the murmuring of the crowds, the smell of burgers wafting from barbecues, the celebrations in front of the dugouts or on the mound.

Mostly, though, I see the face of some little boy or some young man in any one of dozens of uniforms. He's not necessarily one of the All-Stars, or even one of the better players. He's out there playing in a game long forgotten, and he's not rounding the bases after a home run or sliding into the plate with the winning run.

He's just looking at me, smiling, and his face is aglow ... because at that moment, with these people, playing this game in this place, he has never been happier in his life.

Made in the USA